# MURDER AND THE
# REASONABLE MAN

CYNTHIA LEE

# MURDER AND THE REASONABLE MAN

*Passion and Fear in the Criminal Courtroom*

**New York University Press** • *New York and London*

**NEW YORK UNIVERSITY PRESS**
New York and London

Library of Congress Cataloging-in-Publication Data
Lee, Cynthia, 1961-
Murder and the reasonable man : passion and fear
in the criminal courtroom / Cynthia Lee.
p. cm.
Includes bibliographical references and index.
ISBN 0-8147-5115-6 (cloth : alk. paper)
1. Self-defense (Law)—United States.   2. Provocation
(Criminal law)—United States.   3. Murder—United States.
4. Judicial process—Social aspects.   I. Title.
KF9246.L44  2003
345.73'04—dc21          2002155359

New York University Press books are printed on acid-free paper,
and their binding materials are chosen for strength and durability.

Manufactured in the United States of America

10 9 8 7 6 5 4 3 2 1

*In memory of*
*my father*
*Tuck Hop Lee*

# Contents

# Acknowledgments

THIS BOOK COULD NOT have been written without the help of numerous individuals. First, I want to publicly thank my partner, Kenichi Haramoto, for providing me with love and nurture throughout this project. I also want to thank my parents, Tuck Hop and Dorothea Lee, who provided me with the discipline and skills I needed to write this book. Before my father passed away in December 2000, he told me a story that helped me complete this book project. When he was a young man, my father and one of his colleagues drafted seven chapters of what was supposed to be a nine-chapter book. They sent their chapters to an editor who was extremely negative about the project. Demoralized, they never finished the book. Later, the same editor who had been so critical of my father's manuscript published something quite similar to what my father had submitted. My father's story gave me the courage to complete this book project.

Second, I want to recognize and thank Bob Chang, Richard Delgado, and Jean Stefancic, who were instrumental in making this book possible. My friend Bob planted the seed for this project back in 1995, encouraging me to think about writing a book when I was still an untenured professor. After reading some of my written work, Richard and Jean suggested that I submit a book proposal to NYU Press. They then nourished the project from start to finish, providing me with helpful guidance all along the way, reading and commenting on numerous drafts.

This book started as an examination of race and discretion in the criminal justice system. In the summer of 1998, I decided to postpone that project and came up with the idea for the book which you are about to read. I began serious work on this book in 1999 and turned in a completed manuscript to the publisher three-and-a-half years later in July 2002. I am deeply grateful to Niko Pfund, the former director of NYU Press, for providing enthusiastic support for this book project in its various incarnations. I also greatly appreciate the editorial assistance I have received from Alison Waldenberg, editor, and Ginny Wiehardt, editorial assistant, NYU Press.

Third, I want to thank Angela Harris and Andrew Taslitz, the only two colleagues other than Richard and Jean who read the entire manuscript when it was in draft form and provided me with substantive feedback. I also thank my writing buddy, Carol Johnson, for reading and commenting on numerous chapters and providing me with moral support. Carol and I met weekly during the summer of 2000, exchanging rough drafts of our respective books-in-progress and providing each other with useful feedback.

I also want to commend and thank the two George Washington University law students who provided substantial and excellent research assistance on this book project: Zeena Abdi and Missy Grubbs. Zeena and Missy read numerous drafts of the manuscript in various stages of completion, and helped tremendously with research, cite-checking, editing, and proofreading. I want to thank my administrative assistants, Perla Bleisch from the University of San Diego School of Law and Glynis Hammond from the George Washington University School of Law, for providing me with excellent administrative support. I also thank my library liaison, Herb Somers with the Jacob Burns Law Library at the George Washington University School of Law, for truly outstanding research and library support.

I also want to thank the following individuals who read one or more chapters and provided me with helpful comments and suggestions for improvement: Laura Berend, Alafair Burke, Brian Cheu, Joe Colombo, Bob Fellmeth, Cynthia Ho, Jerry Kang, Orin Kerr, Susan Kuo, Carolyn Ramsey, Jeffrey Rosen, Jennifer Russell, and Leti Volpp. I also benefited from conversations with Dwight Aarons, Robin Ballagher, Paul Butler, Bill Bratton, Naomi Cahn, Burlette Carter, David Cruz, Angela Davis, Joshua Dressler, Flora Keshgegian, Mark Morodomi, Janice Nadler, Spencer Overton, Barbara Paige, Natsu Saito, Michael Selmi, Patricia Sun, and J. D. Trout about this book project.

I also benefited from the comments and feedback I received at numerous conferences at which I presented portions of this book when it was in progress. In particular, I thank Dorothy Brown, Alafair Burke, Burlette Carter, Lenese Hebert, Browne Lewis, Alfreda Robinson, and Larry Darnell Weeden for feedback at the 2002 Northeast People of Color Conference. I thank Laura Gomez, Chris Iijima, Ruth Jones, and Peter Kwan for feedback and comments at the 2001 Western Teachers of Color Conference. I thank Taunya Banks, Bob Chang, Neil Gotanda, Cynthia Ho, Jerry Kang, Susan Kuo, and Tayyab Mahmud for comments at the First Asian Pacific American Legal Scholarship Workshop in 1999. I thank Keith Harrison, Lenese Hebert, Ian Haney Lopez, Natsu Saito, Jonathan Stubbs, Eric Yamamoto, and Fred Yen for comments and feedback at the First National People of Color Conference in 1999. I also want to thank Catherine Brady and Mary Jane Moffitt for helpful feedback in the manuscript workshops at the 1999 Foothill Writers Conference.

Even before I began working on this particular book project in 1999, I started doing research on some of the subjects covered in Part II. Therefore, I want to thank the following University of San Diego students who provided research assistance before I started writing this particular book but who nonetheless contributed in some way to the final product: Kendie Chung, Denise Crines, Brian Derdowski, Kathryn Dove, Lise Forquer, David Kim, Natalie Maniaci, Phi Nguyen, Shannon O'Brien, and Xanath Owens. I also thank the following University of San Diego law students who provided research assistance on the actual book: Paul Baelly, Marc Baumgartner, Mike Cordrey, Nicole Davidson, Mo Park, Kelly Smith, Martha Waltz, and Charlotte Wilder. Finally, I want to thank the following George Washington University law students who provided additional research assistance on the book: Sonya Ahuja, David Berman, Megan Kinsey, Tree Martschink, Liza Meyers, Lori Ruk, and Keirston Woods.

Additional thanks go to Dean Michael Young of the George Washington University Law School for providing me with generous research stipends for work on this book. I also thank Dean Daniel Rodriguez, Associate Dean Virginia Shue, Former Dean Kristine Strachan, and Former Acting Dean Grant Morris of the University of San Diego School of Law, all of whom provided me with generous research stipends and time to work on this book project. I also thank Edna Mitchell, former Director of the Women's Leadership Institute at Mills College for giving me a room of my own and board during the calendar year 1999, the year I began writing this book.

Finally, since I wrote most of this book in coffee shops, I want to thank Claire from Claire de Lune in San Diego, California, Dan and Bernie from Twiggs in San Diego, California, and the employees at Politics and Prose in Washington, D.C., for providing me with great nonfat no-foam lattes and a comfortable place to write. I apologize if I have forgotten anyone else who assisted me with this book project.

# Introduction

## FEMALE INFIDELITY

John, a mechanical engineer, finds out that Veronica, his wife of seven years, is having an affair with his best friend. Tormented by images of his wife and his best friend together, John alternates between wanting to shoot himself and wanting to shoot the two of them. Finally, he confronts his wife, tells her he knows she has been unfaithful, and asks what drove her to betray him. Veronica admits she has been unfaithful. She apologizes, but John isn't satisfied. He demands to know why she has done this to him. She tells him that she no longer loves him. In disbelief, John grabs his wife and tries to kiss her. Veronica pushes him away, choking as if she can't stand the way he smells. At this, something in John snaps. John wraps his hands around his wife's throat, like a wedding band that fits snugly around the ring finger. His hurt pours out of his heart into his hands until Veronica lies lifeless before him.

## GAY PANIC

Mike, an honors student at the local junior college, plays quarterback on the football team. Good-looking and well-liked by his classmates, Mike prides himself on being an all-American guy. One day, Mike takes a hard fall on his shoulder during football training. After practice, Mike decides to relax in the school's sauna where he finds his friend and fellow teammate Gary. Gary asks him about his shoulder. Mike tells him that it's pretty sore. Gary, who is openly gay, asks if Mike wants him to massage his shoulder. Mike says that would be great. Mike, clad only in a short white towel, lies face-down on a nearby bench. Gary starts to massage Mike's shoulders and back. Mike tries to muffle a groan of pleasure. The massage feels good, almost too good. Mike starts to feel uneasy. What if another teammate comes in and sees Gary touching his body? What if this teammate tells others that he is gay? What if Gary tries to make a pass at him? As these thoughts are racing through his mind, Mike feels Gary's hands move down to his legs, then up his thighs, underneath the small white towel. Gary starts to rub Mike's buttocks. Mike jumps up and yells, "You pervert! What the f——— do you think you are doing!" Mike starts punching and kicking until Gary falls to the ground. Even though Gary is not fighting back, Mike continues to beat and stomp on him until he stops moving. Gary dies the next day.

## RACIALIZED FEAR

Harry, a White* man, works as a busboy in a restaurant and lives in a low-rent district in the City. He likes to jog in the evenings after work and often passes through high-crime neighborhoods. Just in case, he carries a loaded gun in a fanny pack when he jogs. One evening, Harry sees a group of young Black teenagers on the steps of an apartment building about a block in front of him. As he nears them, two of the youths step out into the street and ask for some money. Harry stops running and tells the kids that he doesn't have any money on him. The teens ask him what he has in his fanny pack. Harry shouts, "I'll show you what I have." Unzipping his fanny pack, he whips out his gun, yelling, "This is what I have. Now back off." Instead of backing off, the boys start laughing at Harry. One named Josh starts to reach into his pants pocket. Thinking that the boy might be reaching for a gun, Harry shoots. The bullet strikes the boy in the chest and kills him instantly.

John, Mike, and Harry are each charged with murder.† Each man argues that he should be found not guilty, either because he was provoked into a heat of passion by the victim's behavior or because he acted in self-defense.

John insists that he should not be found guilty of murder because he was provoked by his wife's adulterous behavior. He simply snapped

---

* I purposely capitalize the word "White" throughout this book to draw attention to the fact that Whiteness is a socially constructed racial category.

† *Murder* is generally defined as the unlawful killing of a human being by another human being with malice aforethought. *Manslaughter,* in contrast, is defined as the unlawful killing of a human being by another human being without malice aforethought.

when Veronica confessed to adultery and pushed him away. Any man, John argues, would lose his self-control and become violent if he found out that his wife was having an affair with his best friend.

Mike also argues that he shouldn't be found guilty of murder. If only Gary had kept his hands where they belonged, he wouldn't be dead now. Mike simply saw red when Gary crossed the acceptable line. Mike argues that he was provoked into a heat of passion by Gary's repulsive behavior and that any "normal" guy would be outraged if another guy started rubbing his buttocks.

Harry maintains he shot Josh in self-defense. There he was, in a high-crime neighborhood, surrounded by Black teens who were demanding money. When Josh reached for his pocket, Harry thought he was reaching for a gun. In fact, Josh was reaching for a pack of cigarettes. Harry admits that had Josh and the other youth been White, he probably would not have leaped to the conclusion that Josh was reaching for a weapon.

John and Mike have asserted the defense of provocation. Harry has argued self-defense. Each of these three men insists he should not be convicted of murder because he felt or acted the way any reasonable man in his shoes would have felt or acted.

This book explores the ways in which social attitudes and beliefs about masculinity, sexual orientation, and race can influence the outcome in murder cases in which a male defendant asserts the defense of provocation or self-defense. Both provocation and self-defense include a reasonableness requirement. If the jury concludes that a reasonable person in the defendant's shoes would have believed it necessary to use force in self-defense or would have been provoked into a heat of passion by the victim's behavior, it generally will find the defendant not guilty of murder. In self-defense cases, a finding of reasonableness leads to an outright acquittal. In provocation cases, such a finding leads to a conviction on a lesser charge, such as voluntary manslaughter.

The open-ended nature of the reasonableness requirement is designed to allow community input on matters involving difficult value judgments and provide greater flexibility and fairness in legal decision

---

*Malice aforethought* is a legal term of art which represents the mens rea for murder. Malice aforethought generally can be proven by establishing one of the following: (1) an intent to kill, (2) an intent to commit grievous bodily injury, (3) gross recklessness plus an extreme indifference to human life, or (4) an intent to commit a felony that meets the requirements of the felony murder rule.

making than is permitted by strict rules. The reasonableness requirement, however, also enables certain criminal defendants to more easily excuse or justify their acts of violence. Because the term "reasonable" is rarely defined or explained, legal decision makers often substitute the words "ordinary" and "typical" in place of the word "reasonable." To decide whether a defendant's beliefs and acts were reasonable, the judge or jury compares the defendant's beliefs and acts to those of the "ordinary" or "typical" person. In this book, I argue that equating reasonableness with typicality can be problematic because views that are popularly held do not always correlate with notions of equality and justice.

As a progressive Asian American law professor who cares about issues concerning race, gender, and sexual orientation, I write from a particular subject position. All of us see the world through the particular prism of our own eyes. Our background and life experiences influence the way we understand particular events. I too see the world through the prism of my own background experiences. Accordingly, I do not purport to represent the truth in these pages. I discuss what I think are problems in the application of the reasonableness requirement in provocation and self-defense doctrines, and use actual criminal law cases to illustrate these problems.

In writing this book, I have two goals. First, I seek to work within the law to prevent the doctrines of provocation and self-defense from becoming havens for sexism, racism, and homophobia. Second, I hope to encourage people interested in criminal justice to think critically about what it means to be "reasonably" provoked and when it is "reasonable" to use force in self-defense. Even if readers disagree with my proposed legal reforms, if I can spark thought and discussion about the meaning of reasonableness, I will have accomplished much of what I set out to achieve in writing this book.

In these pages, I argue that social norms,* particularly those regarding gender, race, and sexual orientation, can influence legal decision makers—judges, jurors, and prosecutors—deciding whether a particular defendant was reasonably provoked or acted reasonably in self-defense. I use three types of criminal cases to illustrate how dominant social norms work to benefit certain defendants over others: (1) cases in which female infidelity, actual or perceived, precipitated the act of

---

* The term "norm" has many different meanings. In this book, I use the term to refer to dominant social attitudes and beliefs.

killing, (2) cases in which the defendant claims that an unwanted homosexual advance triggered the violence, and (3) cases in which racialized fear of the victim led the defendant to use deadly force.

At first glance, these cases appear to be completely separate and unconnected. Different emotions are at issue when a heterosexual man finds out that his female partner is intimate with another man, when a heterosexual man finds himself the subject of a nonviolent homosexual advance, and when an individual kills a person of color and claims self-defense. Feelings of betrayal and jealous rage may lead a heterosexual man to kill in response to female partner infidelity. Outrage and revulsion may lead a heterosexual man to kill in response to a homosexual advance. Fear may motivate an individual to kill a person of color in self-defense.

While superficially disparate, these cases are linked by the defendant's reliance upon social norms to bolster his claim of reasonableness. It is "reasonable" for a man to kill his unfaithful wife when the greater community sees the physical expression of male jealousy as normal and ordinary. It is "reasonable" to beat a gay man to death for making a homosexual advance if society at large sanctions heterosexual male outrage at male homosexual behavior. It is "reasonable" to kill a Black man in self-defense if pervasive race norms stereotype Blacks as dangerous criminals.

Men who kill their female partners and men who kill gay men tend to assert the defense of provocation, rather than self-defense, because dominant norms of masculinity and heterosexuality help make the claim of provocation seem reasonable. A man who kills his woman partner can still be considered a "man" if he claims he killed her because she was cheating on him. It is harder for a man to claim he was afraid of his woman partner and killed her in self-defense because men in this society are supposed to be stronger than women. Similarly, stereotypes about gay men as effeminate make it difficult for heterosexual men to claim they were afraid of a gay man. A heterosexual man who kills a gay man, however, can still be considered masculine if he says he was outraged because a man made a sexual pass at him. Failure to reject a homosexual advance might even call into question his heterosexual masculine identity.

In the self-defense arena, a different, but related problem exists. Here, race norms tend to support claims of self-defense made by individuals who have killed or injured men of color. In this society, Black and Latino men are stereotyped as violent criminals, gang members, and drug dealers. Because of these stereotypes, a man who kills a Black or Latino male may be perceived as having acted reasonably in self-defense even if he would be considered unreasonable had he killed a White man under similar circumstances. Less common, but equally problematic, are claims of self-defense asserted by individuals who use deadly force against unarmed Asian males in the mistaken belief that the victim knew martial arts.

In *The Path of the Law*, Oliver Wendell Holmes wrote that the best way to master a subject is "to get to the bottom of the subject itself" or "to discover from history how it has come to be what it is."[1] In this vein, I start in Part I (Crimes of Passion) by examining the historical evolution of the defense of provocation, a defense rooted in conceptions of masculine honor. I discuss the ways in which norms of masculinity and heterosexuality bolster claims of reasonableness asserted by men who kill in response to female partner infidelity, real or imagined, and men who kill in response to a nonviolent homosexual advance. In Part II (Crimes of Fear), I turn to the doctrine of self-defense and discuss ways in which the reasonableness determination can be influenced by racial stereotypes. In Part III (Rethinking Reasonableness), I offer three tentative suggestions for reform.

One note on choice of subject material before I outline the various chapters in this book. There is a rich and developed literature about battered women who use force in self-defense.[2] I do not purport to add to this literature. While I discuss women who kill their abusers in various places in this book, my primary focus is not on battered women. I have purposely chosen to concentrate on claims of reasonableness asserted by mostly heterosexual male defendants in female infidelity, gay panic, and racialized self-defense cases because these defendants have in common the tendency to rely on dominant social norms to bolster their claims of reasonableness. Women who kill their abusers, in contrast, often need to introduce expert testimony to *dispel* common misperceptions about battered women.[3] While people are more sensitive to the issues facing battered women today than they were fifty years ago, many individuals not familiar with the psychological literature on battered women still tend to view battered women's claims of self-defense with skepticism.

## PART I: CRIMES OF PASSION—
## THE DEFENSE OF PROVOCATION

Part I of this book focuses upon the defense of provocation. The doctrine of provocation, also known as the heat of passion defense, permits a defendant charged with murder to argue that he should not be found guilty of that crime because he was provoked into a sudden heat of passion by something the victim did. One who kills upon being provoked into a heat of passion is not guilty of murder, but of voluntary manslaughter, an offense that carries a lighter sentence than murder.

Chapter 1 provides an historical overview of the provocation defense through the lens of gender. Since its origin, the provocation defense has been biased in favor of male defendants. Initially, courts utilized a categorical approach, permitting mitigation only when the allegedly provocative act fell within one of a few specified categories. One such category benefited husbands who discovered their wives in bed with another man. If the husband responded by killing his wife or her lover, he would be guilty of voluntary manslaughter, not murder. The observation of a wife in the act of adultery was thought to constitute the most serious of all provocations. In some states, a husband who killed under these circumstances was not guilty of any crime. Such a killing was considered justifiable homicide. In contrast, a wife who killed her husband or his mistress after finding them in a sexually compromising position was guilty of murder.

The explicitly gendered categorical approach of the early common law eventually gave way to the modern, ostensibly gender-neutral, approach that permits mitigation if the defendant, male or female, was actually provoked into a heat of passion and a reasonable person in the defendant's shoes would also have been provoked. Even though the modern "reasonable person" approach appears gender-neutral, it still benefits men more than women. Very few women kill their male partners, and those who do are often reacting to domestic violence rather than infidelity. In contrast, approximately 60 percent of the men who kill their female partners admit that they did so in response to female infidelity. Additionally, norms of masculinity which understand male violence and aggression as normal help bolster the male defendant's claim that he was reasonably provoked into a heat of passion by his female partner's infidelity.

Some jurisdictions have moved away from the modern reasonable-person test toward a more subjective test like the one reflected in the Model Penal Code (MPC). This sample code, drafted by judges, lawyers, and law professors, permits mitigation if the defendant was suffering from an extreme mental or emotional disturbance for which a reasonable explanation or excuse exists. The MPC explicitly states that the reasonableness of the defendant's explanation or excuse must be determined *from the defendant's perspective*. By instructing jurors to determine reasonableness from the defendant's subjective point of view, the MPC allows for a more contextualized evaluation of the defendant's provocation claim. The subjective emphasis also makes it easier for jurors to excuse defendants who claim the defense.

Chapter 2 examines what Victoria Nourse calls the hidden normativity of provocation doctrine by focusing on claims of provocation by defendants who are not White, heterosexual, and male. Few documented cases exist, so it is difficult to draw any hard conclusions, but it appears that heterosexual women and gay men who kill in response to male partner infidelity have greater difficulty than their heterosexual male counterparts convincing legal decision makers that they acted reasonably.

This hidden normativity also has a racial dimension. Black men who kill in response to verbal insults of a racial nature are generally precluded from arguing they were reasonably provoked into a heat of passion. The race-neutral rationale for such preclusion is that mere words can never constitute legally adequate provocation. The problem is that this mere words rule has never been applied in a consistent fashion. In the days of slavery, a White man charged with killing another White man's slave could claim that "words of reproach" by that slave provoked him into a heat of passion. A slave who killed a White man for uttering similar words of reproach, however, would not be permitted to argue provocation. In more recent times, men who have killed their female partners in response to a confession of adultery or other verbal provocation have been permitted to argue that they were reasonably provoked into a heat of passion. These cases suggest that the doctrine of provocation, while written in facially neutral terms, is not neutral and unbiased in application.

Chapter 3 examines cases in which heterosexual men have killed gay men in response to a nonviolent homosexual advance. The chapter starts by discussing the historical origins of the concept of gay panic. It then discusses how gay panic is used to support mental defect defenses such as insanity and diminished capacity. Finally, chapter 3 examines cases in which gay panic is used to support defenses with a reasonableness requirement, namely, provocation and self-defense. The defendant, who is typically a young, White, heterosexual male, either asserts that he was reasonably provoked into a heat of passion by his gay victim's sexual advance or insists he acted reasonably in self-defense to ward off a homosexual attack. In both types of cases, the violence of the defendant is constructed as a normal reaction to the gay victim's purported sexual advance. "Normal" (i.e., heterosexual) men in this society are supposed to be offended by homosexual behavior, and violence is an accepted method of dealing with offensive behavior. According to this logic, when a man makes a sexual pass at another man, the reasonable man is offended. He communicates his displeasure and stops further transgressions to his masculinity by responding with violence.

The argument that it is reasonable for a man to react violently to a nonviolent homosexual advance obscures the fact that violence has never been considered a reasonable response for a woman subjected to a nonviolent heterosexual advance. For years, women have been subjected to unwanted sexual advances by men, including having their breasts and buttocks groped and fondled, yet few women subjected to such repulsive behavior respond with violence. Moreover, if these women were to react the way some men have reacted to non-violent homosexual advances, they certainly would not be considered reasonable.

Chapter 4 looks at the use of cultural information in criminal cases. As a general matter, criminal defendants who attempt to mitigate their charges by introducing evidence of cultural difference are unsuccessful. However, when Asian immigrant men kill their female partners in response to infidelity or perceived infidelity, attempts to invoke culture suddenly become more successful. Cultural claims of reasonableness in Asian immigrant female infidelity cases may succeed more often than other attempts to use culture in the courtroom because they parallel the familiar assertions of American men who argue they were reasonably provoked by a female partner's sexual infidelity.

Chapter 4 warns that immigrant and minority defendants are not the only ones who try to mitigate their charges by relying on cultural norms. Every time a White heterosexual male murder defendant argues he was reasonably provoked into a heat of passion by his female partner's infidelity or a nonviolent homosexual advance, he relies on social norms of masculinity and heterosexuality to bolster his claim of reasonableness. These norms, however, are not perceived as cultural because they are embedded in American culture.

Chapter 4 concludes by suggesting that whether or not cultural evidence is deployed successfully in the criminal courtroom may turn on whether the interests of the immigrant or minority defendant converge with the interests of the dominant White majority culture. Using Derrick Bell's interest convergence theory, I examine successful uses of culture by defendants of color and show how the interests of these defendants converged with the interests of the majority.

## PART II: CRIMES OF FEAR—
## THE DOCTRINE OF SELF-DEFENSE

Part II of the book focuses upon the doctrine of self-defense. Chapter 5 provides an overview of this doctrine. Most jurisdictions require the defendant to show that he or she honestly and reasonably believed it was necessary to use deadly force to protect against an imminent threat of death or serious bodily injury. Chapter 5 also discusses alternative formulations of the doctrine that permit exculpation or mitigation even if the defendant's belief in the need to act in self-defense was unreasonable, such as the Model Penal Code's version of self-defense and the imperfect self-defense doctrine.

Chapter 6 explores the influence of racial and ethnic stereotypes upon determinations of reasonableness in self-defense cases involving victims of color. This chapter explains how such stereotypes can influence both the defendant's decision to use deadly force and the determination that this use of deadly force was reasonable. Chapter 6 first describes the Black-as-Criminal stereotype, which links Blackness to criminality, dangerousness, and violence. Social science studies suggest that individuals tend to perceive ambiguously hostile actions by Blacks as violent while viewing the same behavior by Whites as nonviolent, and these findings are reflected in actual cases. For example, racial stereotypes may have helped Bernhard Goetz convince a jury that he acted reasonably in self-defense when he took out a gun and shot four Black youths in a New York subway after two of them asked him for five dollars. Chapter 6 also examines stereotypes about other racialized groups.

Stereotypes that depict Latinos as criminals (e.g., the Drug Dealer stereotype) and foreigners (e.g., the Illegal Immigrant stereotype) can influence legal decision makers to see fatal acts of violence against Latinos as reasonable acts in self-defense. Stereotypes that depict Asian Americans as martial artists and foreigners can also influence the reasonableness determination in self-defense cases.

Chapter 7 examines race and police officer decisions to use deadly force. It is undisputed that racial and ethnic minorities are disproportionately represented as victims of police shootings. Even though Blacks represent approximately 13 percent of the nation's total population, they constitute up to 60 percent of the victims of police shootings in some jurisdictions. Some studies have found that Blacks are more than six times as likely as Whites to be shot by police, and are killed by police at least three times more often than Whites. Latinos are about twice as likely as Whites to be shot and killed by police.

Widespread disagreement exists over the cause of this disproportion. Some believe police officers are not influenced by race or color when they decide to use deadly force. According to this color-blind view of police shootings, Blacks and other minorities are disproportionately represented as victims of police shootings because they are more likely than Whites to engage in behavior that an officer is likely to find threatening, such as resisting arrest or carrying a gun. Others believe police officers and departments intentionally discriminate against Blacks, Latinos, and other racial and ethnic minorities. Undoubtedly, some officers intentionally discriminate in their use of deadly force, but many act without an intent to discriminate. To explain why officers may discriminate without intending to do so, I borrow from Charles Lawrence's important work on unconscious racism to suggest a third view: racial and ethnic stereotypes operate at a subconscious level to influence not only the police officer's decision to use force, but also the jury's decision to acquit. Because of the paucity of research on police use of deadly force against non-Black minorities, this chapter draws mainly from cases involving Black victims.

## PART III: RETHINKING THE CONCEPT OF REASONABLENESS

In the last part of the book, I offer three tentative proposals for theoretical, practical, and doctrinal reform. In chapter 8, I start by discussing the elusive and open-ended nature of the reasonableness requirement. I explore the debate over whether reasonableness standards ought to be objective or subjective. I also discuss the sameness-difference debate in feminist legal theory and the color-blind versus color-conscious debate in legal academia, and show how these debates relate to the question of which characteristics of the defendant should be incorporated into the reasonable person standard. I introduce the concept of switching in this chapter (imagining the facts of the case with the defendant and victim of different genders, different races, or different sexual orientations). Switching provides a practical way to address problems with the reasonableness requirement, avoiding problems that arise from oversubjectivization of the reasonable person standard.

In chapter 9, I discuss two different ways of thinking about reasonableness, two theoretical constructs, which I call positivist reasonableness and normative reasonableness. Under a positivist view, a belief is deemed reasonable if the average or ordinary person would hold that belief. In other words, a positivist conception of reasonableness equates reasonableness with typicality. A normative conception of reasonableness, in contrast, focuses on whether the defendant's belief ought to be deemed reasonable. Another way of thinking about positivist and normative reasonableness is to contrast the "is" and "ought" questions. A positivist conception focuses on what *is* and a normative conception focuses on what *ought* to be.

Currently, legal decision makers in self-defense and provocation cases utilize a positivist conception of reasonableness. I discuss problems with this approach, and argue that the law should recognize both positivist and normative conceptions of reasonableness. To give descriptive content to a normative conception of reasonableness, I argue that courts should give jury instructions which invite jurors to engage in gender-, race-, and/or sexual orientation–switching in cases where dominant social norms operate to bias the jury either in favor of or against the defendant.

In chapter 10, I propose a doctrinal reform which I call the act-emotion distinction. In both self-defense and provocation cases, legal decision makers tend to focus upon the reasonableness of the defendant's emotions (emotion reasonableness), without attending to the reasonableness of the defendant's actions (act reasonableness). Jurors in provocation cases are instructed to mitigate the charges from murder to manslaughter if the defendant's emotional outrage was that of a reasonable or ordinary person. Jurors in self-defense cases are told they may acquit if the reasonable person in the defendant's shoes would have feared death or serious bodily injury (or believed it necessary to act in self-defense). Few jurors are instructed to focus on whether the defendant's acts were reasonable, even though act reasonableness is implied in current self-defense doctrine's proportionality requirement.

I argue that this inattention to act reasonableness is unwise because it ignores important gradations in culpability and makes it too easy for defendants who have intentionally taken a life to escape a murder conviction. To remedy this problem, I argue that juries deciding claims of provocation and self-defense should be required to find not only that the defendant's emotions (or beliefs) were reasonable, but also that the defendant's acts were reasonable. Act reasonableness in provocation, however, does not mean the act of killing must have been reasonable. Act reasonableness simply means paying greater attention to the mode and method of force used by the defendant.

## CONFRONTATION, CONVERSATION, AND CHANGE

Because jurors come to the courtroom with beliefs and attitudes that are shaped in large part by broader community norms, the problems identified in this book can only be resolved by confronting the underlying social attitudes and beliefs that enable certain defendants to be viewed with sympathy. Such confrontation has already begun. Matthew Shepard's death focused national attention on the problem of anti-gay bias. The fatal police shooting of Amadou Diallo led to widespread debate, though little consensus, over the role of race and police use of deadly force. While law reform can and does play an important role in shaping public attitudes, public attitudes are even more likely to be shaped by ordinary people thinking and talking with others about what constitutes reasonable provocation and what constitutes reasonable use of deadly force. My hope is that readers of this book will be prompted to have such conversations, and that these discussions will move our society toward a conception of reasonableness deeper than the prevailing one.

# PART I

# CRIMES OF PASSION
# (THE DOCTRINE OF PROVOCATION)

# 1

# Female Infidelity

Albert Joseph Berry, a forty-six-year-old cook, and Rachel Pessah, a twenty-year-old woman from Israel, were married on May 27, 1974. Three days after the wedding, Rachel went to Israel by herself. When she returned to the United States on July 13, Rachel told Albert that she had fallen in love with a man she met in Israel, that she thought she might be pregnant by this other man, and that she wanted a divorce.

Nine days later, Albert and Rachel went to a movie. According to Albert, they engaged in heavy petting at the theater. When they got home, Albert expected to have sexual intercourse. Rachel, however, refused, telling Albert that although she had earlier intended to make love with Albert, she decided against it because she wanted to save herself for Yako, the man she had been seeing in Israel. Albert got angry and began to leave. When Rachel started screaming at him, he grabbed her by the throat, and choked her into unconsciousness. Two hours later, Albert called for a taxi to take his wife to the hospital. Albert then spent the night with a woman friend.

Three days later, Albert returned to the apartment. It was 3:00 P.M. and Rachel was not in. She did not return to the apartment that night. Throughout the evening, Albert kept thinking about his wife sleeping with another man, and it made him steam with anger. When Rachel finally came home at 11:00 A.M. the next day, she looked at Albert and said, "I suppose you have come here to kill me." Albert replied, "Yes," then "No," and finally "Yes" again, followed by "I have really come to talk to you." Angry words followed. In an explosion of anger, frustration, and exasperation, Albert grabbed his wife and strangled her with a telephone cord.[1]

Albert Berry was charged with first-degree murder and assault by means of force likely to produce great bodily injury. At trial, Berry's attorney requested a jury instruction on voluntary manslaughter, arguing that Berry was provoked into a heat of passion by Rachel's confession of adultery and the ensuing two-week period of sexual taunts and alternating acceptance and rejection. To support this request, Berry's defense attorney called a psychiatrist to the stand who testified that Rachel was a depressed, suicidal girl who sexually aroused Berry and then taunted him into jealous rages by repeated references to her affair with another man in an unconscious effort to provoke Berry into killing her.

The trial court refused to grant the defendant's request for a jury instruction on voluntary manslaughter, and Berry was convicted of first-degree murder. Berry appealed his conviction to the California Supreme Court. That court reversed Berry's conviction, on the ground that sufficient evidence of provocation existed to warrant a jury instruction on voluntary manslaughter.

The *Berry* case is a useful vehicle to understand the provocation defense in its various formulations. Provocation or heat of passion is a partial defense[2] that mitigates a murder charge to voluntary manslaughter.[3] Ordinarily, if a defendant intends to kill his victim, he acts with the malice aforethought required for a murder conviction. In a successful provocation case, however, the defendant, whose claimed loss of self-control negates the malice aforethought required for murder, is instead convicted of voluntary manslaughter. A voluntary manslaughter conviction makes a huge difference in one's possible sentence. In California, for example, a person convicted of voluntary manslaughter may be sentenced to a term of three, six, or eleven years in the state prison.[4] A person convicted of first-degree murder, in contrast, may be sentenced to a minimum of twenty-five years in prison up to a maximum of life imprisonment.[5] One convicted of second-degree murder may be sentenced to fifteen years to life.[6]

In order to receive the mitigation from murder to voluntary manslaughter, the defendant must have been incited to violence by "legally adequate provocation" and must not have had a reasonable opportunity to cool off between the time he was provoked and the time he killed the victim. Over the years, American courts and legislatures have embraced three different approaches to provocation. I call these three approaches the early common law or categorical test, the modern or reasonable person test, and the Model Penal Code's extreme emotional disturbance defense. Most jurisdictions today appear to use the modern reasonable person approach, but a significant number of states have instead adopted the Model Penal Code's extreme emotional disturbance defense.

## THE EARLY COMMON LAW'S CATEGORICAL APPROACH

In the 1700s, courts developed a short list of categories that constituted legally adequate provocation: "(1) an aggravated assault or battery, (2) mutual combat, (3) commission of a serious crime against a close relative of the defendant, (4) illegal arrest, [or] (5) observation by a husband of his wife committing adultery."[7] Only acts falling within these five categories could trigger the provocation mitigation.[8]

Because the categories were clearly defined, the judge would decide whether legally adequate provocation existed and consequently, whether the issue of provocation would even get to the jury. If the judge decided that legally adequate provocation existed, then the jury could return a verdict of murder, voluntary manslaughter, or acquit the defendant of all charges. If the judge decided that the allegedly provocative conduct by the victim did not fall within one of the narrow categories of legally adequate provocation, the jury would have only two choices: murder or complete acquittal.

One court explained the rationale behind the categorical approach as follows:

> To have the effect to reduce the guilt of the killing to the lower grade, the provocation must consist of personal violence. This rule is well established, and we imagine it would not be the part of wisdom to substitute in its place one fluctuating or less rigid, which would require the accused to be judged in each case according to the excitement incident to his natural temperament when aroused by real or fancied insult given by words alone. There must be an assault upon a person, as where the provocation was by pulling the nose, purposely jostling the slayer aside in the highway, or other direct and actual battery.[9]

The personal violence rationale may well explain the reasoning behind the first four categories,[10] but does not explain the fifth—observation by a husband of his wife in the act of adultery. Sexual betrayal might constitute an assault on the husband's ego, but is far from a physical attack upon a person.

If we look carefully at the early common law categories of legally adequate provocation, it becomes apparent that they were created with the hot-blooded man in mind. Men were thought more likely than women to be subjected to an aggravated assault or battery. Men were thought more likely than women to be involved in mutual combat. They were also thought more likely than women to respond with violence to a serious crime committed against a close relative.

The last category of legally adequate provocation, however, was the clearest indication that the early common law categories of legally adequate provocation were created by and for the male half of the population. The husband's observation of his wife having sexual relations with another man was the only category of legally adequate provocation at common law that explicitly applied to male defendants (husbands who killed their wives), and not their female counterparts (wives who killed their husbands).[11] Moreover, this last category was the only kind of provocation that did not involve violent behavior on the part of the victim toward the defendant. Nonetheless, it was considered the paradigmatic example of legally adequate provocation.[12]

A husband's observation of his wife in the act of adultery was thought to be such a grievous injury and affront to the husband that several states, including Georgia, Texas, Utah, and New Mexico, deemed the husband's killing of an adulterous wife or her lover a justifiable homicide—not a crime at all.[13] So strong was this sentiment that a New Mexico court gave a jury instruction on justifiable homicide even though the defendant in that case claimed he shot his wife's lover in self-defense, not because he was outraged and wanted to prevent adultery from taking place. In ruling that the trial court did not err in giving a justifiable homicide instruction, the Court of Appeals explained:

> The purpose of the law is not vindictive. It is humane. *It recognizes the ungovernable passion which possesses a man when immediately confronted with his wife's dishonor.* It merely says the man who takes life under those circumstances is not to be punished; not because he has performed a meritorious deed; but b*ecause he has acted naturally and humanly.* We in New Mexico have enacted [a law], as has been enacted in Texas, that [says], instead of mitigating the homicide to manslaughter, as at common law, such circumstances justify the act.[14]

Interestingly, in three out of the four states that recognized justifiable homicide (Georgia, Texas, and Utah), a husband could claim justifiable homicide only if he killed his rival, not if he killed his wife. In these states, if the husband killed his wife after catching her in the act of adultery, the appropriate charge was voluntary manslaughter. In a twisted way, perhaps the legislators who passed these justifiable homicide statutes were trying to protect wives by encouraging husbands to direct their passion and anger against the lover rather than against the wife herself. One court explained that killing the wife's lover was justifiable because such an act was necessary to protect the marriage; killing the wife, by contrast, was not justified because killing her would terminate the marriage.[15]

Why was a husband's observation of his wife in the act of adultery considered so provocative? Assumptions about married women as property belonging to their husbands contributed to the belief that adultery was an extraordinary affront to the husband's sense of self and his manhood.[16] At marriage, a woman was supposed to become one with her husband. Any property owned by the woman prior to marriage became the husband's property upon marriage. The wife herself was regarded as property of the husband. A wife could not own a credit card in her own name. She could not open an individual checking or savings account. She could not own property separate from her husband, nor could she obtain a home mortgage on her own. In many jurisdictions, a husband could not be convicted of raping his wife because she was considered his property.[17] Reva Siegel explains:

> By law, a husband acquired rights to his wife's person, the value of her paid and unpaid labor, and most property she brought into the marriage. A wife was obliged to obey and serve her husband, and the husband was subject to a reciprocal duty to support his wife and represent her within the legal system. According to the doctrine of marital unity, a wife's legal identity "merged" into her husband's, so that she was unable to file suit without his participation, whether to enforce contracts or to seek damages in tort.[18]

Another reason given for mitigating a killing by a husband who observed his wife in the act of adultery was that sexual infidelity rendered paternity uncertain. If a wife committed adultery with another man, she could then bear that man's child. Given the difficulty of determining the true father under such circumstances, a husband might do all he could, including killing his rival, to avoid having to pay the costs of rearing another man's child. Evolutionary psychologists argue that because men alone face this problem of paternity uncertainty, men are naturally more likely than women to respond to sexual infidelity with violence.[19]

The early common law approach was explicitly biased in favor of men. Only a husband could claim provocation at the sight of his wife in bed with another man. A wife who caught her husband having sexual relations with another woman was not permitted to claim she was provoked into a heat of passion. The law expected a dutiful wife to accept her philandering husband's misbehavior. If a wife killed her unfaithful husband or his lover, she was a murderer. Consider the case of Pearl Reed who killed her husband's mistress after catching the woman in a sexual embrace with her husband. Mrs. Reed tried unsuccessfully to come under Texas's justifiable homicide statute.

> Pearl Reed, a married woman living in Texas in the 1930s, left her husband to live with her parents because of marital difficulties. Later, she returned to her husband, but their relationship remained rocky.
>
> One evening, Pearl and her husband were helping out at a supper for the benefit of the church. A woman named Margaret Washington sent word to Pearl's husband that she wanted to come to the supper, but needed him to come get her. Pearl's husband left the supper without saying anything to Pearl. Pearl soon noticed that her husband was missing from the supper and suspected that he had gone to meet Margaret. Pearl found a pistol in the drawer of the house where the supper was being held and left the supper in search of her husband. She headed towards Margaret's house. About 300 yards from the house, she found her husband and Margaret in a sexual embrace by the side of the road. Pearl cried out, "Oh Bubba." Hearing Pearl's voice, Pearl's husband and Margaret jumped up and started running away. Pearl pulled out the pistol she'd found at the supper and fired at the two lovers, killing Margaret in the process.[20]

Pearl was charged with and convicted of murder. At the time of the shooting, the Texas Penal Code provided, "Homicide is justifiable when committed *by the husband* upon one taken in the act of adultery with the wife, provided the killing takes place before the parties to the act have separated."[21] Appealing her murder conviction, Pearl argued that because a husband had the right to kill his wife's lover if he caught his wife in the act of adultery, she too had the right to kill her husband's lover because she had caught the woman in the act of adultery with her husband.

The Texas Court of Appeals could have rejected Pearl Reed's appeal on the ground that she shot her husband's mistress after, not before, the two had separated. Because the statute required the killing to take place "before the parties to the act have separated," Pearl did not meet the requirements of the statute. Instead, the appellate court refused to apply the statute to Pearl on the ground that it was only intended to benefit husbands, not wives, who killed after catching their wives in the act of adultery. The court explained:

> We cannot agree with the contention of the appellant. No matter what our opinion might be upon the justice or injustice of article 1220, P.C., which justifies a homicide when committed by the husband upon one taken in the act of adultery with the wife, provided the killing takes place before the parties to the act have separated, it does not give the wife justification for her act if she should kill the woman taken in the act of adultery with her husband. The courts are not vested with the power to make laws but under the Constitution such power is vested alone in the Legislature, and the duties of the courts are to take and enforce them as they are written. If the Legislature in their wisdom has not given equal rights to the wife as they have given to the husband under article 1220, P.C., the courts are without power to do so.[22]

The Texas Court of Appeals deferred to the legislature rather than taking action to rectify the gender inequity reflected in the statute. A court hearing this case today might strike down the Texas statute on Equal Protection grounds because it treats similarly situated men and women differently.[23]

Elizabeth Rapaport explains that the mitigation or justification afforded husbands who killed in response to adultery by their wives was really about protecting the husband's sense of masculinity:

> Adultery is sufficient provocation by virtue of being assimilated to assault: The blow administered to the husband is moral, not physical. Adultery derogates from his manhood, which both entitles him and requires him to control his wife, sexually and otherwise. Within the

patriarchal conception of marriage, any challenge to masculine control—adulterous behavior or inclinations, contesting household authority, leaving—is an assault on both legitimate prerogatives and the very masculinity of the husband. Traditionally, violence to reassert possession or punish defiance has been considered legitimate masculine behavior. It is the rootedness of adultery provocation in patriarchal norms which explains why the extension of this mitigation to women who kill adulterous husbands did not occur until the law began to undergo the transition towards gender egalitarianism. It was not pain and anger at betrayal, which either the husband or wife may feel, that mitigated culpability at classical common law; rather, it was the defense of masculinity and its prerogatives and the legitimacy of violence as a vehicle of male control of the family.[24]

Eventually, the early common law's highly rigid categorical approach to provocation came under increasing criticism, not because it was seen as unfair to women who killed their unfaithful husbands, but because it was thought unfair to male murder defendants who could not meet the early common law's stringent requirements. Joshua Dressler explains:

Only a highly unrealistic belief about passion can explain [the common law] rule in terms of excusing conduct. It is implausible to believe that when an actor observes his or her loved one in an act of sexual disloyalty that actor will suffer from less anger simply because the disloyal partner is not the actor's spouse. Instead, this rule is really a judgment by courts that adultery is a form of injustice perpetrated upon the killer which merits a violent response, whereas "mere" sexual unfaithfulness out of wedlock does not. Thus, it has been said that adultery is the "highest invasion of [a husband's] property," whereas in the unmarried situation the defendant "has no control" over his faithless lover.[25]

Not only was the early categorical approach seen as unfair to *unmarried men* who claimed they were provoked into killing their unfaithful fiancées or girlfriends, it was also thought to be unfair to *married men* who learned of their wives' adultery through third parties or through their wives' own confessions. Under the early common law approach to provocation, Albert Berry, although a married man, would not have been entitled to argue that he was provoked into a heat of passion by Rachel's adultery because he did not personally discover Rachel in the act of adultery.[26]

## THE MODERN APPROACH:
## THE REASONABLE MAN STANDARD

Given the restricted nature of the categorical approach to provocation, in the late 1800s many jurisdictions began to abandon it in favor of an approach that employed a reasonableness requirement to determine which types of behavior could be considered legally adequate provocation.[27] Initially, this approach compared the defendant's actions to those of the hypothetical Reasonable Man. Later, in response to criticism that the Reasonable Man approach favored male defendants over female defendants, jurisdictions began to replace the words "Reasonable Man" with "Reasonable Person."

In modern jurisdictions, legally adequate provocation exists if the hypothetical reasonable person in the defendant's shoes would have been provoked into a heat of passion. For a defendant to receive the provocation mitigation, the jury must find that (1) the defendant was actually provoked into a heat of passion, (2) the reasonable person in the defendant's shoes would have been so provoked, (3) the defendant did not cool off, and (4) the reasonable person in the defendant's shoes would not have cooled off between the provocative event and the act or acts that led to the victim's death.[28] Because the defense of provocation is considered a case-in-chief defense attacking the existence of malice aforethought, the mental state required for a murder conviction, the state has the burden of disproving at least one of the above elements beyond a reasonable doubt.[29] In sending the case back to the jury to decide whether Berry's reaction was reasonable, the California Supreme Court's opinion in the *Berry* case reflects the modern approach to provocation.

Unlike the early common law approach which allowed a defendant to claim provocation only if he was responding to something that fell within one of the strictly defined categories of legally adequate provocation, the modern test adopts a context-sensitive approach that permits more defendants to claim provocation as a defense. The defendant need not be married to claim partner infidelity as legally adequate provocation, nor must the defendant personally discover his or her partner *in flagrante delicto* (in the act) in order to assert the defense. Moreover, the defendant doesn't have to be correct in his belief. Even perceived infidelity can constitute legally adequate provocation under the modern test. As long as the fact finder finds that the reasonable man (or woman) in the defendant's shoes would have been provoked into a heat of passion, the defendant may receive the mitigation to voluntary manslaughter.

Another difference between the early common law and the modern approach to provocation lies in who (or which body) gets to decide whether legally adequate provocation exists. As a general rule, judges decide questions of law while juries decide questions of fact. Under the early common law approach, the judge determined whether legally adequate provocation existed because the categories of legally adequate provocation were clearly delineated as a matter of law. In modern jurisdictions, while the judge plays an initial gatekeeper function, deciding whether there is sufficient evidence of provocation to permit defense argument on provocation, the jury ultimately decides whether the thing that provoked the defendant constitutes legally adequate provocation.[30] Legally adequate provocation exists if the Reasonable Person in the defendant's shoes would have been provoked into a heat of passion, and reasonableness is considered a mixed question of law and fact best left to a twelve-person jury reflecting the community's norms and values, rather than a single judge.

The modern approach to provocation appears to establish gender equality by giving men and women equal access to the defense.[31] In practice, however, the modern approach still ends up benefiting men more than women because more men than women kill their partners, and thus have the opportunity to use the provocation defense. According to statistics compiled by the U.S. Department of Justice, nearly 52,000 men and women were killed by someone with whom they shared an intimate relationship between 1976 and 1996.[32] Almost 30 percent of all female homicide victims were killed by husbands, former husbands, boyfriends, or former boyfriends, while less than 6 percent of all male homicide victims were killed by wives, former wives, girlfriends, or former girlfriends.[33] In 1996, approximately 2,000 intimate partner homicides were committed.[34] Of these 2,000 homicides, three out of every four victims were women.[35]

When women kill their male partners, they are not necessarily treated unfairly by the criminal justice system. Government studies indicate that female defendants in spouse murder cases are more likely to be acquitted than male defendants.[36] Additionally, female defendants convicted of killing their husbands tend to receive shorter prison sentences than male defendants convicted of killing their wives.[37] The average sentence for a convicted wife in a spouse murder case is six years. The average sentence for a convicted husband is 16.5 years.[38] While these numbers suggest the system is biased in favor of women and against men, the gender differential may also be due to the fact that grounds for claiming self-defense (e.g., being attacked by one's husband) are more often present in wife defendant cases than in husband defendant cases.*

The factors motivating intimate partner homicide are different for men than they are for women. Studies have found that most women who kill their male partners do so after suffering tremendous physical and psychological abuse.[39] In contrast, men charged with killing their female partners more often than not are motivated by sexual jealousy.[40] Even if these men are initially charged with first-degree murder, the majority end up being convicted of some lesser offense.[41] Because killing in response to female infidelity is seen as a mitigating factor, men who kill their female intimates are rarely charged with or convicted of capital murder. Elizabeth Rapaport calls this the "domestic discount"—a discount given only to men who claim they were provoked into killing their female domestic partners.[42]

Men who kill their wives were not always viewed so favorably. Carolyn Ramsey notes that during the 1800s, more than half of all defendants convicted of capital murder in New York County were men who had killed their wives or female lovers.[43] According to Ramsey, prosecutors were more likely to seek the death penalty for domestic murderers who failed to live up to then prevailing masculinity norms than men who killed male rivals. In Ramsey's view, the District Attorney had an incentive to sate the public's desire for harsh punishment by trying

---

* PATRICK A. LANGAN AND JOHN M. DAWSON, U.S. DEPT OF JUSTICE, SPOUSE MURDER DEFENDANTS IN LARGE URBAN COUNTIES 21 (1995) (noting that grounds for claiming self-defense are more often present in wife defendant cases than in husband defendant cases).

marginal figures, such as unemployed drunks who killed their wives, on capital charges.

Donna Coker observes that many men who kill in response to actual or perceived female partner infidelity have a history of violence that is overlooked or downplayed. Coker observes:

> Contrary to "[t]he popular image of the model citizen who one day goes beserk and kills a family member[,]" police studies have consistently found that men who kill their female partners have a *history* of violent behavior. Roughly 70% to 75% of domestic homicide offenders have been previously arrested and about 50% have been *convicted* [of] violent crimes.[44]

Moreover, according to Coker, men who kill their female partners in response to actual or perceived infidelity and those who abuse their female partners share much in common. Both blame the female victim for causing them to react violently. The man who kills his female partner maintains that her infidelity caused him to lose his self-control. The man who abuses his female partner blames her for failing to act the way a good wife, fiancée, or girlfriend should act.[45]

Coker points to several reasons to question the male abuser's claimed loss of self-control. First, abusive men in heterosexual relationships tend to direct their violence only against current or former wives, girlfriends, or children.[46] They may have similar feelings of frustration and rage in other settings, but do not respond with violence.[47] Coker explains that "[t]his is likely the result of differentially perceived risks as well as social learning that justifies violence against female partners (e.g., 'If I hit my boss, I would get fined and maybe arrested; but my *wife* is *supposed* to do what I say')."[48]

Second, men who beat their wives, but stop short of killing, often explain that the violence was not more severe because they did not want to seriously injure their partner, suggesting a level of control over the degree of violence which is inconsistent with the abuser's claim of loss of self-control.[49] In *Stiffed: The Betrayal of the American Man*, Susan Faludi recounts one convicted batterer's confession to his domestic violence counseling group:

> "I denied it before," he said of the night he pummeled his girlfriend, who had also worked on the base. As he spoke, he studied his massive,

callused hands, lying uselessly on his lap. "I thought I'd blacked out. But looking back at that night, when I beat her with an open hand, I didn't black out. I was feeling good. I was in power. I was strong. I was in control. I felt like a *man*." But what struck me most strongly was what he said next: that moment of control had been the only one in his recent life. "That feeling of power," he said, "didn't last long. Only until they put the cuffs on. Then I was feeling again like I was no man at all."[50]

Like the man who batters his female partner, one who kills his female partner because of infidelity, real or imagined, asserts he could not control himself, excusing his violent action as the result of an understandable loss of self-control. The same factors that cause us to question the abuser's claimed loss of self-control should make us question the man who claims his female partner made him do it. Moreover, often a significant period of time elapses between the event which triggers the claimed loss of self-control and the killing, suggesting the killing was deliberate and planned rather than spontaneous and uncontrolled.

In light of these patterns, Wendy Keller challenges us to answer a number of questions:

> It should be asked, however, why there exists such a large discrepancy between the number of men as opposed to the number of women claiming the killing committed was in response to this scenario of infidelity. Are husbands simply not committing adultery? Or, are women ignorant of their adulterous husbands? Or, alternatively, are women merely choosing not to confront their husbands in a deadly manner? If so, then perhaps manslaughter is just an embodiment of men's excuses and experiences.[51]

Some argue that the reason for the relatively small number of female defendants who kill their male partners in response to infidelity is biological—men have hormones that make them more physically aggressive than women.[52] Supporters of the biological explanation for male violence suggest that women respond to infidelity by turning their anger inward and becoming depressed, whereas men express their jealous anger by lashing out.[53] Moreover, fear of paternity uncertainty may encourage men to react more negatively and more aggressively than women in response to sexual infidelity.[54]

Biological anthropologists explain female passivity in response to male infidelity as a function of the fact that men are more likely than women to commit adultery.[55] According to this view, "the male tendency to commit adultery is caused by the Darwinian drive to produce offspring."[56] Miller explains, "Under this interpretation, men must fight instinct in order to remain faithful."[57]

In suggesting that men who kill in response to female infidelity are not responsible for their actions because their genes made them lose their self-control, the biological explanation obscures the role of socialization in encouraging male violence and aggression in response to sexual infidelity. "[A] man who commits adultery is less aberrant than a woman who does so; a wife who discovers that her husband has strayed is therefore socialized to be less surprised by such behavior."[58] Male infidelity is a common theme in our movies, television shows, and even (real world) politics (Gary Condit, Bill Clinton, Rudy Giuliani, and Gary Hart). Some studies, such as the *Hite Report on Male Sexuality*, report that as many as 72 percent of married men have committed adultery, feeding the perception that male infidelity is something to be expected.[59]

The acceptance of male infidelity as part of human nature is in stark contrast to the condemnation of women with whom these married men stray. Though less so today, many place most of the blame for an extramarital affair between a married man and an unmarried woman on the woman. The "other woman" is considered a homewrecker, even if the house she is accused of wrecking would probably be in a state of disrepair with or without her.

Female infidelity, in contrast, is not expected. Women are supposed to be monogamous. Monogamy as such is very much a matter of male entitlement. The words used to describe female infidelity (she was "cheating" on me, she was sleeping around, she was whoring) suggest the man's entitlement to his female partner's sexuality. Therefore, when a man finds out that his female partner has been unfaithful, his violent reaction is understandable.

The biological explanation for male violence in response to female infidelity fails to account for the growing number of women who, like their male counterparts, are sexually unfaithful. The same report that found up to 72 percent of married men have committed adultery also found that 70 percent of all married women have had at least one extramarital affair.[60] If both men and women are unfaithful sexual partners, then it seems there must be some other reason why we think it is reasonable or at least understandable when a man reacts violently to the discovery of sexual infidelity, but not when a woman does so.

Despite evidence that both men and women can and do cheat on their partners, we continue to assume that men, but not women, have a natural tendency to be sexually promiscuous. This assumption finds its roots, at least in part, in social attitudes and beliefs about what it means to be a man in today's society. As early as junior high school, young boys learn that scoring with as many girls as possible gives them the positive image of being a stud. Although the current directors of the James Bond film series have tried to be more responsive to a female audience that does not want to see women depicted only as sex objects, for many years James Bond (007) was portrayed as a ladies' man, an eligible bachelor who successfully lured into bed all the beautiful women he encountered. In short, Bond was a playboy and it was desirable to be a playboy. Former President Bill Clinton at least at one time was viewed as an extremely sexy and charismatic man. Even though he was caught lying under oath about an extramarital affair with a White House intern, his public approval ratings remained high during his impeachment trial because he was just being a bad boy and well, boys will be boys.

In contrast, consider the things that are said about women who "play around." Women with numerous sexual partners are considered promiscuous and immoral. Women who sleep around are called sluts and whores. The virtuous woman, the kind a man wants to bring home to meet his parents, loves only one man. She controls her sexual desires.

Given these assumptions, when a man finds his female partner in bed with another man, his sense of outrage and betrayal is supported by a society that disapproves of her behavior. A man in this situation who kills his female partner or her lover can appeal to societal expectations to show that his use of violence was a reasonable response to his female partner's infidelity. A woman who finds her man in a compromising position is supposed to either accept his philandering as an expression of human nature or leave him. She is not supposed to kill him.

## THE "MERE WORDS" RULE

Most modern courts have retained the "mere words" rule, a vestige of the early common law approach. Under this rule, words alone can never constitute legally adequate provocation.[61] The "mere words" rule is based on the idea that a reasonable person should be able to tolerate verbal insults rather than respond with physical violence.[62]

Under the early common law approach, the "mere words" rule made sense. Only things included in the short list of categories of legally adequate provocation were sufficient to mitigate a homicide that would otherwise be considered a murder down to manslaughter. Anything off the list was insufficient. Words were not on the list, so they couldn't constitute legally adequate provocation.

The mere words rule makes less sense under the modern formulation of the provocation doctrine. Under the modern test, the jury is charged with determining whether a reasonable person in the defendant's shoes would have been provoked. This means that in most cases the judge defers to the jury on the question of whether the defendant was reasonably provoked into a heat of passion and whether there was a reasonable amount of time for the defendant to cool off. Arguably it would be logical to permit the jury to consider any and all claims of provocation, including claims that extremely insulting or inflammatory words provoked the defendant into a heat of passion. The mere words rule, however, precludes the jury from deciding these issues.

The *Berry* case could have been, but was not, interpreted as a mere words case. Berry never actually observed his wife in the act of adultery. What provoked him was his wife's confession that she had committed adultery. Despite the mere words rule, the California Supreme Court held that Berry should have been given the opportunity to argue to the jury that he was reasonably provoked into a heat of passion because his wife not only confessed to adultery, she also tormented him for two weeks by feigning sexual interest and then rejecting him.[63] The *Berry* case is not the only case of its kind. Other courts have permitted male murder defendants to argue they were reasonably provoked by their wives' confessions of adultery, creating an exception to the rule that mere words do not constitute legally adequate provocation.[64]

Some have tried to explain this inconsistent treatment of words, noting that some courts draw a distinction between informational words (i.e., words that convey information that, if observed directly, would provoke the reasonable person into a heat of passion) and insulting words.[65] Under this distinction, informational words such as confessions of adultery are considered more provocative than verbal insults.

It is not necessarily true that informational words are more provocative than insulting words. Depending on the context, a racial insult can be just as provocative as a confession of adultery. For example, a Black man who has suffered from racial discrimination all his life may be particularly sensitive to being called the N word. In contrast, a man who knows that his wife sees other men may not be outraged by a confession of adultery. If courts are going to permit some defendants to argue they were reasonably provoked into a heat of passion by words uttered by the victim, they should allow other defendants to make the same claim.

## THE MODEL PENAL CODE APPROACH: EXTREME MENTAL OR EMOTIONAL DISTURBANCE

It appears that at least twenty states have adopted the Model Penal Code's approach to provocation.[66] Under the Model Penal Code, a person who would otherwise be guilty of murder is guilty of manslaughter if he killed another person while suffering from an "extreme mental or emotional disturbance for which there is a 'reasonable explanation or excuse.'"[67] Section 210.3(1)(b) of the Code provides:

(1) Criminal homicide constitutes manslaughter when:

\* \* \*

(b) a homicide which would otherwise be murder is committed under the influence of extreme mental or emotional disturbance for which there is reasonable explanation or excuse. The reasonableness of such explanation or excuse shall be determined from the viewpoint of a person in the actor's situation under the circumstances as he believes them to be.[68]

While the burden of proving or disproving the elements of this defense can be placed on either the government or the defendant, many states that have adopted the Model Penal Code's extreme emotional disturbance defense place the burden of proving the elements of this defense on the defendant.[69]

Like modern formulations of the provocation defense, the Model Penal Code version lets the jury, rather than the judge, decide whether the defendant ought to receive the mitigation.[70] Apart from this one similarity, the two approaches are significantly different. Unlike the modern test, the Model Penal Code does not require proof of legally adequate provocation triggering the defendant's loss of self-control.[71] Rather than focus on the nature of the provocation, the Model Penal Code approach focuses on the defendant's subjective state of mind— whether the defendant was suffering from an extreme mental or emotional disturbance. Additionally, the Model Penal Code does not require the absence of a cooling off period.[72] A defendant may receive the partial mitigation even if the killing took place after a long period of tension-building.[73] Finally, the Model Penal Code rejects categorical restrictions on the defense of provocation still viable in many modern jurisdictions, such as the mere words rule and the misdirected retaliation rule.[74]

Under the Model Penal Code formulation of the heat of passion defense, the defendant must have actually (or subjectively) suffered from an extreme mental or emotional disturbance for which he or she has a *reasonable* explanation or excuse. Because the reasonableness of the defendant's explanation or excuse is determined from the viewpoint of a person in the defendant's situation under the circumstances as the defendant believes them to be, the Code subjectivizes the reasonableness inquiry to a greater extent than permitted by the modern approach. The drafters explained that they were purposely introducing more subjectivity into the reasonableness determination while attempting to retain the determination's objective character:

> There is a larger element of subjectivity in the standard than there was under prevailing law, though it is only the actor's "situation" and "the circumstances as he believes them to be," not his scheme of moral values, that are thus to be considered. The ultimate test, however, is objective; there must be "reasonable" explanation or excuse for the actor's disturbance.[75]

Although the drafters of the Code may have intended to retain the objective nature of the reasonable person standard, any objectivity gained by using the term "reasonable" is undermined by requiring a subjective evaluation of the defendant's explanation or excuse. By stating that the reasonableness of the explanation or excuse for the actor's extreme mental or emotional disturbance must be "determined from the viewpoint of a person in the actor's situation under the circumstances as he believes them to be,"[76] the Code allows the defendant's subjective perspective to control the outcome. Subjectivizing the reasonableness standard is almost as good as getting rid of it altogether.[77]

The subjective Model Penal Code approach has led to some shocking verdicts.[78] In a few cases, juries have rejected murder charges in favor of manslaughter when the provocation consisted of a female partner dancing with another man.

> January 16, 1979. Little Rock, Arkansas. Randall Dixon and Rebecca Newman went to a bar to celebrate their engagement to marry. Randall became jealous when Rebecca asked a male friend to dance with her. Randall stormed off and went home. He returned to the bar only after his sister asked him to return. Upon entering the bar, Randall saw that his fiancée was still dancing and having a good time with her male friend. Randall charged onto the dance floor and knocked Rebecca down. He then hit her so hard that a waitress said it could be heard all over the bar. By this time, it was almost 2:00 A.M. Randall was ejected from the bar. Randall insisted that Rebecca come home with him to his apartment. Once there, he continued to beat her. Randall's thirteen-year-old niece and her girlfriend were at the apartment and testified that Rebecca had bruises all over her face. Her eyes were black, her jaws were swollen, and her nose was bleeding. Rebecca begged Randall to stop hitting her, and then passed out. Subsequently, Rebecca died of cranial cerebral injuries.[79]

Dixon was charged with murder in the second degree. At trial, he claimed that he should be found guilty of manslaughter rather than murder because at the time of the incident, he was suffering from an extreme emotional disturbance. Dixon explained that the reason he became so emotionally distraught was because Rebecca had asked another man to dance with her. Dixon felt Rebecca was not acting the way a fiancée ought to behave. When he came back to the bar and saw Rebecca laughing and dancing with the same man, he simply lost his self-control. Instructed to decide the reasonableness of Dixon's explanation from his perspective, the jury returned a verdict of manslaughter.

Because the only information about this case appears in a short three-page court opinion, little is known about Dixon except that he was a man living in Arkansas at the time of the killing. It is unlikely that he belonged to a religious group that frowns upon drinking and dancing, given that he was celebrating his upcoming marriage in a bar. We do not know his class status or race. We only know that this incident took place in the South.

Place seems to play a role both in terms of an individual's propensity toward violence upon taking offense and the jury's willingness to excuse such violence. In *Culture of Honor: The Psychology of Violence in the South*,[80] Richard Nisbett and Dov Cohen seek to explain why homicide rates are higher for White males in the South than they are for White males in the North. After examining Southern and Northern male attitudes toward violence and their comparative behavioral responses to insult, Nisbett and Cohen found that Southern men are more likely than their Northern counterparts to approve of the use of force in response to insults. In the South, "[i]nsults cannot be ignored, because a man's reputation for strength and toughness is compromised until he proves himself through violence, or at least through dominant or aggressive behavior signaling a capacity for violence."[81] In laboratory experiments, Southerners actually experienced physiological changes when they were insulted. Their cortisol and testosterone levels increased more than their Northern counterparts, and they were more likely to end the incident with verbal or physical aggression. Nisbett and Cohen's work on the psychology of violence in the South suggests that individuals from that region tend to take offense more easily than individuals from other parts of the country, and have a greater tendency to resort to violence in response to insults to honor.[82] This may help explain why Dixon felt that his outrage upon seeing his fiancée dancing with another man was reasonable and why his jury agreed with him.

Place, however, only goes so far in explaining why juries sometimes accept claims that seem patently unreasonable. In a similar case arising in Connecticut, a man became distraught at the sight of his *former* girlfriend dancing with another man. This man stalked his former girlfriend for two weeks, watching her apartment to see who visited her and who spent the night. After two weeks of stalking, this man accosted his former girlfriend at her apartment and then killed her.

June 21, 1987. 4:00 A.M. Bridgeport, Connecticut. Forty-four-year-old Hipolito Martinez waited outside Esther Grajalez Perez's house at 407 Nichols Street. She wasn't home. What was she doing out this late? Who was she going out with at four o'clock in the morning? As he waited, Hipolito became increasingly agitated. Even though he was a married man, Hipolito had gone out with Esther for approximately four years. The last year-and-a-half of their relationship, Hipolito stayed at Esther's place on the weekends and the YMCA during the week. In November 1986, Esther told Hipolito she wanted to break up. He moved out after a loud argument. He was bitter and angry about the breakup. He had wanted so much for the two of them, but Esther had only wanted him on the weekends. She just wanted to party. After Esther broke up with him, she dated other men. This bothered Hipolito tremendously.

The first weekend in June, Esther called Hipolito and asked him if he wanted to go dancing. They met at the Calypso. There, another man asked Esther to dance. Hipolito was furious. The way the two were dancing made Hipolito think they were dating. In fact, the man dancing with Esther was Leonardo Mieles, Esther's brother. Hipolito told Esther that he would shoot her one day.

After the incident at the Calypso, Hipolito started hanging around Esther's apartment building. He wanted to find out who was spending the night with her. He was also agitated because Esther telephoned his wife and told her that Hipolito wanted to get back together with her, that he had made trouble for her at the Calypso, and that she didn't want Hipolito because she had a new boyfriend. At midnight on June 20, Hipolito stood outside Esther's apartment and threw rocks at her window.

June 21. 4:00 A.M. Hipolito waited for Esther in front of her apartment. His .32 caliber gun was in a holster on his belt. Finally, a car pulled up. Hipolito saw Esther in the passenger's seat. Esther spotted Hipolito and asked her brother, Leonardo, who had just taken her and her sons to the airport, to come up with her to her apartment. As she approached her front door, Hipolito grabbed her arm and pointed a gun at her. Leonardo tried to separate the two, but Hipolito turned the gun on Leonardo and said, "This isn't between you and me, it's between her and me." Leonardo backed off and went to the car to call the police. Hipolito dragged Esther from her doorway, and forced her to walk across the street, muttering repeatedly, "You made me do this." He then struck Esther in the face and shot her five times. Shortly after the shooting, Hipolito told police, "I shot her and I hope she dies."[83]

Martinez was charged with murder. At trial, he argued he was suffering from an extreme emotional disturbance. The sight of his former girlfriend dancing with another man was Martinez's "reasonable" explanation for his emotional disturbance even though this observation took place two weeks before he killed her. The jury returned a verdict of manslaughter, agreeing with Martinez that, from his perspective, his explanation was reasonable.

The Model Penal Code's subjective approach, permitting mitigation whenever a defendant can show he (or she) was actually suffering from an extreme mental or emotional disturbance at the time of the homicide, is extremely problematic because it provides an excuse to almost any defendant who appears credible on the stand. The requirement that the defendant's explanation or excuse be reasonable does not provide much of a check on the defendant's subjective showing, since the Code directs the trier of fact to determine the reasonableness of the defendant's explanation from the viewpoint of a person in the defendant's position viewing the circumstances as the defendant believed them to be.

A third case, also from Connecticut, highlights the problematic nature of the Model Penal Code approach to provocation.

Mark Chicano and Ellen Babbit were involved in a romantic relationship that had deteriorated by the end of 1986. At approximately 2:00 A.M. on February 28, 1987, Mark went to Ellen's home in East Windsor, Connecticut. While outside the house, Mark saw Ellen's new boyfriend, Raymond Arnold, arrive and enter the house. Mark then walked around the house and stood outside Ellen's bedroom where he could hear Ellen and Raymond making love. After thirty minutes of standing outside the bedroom window, Mark quietly entered the house and hid in the bathroom for an hour. Once he was certain Ellen and Raymond were asleep, Mark crept into the bedroom and struck Raymond on the head with a crowbar. Ellen cried out and tried to protect Raymond. This only enraged Mark who continued to strike Raymond with the crowbar until Raymond was lifeless. Mark then started kicking and punching Ellen. Because she was resisting so fiercely, Mark tried to tie Ellen's hands. At this point, Ellen's eleven-year-old son entered the room and started screaming. Mark turned to the boy, grabbed him by the throat to quiet him, and then strangled him to death. Mark turned back to Ellen and struck her on the head twice with the crowbar, killing her almost instantly.[84]

Chicano was charged with three counts of murder, felony murder, and other crimes. At trial, he intimated he was acting under an extreme emotional disturbance caused by hearing his former girlfriend Ellen and her new boyfriend making love. One heavily contested issue was where Chicano got the crowbar which he used to kill two of the three victims. The government contended that Chicano brought the crowbar with him in his car to Ellen's house. If this were the case, Chicano likely planned to kill his former girlfriend. A planned killing usually constitutes first-degree murder. The defense, however, claimed Chicano found the crowbar in Ellen's home and used it because it was handy. Of course, even if it were true that Chicano used a crowbar which he found in the house, it still would have taken some thought and effort on his part to locate and use it in the fatal attack. A three-judge panel, however, focused on whether Chicano brought the crowbar with him to Ellen's home and found insufficient evidence that he did. After concluding that Chicano met the requirements of the affirmative defense of extreme emotional disturbance, the panel found Chicano guilty of three counts of manslaughter in the first degree, rather than murder.[85]

As these cases illustrate, the Model Penal Code's subjective approach permits the mitigation in many cases in which the early common law approach and the modern approach would not. In a Model Penal Code jurisdiction, as long as the jury believes the defendant was acting under an extreme emotional disturbance for which there is a "reasonable" explanation or excuse (from the defendant's perspective), the jury may return a manslaughter verdict. When killing a former girlfriend or a fiancée for dancing with another man is partially excused, the law sends a message that men who react violently, even fatally, to such activity deserve sympathy rather than condemnation for their actions.

## POST–MODEL PENAL CODE ATTEMPTS TO ADDRESS PROBLEMS WITH THE DOCTRINE OF PROVOCATION

Some jurisdictions are changing their laws to make it more difficult for men who kill in response to female infidelity to assert that they acted in a heat of passion. These reforms have taken one of two forms. First, in what appears to be a return to the early common law's categorical approach, some states are adopting categorical exclusions. Unlike the early common law which named categories of legally adequate provocation, these states identify categories of inadequate provocation.[86] Second, at least one state has attempted to abolish the defense of provocation.[87]

In an example of categorical exclusion, the Maryland legislature in 1997 added a statutory provision to Maryland's Penal Code. Section 387A of the Annotated Code of Maryland (Criminal Law) provides, "The discovery of one's spouse engaged in sexual intercourse with another person does *not* constitute legally adequate provocation for the purpose of mitigating a killing from the crime of murder to voluntary manslaughter."[88] In essence, Maryland has ruled that as a matter of law the discovery of one's spouse in the act of adultery is not legally adequate provocation.[89] The Kenneth Peacock case was probably the motivating force behind this change.

> February 8, 1994. Towson, Maryland. 5:00 P.M. Kenneth Peacock, a thirty-six-year-old truck driver, called his thirty-one-year-old wife Sandy to let her know that the roads were icy and he wouldn't make it home that night. An outgoing, fun-loving spirit, Sandy decided to go to a new bar in the town of Maryland Line where she ran into her friend Bruce Leslie Morgan. Sandy and Bruce both had a lot to drink before leaving the bar and going to Sandy's home. According to Bruce, Sandy promptly took off all her clothes and jumped into bed. Bruce was so drunk, he passed out before climaxing.
>
> Midnight. Bruce was knocked awake by an angry Ken Peacock, who had come home earlier than expected and was pointing a rifle at him. Ken yelled at Bruce to get out of his house. He then shouted to his sobbing wife, "Shut up, bitch. I can't believe you did this to me." Still drunk, Bruce stumbled out of the house.
>
> Once alone, Ken and Sandy proceeded to argue. At a lull in the argument, Sandy called her mother and told her she was moving out. Ken grabbed the phone and told his mother- in-law, "She's lucky if I let her live to leave." Ken, still holding onto his rifle, was so upset that he proceeded to drink a gallon of wine and four beers.
>
> February 9, 1994. 4:00 A.M. Ken leveled his rifle at his wife who was lying on the sofa. A shot rang out. Ken dialed 911 and told the police that he shot his wife in the head because she was sleeping around on him.[90]

Peacock was initially charged with first-degree murder. Later, prosecutors permitted him to plead guilty to voluntary manslaughter be-

cause they believed his claim that he was provoked into a heat of passion by finding his wife in bed with another man. At Peacock's sentencing hearing, prosecutors argued for a sentence of three to eight
years. The defense asked for probation on the ground that Peacock did
not intend to shoot his wife. Peacock maintained he pointed his rifle at
Sandy merely to frighten her and the gun accidentally discharged. Undermining Peacock's claim of an accidental shooting was a history of
domestic violence. According to Sandy's mother, her daughter spent
one night in a motel with a guard outside her door because she was so
afraid of her husband.

On October 17, 1994, Judge Robert Cahill sentenced Peacock to
eighteen months in prison and fifty hours of community service.[91] Because Peacock received credit for time served, he was out of jail within
two weeks. Judge Cahill explained that he was reluctant to give any jail
time at all to Peacock, explaining, "I seriously wonder how many men
married five, four years would have the strength to walk away without
inflicting some corporal punishment. I am forced to impose a sentence
only because I think I must do it to make the system honest."[92]

Judge Cahill's remarks provoked an angry response from many
women. Baltimore District Court Judges Teaette Price and Sandra Gray
noted that Judge Cahill's comments reflect "a stereotypical view of the
proper or expected behavior of a husband who finds his wife engaged
in infidelity."[93] Melinda Towne, Maryland Chapter President for the
National Organization for Women, criticized the characterization of the
event as a heat of passion killing:

> Most people might be angry and upset [if they found their spouse in
> bed with someone else], but we have to remember that this man
> waited [four hours] before going back and killing his wife. This was
> not a spur-of-the-moment emotional response. We don't think a
> woman would have been treated the same way if she went back and
> killed her husband the same way.[94]

Kim Gandy, Executive Vice President for the National Organization for
Women, echoed these sentiments, commenting, "The sentencing reflects the judge's attitude toward this woman, that she was [her husband's] property, that he had the right to be judge, jury and execu-
tioner."[95] The public outrage following Judge Cahill's remarks likely led
the Maryland legislature to add section 387A to the Maryland penal

code, providing that the observation of a spouse in the act of adultery does not constitute legally adequate provocation.[96]

One might think that disallowing the provocation defense only in certain situations, such as the observation of a spouse in the act of adultery, does not go far enough, and that the best way to deal with the gender bias inherent in the doctrine is to completely abolish provocation as a defense to murder.[97] The state of Texas attempted to do something of this sort in the mid-1990s. In September 1994, the Texas legislature revised its penal code to eliminate heat of passion as a partial defense to murder.[98] Under Texas law, sudden passion no longer acts to mitigate a murder down to manslaughter and may only be considered at the penalty phase of the trial. If the jury finds sudden passion in the penalty phase, the defendant will be convicted of second- rather than first-degree murder.[99]

Despite this change, a Texan who shot and killed his wife in December 1998 because she had invited her lover into the family home was able to receive a sentence of probation because the jury found he had acted in a sudden heat of passion:

December 1998. Fort Worth, Texas. Jimmy Watkins, a thirty-three-year-old supervisor of a waste disposal company, and his thirty-year-old wife, Nancy, were married in 1984. In 1997, the couple began having marital problems. Nancy, who worked at a Wal-Mart store, began seeing one of her coworkers, Keith Fontenot. On December 21, 1998, Nancy kicked Jimmy out of the house after he sexually assaulted one of her relatives. Keith Fontenot moved in the same day. Following his removal from the house, Jimmy started calling Nancy using his cellular phone every few minutes. He called her at 11:25 P.M., 11:29 P.M., 11:30 P.M., 11:31 P.M., 11:37 P.M., and 11:43 P.M. He stopped calling her for about three hours, then called her again at 3:24 A.M. on December 22. Later that day, he called his wife three more times. The last time he called, it was 3:30 P.M. Jimmy called Nancy from his cellular phone while he was just outside the family home. He asked his wife where she was in the house. When she told him she was in the kitchen, he kicked in the kitchen door, burst in, and shot her in the head with a 9 millimeter handgun while their ten-year-old son watched. He then turned his gun on Keith, shooting him twice. The third time he pulled the trigger, the gun didn't go off. Thinking he was out of bullets, Jimmy fled in his green GMC pickup truck. While driving, Jimmy discovered he still had bullets left. His gun had simply jammed. He pulled over to the side of the road to fix his gun, then headed back to the house. While his wife was on the phone with 911 dispatchers pleading for help, Jimmy shot her five more times, killing her.[100]

Watkins was charged with murder. At trial, he argued that he was distraught over his wife's affair and simply snapped when he found out that his wife's lover had moved into the family home. The jury found Watkins guilty of murder, but then recommended a sentence of probation because he killed his wife in a sudden heat of passion.[101] In October 1999, Judge Robert Gill sentenced Watkins to ten years of probation. As a condition of probation, Watkins was ordered to serve four months in custody and pay a $10,000 fine.

Watkins did not walk in on his wife while she was in bed with another man. He shot her in the kitchen of the family home in front of their ten-year-old son. Watkins stopped shooting only because his gun jammed. After he fixed the jam, he returned to the house to finish the job, pumping five more bullets into his wife while she was on the phone with 911, pleading for help. Watkins's probationary sentence for murdering his wife is a reminder that even today, some people think a man's violent reaction to female partner infidelity is normal or reasonable.

## REVISITING THE *BERRY* CASE

The story told at the beginning of this chapter was largely Albert Berry's story, the one he told when he testified at trial and the one his attorney told when he appealed Berry's murder conviction to the California Supreme Court. Berry asserted that Rachel was screaming at him before he choked her into unconsciousness the first time and before he strangled her with a telephone cord several days later. Yet how do we know whether Rachel was actually screaming? Perhaps Albert heard screaming when Rachel was trying to talk to him. Perhaps Albert remembered screaming when there was only noise and confusion. Perhaps Albert made up a screaming Rachel to support his assertion that he was provoked into a heat of passion. Rachel Pessah, the only other person to witness the events preceding her death, can't tell us what happened because she is dead. Her side of the story was never heard. Yet Berry's version of what happened was the only one represented in the California Supreme Court's opinion.

If one digs beneath the surface and goes beyond the facts as reported in the California Supreme Court opinion, as law professor Donna Coker did by reviewing the transcripts of the trial testimony, one discovers that Berry had a history of prior violence against his other female partners. Before he married Rachel Pessah, Berry stabbed his second wife eleven times in the abdomen with a butcher knife after she called out the name of another man while she and Berry were having sex.[102] In other relationships, Berry destroyed property and threatened physical violence against his female partners to keep them in line.[103] In Berry's statement to the police, he admitted, "I deliberately waited to kill [Rachel]. No pretense, no bullshi[t], no nothing."[104] With this additional information, Berry's claim that he was reasonably provoked by Rachel's behavior is disingenuous.

The *Berry* case is often cited for its "extremely elastic interpretation of the cooling-off requirement."[105] The "no time to cool off" requirement in the modern test is intended to ensure that the defendant truly acted in a heat of passion, not as the result of premeditation and deliberation. As Donna Matthews and Caroline Forell note, "Most courts require that a relatively short interval—usually only a few minutes—occur between the provocation and the killing. However, like the expanded scope of provocation . . . many courts stretch the cooling-off time when men kill their intimates."[106] Even though Albert Berry found out about his wife's infidelity two weeks before he killed her, and waited in Rachel's apartment for twenty hours before strangling her with a telephone cord, the California Supreme Court thought a rational jury could find that a reasonable man in Berry's shoes would not have cooled off during this time period.

Under the Model Penal Code approach, not only would Berry be permitted to argue extreme emotional disturbance to the jury, most likely he would be successful in receiving a manslaughter verdict. Arguably, only an extremely disturbed individual would strangle his wife to death with a telephone cord. Berry's excuse would be Rachel's confession of adultery and her subsequent behavior, teasing him sexually and then rejecting him. Because the reasonableness of this explanation would be determined from Berry's perspective, the trier of fact would likely conclude that this was a reasonable explanation for Berry's extreme emotional disturbance.

Of course, not all claims of provocation are so unsympathetic. The *Berry* case may be included in most criminal law casebooks and taught to first-year law students precisely because it is so outrageous. The case makes us question the modern approach to provocation. It makes us question the desirability of an open-ended reasonableness requirement that permits defendants like Berry to argue they were reasonably provoked by a confession of marital infidelity.

Finding out that one's partner, male or female, has been unfaithful is a devastating experience. The infidelity reflects a profound betrayal of trust and in most cases damages the relationship beyond all hope of repair. Discovering one's partner in bed with another person only multiplies the feelings of anger, outrage, betrayal, and profound sadness that accompany the information conveyed. It is thus understandable why lawmakers, judges, prosecutors, and jurors sympathize with the man who lashes out in anger in response to his female partner's infidelity. The provocation defense allows the jurors to translate their sympathy for the defendant into a verdict that relieves the defendant of murder liability. The defense also allows jurors to register their disapproval of the act of killing by returning a verdict of voluntary manslaughter.

While the provocation defense offers the benefit of allowing the law to reflect gradations of culpability, unfairness can result when certain defendants and not others are able to bolster their claims of reasonableness by relying on commonly held beliefs and attitudes about what it means to be a man in today's society. The reasonableness requirement, while providing a useful and necessary check on the defendant's subjective emotional distress, opens the door to inconsistent treatment of similar claims. What is reasonable to an American jury is a function of what is considered typical or normal in America. As we shall see, normality in America has an overlooked gender, race, and sexual orientation.

# 2

# Unreasonable Women, Gay Men, and Men of Color

## HETEROSEXUAL MALE INFIDELITY

Betty was seventeen when she met Dan. It was love at first sight. Dan, who had just been accepted to Cornell Medical School, began writing to Betty every day, signing his letters, "Love, D" with an "X" representing a kiss. They were married in April 1969, and soon Betty was pregnant with the first of four children. After receiving his medical degree, Dan decided to go to law school so he could realize his dream of becoming a millionaire before the age of forty. It was Betty's dream too. Whatever her husband wanted, she was there to support him. The two moved to Cambridge where Dan attended Harvard Law School. Betty worked a part-time night job at a department store and babysat during the day to pay the bills. She got pregnant again and bore their second child. After Dan graduated from law school, he landed a job as an associate at Gray, Cary, Ames and Frye, a large law firm in San Diego. Because his income was only $30,000 per year, the family lived in a low-rent apartment and Betty worked nights at a restaurant to help pay the bills. Once they had saved enough money, the family moved to La Jolla, and Betty bore a third child.

In 1978, Dan decided to leave Gray Cary and set up his own law practice. Dan was an instant success. In the first three months on his own, he made more money than he had ever made in one year at the law firm. Soon after, Betty became pregnant with their fourth child. Although Dan's law practice was booming, Dan began coming home later and later. Sometimes he would sneak out at nights after Betty had gone to bed. Betty suspected Dan was having an affair with Linda Kolkena, a young woman who worked as a receptionist in Dan's office building (and bore an uncanny resemblance to Betty in her younger days). In 1983, Dan hired Linda to work as his personal office assistant. Soon Betty began hearing from friends that Dan and Linda were being seen around town, having lunch together at expensive restaurants, and attending black-tie events. Yet every time Betty confronted Dan, he denied there was anything going on between him and Linda. In November of that year, Betty decided to surprise Dan on his birthday. She got dressed up and went to his office with a bottle of champagne, but was told that Dan and Linda had gone out to lunch. She waited all afternoon, but Dan never came back to the office. She saw Linda's office next to Dan's, beautifully furnished with a view of the bay and a framed picture of Dan on a white horse, and she knew that Linda was not simply Dan's office assistant. Betty marched back home, took Dan's clothes out of his closet, threw them in a pile in the yard, and set them on fire. Then she poured black paint on the smoldering remains.

In 1985, Dan finally told Betty that he had been having an affair with Linda Kolkena for the past three years. Dan also told Betty that he wanted a divorce. To add insult to injury, Dan told Betty he thought she should be committed to a mental institution. Betty refused to be committed. After being served with divorce papers, Betty's mental condition, already unstable, deteriorated rapidly. When Dan sold the home they had owned together without her consent, she drove her car through the door of his new house. When he took Linda and the kids on a "family" vacation, she went to Dan's home and threw a bottle of wine through the living room window. She left obscene messages on Dan's home answering machine, calling Dan "F———head" and Linda "The Cunt." She acted out, all the while hoping that somehow someday her Dan would come back to her.

Finally, on November 5, 1989, Betty drove to Dan and Linda's new home at 5:30 in the morning. She brought a gun with her to make sure Dan listened to her this time. If he didn't listen to her and give her custody of the kids, she was going to blow her own brains out in front of him to make him suffer. When she got to the house, she quietly let herself in with a key she had surreptitiously taken from her daughter's key ring. She went up the stairs into the master bedroom and entered the room, gun in hand. She wasn't emotionally ready for what she saw. Her ex-husband Dan was lying there in his boxer shorts with his new wife. Linda, thin and beautiful, was wearing black-and-white polka-dot short pajamas. Hearing Betty rustle, Dan and Linda woke up and saw Betty in their bedroom with a gun. One of them yelled, "Call the police." Suddenly, she was shooting. One shot tore into Linda's chest and another into the back of her head. A third shot hit Dan's back. Betty's two remaining bullets narrowly missed hitting Dan and

Linda. One went into the wall. The other went into the bed stand near Linda's head. Betty could hear Dan gurgling on his own blood as he tried to reach for the phone. Without hesitating, she marched over to the other side of the bed, ripped the phone out of the wall, and fled.[1]

Betty Broderick was charged with two counts of first-degree murder. At trial, her attorney argued that psychological abuse by her former husband and his new wife provoked her into a heat of passion that led to the killings.[2] Broderick's first jury couldn't reach a unanimous verdict. Ten of the jurors felt Broderick should be convicted of murder. Two jurors felt manslaughter was a more appropriate verdict. The jury's indecision resulted in a mistrial. Broderick's second jury rejected her provocation argument and found her guilty of second-degree murder.

Was Broderick reasonably provoked into a heat of passion? Many facts suggest she was not. Broderick did not walk in on her husband while he was being unfaithful with another woman. They were already divorced when she killed him. Moreover, Broderick went to her former husband's house at 5:30 in the morning, when she knew he and his new wife would be asleep. She didn't ring the doorbell. She let herself in with a key she had stolen from one of her daughters. She brought a loaded gun into his house and headed straight to the bedroom. As soon as she entered the bedroom, she started firing. She pulled the trigger five times. Not only had Betty Broderick threatened to kill Dan Broderick several times, she was an excellent shooter and had been to the firing range to practice several times before she killed her former husband. Premeditated first-degree murder without a doubt.

On the other hand, some facts support the defense theory that Betty Broderick exploded in a heat of passion brought on by years of being a good wife followed by psychologically cruel behavior by her former husband. Betty Broderick had given her life to Dan Broderick. She supported him while he attended Harvard Law School. She worked part-time and took care of his babies while he studied, worked, and went out with his friends. She continued to work even after he received his law degree because they needed the money. And when he finally started making money, he began seeing another woman. But Dan Broderick didn't tell his wife that he was being unfaithful. He lied to her for three years, denying his affair while flaunting it around town. When he finally confessed, he decided he no longer needed Betty in his life. Dan not only divorced her, but he manipulated the legal system so she would receive only a fraction of his income. He also fought against Betty getting custody of the four children. He took away his love and her children, and did so coldly and callously. She just wanted her family back. She just wanted him to love her the way he once had, but instead she received contempt orders, fines, and jail time. She finally exploded when she saw the man who had promised to love her forever, with his new wife, in the bed that was supposed to be their bed.

According to Betty, speaking from prison, her anger was eminently reasonable:

> They all keep saying to me that I'm still angry. . . . Like that's a fault? You bet, boys—my frustration and anger is off the graphs! Totally. How many times can you bend over and get fucked and not get mad? What man wouldn't have been angry? Angrier sooner. But women aren't allowed to get angry, because that's an unfeminine trait, you know. . . . It's always, "Oh, well, of course she's crazy, she uses naughty words, and she's in contempt of court, so we better arrest her." But, see, that's because the men write the rules. And the rules are that you're allowed to defend yourself— if you're a man. You're allowed to defend your home and your family and your property from thievery or people—if you're a man. But if you're a woman, you're supposed to go in the corner and cry and get fat and take pills and kill yourself.[3]

I happen to think Betty Broderick was lucky to receive a second-degree murder conviction because the facts suggest she planned in advance to kill her former husband and his new wife. Normally, a killing committed with advance planning is considered a first-degree murder. But men whose provocation claims have been as weak or weaker than Broderick's have succeeded in getting their murder charges reversed or reduced to manslaughter.[4]

Broderick's provocation claim was a difficult sell, not only because it appeared that she planned to kill her former husband and his wife, but also because Broderick did not fit the image of the Reasonable Woman. She didn't act like most of the upper class La Jolla women who had either been dumped or betrayed by their wealthy husbands. They tried to persuade Broderick to move on with her life, to stop obsessing over Dan Broderick and Linda Kolkena. Instead of taking their advice, Broderick stopped paying attention to her appearance and put on a lot of weight. She acted out, not only verbally, but also physically, engaging in unusually aggressive actions such as driving her car through the door of her former husband's new house and throwing a bottle of wine through his living room window. Given her behavior, it was easier to see Broderick as a mentally unstable, crazy woman, quite the opposite of reasonable.

Even if Broderick had not been so aggressive, she still would have faced obstacles in the courtroom. Women who kill in response to male partner infidelity are not considered reasonable in this society. The Reasonable Woman in the American imagination responds to male infidelity in a myriad of ways, but not by lashing out in a fit of fatally violent anger. This understanding of the Reasonable Woman is reflected in our movies, our politics, and our courts. Take for instance the heroine played by Gwyneth Paltrow in *Sliding Doors*, a late 1990s film about a woman who, in one version of the story, catches the subway home in time to find her live-in boyfriend in bed with another woman. In this version of the story, Paltrow cries and hits her boyfriend after catching him in the act, but does not try to kill him. Paltrow simply leaves her unfaithful partner and starts a new life as a successful career woman.[5]

The hypothetical Reasonable Woman is also a reflection of how we think reasonable women ought to conduct themselves regardless of how ordinary women actually behave. Senator Hillary Clinton might be considered a good example of how the modern-day Reasonable Woman ought to behave when she finds out that her male partner has been unfaithful. Hillary Clinton's husband, former President Bill Clinton, engaged in a highly publicized extramarital affair with Monica Lewinsky while in the White House. Although Hillary Clinton likely expressed her anger toward her husband privately, publicly she defended him against accusations of perjury and obstruction of justice arising from his denials of the affair, attributing such accusations to a right-wing conspiracy. Long after the impeachment hearings, she defended her husband as "a very, very good man" with weaknesses who simply needed "to be more responsible, more disciplined."[6] Hillary Clinton's stand-by-your-man response to her husband's infidelity was quite the opposite of what we would expect of a man in the same position. A man who stands by and does nothing in the face of knowledge that his wife has been sexually unfaithful is viewed as a cuckold and a fool. Hillary Clinton's actions, however, conformed to dominant societal expectations regarding the appropriate way for a wife to react after finding out about her husband's marital infidelity, and her approval ratings skyrocketed during her husband's impeachment trial. Her measured response to her husband's infidelity may have helped her candidacy for the New York Senate race in November 2000.[7] Had she taken a knife to either her husband or his intern, many would have seen her as an emotionally unstable woman, unfit for public office.

Given the unique circumstances of the Betty Broderick case, it is probably not the best example of the double standard that favors men who kill in response to female infidelity over women who kill in response to male infidelity. Consider another Betty Broderick-like story, although this time a wife caught her husband right after he finished a sexual tryst with two women. This woman, like Betty Broderick, claimed that her husband's adultery provoked her into a heat of passion and that the reasonable person in her shoes would have been provoked as well. Like Betty Broderick, this woman's assertion that she was reasonably provoked into a heat of passion was rejected and she was convicted of murder.

> George and Robin Williams were a married couple, living together in an apartment at 5419 West Washington Street in Cook County, Illinois. George was the janitor for that apartment building.
>
> On April 20, 1986, Robin came home to her apartment. As she walked towards the bedroom, she saw two women and her husband, stark naked, leaving the bedroom. Putting two and two together, Robin started yelling at George. George told her to shut up and went back into the bedroom to put on some clothes. In the meantime, the two women quickly left the apartment.
>
> Shaking with anger, Robin went into the kitchen and started to fry some chicken. After putting on a pair of pants, an angry George came into the kitchen and started yelling at Robin. Robin yelled back. George slapped Robin in the head. In response, Robin grabbed a kitchen knife, and stabbed George many times. She continued stabbing him even after he turned his back on her and tried to get away.[8]

Robin was charged with murder. At trial, Robin's attorney argued that she killed her husband in a sudden and intense passion resulting from serious provocation.[9] The relevant Illinois statute provided, "A person who kills an individual without lawful justification commits voluntary manslaughter if at the time of the killing he is acting under a sudden and intense passion resulting from serious provocation by [t]he individual killed. . . . Serious provocation is conduct sufficient to excite an intense passion in a reasonable person."[10] Robin waived her right to a jury trial and was tried before a male judge who did not think catching one's husband naked with two women constituted serious provocation or conduct sufficient to excite an intense passion in a reasonable person. After Judge John Crilly found Robin guilty of murder, an appellate court affirmed the conviction, holding that a rational trier of fact could have found beyond a reasonable doubt that Robin did not act under a sudden passion resulting from legally adequate provocation.

Underlying the *Williams* case is the notion that the Reasonable Woman does not react with violence when she catches her husband in the act of adultery. According to the judges who heard the *Williams* case, it is not reasonable for a woman to lose her self-control after catching her husband coming out of the bedroom naked with two women.

Caroline Forell and Donna Matthews recount another case of a woman who shot and killed her estranged husband after he had just finished having sexual intercourse with another woman. Shirley Quick was convicted of first-degree murder.

> [I]n September 1998, Shirley Quick was released to a halfway house after spending twenty-three years in prison for killing her estranged husband. There was evidence that he had asked her to bring his handgun to the mobile home where he was living. By Shirley Quick's account, when she arrived he came to the door zipping up his pants. An editorial in the *Lakeland (Florida) Ledger* on July 20, 1998 quoted her as saying: "His shirt was open. I started to come in and he blocked me and I saw, in side vision, this girl; she was naked, going down the hallway." Quick shot him four times, killing him. She was convicted of first-degree murder—an inconceivable outcome had the genders been switched, particularly in 1975. . . . In 1975, a man might well have not even been charged.[11]

## SAME-SEX PARTNER INFIDELITY

Very little published case law exists on the subject of whether a gay man who kills after finding out that his lover has been unfaithful should be held to the same standard as a heterosexual man who kills his female partner after finding out she has been unfaithful. The modern approach appears to be neutral as to sexual orientation. Any individual, gay or straight, can assert the provocation defense.

The law, however, is silent on the question of whether a gay male defendant who kills his male lover after finding him in bed with another man should be compared to the average gay man or the average straight man, or whether the defendant's sexual orientation ought to be incorporated into the Reasonable Person standard. In one of the few reported cases in this country concerning a gay man who killed his lover and claimed he was provoked by his lover's infidelity, Merle Francis Washington shot and killed his lover Owen Wilson Brady on August 10, 1974, while the two were riding in Brady's car.[12] Washington was charged with murder and tried in the Superior Court of Los Angeles County before the Honorable Billy G. Mills. At trial, Washington admitted to killing Brady after a lover's quarrel, but argued that he was reasonably provoked into a heat of passion by Brady's unfaithfulness and his expressed desire to end the relationship. The jury did not believe Washington was reasonably provoked, and found him guilty of second-degree murder.

On appeal, Washington argued that the trial court erred in using a Reasonable Man standard when instructing the jury on provocation. Washington argued that the trial court should have used an "average servient homosexual" standard or an "average female" standard, rather than a "Reasonable Man" standard. The Court of Appeals rejected Washington's argument and affirmed his second-degree murder conviction.

It is unclear why Washington sought a jury instruction comparing him to a "reasonable servient homosexual." The term "servient" is defined as "subject to some person or thing that dominates, rules, or controls."[13] Washington probably wanted the jury to think that he was the less powerful party in the relationship. Being the less powerful party, however, does not seem to help in provocation cases. Women who kill their more powerful male partners are not necessarily granted the provocation mitigation.

Given the long-standing tradition of juries and judges sympathizing with straight men who have killed their female partners in response to infidelity, it probably would have been easier for Washington to convince the jury that he was "reasonably" provoked by arguing that the average heterosexual male would have been upset if he found out his girlfriend or fiancée was sleeping with another man, rather than asking the jury to imagine what the reasonable servient homosexual man would have done in the same situation. Stereotypes about gay men as promiscuous and eager for sex with as many partners as possible, even to the extent of engaging in unsafe sex with anonymous partners in public restrooms and bathhouses, might have undermined Washington's assertion that he was shocked and outraged at his male lover's infidelity.

Washington's alternative request for a Reasonable Woman instruction is interesting in light of recent case law in the sexual harassment arena. Some courts have applied a Reasonable Woman standard to claims of sexual harassment, holding that the key question is whether a reasonable woman would have found the defendant's conduct objectionable.[14] In their recent book, *A Law of Her Own: The Reasonable Woman as a Measure of Man*, Donna Matthews and Caroline Forell argue that a Reasonable Woman standard should be used across the board in all sexual harassment, stalking, and domestic homicide cases, regardless of the gender, race, or sexual orientation of the parties.[15]

In Washington's case, it is doubtful that a Reasonable Woman standard would have resulted in a more favorable verdict for him. Women who kill their philandering male partners are rarely considered reasonable. Robin Williams virtually caught her husband in the act, yet the judge presiding over her trial felt she was not reasonably provoked by her husband's act of adultery with two other women at the same time. Shirley Quick, the woman who killed her estranged husband after finding him with a naked girl, zipping up his pants, was convicted of first-degree murder. No one thought Quick was *reasonably* provoked by her husband's behavior.

Heterosexual women, lesbian women, and gay men who kill in response to partner infidelity may end up with more lenient sentences if they insist upon a Reasonable (Heterosexual) Man standard, rather than seeking a gender- or sexual orientation–specific standard. Comparing the heterosexual female, lesbian, and/or gay male defendant to the hypothetical Reasonable (Heterosexual) Man encourages jurors to treat heterosexual female and gay male defendants the same way they would treat a heterosexual male defendant. If the jury would grant the provocation mitigation to a heterosexual male defendant using a Reasonable Man standard, then arguably they should grant the same mitigation to a heterosexual female, lesbian female, or gay male defendant.

Whether an increase in voluntary manslaughter convictions and a corresponding decrease in murder convictions is a good or bad result depends in part upon whether one thinks the claims of all provoked defendants should be closely scrutinized or whether one thinks heterosexual females, gays, and lesbians should be given the same breaks that are given heterosexual men who kill. When an individual has taken another's life and seeks mitigation by arguing that he (or she) was reasonably provoked, good reasons weigh in favor of ratcheting up rather than down the level of scrutiny applied to that individual's claim of reasonableness. Rather than lowering the bar by applying an easy-to-meet Reasonable Man standard across the board, the bar should be raised. All claims of reasonableness in provocation cases, particularly those made by men who kill in response to female partner infidelity, ought to be subjected to the same critical scrutiny that is applied to claims of reasonableness made by heterosexual women and gay men who kill in response to partner infidelity.

A search for homicide cases stemming from killings in response to lesbian infidelity turned up only one case from Scotland, which seems to support the theory that heterosexual women, gay men, and lesbians who kill in response to partner infidelity can benefit from a Reasonable (Heterosexual) Man standard. Vikki McKean, a lesbian woman who killed a man who was sleeping with her estranged lesbian lover, was able to receive the provocation mitigation by convincing jurors that she reacted the way the ordinary heterosexual male would have reacted if he found his wife with another.

Vikki McKean and Connie Andrew were childhood friends who became lovers and began living together in 1991. Connie worked as a massage girl at a sauna while Vikki stayed home and looked after Connie's children.

On June 30, 1995, the two women expressed their commitment to each other in a marriage ceremony. Shortly after the wedding, the two women began having problems stemming from Connie's conflicted feelings about whether she wanted to be with a woman or a man. While working at the sauna, Connie, who was twenty-seven at the time, met a forty-year-old man named Stephen Blackwell, a Londoner who had just come to Scotland after separating from his wife. Initially, Connie provided Stephen with sexual services in exchange for money. Eventually, Connie began to see Stephen as more than just a paying customer. By the end of the summer, Connie decided to leave Vikki and moved out with her kids. She invited

Stephen to stay at her new flat. Stephen slept with Connie in her bed during this time.

In September 1995, Connie met Vikki in a bar and told her she was seeing a man, but she wasn't sure whether she wanted a man or a woman. The two women ended up making love in the bar's restroom.

Four days later, Vikki arrived at Connie's flat and was met at the door by one of Connie's children who told Vikki that Connie was sleeping with a man. Vikki stormed into the house, picked up a knife from the kitchen, and marched into the living room. There she saw Stephen Blackwell, Connie, and Connie's cousin, Donna Purdon. Vikki, white-faced and distraught, turned to Connie and said, "I thought he wasn't staying here." Then she turned to Stephen Blackwell and screamed, "Are you fucking my wife? What are you doing sitting in my seat?" Stephen denied that he and Connie were lovers, but before anyone knew what was happening, Vikki was stabbing Stephen. She stabbed him eleven times before she stormed out of the house, swearing Blackwell would never sleep in her bed again.[16]

McKean was charged with murder. At trial, the twenty-eight-year-old defendant argued that just as a heterosexual man could be reasonably provoked into a heat of passion upon learning of his wife's infidelity, she was reasonably provoked into a heat of passion upon finding out that *her* wife had been unfaithful. Even though the provocation defense had never before been applied in a case in which a lesbian was charged with murdering a man for sleeping with her female lover, the judge allowed McKean to argue provocation, and the jury found her not guilty of murder. The jury convicted McKean of the lesser offense of culpable homicide, and she was sentenced to eight years of imprisonment.

Vikki McKean was fortunate to have a judge who thought it unfair to restrict the provocation defense to male defendants who kill in response to female partner infidelity. The judge explained to the jury that what was good enough for heterosexual men was good enough for lesbian women:

> In these somewhat more enlightened days of sexual equality I can see no reason why the law should not extend uniformly to a man and a woman. In other words, a wife or female companion should have the benefit of the mitigating plea of provocation equally with the husband or male partner.
>
> I also see no reason why, in the modern context, the plea should not

also be available to homosexual couples who live together and are regarded in the community as partners bound together by ties of love,
affection and faithfulness—although I have to say that, until this case,
the law has not so far been extended to them.[17]

It is unclear whether a lesbian woman in an American court would
be as fortunate as Vikki McKean. While American views on homosexuality are much more tolerant today than they were thirty years ago, negative attitudes toward gay men and lesbian women persist. According
to a general social survey conducted in 1994, a majority of Americans
think engaging in homosexual sex is immoral.[18] A 2000 Gallup poll
found that 62 percent of Americans polled believe same-sex marriages
"should *not* be recognized by the law as valid, with the same rights as a
traditional marriage."[19] Only one state, Vermont, permits gay men and
lesbians to enter into civil unions; no state currently permits gay couples to marry.[20]

Many Americans still believe gays and lesbians should not teach or
serve as role models. In 1992, James Dale, an Assistant Scoutmaster,
sued the Boy Scouts of America after he was expelled from the organization because of his sexual orientation.[21] Dale was serving as co-Presi-
dent of the Rutgers University Lesbian and Gay Alliance when he was
interviewed by a newspaper about his views on the need for gay role
models for gay and lesbian teens. Shortly after this interview was published, Dale received a letter from the Boy Scouts informing him that the
organization was revoking his membership. When Dale asked why he
was being expelled, he received a letter stating that the Boy Scouts
"specifically forbid[s] membership to homosexuals."[22] Dale sued the
Boy Scouts, arguing that the organization had violated New Jersey's
public accommodations law by revoking his membership solely on the
basis of his sexual orientation. The Boy Scouts countered that since it
was a private organization, it had the right to exclude Dale because his
presence undermined "the values embodied in the Scout's Oath and
Law, particularly those represented by the terms 'morally straight' and
'clean'" and the organization's desire not to "promote homosexual conduct as a legitimate form of behavior."[23] On June 28, 2000, the U.S.
Supreme Court upheld the right of the Boy Scouts, as a private organization exercising its First Amendment freedom of expressive association, to exclude Dale on the basis of his sexual orientation.[24]

Hostility toward gays and lesbians is also manifested in physical violence and threats of physical violence. In March 1996, the Rhode Island Department of Health and Education reported that 41 percent of lesbian and gay youths had been violently attacked at school.[25] In a 1997 survey of about four thousand students at fifty-eight high schools in Massachusetts, 22 percent of the gay students said they had skipped class because they felt unsafe at school, and 31 percent said they had been threatened or injured at school in the last year.[26] These percentages were about five times greater than the percentages for straight students. In a 1998 study of approximately five hundred community college students in the San Francisco Bay Area, a region known for its tolerance for gays and lesbians, 32 percent of male respondents admitted they had verbally threatened gays and/or lesbians and 18 percent admitted they had physically threatened or assaulted gays and/or lesbians because of their sexual orientation.[27] Three out of every ten male respondents who had not verbally or physically threatened a gay person, reported that they would likely respond with violence if a gay man flirted with or propositioned them.

## RACIAL INSULTS

Heterosexual women, lesbians, and gay men charged with murdering their intimate partners are not the only ones who face difficulty when they assert claims of reasonableness in defense of acts of violence. Black men who kill in response to a racial insult also face obstacles when they seek to argue provocation. Heterosexual women, lesbians, and gay men who kill in response to partner infidelity, however, generally are allowed to argue provocation to the jury, which can then accept or reject the defense. Blacks and other persons of color who kill in response to a racial insult generally are precluded from arguing provocation because of the "mere words" rule.

The mere words rule is a vestige from the early common law's categorical approach. Under this rule, words alone can *never* constitute legally adequate provocation. Accordingly, a person who kills in response to a verbal insult or other verbal provocation is not entitled to a jury instruction on heat of passion or voluntary manslaughter.

However, never doesn't really mean never. The mere words rule suggests a strict ban on the use of words to substantiate a heat of passion defense. Yet, as discussed in chapter 1, courts have relaxed the rule when the provoking words are a wife's confession of adultery or verbal insults regarding the husband's sexual ability.[28] Courts have permitted a heat of passion/provocation argument in other cases involving words. In *State v. Erazo*,[29] for example, the defendant killed his wife after she threatened to report him to the authorities so they would revoke his parole. Although there were other things creating tension in the relationship between the defendant and the victim prior to the homicide, the last straw constituted the victim's verbal threats. In a subsequent case, a New Jersey court explained:

> The defendant in *Erazo* had killed his wife. The Court observed that "the tension between defendant and the victim on the night of the slaying . . . was . . . a continuing strain in a marriage fraught with violence." But the final provocation was "words," the victim's threatening defendant that she would induce the revocation of his parole by reporting that he had caused her what was in fact a self-inflicted cut. *Erazo* thus recognizes that although "words" are not legally sufficient for passion/provocation manslaughter when they are mere insults, "words" may be sufficient when they convey a significant threat, even one that does currently not put the defendant's own life at risk.[30]

At one time, North Carolina and Tennessee courts recognized another exception to the mere words rule.[31] If a slave uttered "aggravating words of reproach" to a White man, prompting the White man to kill the slave, the White man could argue that he was provoked into a heat of passion by the slave's words. In *State v. Jarrott*,[32] the Supreme Court of North Carolina explained the reason for this exception. According to the court, the mere words rule applied only to words spoken among equals, not to words uttered by a slave to a White person:

> Among equals, the general rule is, that words are not, but blows are, a sufficient provocation; while in Tackett's case, it was declared that there *might be* words of reproach, so aggravating when uttered by a slave, as to excite the temporary fury which negatives the charge of malice. This difference in the application of the same principle, arises from the *vast* difference which exists, under our institutions, between the social condition of the white man and of the slave; in consequence of which difference, what might be felt by one as the grossest degradation, is considered by the other as but a slight injury.[33]

This exception to the mere words rule only worked when a White man killed a slave, not when a slave killed a White man. The Supreme Court of Tennessee explained why in *Nelson v. State*:

> [I]t is manifest, that the same indignity which would excite the passions of a white man, would not have a like effect upon a slave. That which would be a grievous provocation to the one, would provoke the other but slightly. This difference arises from the different habits of feeling, and modes of thought, of the two races. In view of reason, then, the common law cannot hold that an act, constituting a provocation, which would mitigate a homicide committed by a white man to manslaughter, shall have a like effect when the homicide is committed on a white man, by a slave.[34]

The words-uttered-by-a-slave exception to the mere words rule recognized by the Supreme Courts of North Carolina and Tennessee has long since been abandoned, but it is still the case that a Black man who kills a White man in response to words of reproach is guilty of murder. Black defendants who kill in response to a racial insult rarely seek the provocation mitigation because of the mere words rule, and in the few cases in which such defendants have sought a provocation instruction, the trial court has refused their request. For example, in the 1994 case of *People v. Green*,[35] an African American man named Green was charged with murder after he stabbed his neighbor to death for using the N word to describe him. Just before the fatal stabbing, the neighbor told Green that he was the one who had shot Green's dog two weeks earlier. The neighbor explained, "it was bad enough living around niggers, much less dogs."[36] Green tried to argue that the neighbor's inflammatory words provoked him into a heat of passion, but the trial judge refused to give the jury an instruction on heat of passion voluntary manslaughter. Green was convicted of murder, and his application for leave to appeal the failure to give a voluntary manslaughter instruction was denied.[37]

In his recent book, *Nigger*, Randall Kennedy discusses another case, *State v. Watson*,[38] in which a Black male prisoner, Rufus Coley Watson, Jr., killed a White male prisoner, Roger Dale Samples, who had used the N word to insult him.[39] The rumor among inmates was that Watson and Samples had been swapping out, a prison term for having sex. On the night in question, the two men argued. Samples told Watson, "N———.

N————. You're just like the rest of them."[40] Samples also suggested that Watson was too scared to fight, made several derogatory references to Watson's mother, and called Watson a "black mother f————er."[41] In response, Watson stabbed Samples to death.

At trial, Watson's attorney asked for a jury instruction on manslaughter, arguing that his client was provoked into a heat of passion by the White inmate's use of the N word. Relying on the mere words rule, the judge denied the defense request. The court then told the jury, "[L]et me say here, that mere words will not form a justification or excuse for a crime of this sort . . . words and gestures alone, where no assault is made or threatened, regardless of how insulting or inflammatory those words or gestures may be, does [sic] not constitute adequate provocation for the taking of a human life."[42] Watson was convicted of second-degree murder.

In both these cases, the jury was not permitted to consider the defendant's claim that he was reasonably provoked into a heat of passion because the provocation at issue was a verbal insult. Racial insults, however, may be more harmful to the recipient and others belonging to his or her racial group than other verbal insults. Richard Delgado explains that "racial insults are in no way comparable to statements such as, 'You are a God damned woman and a God damned liar,' which the Restatement gives as an example of a 'mere insult.' Racial insults are different qualitatively because they conjure up the entire history of racial discrimination in this country."[43] Similarly, Mari Matsuda observes that "[t]he typical reaction of target-group members to an incident of [racial harassment] is alarm and immediate calls for redress. The typical reaction of non-target-group members is to consider the incidents isolated pranks, the product of sick- but-harmless minds."[44] Matsuda notes that "[h]owever irrational racist speech may be, it hits right at the emotional place where we feel the most pain."[45] Arguably, the N word is worse than other racial insults. As Randall Kennedy notes, the N word has been described as "the nuclear bomb of racial epithets" and "the most noxious racial epithet in the contemporary American lexicon."[46]

In my opinion, the convictions in the above-described cases were appropriate. The law should discourage violence in response to verbal provocations. If, however, the law seeks to discourage people from responding to verbal provocations with violence, it ought to be consistent. If courts disallow the provocation defense when a racial insult triggers the violence, they should do the same when a confession of adultery is the provoking factor. No good reason exists for treating one set of words less favorably than the other.

An alternative, and perhaps better, way to resolve the inconsistency would be to abolish the mere words rule. The move from the early common law categorical approach to the modern Reasonable Man test was supposed to give juries more, not less, discretion to decide whether legally adequate provocation existed. Focusing on whether the reasonable man in the defendant's shoes would have been provoked rather than on whether the provocative act or event fits into one of a few limited categories enables juries to contextualize and individualize the provocation inquiry. When courts rule as a matter of law that certain things, like words, do not and can never constitute legally adequate provocation, they preclude jurors from considering the full context in which the killing took place. A Black person who kills in response to a racial insult may do so as a result of an outpouring of frustration and outrage over past and present discrimination.

Blacks in America have been subject to a long history of enslavement, Jim Crow laws, and persistent discrimination despite laws aimed at guaranteeing equality. Even today, Blacks suffer the effects of conscious and unconscious racism.[47] Blacks are often pulled over for minor traffic violations and subjected to intrusive searches. Blacks are disproportionately subjected to police use of deadly force.[48] Many Blacks have experienced the humiliation of not being able to catch a cab, passed up by taxi drivers who believe they are more likely to be robbed or stiffed by a Black person than a non-Black person. Others have experienced the snub of someone refusing to ride an elevator with them or crossing the street. As Peggy Davis notes, Blacks in America are subject to almost daily microaggressions or put-downs.[49]

A racial insult may be the last straw for a Black person who has suffered a lifetime of microaggressions. When that racial insult triggers a violent reaction, the response may seem unreasonable to those who have not experienced such a history. As Camille Nelson notes, "If it strains credulity to imagine what the 'ordinary white man' would do in the position of a black man bombarded with racial slurs, it is probably because white men do not typically find themselves in that situation."[50] Given the modern test's focus on context, the defendant who kills in response to a racial insult should be permitted to explain to the jury why his reaction was reasonable in light of the circumstances.[51]

Allowing defendants to make the provocation argument to the jury does not mean the jury will end up mitigating the charges. In a fairly recent case, a Black inmate named Stephen Beverly fatally stabbed a White prison guard after the guard made anti-gay comments and racial insults. Beverly was permitted to argue that he was provoked into a heat of passion by the guard's remarks.[52] On July 30, 1997, Corrections Officer Fred Baker, a man who had harassed Beverly for many months, came to Beverly's cell and told Beverly and his cell mate and partner, Favors Ali, to pack up their belongings because they were being moved to different cells. According to other inmates, Officer Baker first told Beverly, "both you and your homo lover are out of here!"[53] He then told Ali, "Your homo ass is out of here!"[54] When Beverly asked Officer Baker for a box to pack his possessions, Officer Baker refused Beverly's request, stating, "No, I don't give boxes to niggers."[55] At this, Beverly snapped and became overwhelmed with rage. He went straight into the yard, where he knew a shank was buried, dug up the shank, then returned to find Officer Baker talking on the telephone. Beverly stabbed Baker once in the back, killing him.

Beverly was charged with capital murder. Before trial, the prosecution filed a motion to preclude the defense from arguing passion-provocation. The judge ruled against the government, permitting the defense to argue to the jury that Beverly was provoked into a heat of passion by a racially hostile prison environment, a prison administration that did nothing in response to Beverly's numerous complaints of unfair harassment by Officer Baker, and being called the N word by Officer Baker. The jury, however, was not persuaded that Beverly was reasonably provoked into a heat of passion sufficient to reduce the charge to manslaughter, and found Beverly guilty of first-degree murder.[56]

Hostility to race-based provocation claims by persons of color runs so deep that one court has even held that racial antagonism, not merely words of a racially insulting nature, cannot constitute legally adequate provocation. In *State v. Madden*,[57] a White police officer was killed by a group of Blacks after he shot and wounded a Black man in an area of Plainfield, New Jersey, that had recently experienced serious racial rioting.[58] Twelve persons were indicted. Two of the twelve were convicted of first-degree murder. On appeal, those two defendants argued, among other things, that the jury should have been instructed that racial antagonism *may* constitute legally adequate provocation. Writing for the

Supreme Court of New Jersey, Chief Justice Weintraub rejected this argument out of hand, calling it frivolous.

> Defendants now urge that the jury should have been told (1) that racial or like antagonism or grievances may constitute provocation, and may so serve whether or not the officer was acting in the execution of his duty; and (2) that the illegal arrest or the shooting of Williams could constitute a provocation of bystanders. *The first proposition is frivolous.* It is no more than this: that racial, ethnic, religious, economic, political, or like grievances within our social order should be deemed sufficient to provoke a member of one group to kill a member of a group he deems opposed to him, or to kill every police officer as a symbol of the social order within which such grievances exist. The proposition is foreign to the subject of voluntary manslaughter. Voluntary manslaughter is a slaying committed in a transport of passion or heat of blood induced by a provocation the law deems adequate to arouse such passion in a man of ordinary firmness, and then only if the killing occurs before the passage of time sufficient for an ordinary person in like circumstances to cool off. The conventional picture is that of a defendant who exploded in response to some injury or affront to which he was subjected by the deceased. None of this can be found in the proposition defendants now advance.[59]

Even though the modern test's focus on context rather than categories is supposed to encourage deference to juries, Judge Weintraub had no qualms about deciding, as a matter of law, that racial antagonism did not constitute legally adequate provocation, thus precluding the jury from even considering the possibility that the defendants were provoked into a heat of passion.

## THE HIDDEN NORMATIVITY
## IN THE DEFENSE OF PROVOCATION

The doctrine of provocation looks a lot different today than it did at its inception. In abandoning the early common law's categorical approach, judges and legislators tried to make the doctrine less rigid and more responsive to context. Yet the doctrine, even today, appears to benefit heterosexual men who kill in response to female infidelity over others. Reva Siegel describes the phenomenon of things staying the same despite changes in the law as "preservation through transformation."[60] Even when efforts are made to address inequities by changing or transforming the law, inequities may persist because of deeply entrenched social attitudes. Transforming the law of provocation by moving from rigid categories to a more fluid Reasonable Person approach has not eliminated bias in favor of heterosexual men who kill in response to female infidelity, because some judges and jurors still see heterosexual male sexual jealousy and violence as reasonable.

In 1997, Victoria Nourse published the results of a thorough study of cases in which male defendants who had killed in response to perceived female infidelity were permitted to argue provocation or extreme emotional disturbance to the jury.[61] Nourse argues that the early common law approach to provocation is more protective of women than either the modern (Reasonable Man) test or the Model Penal Code's extreme emotional disturbance approach. Under the modern approach, acts of separation or perceived infidelity, such as leaving, seeking a divorce, dancing with another man, deciding to date others, or seeking a protective order, may constitute legally adequate provocation and lead to a voluntary manslaughter conviction as long as the jury determines that a reasonable man in the defendant's shoes would have been provoked by the female victim's acts. Similarly, under the Model Penal Code approach, such acts may lead to the manslaughter mitigation if the jury finds the defendant's explanation for extreme mental or emotional disturbance reasonable.[62] In contrast, under the early common law approach, such acts could not support a reduced charge because they did not fit into one of the discrete categories of legally adequate provocation.

Nourse observes that the current law of provocation, while purporting to be neutral and objective, in fact makes judgments about the equities of relationships. Just as it did in the past, the provocation doctrine today protects certain losses of self-control over others. Men who lose control over their female partner's infidelity (or perceived infidelity) are protected; women who lose control over their male partner's infidelity are not. Heterosexual men who lose control after being told they are lousy lovers are protected; men of color who lose control after being subjected to racial insults are not. Nourse explains:

When, for example, a young man argues that he was grievously insulted by friends, judges easily conclude that the man's rage is irrational and refuse a jury instruction. Similarly, when an employer has insulted a defendant, a judge will find it difficult to believe that such an insult could rationally lead to murderous violence; this defendant, too, will be denied a jury instruction. Take away the intimacy of a relationship and passion's "rationality" disappears. Return that same claim to intimacy, however, and the emotion becomes "rational" again. An insult by a wife, ex-wife, girlfriend, or even a casual sex partner constitutes precisely the "humiliation" necessary for a court to believe the emotion is sufficiently "rational" to send the case to the jury.[63]

Not all the news on this front is bad. American attitudes about male jealousy have evolved from the days when jealousy was regarded as a virtue and jealous anger as a sign of love.[64] Today, excessive jealousy is often seen as a sign of personal immaturity.[65] This shift in American attitudes about jealousy correlates with a decline in the number of intimate homicides committed each year. According to the U.S. Department of Justice, nearly three thousand intimate partner homicides were committed in 1976, 13.6 percent of all homicides.[66] By 1996, the number of intimate partner homicides had declined to just under two thousand, only 8.8 percent of the total.[67] Unfortunately, the government has not compiled statistics mapping the success rate of provocation claims based on partner infidelity, so it is impossible to tell whether juror attitudes about the reasonableness of male sexual jealousy have changed as well.

# 3

# Gay Panic

March 1, 1995. Pontiac, Michigan. Jonathan Schmitz, a twenty-four-year-old employee at the Fox and Hounds restaurant in Pontiac, Michigan, was looking forward to his upcoming appearance on the *Jenny Jones Show*. The nationally televised show was airing a segment on "Secret Admirers" and John had been invited to Chicago to appear as a guest. John hoped that his secret admirer would be his former girlfriend, Kristen. John wanted to resume a relationship with his ex and had told friends that if Kristen was his secret admirer, he would propose to her.

March 6, 1995. Chicago, Illinois. Showtime. John sat on stage, waiting to see his former sweetheart. Then Scott Amedure appeared. John was taken aback. What was his friend Scott doing on the show? Then he realized— Scott was his secret admirer. John managed a smile and hugged Scott for the sake of the cameras. He even laughed when Scott recounted a fantasy that involved John, whipped cream, strawberries, and champagne.

On his way back to Michigan, John told his friend Donna Riley, who had worked with Scott Amedure to arrange the taping, that he could get angry about his appearance on the *Jenny Jones Show* if he thought about it. On the plane, John struck up a conversation with Patricia Cielinski, who was sitting next to him. John told her about his experience on the show and said he was disappointed that his friends Donna and Scott had set him up. He told Patricia that he had spent $600 on new clothes and other things, thinking that his secret admirer would be his ex-girlfriend or another woman. John repeated that he could get angry about Scott's appearance on the show if he thought about it. Yet after returning to Michigan, John went out for drinks with Scott and Donna.

March 9, 1995. Pontiac, Michigan. John came home from work to find a flashing construction light and an anonymous note in front of his apartment. The note read, "John, if you want it off, you'll have to ask me. P.S. It takes a special kind of tool. Guess Who." Believing the note was a crude sexual come-on from Scott, John drove to his bank and withdrew $350. He then went to two different gun stores where he purchased a 12-gauge pump-action shotgun and ammunition. Next stop, Scott's trailer home, seven miles away. Leaving the gun in his car, John walked up to the trailer and knocked on the door to make sure Scott was home. Scott answered the door. He let John in. John told Scott he needed to go back to his car because he had left the engine running, and promised to come right back. Then John went to his car, got his shotgun, and came back into the trailer. Scott saw the shotgun and tried to hide behind a wicker chair, but it was an ineffective shield. The first bullet tore through the chair and into Scott's chest. Scott fell to the ground. Scott's roommate came out into the front room and watched in horror as John walked up to Scott, who was writhing on the floor and screaming in pain, manually racked the shotgun, and fired again.[1]

When a heterosexual man kills a gay man and is charged with murder, a common defense strategy is to use the concept of "gay panic" to explain the killing.[2] As one court has explained, "homosexual panic" is "the idea that a latent homosexual—and manifest 'homophobe'—can be so upset by a homosexual's advances to him that he becomes temporarily insane, in which state he may kill the homosexual."[3] Although the term has appeared several times in recent popular literature, gay panic is not an officially sanctioned criminal law defense. Gay panic nonetheless is used by criminal defendants to bolster many different criminal law defenses, including temporary insanity, diminished capacity, provocation, and self-defense.

The Jonathan Schmitz case, also known as the Jenny Jones case because the initial incident which triggered Schmitz's panic was his appearance on the *Jenny Jones Show,* is unusual because Schmitz used the idea of gay panic first to bolster a claim of diminished capacity, a mental defect defense which essentially admits the *unreasonableness* of the defendant's actions, and later a claim of provocation, a defense which rests upon an assertion of *reasonableness*.[4] Because diminished capacity and provocation rest upon inconsistent claims regarding the reasonableness or normalcy of the defendant, defendants usually will choose one defense or the other, but not both. Schmitz used a diminished capacity defense at his first trial to reduce his first-degree murder charge to second-degree murder. He successfully appealed and his second-degree murder conviction was vacated because the trial court had refused to allow the defense to remove a juror they found problematic. On retrial, Schmitz was not able to reassert the diminished capacity defense that had helped him at his first trial because Michigan law only permits diminished capacity as a defense to first-degree murder. Schmitz's attorney instead argued that Schmitz was reasonably provoked into a heat of passion by Amedure's actions and therefore should be found guilty of manslaughter rather than murder. This time, Schmitz's attempt to use a gay panic argument was unsuccessful. Schmitz was again convicted of second-degree murder, and sentenced to twenty-five to fifty years in prison.

In this chapter, I start by examining the historical origins of the concept of gay panic. I discuss the use of gay panic to bolster claims of mental defect. I then discuss the use of gay panic to support claims of reasonableness through the defenses of provocation and self-defense. I conclude by returning to the Jonathan Schmitz case, examining the ways in which masculinity, race, and sexual orientation interacted to produce the outcome in that case.

## "HOMOPHOBIA"—A MISNOMER

Many use the term "homophobia" to describe anti-homosexual attitudes. I too use the term for this purpose, but try to do so sparingly because of its problematic nature. Attaching the prefix "homo" to the word "phobia" suggests that individuals with negative attitudes about homosexuality are fearful of homosexuals, although anti-homosexual sentiments are often driven more by prejudice than fear.[5] Colleen Logan warns that "the continued use of homophobia as a descriptor for anti-homosexual response may be seen by society as implicit permission to continue the oppression of homosexuals, excused by its being the result of inescapable fear."[6] Similarly, Gregory Herek remarks, "Characterizing hostility toward homosexual persons in terms of a phobia implies that those attitudes are based upon an irrational fear, similar to the fear some people experience when confronted with snakes, spiders, or open spaces."[7] Stephanie Shields and Robert Harriman note, "The great difference between the unreasonable fear of spiders (or mutilation, snakes, etc.) and fear of homosexuality lies in the assignment of responsibility for such acquired pathologies. Whereas spider phobics typically accept responsibility for their fear and even seek treatment, homophobics do not. To the homophobic, it is homosexual men who are sick."[8]

## HOMOSEXUAL PANIC DISORDER

The use of gay panic in murder cases has its roots in theories about latent homosexuality as a mental disorder. The term "homosexual panic" was coined by Dr. Edward Kempf, a clinical psychiatrist, in 1920.[9] After treating several hundred patients who exhibited similar characteristics, Kempf came to the conclusion that certain troubled individuals who thought of themselves as heterosexual were actually latent homosexuals. These individuals suffered from an internal conflict between their feelings of attraction to individuals of the same sex and societal views of such feelings as perverse. They also experienced a heightened sense of anxiety in same-sex environments, caused by this tension between their true feelings of attraction to members of the same sex and what they perceived as the socially acceptable feelings they were supposed to have—attraction to members of the opposite sex.[10]

According to Kempf, Homosexual Panic Disorder was marked by two factors: (1) a patient's terror of his attraction to homosexuality, and (2) his or her fear of heterosexuality.[11] Interestingly, a panic state was typically precipitated by *separation* from an individual of the same sex to whom the patient was emotionally attached, not by a sexual advance.[12]

Homosexual Panic Disorder was listed in the 1952 edition of the *Diagnostic and Statistical Manual of Mental Disorders,* the official list of psychiatric disorders published by the American Psychiatric Association. It has not appeared in that manual since 1952.[13] Even then, Homosexual Panic Disorder was not recognized as an existing psychiatric disorder by many of the standard psychiatric and psychological dictionaries.[14]

Some modern support for Dr. Kempf's theory exists. In 1996, Henry Adams conducted a study to find out whether heterosexual men who exhibited strong anti-gay sentiments would be aroused by homosexual erotica. Adams started by measuring sixty-four Caucasian self-described heterosexual male participants' feelings toward gays. After evaluating their responses, he divided the participants into two groups which he labeled "homophobic" (those who were hostile toward gays) and "not homophobic" (those who were not hostile toward gays). He then placed a sensor on the penises of all the participants, and measured penile response to erotic videotapes involving heterosexual, female homosexual, and male homosexual activity. Only the men in

Adams's homophobic category, those who had earlier expressed strong anti-gay sentiments, showed an increase in penile erection in response to male homosexual erotic stimuli.[15] Like Kempf's patients, the homophobic men in Adams's study generally were not aggressive toward others.

Even if self-identified straight men who express strongly negative feelings about homosexuality are actually latent homosexuals repressing their own homoerotic desires, the idea that gay panic should excuse the killing of a gay man is problematic for several reasons. First, treating gay panic as a mental disorder can lead to the assumption that *homophobia* stemming from latent homosexuality is a mental illness.[16] However, many individuals who are of sound mental ability believe that homosexual activity is immoral and deviant. Studies indicate that negative attitudes about homosexuality tend to come from two sources: sexual conservatism and prejudice against those who are different.[17] Sexually conservative individuals and prejudiced individuals are not necessarily mentally ill.

Second, the idea that *homosexuality* itself is a mental illness has long been discredited. In December 1973, after a review of the scientific literature and consultation with experts in the field, the Board of Trustees for the American Psychiatric Association deleted homosexuality from the *Diagnostic and Statistical Manual of Mental Disorders*, Second Edition (DSMII), its official list of mental disorders.[18] The Board recognized that a significant proportion of the gay and lesbian population were "clearly satisfied with their sexual orientation and showed no signs of psychopathology."[19] The American Psychological Association followed suit in January 1975, adopting the following resolution:

Homosexuality per se implies no impairment in judgment, stability, reliability, or general social and vocational capabilities; [f]urther, the American Psychological Association urges all health professionals to take the lead in removing the stigma of mental illness that has long been associated with homosexual orientations.[20]

Even though more than twenty-five years have passed since both the American Psychiatric Association and the American Psychological Association rejected the characterization of homosexuality as a mental illness, the idea that it might be normal for someone to be sexually attracted to another person of the same sex still arouses controversy today. In November 1999, a coalition of medical, mental health, educational, and religious organizations announced that it would be sending school superintendents across the country a booklet entitled "Just the Facts about Sexual Orientation and Youth." Among other things, the booklet informed readers that mental health and health professional organizations do not support the idea that homosexuality is abnormal or mentally unhealthy.[21] Negative reaction to the booklet was strong and swift. Janet Parshall, spokeswoman for the conservative Family Research Council, stated, "If they're going to talk about 'the facts,' here's a fact: All the major religions of the world consider homosexuality wrong."[22] John Paulk, a "homosexuality and gender analyst" for Focus on the Family, a Christian group based in Colorado, commented, "They're saying they want to present factual information on homosexuality, but we believe that they're presenting propaganda."[23]

Negative attitudes about homosexuality are not limited to the private sector. The U.S. military's "don't ask, don't tell" policy forces gays and lesbians who wish to join or remain in the military into the closet. Until as recently as 1990, federal law barred gays and lesbians, along with convicted felons, epileptics, and drug addicts from immigrating to the United States.[24] In 1996, Congress passed the Defense of Marriage Act (DOMA) which declared that marriage is the union of man and woman.[25] Implicit in the Act is the idea that marriage is *not* the union of man and man nor of woman and woman.

A third problem with using gay panic to support a mental defect defense in a murder case is that the psychological profiles of the defendants in these cases seem very different from the patients Dr. Kempf diagnosed.[26] Men who kill gay men often appear to be quite normal, whereas Kempf's patients tended to have a history of psychological problems.[27] Moreover, Kempf's patients were not aggressive toward others. If physical at all, they tended to inflict punishment upon themselves, not on others.[28] As Adrian Howe observes:

> [T]here was a considerable discrepancy between cases reported in the psychiatric literature and the cases involving immediate reaction or sudden panics described in the legal defenses. Patients diagnosed with acute homosexual panic demonstrated "a helplessness, passivity, and inability to be aggressive" far removed from the picture of the explosively violent man constructed by lawyers deploying a HPD

[Homosexual Panic Disorder] defense. The legal argument that this disorder was likely to result in extreme violence therefore had no psychiatric basis.[29]

A fourth problem with the use of gay panic as a mental disorder is the gendered nature of its use. The murder defendants who claim that Homosexual Panic Disorder made them do it are almost exclusively male.[30] According to Kempf, however, Homosexual Panic Disorder is a mental disease that afflicts both male and female patients. Gary Comstock, one of the nation's leading authorities on violence against gays and lesbians, questions why we should accept claims of gay panic made by men who kill in response to gay male sexual advances when women apparently do not kill in response to lesbian sexual advances:

> [I]f the homosexual panic defense is premised on the disorder's causing murderous behavior in those it afflicts, why have female patients not been driven to kill? The soundness of the defense's premise should be challenged according to its inability to reflect the behavior of the universe of those who suffer from the disorder. If only some are driven to murder, the defense should be pressed to present a scientific, medical explanation for the differential behavior. To be used convincingly as a cause for killing, the disorder would have to be documented with evidence that both male and female patients have killed.[31]

While it is not inconceivable that a woman might panic and respond violently to a lesbian sexual advance, a search for lesbian panic homicide cases turned up no such cases. The lack of such cases suggests that gay panic is the product of a specific construction of masculinity, one that values heterosexism and violence as traits of the masculine.

## GAY PANIC AND MENTAL DISORDER

A defendant claiming mental defect in the form of an insanity defense or a diminished capacity defense typically argues that the victim's (homo)sexual advance caused him to lose control over his mental abilities.[32] Insanity, a complete defense which results in a not guilty by reason of insanity (NGI) verdict, requires proof that the defendant, because of a mental disease or defect, lacked the ability to determine right from wrong or the ability to control his conduct to conform to the law. Diminished capacity, a partial defense to murder which results in a manslaughter conviction, generally requires proof that the defendant was acting under the influence of a mental disease or defect which affected his capacity to premeditate and deliberate or form the intent to kill required for murder.[33] Two high-profile cases illustrate how the concept of gay panic and mental disorder can be deployed in the courtroom.

### Matthew Shepard

October 6, 1998. Laramie, Wyoming. Around 10:30 P.M. Matthew Shepard, a twenty-two-year-old openly gay political science student at the University of Wyoming, arrived at the Fireside Bar and ordered a beer. Around midnight, Shepard met Russell Henderson and Aaron McKinney, two high school dropouts also in their early twenties, who were sharing a pitcher of beer. Henderson and McKinney pretended they were gay and invited Shepard to join them for a drive in McKinney's truck.

Once McKinney and Henderson had Shepard alone in their truck, McKinney pulled out a gun and told Shepard, "We're not gay, and you're getting jacked." He then ordered Shepard to hand over his wallet. Shepard complied, but this did not end the incident. McKinney proceeded to hit the 5 foot 2, 102 pound Shepard repeatedly on the head with the butt of his .357 Magnum pistol. During this time, Henderson drove the truck to a deserted field about one mile outside of Laramie. Once there, McKinney ordered Shepard out of the truck. McKinney asked Shepard whether he could read the license plate on the truck. Shepard replied, "Yes, I can read it," and then recited the license plate number. McKinney responded by kicking Shepard between his legs and striking him over the head, causing Shepard to lose consciousness. Then McKinney and Henderson stripped Shepard of his shoes and tied him to a wooden fence.

Shepard remained tied to the fence in near-freezing weather for approximately eighteen hours before Aaron Kriefels, a freshman at the University of Wyoming, found him. Shepard, who was so badly beaten that he was recognizable only by a distinctive bump on his ear, died five days later.[34]

After leaving Shepard tied to the fence, Henderson and McKinney headed back into town. There, McKinney picked a fight with two Latino youths, Emiliano Morales and Jeremy Herrera. McKinney threw the first punch, hitting Morales in the head. He proceeded to pummel Morales until Herrera intervened, striking McKinney with a stick. According to one police officer, if Herrera had not intervened, Morales might have ended up a homicide victim like Shepard.[35] Police officers who responded to a 911 call about the fight found Henderson and McKinney in McKinney's truck. They also found the bloody gun used to beat Shepard, Shepard's credit card, and one of Shepard's shoes.[36] Henderson and McKinney were arrested and charged with first-degree murder, felony murder, kidnapping, and aggravated robbery.[37] On the eve of trial, Henderson pleaded guilty to murder to avoid the death penalty. McKinney, however, decided to take his chances with a jury, hoping for an outright acquittal or mitigation of the charges.

Initially, McKinney denied that Shepard made any sexual advances toward him.[38] Later, McKinney told several people that Shepard placed his hand on McKinney's crotch and stuck his tongue in McKinney's ear while in McKinney's pickup truck.[39] In a letter McKinney sent from prison to the wife of a fellow inmate, McKinney described the events of the evening as follows:

> When we got out to where he was living, I got ready to draw down on his ass, and all of the [sic] sudden he said he was gay and wanted a piece of me. While he was "comming [sic] out of the closet" he grabbed my nuts and licked my ear! Being a verry [sic] drunk homofobic [sic] I flipped out and began to pistol whip the fag with my gun, ready at hand.[40]

It is hard to believe that an unarmed Shepard, who was much smaller than McKinney and Henderson, would attempt a sexual advance upon a man with a gun who had just announced that he wasn't gay and that Shepard was getting robbed.

McKinney's murder trial began on October 25, 1999. Despite McKinney's initial denial that Shepard made any sexual advances, Jason Tangeman, McKinney's attorney, used a gay panic argument before the jury of seven men and five women.[41] During his opening statement, Tangeman argued that Shepard made a (homo)sexual advance upon McKinney and that this sexual advance was particularly upsetting to McKinney because of his past history with unpleasant homosexual encounters. According to Tangeman, when McKinney was five years old, he was forced to perform oral sex on a neighborhood bully. As a teenager, McKinney engaged in homosexual acts with a cousin, and at the age of twenty, McKinney was traumatized when he accidentally entered a gay and lesbian church in Florida.[42] These "sexually traumatic events" combined with his use of alcohol and methamphetamine[43] caused McKinney to lose his self-control.

Tangeman's opening statement was somewhat of a surprise. McKinney's attorneys had not mentioned plans to use a gay panic defense in any of the pretrial hearings.[44] Judge Barton Voigt quickly called a hearing to decide whether the defense attorneys should be permitted to introduce evidence of gay panic in support of a mental disorder defense. After hearing arguments from both sides, the judge ruled against the defense. First, Judge Voigt observed that despite their protests to the contrary, the defense attorneys were in fact trying to assert what he called a "homosexual rage" defense. He explained:

> Defense counsel have tried valiantly to convince the Court that their defense is not a homosexual rage defense. But what they hope to do is to present testimony that, because of homosexual experiences in the Defendant's past, he flew into a rage and killed Matthew Shepard, without specific intent to kill, but voluntarily in a sudden heat of passion. This is the homosexual rage defense, nothing more, nothing less. The fact that the Defendant attempts to raise it through lay witnesses, rather than through experts, is inconsequential.[45]

The judge then ruled that McKinney's prior homosexual experiences could not be considered by the jury on the issue of provocation because provocation is supposed to be based upon an objective Reasonable Person standard and McKinney's personal experiences bore only upon his subjective state of mind. The judge also ruled that the defenses of temporary insanity and diminished capacity were not recognized by Wyoming law, and accordingly were unavailable to the defense.[46]

Despite the judge's attempts to limit the defense's use of gay panic, Tangeman called two witnesses to the stand whose testimony was used to convey the idea that Matthew Shepard was sexually aggressive and deserved the beating he got, playing on stereotypical images of gay men as sexual deviants and sexually aggressive predators.[47] One witness testified that he was at the Fireside Lounge Bar the night Shepard was killed. According to this witness, Shepard approached him, whispered something in his ear, and licked his lips in a sexually suggestive manner.[48] After he agreed to let Shepard sit with him, this witness testified that he "began to feel really uncomfortable. I didn't like the thoughts I was having about the motives for him sitting with me."[49]

A second witness testified that Shepard was sexually aggressive toward him when they went on a trip to a lake with others in the summer of 1998. According to this second witness, Shepard tugged on his shirt and asked him to go for a walk. He responded by punching Shepard twice, knocking him out.[50]

These two witnesses were used by the defense not only to give credibility to McKinney's otherwise hard to believe claim that Shepard had made a sexual advance upon him, but also to suggest that it was reasonable for McKinney to be offended by Shepard's advance and for him to respond to the alleged homosexual advance with violence. During closing arguments to the jury, Tangeman again argued that Shepard's sexual advance upon McKinney triggered the subsequent beating.

Some have speculated about the role of class in the murder of Matt Shepard. Henderson and McKinney were seasonal roofers who brought home about $900 a month after taxes.[51] Both were frequent users of methamphetamine, the drug of choice for drug users without a lot of money.[52] Shepard, on the other hand, was a student at the University of Wyoming who reportedly wore stylish leather shoes and could afford to drink imported beer.[53] Henderson and McKinney could have been hostile to Shepard because of his higher class and wealth. According to University of Wyoming professor Beth Loffreda, however, most residents of Laramie did not believe class resentment caused McKinney to kill Shepard. One resident told Loffreda that he believed class resentment was not a factor contributing to Shepard's beating, because most people in Laramie are not wealthy and those who are don't flaunt it.

Even if class did not motivate McKinney to kill Shepard, race and class together may have influenced the public's perception of the case. Shepard was young, White, and middle class. Henderson and McKinney, in contrast, were working class or unemployed, high school dropouts, and methamphetamine users—viewed as "White trash" by some. According to Jay, a gay Shoshone-Northern Arapahoe-Navajo American Indian from the Wind River Reservation in Wyoming, people were outraged by the killing of Matt Shepard because "it was as if white, middle-class America finally had its own tragedy." Jay continued, "If that was me hung on the fence, they'd just say, oh, another drunk Indian."[54] Jay's intuition about public sentiment may be accurate. That McKinney brutally beat a Latino shortly after beating Shepard was barely reported in the press. Had Morales, a young Latino with a criminal record, died of his injuries, one wonders whether middle America would have been as outraged as they were following Shepard's murder.

At the end of the trial, the jury had to decide whether to convict McKinney of first-degree murder (which requires proof of premeditation and intent to kill), second-degree murder (which requires proof that the defendant purposefully killed the victim), or felony murder (which merely requires proof that a killing occurred during the commission or attempted commission of a felony). The jury found McKinney guilty of two counts of first-degree felony murder (one based on the underlying felony of kidnapping and the other on the felony of robbery) and one count of second-degree murder.[55] Despite repeated attempts to use gay panic as a mitigating factor, McKinney was not able to escape liability for murder.

### Billy Jack Gaither

A gay panic argument was used in another high-profile case by a man named Charles Butler who was charged with murder in the death of Billy Jack Gaither, an openly gay man. Butler and his friend, Steven Mullins, beat Gaither and then set his body on fire atop a pyre of tires, claiming they did so because Gaither propositioned them.

> February 19, 1999. Coosa County, Alabama. Steven Mullins asked Billy Jack Gaither, a thirty-nine-year-old textile worker, to pick him up and take him to the Tavern, a local bar which both men frequented. Mullins was unemployed and often asked Gaither for rides and money. Mullins told Gaither that his friend Charles Butler was interested in a sexual threesome and that they were supposed to meet Butler at another bar. In fact, Mullins and Butler had no intention of having a sexual threesome with Gaither. As Mullins later explained, he decided to kill Gaither for propositioning him two weeks earlier, and invited Butler to join him because he knew how much Butler despised homosexuals. Gaither and Mullins picked up Butler, and drove to a secluded place in the woods.
>
> The three men got out of the car, and started drinking beer. Butler was the first to hit Gaither, claiming he did so only after Gaither talked about

his interest in a sexual threesome. Butler told sheriff's investigator Kelley Johnson, "Well, sir, he started talking, you know, queer stuff, you know, and I just didn't want no part of it. That's when I kicked him, and he went down. I kicked him maybe two or three more times, then he got up, and then I went to use the bathroom, and that's when Steve jumped on him."[56]

As Butler was relieving himself at the front of the car, Mullins grabbed Gaither, threw him on the ground, and slashed his throat with a pocket knife. He then stabbed Gaither in the ribs. Mullins told Butler to pop the trunk of Gaither's car, then ordered Gaither to climb in.

With Gaither in the trunk of the car, Mullins and Butler drove to a trailer where they picked up tires, kerosene, a box of matches, and an ax handle. The two men then got back in the car and drove to Peckerwood Creek. Once there, Mullins and Butler took the tires out of the trunk and propped the ax handle against the car. Butler started to light the tires. Mullins dragged Gaither out of the trunk and left him on the ground. While Mullins's back was turned, Gaither managed to get up and knock Mullins down the embankment. Gaither crawled back to the car and tried to escape. Mullins got up, followed Gaither, and dragged him out of the car. He then grabbed the ax handle and beat Gaither in the face until his face collapsed. In the meantime, the tires had caught fire. Mullins dragged Gaither's body into the flames and he and Butler watched Gaither's body burn.[57]

That night, Butler confessed to his father, "Daddy, we kicked a queer's ass." Butler's father told this to a friend, and within a week Butler and Mullins were in custody. The two men were each charged with capital murder. In June 1999, Mullins pleaded guilty to capital murder and agreed to testify against Butler in exchange for a life sentence without the possibility of parole.

At his arraignment, Butler pleaded not guilty by reason of mental disease or defect.[58] Before trial, however, Butler withdrew his mental defect defense,[59] arguing instead that he should be found not guilty of murder because it was Mullins who actually killed Billy Jack Gaither.

Even though Butler formally withdrew his mental defect defense, gay panic was prominently featured at his trial. Butler claimed he hit Gaither only after Gaither told him he was interested in a sexual threesome with Butler and Mullins. Mullins too asserted that the reason he killed Gaither was because Gaither had propositioned him two weeks earlier.

Gaither's friends, however, said it was highly unlikely that Gaither would proposition either man. According to one friend, "[Billy Jack] didn't walk around acting, looking, or talking gay. If anybody was asking for sex, it wasn't him—it was them. We've got a lot of rednecks in here. You don't make advances with them around."[60] Marian Hammonds, owner of The Tavern, a straight bar which Gaither frequented, described Gaither as a likable man who, while never denying he was gay, "made a point of never doing the gay thing when he was at our place. . . . My husband, Larry, didn't even know he was gay until about a year ago, and I had to tell him."[61] Hammonds further remarked, "He [Gaither] never put anybody in [an awkward] position."[62]

Mullins may have had a different reason for wanting Gaither dead. Friends of Gaither have asserted that Mullins and Gaither had a sexual relationship which Mullins didn't want anyone to know about, and that Mullins killed Gaither in order to ensure that he never would tell anyone about their homosexual affair. At Butler's trial, Mullins adamantly denied having sex with Gaither or any other man. Yet Butler's attorneys presented several witnesses who testified that Mullins had a secret gay sex life. One man, Jimmy Lynn Dean, testified that he and Mullins had oral sex about four months before Billy Jack Gaither was killed.[63]

In Butler's case, neither gay panic nor the "it wasn't me" argument worked. The jury convicted Butler of capital murder. Even though this made Butler eligible for the death penalty, Gaither's family requested that Butler be spared capital punishment. Butler was sentenced to life in prison without the possibility of parole.

It is comforting that attempts to link gay panic to mental disorder in these two very high-profile cases did not work. In large part, the gay panic argument probably failed in both cases because the facts clearly demonstrated a premeditated and deliberate intent to kill. Additionally, gay and lesbian activists focused media attention on these cases, which helped to delegitimize defense attempts to blame the victim.

Over time, the use of mental defect defenses in gay victim homicide cases has fallen out of favor for a number of reasons, not the least of which is the difficulty of securing a favorable jury verdict with a mental defect defense.[64] Jurors are often skeptical of defense claims of insanity.[65] Additionally, a verdict of not guilty by reason of insanity (temporary or otherwise) does not mean the defendant goes free. The defendant who is found insane is usually committed to a mental institution for an indefinite period of time. This period of confinement can exceed the length of the prison sentence the defendant would have received if he or she had been convicted. Many individuals would rather serve a definite prison sentence than endure the stigma and uncertainty of an indefinite period of commitment in a mental institution. Moreover, asserting a mental defect defense is often seen as an unacceptable admission of mental deficiency.

Another reason for the shift away from mental defect defenses is the unavailability of those defenses in certain jurisdictions. At least three states do not recognize the defense of insanity.[66] A number of states have either abolished the defense of diminished capacity or substantially restricted its use. For example, diminished capacity is not officially recognized as a defense in California[67] or Wyoming.[68] In some states, such as Michigan, diminished capacity is only allowed as a defense to first-degree murder.[69]

## GAY PANIC AND CLAIMS OF REASONABLENESS

Because of the above-described difficulties associated with mental defect defenses, male defendants charged with murder may claim instead that they were provoked into a heat of passion by the victim's homosexual advance.[70] Alternatively, they may claim they acted in self-defense. Both defenses require a showing of reasonableness. The defendant will not succeed unless the jury finds that a reasonable man in the defendant's shoes would have been provoked or would have used deadly force in self-defense.

The idea that a homosexual advance constitutes legally adequate provocation is almost as deeply rooted in Anglo-American law as the idea that the observation by a husband of his wife in the act of adultery constitutes legally adequate provocation. At early common law, one of the categories of legally adequate provocation was a serious crime committed against a close relative. Some courts limited this category to cases in which a father discovered someone committing sodomy on his son.[71] The discovery by a father of someone committing sodomy on his son and the observation by a husband of his wife in the act of adultery were the only two categories of legally adequate provocation which did not involve actual violence by the deceased victim against the defendant. Both these categories involved observations of offensive sexual behavior.

Not all observations of sexually offensive behavior are considered legally adequate provocation. In one case, a man named Stephen Carr, charged with first-degree murder for killing a woman after watching her engage in lesbian lovemaking, tried unsuccessfully to assert a provocation defense.[72] Carr encountered Claudia Brenner and Rebecca Wight on May 13, 1988, as they were hiking on the Appalachian Trail. Carr decided to follow the two women, and watched from a hidden vantage point as they began to engage in lovemaking. For no apparent reason, Carr aimed his single-gauge shotgun at the two women and shot eight bullets, killing Wight and injuring Brenner. He was charged with first-degree murder.

In defense of his actions, Carr argued that he was provoked into a heat of passion after observing the two women engage in nude lesbian lovemaking.[73] To support his heat of passion argument, Carr argued that he had a history of constant rejection by women, starting with his mother who was involved in a lesbian relationship. Prior to trial, the prosecutor filed a motion in limine, arguing that the defendant should be precluded from arguing he was provoked by the women's lovemaking. At the hearing on this motion, defense counsel argued that Carr should be permitted to introduce evidence of his personal, psychological, and sexual history to support his claim of provocation. The Honorable Oscar Spicer found such evidence irrelevant, and granted the prosecution's motion.[74] After a non-jury trial, the judge found Carr guilty of first-degree murder. Carr appealed his conviction, arguing that Judge Spicer erred in disallowing evidence of his psychosexual history to show that he was provoked into a heat of passion. The appellate court affirmed Carr's conviction, explaining that "The sight of naked women engaged in lesbian lovemaking is not adequate provocation to reduce an unlawful killing from murder to voluntary manslaughter. It is not an event which is sufficient to cause a reasonable person to become so impassioned as to be incapable of cool reflection. A reasonable person would simply have discontinued his observation and left the scene; he would not kill the lovers."[75]

Unlike Carr who killed a lesbian woman after merely observing her engage in lovemaking, heterosexual men who have killed gay men in response to unwanted nonviolent sexual advances have had much better luck arguing that they were reasonably provoked into a heat of passion. Perhaps this is because the argument that a nonviolent homosexual advance constitutes legally adequate provocation conforms to dominant norms of masculinity. A male-on-male sexual advance threatens a heterosexual man's sense of identity as a man in several ways. First, men in this society are supposed to be interested in women, not men. Second, men are supposed to be the sexual aggressors, not the ones aggressed upon.[76]

Masculinity norms also bolster the heterosexual male's claim that he was reasonably outraged by the nonviolent homosexual advance. Roy Scrivner notes that men in this society are supposed to be "fearful and disdainful of homosexuals," and "are taught to reject any personal same-gender sexual feelings."[77] James Harrison observes that many heterosexual men are so terrified of being perceived as gay that they avoid expressing qualities that they think seem feminine, like being loving, caring, gentle, and nurturing, and enjoying beauty.[78]

Finally, dominant masculinity norms legitimize the use of physical violence in response to nonviolent homosexual advances. Men in this society who are physically strong, aggressive, and willing to use force when necessary are admired by women and other men.[79] When a heterosexual man finds his masculinity threatened by a homosexual advance, aggression and violence are considered appropriate ways to respond.[80] The feeling of threat in such cases is analogous to the threat to male identity and honor that arises when a wife is unfaithful.

The perceived threat to male identity may be heightened if the advance occurs in front of other people, rather than in a private setting. JoAnn Wypijewski recounts the following conversation she had with a young man from Laramie, Wyoming, the town where Matthew Shepard was killed:

> "If a guy at a bar made some kind of overture to you, what would you do?"
>
> "It depends on who's around. If I'm with a girl, I'd be worried about what she thinks, because, as I said, everything a man does is in some way connected to a woman, whether he wants to admit it or not. Do I look queer? Will she tell other girls?"
>
> "If my friends were around and they'd laugh and shit, I might have to threaten him."
>
> "If I'm alone and he just wants to buy me a beer, then okay, I'm straight, you're gay—hey, you can buy me a beer."[81]

In both the Matthew Shepard and Billy Jack Gaither cases, however, the alleged sexual advance occurred in private (in a pickup truck or out in the woods) when the defendant was with the victim and only one other man, yet the alleged sexual advance still triggered a violent response. Perhaps the private nature of these encounters encouraged the juries in these cases to see the defendants' actions as unreasonable.

The claim of reasonableness linked to anti-gay violence is very much the product of a culture that privileges *heterosexual male* violence over other types of violence. A man who responds to a (homo)sexual advance with violence resulting in death claims he acted as any ordinary (i.e., heterosexual) man would have acted. A woman who tries to make a similar claim would find it pretty difficult to succeed. A woman who responds with deadly force to a man who whistles at her, tries to kiss her, grab her buttocks, or fondle her breasts is quite unusual, not at all typical. Ordinary or reasonable women are supposed to accept a certain amount of unwanted male attention, and while they might frown, struggle, or protest, they are not supposed to use lethal violence to dissuade or thwart men who suggest sexual interest. Moreover, women are taught to believe that a man who expresses his sexual attraction to a woman is merely behaving the way a man is supposed to behave. The woman who is the target of male attention is supposed to be flattered. Even if the woman is a lesbian, and is just as offended by a male sexual advance as a heterosexual male might be, she is unlikely to convince the average juror that a violent response to a nonviolent heterosexual advance is reasonable, because women are not supposed to be violent. David Wertheimer, former Executive Director of the New York City Gay and Lesbian Anti-Violence Project, wryly points out, "If every heterosexual woman who had a sexual advance made to her by a male had the right to murder the man, the streets of this city would be littered with the bodies of heterosexual men."[82]

The heterosexual man's claim of reasonableness does more than privilege men over women. It privileges heterosexual men over gay men. If a heterosexual man responds violently to a homosexual advance, he enjoys a presumption of reasonableness. A heterosexual man is supposed to be disgusted and outraged when another man attempts a sexual advance. If, however, a *gay* man responds violently to a heterosexual female's sexual advance, he will have a difficult time convincing anyone that he was *reasonably* provoked into a heat of passion even if a heterosexual woman's sexual advance is just as disgusting to him as a gay man's sexual advance might be to a heterosexual man. Men in this society are supposed to be happy if a woman shows she is sexually attracted to him by taking off her clothes, kissing him on the mouth, or grabbing his crotch. If a man, however, shows his sexual interest in another man by acting in a similar manner, he is asking for a violent response.

Charles Butler, the man convicted of capital murder for his part in the slaying and burning of Billy Jack Gaither on a pyre of tires, admitted he would have reacted differently had Gaither been a woman. In an interview with *Frontline,* Butler admitted that Billy Jack did not attempt to grab him or touch him in any way. Billy Jack's *verbal* suggestion of a sexual threesome made Butler feel disrespected and led him to beat Billy Jack. Butler admitted that had a woman made a similar suggestion, he would not have viewed her remarks as disrespectful. Because the verbal come-on came from a man, Butler felt he had to react with physical violence.

Race and age also play a part in gay homicide cases. Sixty-seven percent of the perpetrators of anti-gay/lesbian violence are White and 94 percent are male.[83] A majority of the perpetrators are in their teens or twenties. These young, White, male defendants are often described at trial as well-liked, normal young men.[84] In many cases, the victim is much older than the defendant. Stereotypes about gay men as sexual deviants who prey on young boys and cannot be trusted to work in positions of supervisory authority, the message of both the Religious Right and the Boys Scouts, might lead jurors to feel that a young male defendant's violent response to an older male's sexual advance is reasonable. Even though the concept of reasonableness is usually associated with reason and calm deliberation, the opposite of violence driven by emotion, a young heterosexual man nonetheless is considered reasonable if he responds violently to an older male's nonviolent homosexual advance.

### Randy Eklund

One problem that arises in murder cases in general is the absence of the victim's testimony. Since the victim is dead, the jury often hears only the defendant's account of what happened. This is particularly true in cases in which the defendant and the victim were alone at the time of the homicide.

February 26, 1991. Rockford, Illinois. Johnny Mangum, a thirty-year-old ex-convict and former Golden Gloves boxer, met Randy Eklund, a gay man twelve years his senior, at Pribby's Tavern in Rockford. The two men began talking, and Eklund bought a number of drinks for Mangum. Eventually, Eklund invited Mangum to come home with him. Mangum accepted the invitation. The two continued drinking in Eklund's kitchen. After several more drinks, Eklund reached over, placed his hand on Mangum's crotch, and squeezed. Mangum pushed Eklund's hand away and told him to stop. Eklund retorted, "I bought you all those drinks, and I want to suck your dick." In response, Mangum began to hit Eklund. When Eklund tried to escape, Mangum followed Eklund and continued to beat him until he fell to the ground. Mangum then forced Eklund to lie face down and tied Eklund's hands and feet together behind his back. With Eklund disabled, Mangum took Eklund's car keys, filled a garbage can with bottles of Eklund's liquor, loaded the garbage can and Eklund's microwave into Eklund's car, and drove it away. Later that evening, Mangum bragged to a friend that he had "robbed a faggot and beat the guy up."[85]

After Ecklund's dead body was discovered, Mangum was charged with first-degree murder. At trial, he claimed that Eklund's homosexual advance provoked him into a heat of passion. According to Mangum, when Eklund grabbed his crotch and said he wanted to suck his penis, he got so angry that he couldn't stop himself from the brutal beating that followed.[86]

Mangum's claim that he killed Eklund in a heat of passion was partially successful. The jury found him guilty of murder in the second degree, implicitly acquitting him of first-degree murder.[87] A journalist who sat through the trial looked over at the jury when the verdict was read and noticed that several of the jurors looked at Mangum with sympathy. After the trial, this journalist interviewed several of the jurors to ask about their decision. One male juror called the deceased victim a "deviate," and added, "I think anyone of his sexual persuasion invites a certain amount of grief."[88] Another male juror said he would have clobbered any guy who hit on him.[89]

Mangum's class likely had some influence on his verdict. Jurors are not usually sympathetic to poor defendants with criminal records. In this case, however, at least some of the jurors were sympathetic to Mangum even though he was a transient and convicted criminal who apparently "hung out with alcoholics and drug users along a strip of seedy bars in one of Rockford's two 'red light' districts."[90] The jurors may have felt it was particularly believable that a lower-income man like Mangum would panic and respond violently to a (homo)sexual advance.

Mangum's status as a convicted felon may have worked against him as well, encouraging the jury to return a conviction for second-degree murder rather than the lesser offense of voluntary manslaughter. Studies indicate that lower- and working-class men convicted of assaulting or killing gay men tend to receive more severe sentences than middle- and upper-class men convicted of similar crimes.[91] If Mangum had been an upper-middle-class or wealthy man, the jury might have returned a more favorable verdict, such as a manslaughter conviction.

Mangum's story may have sounded credible to his jury because it resonated with stereotypes about gay men as sexual deviants and predators. However, in this case as in most homicides, the only version of the facts the jury heard was the defendant's version. Mangum claimed that Eklund grabbed his crotch and started squeezing. Mangum claimed that Eklund threatened to "suck his dick," but we will never know what really transpired the night Randy Eklund was beaten to death. Eklund is not alive to contest Mangum's version of events and no eyewitnesses saw the homicide.

At Mangum's sentencing hearing, Mangum's former wife testified that Mangum did not like homosexuals. She also testified that Mangum told her that before he met her, he used to go into the Seventh Avenue area of Rockford and walk the streets on a regular basis, posing as a homosexual in order to encourage gay men to pick him up. After being picked up, Mangum would wait until the gay stranger made a sexual advance, then he would beat and rob him.[92] Given this history, Mangum may have pretended interest in Eklund to encourage some kind of sexual advance from Eklund, so that he would have an excuse to beat him. Mangum not only beat Eklund to death, he also stole his belongings. If Mangum was as out of control as he claimed to have been, it is unlikely that he would have had the presence of mind to steal Eklund's liquor, microwave, and car.

For some reason, the jury seemed to ignore Mangum's history as a former boxer who had fought in a "Golden Gloves" competition. Given this history, one might have concluded that Mangum was capable of leaving Eklund's home as soon as the situation got uncomfortable for him. Even if Eklund had made some kind of sexual advance, Mangum could have gotten out of the situation without beating him to death.

### Stephen Lamie

August 6, 1988. Lafayette, Indiana. Seventeen-year-old Timothy Schick went out with friends to drink and look for women. After his friends asked to be dropped off, Schick continued to drive around. His car broke down, so he stuck out his thumb and tried to hitchhike a ride. Thirty-eight-year-old Stephen Lamie saw Schick and offered him a lift. Schick climbed in Lamie's car and asked him if he knew where they could find some loose women. Lamie said he couldn't help him. Schick then asked Lamie if he knew where one could get a blow job. Lamie told Schick he could handle that request. Lamie drove to a local high school baseball field and told Schick this was where he would get his blow job. As the two were walking toward the field, Lamie pulled down his own shorts and underwear, grabbed Schick around the waist, and reached for Schick's penis. Shocked by Lamie's forwardness, Schick kneed Lamie in the stomach and hit Lamie in the face. Lamie fell to the ground without fighting back, but Schick continued to kick and beat Lamie. When he heard gurgling sounds coming from Lamie's throat and chest, Schick removed Lamie's watch, some cigarettes from Lamie's pocket, and $26 from Lamie's wallet. He raced back to Lamie's car and wiped the dashboard and seat to get rid of his fingerprints, then ran away.[93]

Schick was charged with murder and other offenses. At trial, Schick claimed he was provoked into a heat of passion by Lamie's sexual overture and therefore should be convicted of manslaughter rather than murder. The jury agreed, and found Schick guilty of voluntary manslaughter.

In analyzing the jury's verdict, it is important to consider several factors besides the gender and sexual orientation of the parties. The relative ages of the defendant and victim may also influence the jury's decision as to reasonableness. More than 50 percent of the perpetrators of anti-gay and anti-lesbian violence are under the age of twenty-eight.[94] Given the stereotype of the gay man as a sexual predator who preys on young boys, Lamie's status as a gay man more than twice Schick's age may have influenced the jury to see Schick's violent reaction as reasonable. Additionally, Lamie's explicit sexual advance (as described by Schick) may have convinced the jury that Schick's violent acts were necessary to protect himself from a sexual assault. If an older man pulled down his underwear, exposed his penis to a teenage girl, grabbed her around the waist, and tried to grab her breasts or crotch, we would probably sympathize with the girl if she used non-lethal violence (a kick or a punch) to escape the older man's sexual advance.

The problem is that even under Schick's version of events, Schick did more than simply use nonlethal violence to escape Lamie's alleged sexual advance. After Lamie was down on the ground with his underwear around his ankles, Schick proceeded to punch, kick, and stomp Lamie to death. If Schick had been a teenage girl, it is doubtful that a jury would find such a response ordinary or reasonable, although they might grant her leniency out of sympathy. Moreover, Schick's claim that the alleged homosexual advance provoked him into such a heat of passion that he completely lost his self-control must be called into question, given that Schick had sufficient presence of mind to take Lamie's watch, cigarettes, and cash, and wipe his fingerprints from Lamie's car before fleeing the scene.

### Billy Francis Brinkley

July 13, 1973. Mecklenburg, North Carolina. Seventeen-year-old David Mills met forty-three-year-old Billy Francis Brinkley at a bar. According to Mills, Brinkley offered to pay Mills $20 if Mills would "commit a homosexual act" with Brinkley. Mills agreed, and the two men drove to Paw Creek Cove in Brinkley's car. Once there, according to Mills, Brinkley proceeded to grab Mills's privates. Mills demanded his $20, but Brinkley said he didn't have $20 with him. Because Brinkley did not have the money he had promised, Mills fought Brinkley off. When Brinkley persisted, Mills pushed Brinkley out of the car. Mills then chased Brinkley, knocked him down, kicked him, and pulled Brinkley's clothes down to hinder his escape. Mills then took Brinkley's jewelry and fled in Brinkley's car. Brinkley's body was later found in a cove in Mecklenburg County, North Carolina. Brinkley had died from head injuries and a massive crushing injury to his chest consistent with having been kicked and then thrown against rocks. Mills was found a few hours after Brinkley's death with Brinkley's automobile, watch, ring, and bracelet.[95]

Mills was charged with second-degree murder. Mills maintained he was reasonably provoked by the older man's attempt to have sex with him. The jury agreed that Mills was reasonably provoked, and convicted him of voluntary manslaughter.

Mills's voluntary manslaughter verdict is troubling for several reasons. First, it suggests that the jury believed it was reasonable for Mills to become enraged at Brinkley's conduct (grabbing Mills's private parts and making a pass at him), even though Mills had previously agreed to engage in sexual activity with Brinkley. Mills willingly accompanied Brinkley to Paw Creek Cove, knowing that the purpose of the trip was sex. Generally speaking, the criminal law does not excuse a defendant who creates the conditions of his own defense.

Second, the verdict suggests the jury believed Mills's claim that he was genuinely afraid of being sexually assaulted by Brinkley, even though Mills's behavior—pushing Brinkley out of the car, chasing Brinkley, knocking Brinkley down, kicking him, and pulling his pants down to hinder Brinkley's escape—seems more consistent with the behavior of someone who intends to seriously injure than the behavior of one who is afraid. If Mills had been afraid of Brinkley, he might have tried to get away by driving off in Brinkley's car as soon as he pushed Brinkley out of the car. Instead, Mills chased after Brinkley, knocked him down, and kicked him repeatedly. Once Brinkley was down, he no longer posed an immediate threat to Mills. Nonetheless, Mills proceeded to pull down Brinkley's clothes to hinder Brinkley's escape. He then either pushed or threw Brinkley onto the rocks in the cove where the body was later found.

Finally, Mills's claim that the alleged sexual advance by Brinkley so provoked him that he lost his ability to control his actions is belied by his having the presence of mind to take several items of value belonging to Brinkley, including his watch, ring, bracelet, and car.

One pattern that emerges from gay homicide cases is that the perpetrator who claims he was provoked into a heat of passion often takes money or other items of value from the victim after killing him. Stealing the victim's belongings suggests an economic motivation for the killing, rather than panic or fear. Johnny Mangum took off with Randy Eklund's liquor, microwave oven, and car after beating him to death. Timothy Schick took Steven Lamie's watch, cigarettes, and money, then wiped off his fingerprints from the dashboard of Lamie's car in an attempt to avoid detection and arrest. David Mills took Billy Francis

Brinkley's watch, ring, bracelet, and car. As one observer of gay panic killings has noted, "the number of cases where [gay] murders have been accompanied by robbery suggests that criminal opportunism is a frequent motive for these killings."[96]

Also undermining claims of provocation in gay homicide cases is the fact that the defendant often places himself in a situation in which a homosexual advance is likely. Johnny Mangum accepted Randy Eklund's invitation to come home with him. Timothy Schick hitched a ride from Stephen Lamie, a total stranger, and stayed in the car even after Lamie suggested he could handle a blow job for Schick. David Mills agreed to have sex with Billy Francis Brinkley in exchange for $20. Yet in case after case, jurors seem to overlook these facts undermining the defendant's claim that he was actually and reasonably provoked when they give the defendant the manslaughter conviction he seeks.

Less common, but sometimes successful, are claims of gay panic and self-defense. Just as in the provocation cases discussed above, the defendant claiming self-defense draws upon masculinity norms, heterosexuality norms, and stereotypes about gay men to bolster his claims of reasonableness.

### Kenneth Brewer

September 30, 1997. Oahu, Hawaii. After an afternoon and evening of drinking beer and bar hopping, Stephen Bright, a thirty-year-old construction worker, decided to check out Hula's, a gay bar on Kuhio Street. There he met Kenneth Brewer, a retired fifty-eight-year-old former hotel executive. Brewer offered to buy Bright some drinks and the two men chatted. After midnight, Brewer invited Bright to spend the night at his Hawaii Kai condominium. Bright agreed to accompany Brewer back to his condo. Once they arrived, the two men went to Brewer's bedroom where they had a few gin and tonics.

After several drinks, Brewer excused himself. According to Bright, Brewer came back into the bedroom, completely naked with an erection, approached Bright, and told him he wanted to "fuck." Then Brewer grabbed Bright's throat with one hand and his crotch with the other, saying, "Take your clothes off. I want to suck your cock." Bright punched Brewer to get him off of him. He then beat Brewer until Brewer was a bloody mess at the foot of the bed.[97]

Bright was charged with second-degree murder. At trial, Bright claimed he acted in self-defense, beating Brewer to ward off a sexual assault. Self-defense as a defense to murder requires proof that the defendant honestly and reasonably believed it was *necessary* to use deadly force to protect against an imminent threat of death or serious bodily injury. If the defendant could have avoided the threatened harm by taking less fatal action, the defendant cannot claim self-defense. Self-defense doctrine also requires proportionality. An individual cannot use deadly force to counter nondeadly force.

Interestingly, Bright's attorney, Deputy Public Defender Jack Tonaki, did not argue that his client's fear of sexual assault was somehow worse because his attacker was a man. Instead, in a sophisticated appeal to the women on the jury, Tonaki argued that fighting back in self-defense against the threat of sexual assault is the same whether by a man or a woman. Engaging in a bit of veiled gender- and sexual orientation–switching, Tonaki further argued that it makes no difference whether the sexual assailant is gay or straight, because an individual has the right to fight off an unwanted sexual attack.[98] The jury, encouraged to imagine Bright as a woman being sexually attacked by an older man, sympathized with Bright.

It is true that a woman threatened with imminent rape or other forcible sexual assault is generally justified in using deadly force in self-defense. However, the woman is justified only if deadly force is necessary to avoid being killed or seriously injured. Use of deadly force to protect against death or serious bodily injury is considered proportionate force. It is doubtful that Stephen Bright had to kill Kenneth Brewer in order to avoid the alleged sexual advance. Bright was younger by almost thirty years and much stronger than Brewer. According to Wayne Tashima, the prosecutor who tried the case, Bright's body was muscular and stocky. It was obvious that he worked out, and his job as a construction worker required him to lift heavy objects. Brewer, in contrast, was overweight and weak. Bright did not have to beat Brewer to death in order to avoid a sexual assault.

Further undermining Bright's claim of self-defense was that Brewer's blood was found on the inside of Bright's jeans, suggesting that Bright had his pants off during the beating and may have engaged in some form of consensual sexual activity before the killing. Bright, however, denied taking off his pants during the evening. His attorney suggested Brewer's blood could have gotten on the inside of Bright's jeans after he took off his clothes and threw them together in a laundry basket. According to the prosecutor, however, Bright did not remove his clothes until at least four hours after the killing. Any blood from the beating probably would have dried by that time, and would not have transferred from one piece of clothing to another.

The blood on the inside of Bright's jeans suggests Bright may have allowed Brewer to orally or manually copulate him before he beat Brewer to death. If so, Bright's claim that he was afraid of Brewer and only beat him to ward off a sexual attack is suspect. It seems more plausible that Bright went to Brewer's home knowing that Brewer expected some kind of sexual activity in exchange for all the drinks he had purchased for Bright that evening. The two may have started to engage in sexual activity. Then Bright may have started feeling disgusted with himself and took his feelings of shame and guilt out on Brewer. Alternatively, Bright may have engaged in consensual sex in order to make it easier for him to kill Brewer. The brutality of the beating suggests a rage that far exceeds the force needed to protect oneself from a sexual assault.

The jury deliberated for three-and-a-half days before acquitting Bright of murder, finding him guilty of only third-degree assault, a misdemeanor. The maximum punishment for third-degree assault was one year in jail.* Because Bright had already been in jail for one year pending trial, he was released from jail the same day he was convicted.[99]

## REVISITING THE *JENNY JONES* CASE

Heterosexism, racism, and sexism often work in tandem, privileging White (race) heterosexual (sexual orientation) males (gender) over others who are seen as different from the norm.[100] One of the goals of this project is to highlight the ways in which masculinity, race, and sexuality norms work in tandem to privilege certain claims of reasonableness over others. To the extent possible, I have tried to engage in what Peter Kwan calls a cosynthetic analysis, one that takes into account differing axes of subordination.[101] In like vein, Darren Hutchinson calls upon

---

* Bright was sentenced to time served and four hundred hours of community service.

legal scholars to apply a "multidimensionality" approach, recognizing the interrelationships between racism, patriarchy, and heterosexism.[102]

It is often difficult to perform a multidimensional analysis because the written accounts of most cases focus on only one axis of discrimination, if any.[103] For example, court opinions in gay panic cases rarely identify the race of the defendant or victim because the court is focused on sexual orientation. Similarly, court opinions in racialized self-defense cases rarely identify the class status or sexual orientation of the parties.

How might a cosynthetic or multidimensional analysis be applied to the *Jenny Jones* case? Such analysis would evaluate how norms of heterosexuality, masculinity, and race interacted to support Schmitz's claim that appearing on the *Jenny Jones Show* with a gay secret admirer was deeply humiliating. For example, Jonathan Schmitz's claim of outrage and embarrassment by a gay secret admirer makes sense only if we accept as reasonable his expectation that his secret admirer would be a woman. A gay man wouldn't necessarily expect a woman to be *his* secret admirer. But in this society, heterosexual orientation is the norm and therefore most people think it reasonable for a man to expect that a secret admirer will be a woman.

Schmitz's resort to violence as an expression of outrage at Amedure's expression of sexual interest could also be seen as reasonable given the masculinity norm of violence and aggression. Men in this society are socialized to respond to threats to masculinity with force. A boy who turns the other cheek when hit is considered a sissy.[104] Because men are not supposed to be anything like women, the fact that women rarely resort to violence when they are confronted with unwanted sexual attention from male admirers does not detract from the male claim of reasonableness. Scott Amedure, however, did not make an unwanted homosexual advance upon Schmitz, unless we stretch the meaning of sexual advance. There was no attempted kiss, no grabbing or stroking of a private part. Schmitz's response to the note he received on his doorstep, which he assumed was a crude come-on from Amedure, was grossly disproportionate, which was probably why Schmitz's second jury rejected his claim of reasonable provocation.

The racial implications of the *Jenny Jones* case are less apparent. Both Schmitz and Amedure were White men, so the case seems devoid of racial content. Race most likely had an effect on public perception in the negative. Because Schmitz was a White male, his resort to violence was *not* attributed to all White males as a class. Had Schmitz been a Black man or a foreigner, his resort to violence might have been seen as typical of all Black men or all men from his particular country. Instead, Schmitz's resort to violence was viewed as the act of a distraught individual.

In the end, the jury rejected Schmitz's claim of provocation. Apparently, they did not believe Schmitz's claim that being taped on the *Jenny Jones Show* with a male secret admirer would cause a reasonable man to be provoked. The legal hook that helped Schmitz reduce his murder charge from first degree to second degree was diminished capacity, a mental defect defense. Given that Schmitz clearly met the requirements for first-degree murder—he intended to kill and premeditated and deliberated on how to do so—Schmitz was lucky to receive a second-degree murder conviction.

# 4

# Culture and Crime

In 1986, Dong Lu Chen immigrated to the United States from mainland China with his wife, Jian Wan Chen, and their three children. Dong Lu, fifty-three years old at the time, had been a farmer in China, but was only able to find work as a dishwasher in Maryland. Dong Lu lived in Maryland. His wife and three children lived in New York where Jian Wan worked part-time at a garment factory. On his days off, Dong Lu would travel to New York to be with his wife and family. During one visit, Jian Wan refused to have sex with Dong Lu. Dong Lu began to suspect that his wife was having an affair.

In June 1987, Dong Lu decided to move back to New York to live with his family. He noticed that his wife seemed cold and distant. Dong Lu continued to suspect his wife of infidelity. Finally, on August 25, Dong Lu asked Jian Wan whether she was seeing another man. Jian Wan confessed that she was. Dong Lu walked away without saying anything more. Two weeks later, on September 7, Dong Lu tried to have sex with his wife. According to Dong Lu, Jian Wan refused, telling him, "I won't let you hold me because I have other guys who will do this." This retort angered Dong Lu who grabbed his wife and pressed her down. "How long has this been going on?" he shouted in Chinese. Jian Wan, who could barely breathe, gasped, "For three months." Her honesty only enraged Dong Lu further. Dong Lu went into the next room, grabbed a claw hammer, came back to the bedroom, and struck his wife eight times on the head.[1]

Dong Lu Chen was charged with second-degree murder in the death of his wife. At trial, Chen's attorney argued that Chen should be found not guilty of murder because he was temporarily insane at the time of the crime. Chen's attorney further argued that Chen's cultural background negated his culpability in two ways.[2] First, according to the defense, any reasonable or ordinary Chinese man would have reacted the way Chen did when he learned of his wife's infidelity. Second,

Chen's attorney argued that if Chen had been in China when he found out about his wife's infidelity, his family would have stopped him from killing his wife. Because he was here in America, without his usual base of familial support, Chen had no one to hold him back when he lost his self-control.[3]

Chen's attorney relied primarily upon the testimony of Burton Pasternak, an American anthropologist who had studied Chinese culture, to make these points. Pasternak explained that in Chinese culture adultery by a wife was a stain on the husband, indicating that the husband had only minimal control over his wife.[4] According to Pasternak, Chen's behavior "would not be unusual at all for [a] Chinese in that situation, *for a normal Chinese* in that situation. . . . If it [*sic*] was a normal person, it's not the United States, they would react very violently. . . . I've witnessed such situations myself."[5] He continued, "In general terms, I think that one could expect a Chinese [man] to react in a much more volatile, violent way to those circumstances than someone from our own society."[6]

While Pasternak testified on direct examination that he had witnessed *similar* incidents in China, suggesting personal knowledge of incidents in which other Chinese men had killed their adulterous wives, he later admitted on cross-examination that he could not recall a single instance during the six years in which he had lived in China where a Chinese man had killed his wife for being unfaithful.[7] Nonetheless, Brooklyn Supreme Court Justice Edward Pincus found Chen guilty of second-degree manslaughter, rather than murder, and sentenced him to five years of probation and no additional jail time. Explaining his decision, Justice Pincus wrote:

> Were this crime committed by the defendant as someone who was born and raised in America, or born elsewhere but primarily raised in America, even in the Chinese American community, the Court would have been constrained to find the defendant guilty of manslaughter in the first degree. But, this Court cannot ignore . . . the very cogent forceful testimony of Doctor Pasternak, who is, perhaps, the greatest expert in America on China and interfamilial relationships.[8]

Justice Pinkus continued, "[Dong Lu Chen] was the product of his culture. . . . The culture was never an excuse, but it is something that made him crack more easily. That was the factor, the cracking factor."[9]

## THE MEANING OF CULTURE

When we talk about culture, what do we mean? In 1871, Edward B. Tylor defined culture as "that complex whole which taken [together] includes knowledge, belief, art, morals, law, custom, and any other capabilities and habits acquired by man as a member of society."[10] According to Madhavi Sunder, this traditional definition "conceived of culture as a 'thing' that survives and is imposed on generation after generation."[11] The traditional view was that culture was something "static, homogeneous, bounded, and distinct."[12]

Sunder notes that most anthropologists today "dismiss Tylor's view as mistaken in its characterization of culture as a static, unchanging set of beliefs that is imposed upon individuals generation after generation."[13] Modern anthropologists see culture as "increasingly fluid, heterogenous, and contingent."[14] Postmodernists have redefined the term culture as reflecting "a discourse or a set of social relations between individuals and groups attempting to define and redefine themselves in relation to one another and within a social context."[15]

One thing missing from these attempts to define culture is recognition that culture is something we Americans tend to ascribe to others, namely immigrants and racial minorities, not to ourselves. As Leti Volpp explains:

> [B]ehavior that we might find troubling is more often causally attributed to a group-defined culture when the actor is perceived to "have" culture. Because we tend to perceive white Americans as "people without culture," when white people engage in certain practices we do not associate their behavior with a racialized conception of culture, but rather construct other non-cultural explanations. . . . Thus, we consider early marriage by a Mexican immigrant to reflect "Mexican culture." In contrast, when a white person commits a similar act, we view it as an isolated instance of aberrant behavior, and not as reflective of a racialized culture. Under this schema, white people are individual actors; people of color are members of groups.[16]

Think about it. When someone says, "I'm going to talk about the role of cultural norms in the criminal courtroom," as I've said often enough when describing this book project, the first thing one thinks about is a foreign immigrant defendant or other defendant of color attempting to excuse a criminal act by saying what he did would have been okay in his country or community. Dong Lu Chen's claim that what he did was normal for an ordinary Chinese man in his situation is believable because we think of China as a patriarchal society where men can do whatever they want and women are killed for the slightest transgression. Popular films contribute to our vision of China as a patriarchal society. For example, the film *Raise the Red Lantern*,[17] set in China during the 1920s, depicts the life of a self-centered, wealthy, Chinese man with several wives, including one about his age and several who are much younger. The husband sleeps with a different wife every night. The wife he chooses to sleep with is treated to extra special attention from the servants that day in preparation for the big night, while the other wives are ignored or treated like second-class citizens. Instead of recognizing the unfairness of the situation and getting angry at the husband, the women compete for his nightly attentions. Tired of being left alone night after night while her husband enjoys the company of other women, one of the younger wives decides to take on a lover herself. When the husband discovers her adultery, he has her killed. The China depicted in *Raise the Red Lantern* is the China in the American imagination. We Americans tend not to think of China as a place where men and women both work and share domestic responsibilities, even though this state of affairs is more reflective of modern-day China.

Even though numerous American men have killed their wives for committing adultery, we don't think of America as a patriarchal society. We think our country is progressive, especially compared to countries in Asia and Africa.[18] We don't think American men who beat their wives are representative of American culture, even though domestic violence is a serious problem that affects a significant number of American women. We don't see the actions of White, heterosexual, American men who kill their unfaithful wives as reflecting the cultural norms of American society. The irony is that while we see men who kill their female partners as aberrant individuals, not cultural icons, we also find credible their claims of normality or reasonableness.

## THE ROLE OF CULTURE IN THE CRIMINAL COURTROOM

Although it is common to hear the term "the cultural defense," there is no separate cultural defense per se. Typically, a defendant will offer lay or expert testimony regarding her cultural background to support a traditional defense, such as insanity, provocation, or self-defense. Cultural evidence may also be offered as a mitigating factor during plea negotiations or at sentencing.

It is difficult to assess the extent to which cultural information influences criminal cases. No nationwide database keeps track of criminal cases in which cultural evidence is presented and it is virtually impossible to independently track all the criminal cases in which cultural evidence helped secure an acquittal, a reduction in the charges, or a lighter sentence. Nonetheless, it appears that most attempts to use culture to exonerate or mitigate are not successful.[19] According to Holly Maguigan, defendants who are not from the dominant culture are convicted more frequently and sentenced more severely than dominant-culture defendants.[20]

Attempts to use culture in the criminal courtroom may fail because judges and jurors have difficulty placing themselves in the shoes of the other. It is hard for someone who is not part of a given community to understand that community's beliefs and customs. Moreover, a defendant who comes from a different country or a minority community in the United States does not fit mainstream America's vision of the average ordinary person.

Judges may also exclude cultural evidence because they believe it is irrelevant. Judges may assume that Americans have a shared understanding of what reasonable people think and do. Admitting evidence regarding a defendant's cultural background would muddy the otherwise clear waters of reasonableness.

To a large extent, these judges are correct in thinking that Americans have shared understandings. Some attitudes and beliefs are so pervasive in American society that they influence the way all of us see things. Nonetheless, Americans are not a homogeneous group. People who are exposed to the same testimony and evidence can and do come to vastly different conclusions. O.J. Simpson's double murder trial was televised and watched by thousands of Americans, each of whom interpreted the evidence in a different way. Even though exposed to the same testimony, the same DNA evidence, and the same arguments by the attorneys, Americans disagreed over Simpson's culpability as if they had seen two different trials.

Reasonableness is a vague, open-ended standard. In many cases, jurors will not agree that the defendant acted reasonably or unreasonably.

In such cases, jurors should be guided by more than simply the influence of dominant American cultural norms which are likely to lead to one result. Information about the defendant's cultural background may be useful to help jurors understand why the defendant acted the way he did. Jurors don't have to agree that the defendant's actions were reasonable, but they should at least hear what the defendant has to offer in his defense. When the defendant is American, the jurors already understand the defendant's cultural background because the jurors are part of the same culture. The American defendant doesn't have to ask for special consideration because he already gets it.

Culture is sometimes thought to be less relevant than gender. For example, Yvonne Wanrow tried unsuccessfully to present evidence of her Native American background in support of her claim of self-defense.[21] Wanrow, charged with killing a man she believed had molested her child, wanted to show that because Native American culture places heavy emphasis on the importance of family and abhors unnatural sex acts, it was reasonable for her to be startled and afraid when she found the man she believed had engaged in unnatural sex acts with her child directly behind her.[22] The trial judge excluded Wanrow's proffered evidence on the ground that it was not relevant. Although Wanrow was later able to get her conviction reversed because of the trial court's erroneous use of the male pronoun when describing the Reasonable Person,[23] both the intermediate court of appeals and the Washington Supreme Court agreed that the trial court acted properly in excluding evidence of Wanrow's Native American culture.

Other Native Americans have attempted unsuccessfully to persuade judges that their beliefs or actions were reasonable in light of their cultural background and experiences. In *State v. Williams*, for example, a Native American couple charged with manslaughter in the death of their infant baby tried unsuccessfully to argue that their failure to take their baby to a doctor was due to a reasonable fear that the doctor would tell governmental authorities that they were bad parents, and then the government would come and take away their child.[24] Surveys of states with large Native American populations, conducted by the Association on American Indian Affairs around the time of the trial, indicated that approximately 25 to 35 percent of all Native American children were separated from their families and placed in foster homes, adoptive homes, or institutions.[25] In some states, the rate of adoption and foster placement for Native American children was even higher. In

Minnesota, Native American children were placed in foster or adoptive homes at a per capita rate five times greater than non–Native American children, and nearly one in every four Native American children under one year old was adopted.[26] In Montana, the ratio of foster-care placement for Native American children was at least thirteen times greater than that for non–Native American children.[27] In South Dakota, 40 percent of all adoptions made by the State's Department of Public Welfare were of Native American children, even though Native Americans made up only 7 percent of the entire state's juvenile population.[28] Given these statistics, the Williamses argued that their fear that their infant would be taken away from them was reasonable. The trial judge was not persuaded by this argument and found the parents guilty of manslaughter.

In affirming the convictions, the appellate court explained that the crime of manslaughter is committed by one who fails to exercise ordinary caution and thereby causes a death. According to the court, "Ordinary caution is the kind of caution that a man of reasonable prudence would exercise under the same or similar conditions."[29] Focusing on whether a "man of reasonable prudence" would have failed to take the baby to the doctor, rather than on whether the Native American parents' fear that their baby would be permanently taken away from them was reasonable, the appellate court found that the parents acted unreasonably.[30]

When I teach *State v. Williams* in my criminal law classes, my students generally defend the appellate court's decision.[31] Many will argue that all individuals should be held to the same (i.e., American) standard of reasonableness. In their view, the "reasonable parent" would have taken the baby to the doctor. Because the Williamses failed to do so, they acted negligently and therefore satisfied the conditions for conviction. Like the trial and appellate courts, many students do not think the Native American parents' fear of having their baby taken away is relevant. Perhaps the parents' fear is not considered relevant because most Americans never have to worry about the government permanently taking their young children away from them.

## PROBLEMS WITH THE USE OF CULTURE
## IN THE CRIMINAL COURTROOM

Although cultural evidence is often excluded, it is sometimes allowed under problematic circumstances. We've seen how courts sometimes privilege gender over race. When courts admit evidence of culture, the opposite occurs. Race (or the defendant's culture) is privileged over gender. As Dana Chiu notes, "When we privilege the voices of Asian men, who rely on their cultures' traditions of beating and killing their wives to excuse their acts, women are silenced."[32] Dong Lu Chen's sentence of probation with no jail time created concern in the Asian Pacific American community that other Asian immigrant men would view the verdict and sentence as a license to beat and kill their wives. Sharon Hom, commenting upon the Chen case, notes, "This kind of thinking reinforces patriarchal and racial stereotypes—*which don't even exist in China today*. This is like saying, 'My goodness, Americans lynch blacks, let's let them do it,' just because lynchings have happened in the past."[33]

A second, related, problem is that culture is often presented as uncontested or one-dimensional. The Asian immigrant male defendant claims he comes from a culture that condones male violence against women. Asian immigrant women from the same country, however, might contest his depiction of their culture. Leti Volpp explains how this occurred in the Dong Lu Chen case:

> Pasternak's perspective was "male," obviating the possibility that a woman, and specifically a Chinese immigrant woman, might describe divorce, adultery, and male violence within "Chinese culture" very differently.... Thus, the "cultural defense" served in this case to legitimize male violence against women by glossing over the gendered aspects of Pasternak's testimony.[34]

Volpp further notes that the defense strategy in the Chen case turned the tables by portraying Dong Lu Chen, the husband, as the victim, thus rendering the real victim, Jian Wan Chen, invisible:

> But where was Jian Wan Chen in this story? The defense strategy rendered her invisible. She was most notably present in the testimony as a dead body and as a reputed "adulteress," bringing a "stain" upon

her husband. Jian Wan Chen did not exist as a multi-faceted person but was instead flattened into the description "adulteress." Any discussion of her at trial was premised upon her characterization as a woman who provoked her husband into jealousy. How should this flattening be interpreted? This invisibility and erasure of the woman, Jian Wan Chen?[35]

A third problem is the assumption that the culture of others is fixed and static. Cultural practices, however, are not fixed, but change over time.[36] At one time, Chinese women had their feet bound so they could barely walk. Small feet were considered pretty, delicate, childlike. Women in China no longer follow this practice. Similarly, American women once wore corsets with "whalebone or metal stays that were laced so tightly the wearer could barely breathe" so they could achieve the "perfect" sixteen-inch waist.[37] While American women today do other things to their bodies to look beautiful, including breast augmentation and plastic surgery, they no longer commonly wear the unbearably tight corsets that once were popular.[38]

That cultural norms are in a constant state of flux is evident if we look at our own evolving attitudes about men and masculinity in American society. At one time, being a man in American society meant being in control, being physically strong, being the breadwinner, not exhibiting anything that might be seen as feminine, and not showing one's emotions. In the 1970s, Deborah David and Robert Brannon identified the four primary elements of the "male sex role" in America:

No Sissy Stuff: The stigma of all stereotypical feminine characteristics and qualities, including openness and vulnerability.

The Big Wheel: Success, status, and the need to be looked up to.

The Sturdy Oak: A manly air of toughness, confidence, and self-reliance.

Give 'Em Hell? The aura of aggressiveness, violence, and daring.[39]

Today, what it means to be a man is much less clear. Ronald Levant notes, "To many [American] men, particularly mid-life men, the question of what it means to be a man today is one of the most persistent unresolved issues in their lives."[40] American men today feel pressure from their female partners to be more emotional and sensitive. Many (though, unfortunately, not all) have begun to help with the domestic chores of cooking and cleaning, tasks previously delegated to the female partner. Men are no longer the sole breadwinners in many households. The reality of women in the workplace and the need for dual incomes to afford a comfortable standard of living have made some of the traditional traits of masculinity obsolete. Accordingly, young American men today do not endorse many of the traditional norms of masculinity.[41]

Some masculinity norms, however, have survived even the passage of time. According to Levant, most young American men still endorse the norm of male aggression.[42] Susan Faludi, who agrees with Levant that the meaning of manhood is much less clear today than it was eighty years ago, opines that the current prevailing norm of masculinity is the man in control of his environment. The man in control sounds a lot like "The Big Wheel" and "The Sturdy Oak" male sex role norms described by David and Brannon. According to Faludi:

> The man controlling his environment is today the prevailing American image of masculinity. A man is expected to prove himself not by being part of society, but by being untouched by it, soaring above it.[43]

In China, as in America, masculinity norms have likely changed over time. Even if a cultural practice of killing one's wife for being unfaithful once existed in China, it is doubtful that this practice was in force in 1986 when Dong Lu Chen emigrated to the United States from mainland (communist) China.

Another problem with the way culture is deployed in the criminal courtroom is the perpetuation of negative stereotypes. Cultural evidence which is used to help a particular criminal defendant often ends up hurting others from the defendant's community by creating or reinforcing negative stereotypes. The Dong Lu Chen case, for example, sent the message that it is normal for Chinese men to be more volatile and violent than American (or, more precisely, non-Chinese) men. Recall Burton Pasternak's testimony: "In general terms, I think that one could expect a Chinese [man] to react in a much more volatile, violent way to those circumstances than someone from our own society."[44] Even if untrue, individuals who heard about the case might have been left with the impression that all Chinese men are extremely jealous and prone to physical violence. The problem is compounded when other Asian immigrant men are able to use culture to excuse their acts of violence against women.[45]

Anthony Alfieri argues that defense attorneys should be sensitive to the risk that when they assert "deviance" defenses such as "Black Rage" or mob contagion, on behalf of their Black criminal defendant clients, they hurt the entire African American community by sending the message that all African Americans are deviants who cannot control their impulse toward violence.[46] For example, attorneys for Damian Monroe Williams and Henry Keith Watson, who were charged with attempted murder, aggravated mayhem, torture, and second-degree robbery arising from their assault upon Reginald Denny,[47] argued that their African American clients lacked the specific intent to kill Denny (a necessary element of attempted murder) because the beating of Denny was the result of Black Rage and mob contagion.[48] Williams was acquitted of attempted murder and convicted of mayhem, a felony, and four misdemeanor assaults.[49] Watson was also acquitted of attempted murder and convicted of a misdemeanor assault. The jury deadlocked on the other charges against Watson, leading the judge to declare a mistrial on those counts.[50]

Being sensitive to the defendant's community, while a good idea in theory, may conflict with the practical realities of criminal defense practice and the ethical duty to zealously represent the client. All attorneys owe a duty of loyalty to their clients, but criminal defense attorneys, more so than other attorneys because of the stakes involved (the client's life or liberty), must put their clients' interests above all other interests. Abbe Smith points out that lawyers are not supposed to forsake their clients for larger causes.[51] Attorneys, civil and criminal, are not supposed to place restrictions on their advocacy based on their own personal moral values.[52] Criminal defense attorneys have a special duty to use "all means and expedients . . . at all hazards and costs to other persons" to save their clients.[53] Smith concludes that if criminal defense attorneys were to follow Alfieri's advice and refrain from advancing defenses which could help their clients, they would not only breach their ethical duty of loyalty to the client, but also contribute to the problem of massive incarceration of young Black men.

Criminal defense attorneys, however, can be sensitive to racialized narratives without selling out their clients.[54] For example, the attorneys for Damian Williams and Keith Watson could have advanced the Black Rage and mob contagion arguments while acknowledging that not all young Black males are violent criminals. Making such an admission likely would have enhanced the defense attorneys' credibility with the jury. It isn't clear from the press accounts whether the prosecutor made any effort to educate jurors about the dangers of racial stereotyping, but such education certainly would have been worth the effort. Prosecutors in other cases have successfully rebutted defense attempts to use racial stereotypes to their client's advantage. Holly Maguigan points out that the rape trial of African American boxer Mike Tyson is one example of "successful prosecutorial response to stereotyped cultural information presented and argued by a defense lawyer."[55] In that case, the defense tried to depict the complainant, Desiree Washington, an African American woman, as a "lascivious, hot-blooded, willing young thing who could not wait to screw the savage."[56] As Joan Morgan notes, Tyson's attorneys "used a characterization of African American female sexuality that has plagued [Black women] since slavery."[57] The defense attorneys also depicted Tyson as an out-of-control Black sex maniac, hoping that the jury would think Washington was asking for it when she accompanied Tyson to his hotel room at 2:00 in the morning. Instead, the jury convicted Tyson of rape.[58]

## THE DEBATE OVER ADMISSIBILITY OF CULTURAL EVIDENCE

No universal rule governs the admissibility of cultural evidence in the criminal courtroom.[59] Some judges admit cultural evidence while other judges view it as irrelevant. This has led Deirdre Evans-Pritchard and Alison Dundes Renteln to opine that "whether a defendant can invoke a cultural defense depends almost entirely on the luck of the draw, that is, on who the judge is."[60]

Whether cultural evidence should be admitted at trial is hotly contested. Those who oppose the admission of cultural evidence argue that the behavior of individuals who choose to live in the United States should conform to the laws and customs of this country. Ignorance of the law generally is not an excuse, and a person who lives in this country shouldn't be excused simply because what he or she did would not be a crime in his or her country.

Proponents argue that cultural information should be admitted at trial if relevant. A person's cultural background might be relevant in many different ways. Culture might inform the question of whether the defendant acted with the requisite mental state. If, for example, the defendant believed she was helping the victim, she may not have acted with an intent to kill or inflict grievous bodily injury.[61] Some Southeast Asians believe that coining, rubbing a serrated coin about the size of a quarter on the skin of a child until mild bruising occurs, is a way to cure the flu and other ailments.[62] When a Southeast Asian parent is charged with child abuse or child endangerment because of coining, evidence of this cultural belief may demonstrate a lack of intent to harm.

If the defendant asserts a defense with a reasonableness requirement, such as provocation, self-defense, mistake of fact, or consent as a defense to rape, his or her criminal liability will turn upon whether the jury thinks a reasonable person *in the defendant's shoes* would have believed or acted the way the defendant did. Ordinarily, factors such as the defendant's age, height, weight, and gender are taken into account when determining whether the defendant acted reasonably. Arguably, a defendant's cultural background is an equally important consideration.

Holly Maguigan notes that the debate over admissibility of cultural evidence has sometimes pitted multiculturalists against feminists.[63] Multiculturalists believe in the importance of cultural difference and critique the idea that assimilation into the dominant culture is always best. They "argue that the old 'melting pot' social metaphor, which privileges the erosion of cultural distinctiveness in the dominant cultural stew, is obsolete and at times discriminatory."[64] Multiculturalists believe that admitting cultural evidence in criminal cases is necessary "to counteract the injustice of applying the dominant culture's legal standards to defendants from other countries."[65]

In contrast, some feminists argue against the admission of cultural evidence, especially in cases involving male violence against women, because admission "condones such violence."[66] Feminists who oppose the admission of cultural information find themselves in an awkward situation. Feminists generally believe in the importance of individualized and contextualized adjudications. They are generally supportive of social framework evidence, evidence which helps the jury understand the context in which the defendant was acting. For example, feminists have generally supported battered women's attempts to introduce expert testimony regarding the effects of battering on an abused victim's state of mind. Yet when a male immigrant defendant attempts to introduce expert testimony about the effects of his cultural upbringing on his state of mind, some feminists argue that such evidence should be excluded because it reinforces patriarchal practices and the subordination of immigrant women.

Some feminists have argued that it is unfair to give immigrants and members of minority communities in America a special defense that is unavailable to members of the dominant culture. For example, Doriane Coleman argues that recognition of a cultural defense violates the antidiscrimination principle by treating immigrant defendants more favorably than dominant culture defendants.[67]

The special treatment argument is misguided for two reasons. First, courts generally do not recognize a separate cultural defense. Cultural evidence is usually introduced to provide support for a traditional criminal defense. Second, as Holly Maguigan notes, the special treatment argument "ignores the work of scholars who explain that the standards of the dominant culture operate now as a cultural defense."[68] Americans who commit crimes don't have to specially argue that their cultural background influenced their actions because dominant social norms already support their claims of reasonableness. Moreover, there is no risk of inadequate translation because all the relevant decision makers—the judge, jury, and prosecutor—are part of the same culture.

Coleman calls the question of how to resolve the competing values of respect for cultural difference and the protection of women and children the "Liberals' Dilemma" because liberals, who generally respect both cultural difference and feminist concerns, have to choose one over the other when it comes to the question of whether cultural evidence should be admitted in criminal cases.[69] Several scholars have contested Coleman's characterization of the issue, arguing that the values of multiculturalism and feminism are not hopelessly conflicted. Leti Volpp, for example, notes that the reason Coleman is able to pit multiculturalism against feminism is by depicting feminism as "Euro-American" and non-European culture as patriarchal.[70] Volpp points out that feminism is not exclusively Euro-American, and Euro-American culture is also patriarchal.[71] Volpp argues that Coleman's "bifurcation of race and gender leads to the mistaken conclusion that the goals of multiculturalism and feminism are antithetical."[72] Andrew Taslitz argues that permitting immigrant defendants, such as Hmong men charged with rape, to offer cultural evidence is actually consistent with the values of feminism *and* multiculturalism.[73] He explains:

> Postmodern multiculturalists view objective truth in the law as a fiction, with the law and its products merely reflecting the drafters'

voices. Anglo-American law thus embodies dominant white male culture, rather than some grander truth. Because all cultures deserve respect, postmodern multiculturalists argue that we cannot judge those of another culture without at least giving their culture's perspective a voice in the judgment process. Cultural evidence serves that purpose. Indeed, at their most extreme, postmodern multiculturalists conclude that a culture's people can be judged only by that culture's standards. Evidence of Hmong marriage-by-capture customs should thus be relevant not only to show that Hmong men believed that the captured women were consenting, but also to show that their belief was reasonable. Emphasizing respect for the disempowereds' voices and for their cultural differences from the mainstream is consistent with some branches of feminism. Some feminists have thus endorsed the cultural defense in selected contexts.[74]

## CULTURE ISN'T LIMITED TO FOREIGNERS AND MINORITIES

Contrary to popular perception, immigrant and racial minority defendants are not the only ones who try to mitigate their criminal charges by relying on cultural norms. Every time a White heterosexual male murder defendant argues he was reasonably provoked into a heat of passion by his female partner's infidelity or by a gay man's sexual advance, he seeks to mitigate his charges by relying on cultural norms. The White heterosexual male defendant, however, has an advantage over the defendant of color because the cultural norms he relies upon are dominant social norms. These norms are so embedded in American culture that we Americans do not perceive them as cultural per se.

Why is it so easy to see the culture in immigrant and minority defendant claims of reasonableness, and so difficult to see the culture in similar claims asserted by Americans, especially White heterosexual American men? Leti Volpp explains that when White people engage in criminal behavior, we tend to see their acts "as an isolated instance of aberrant behavior, and not as reflective of a racialized culture."[75] To illustrate her point, Volpp compares and contrasts the way we view dowry murders in India with the way we view domestic violence homicides in the United States. "Dowry murders are thought of as a peculiar indicator of the extreme misogyny of India,"[76] while an American man who beats his wife to death is seen as an individual acting wrongfully. His acts are his own, not a reflection of U.S. culture. Volpp explains:

> We identify sexual violence in immigrants of color and Third World communities as cultural, while failing to recognize the cultural aspects of sexual violence affecting white mainstream women. This is related to the general failure to look at the behavior of white persons as cultural, while always ascribing the label of culture to the behavior of minority groups.[77]

Government action in the wake of two of the most devastating acts of terror on American soil provides support for Volpp's theory that we Americans tend to see the culture in others while failing to see the culture in ourselves. On April 19, 1995, the Alfred P. Murrah Federal Building in Oklahoma City was destroyed by a bomb blast that left 169 dead and more than 600 injured.[78] Initially, the public thought the bombing was the work of an Arab terrorist group.[79] When law enforcement officials discovered that the bombing of the Oklahoma City federal building was the work of White supremacist Timothy McVeigh, McVeigh's act of terror was not attributed to all White men with right-wing supremacist ideas. The FBI did not round up all the known White supremacists and detain them for months on end. McVeigh and his alleged coconspirator Terry Nichols were seen as individuals with extreme ideas rather than as representatives of the entire White American male population.

In contrast, when nineteen men from Saudi Arabia, Egypt, and other Middle Eastern countries hijacked three American planes on September 11, 2001, and flew them into the World Trade Center and the Pentagon, killing close to three thousand people, the government rounded up more than a thousand men, most of whom were of Arab and South Asian descent, and detained them for months with little or no evidence that these men were actually linked to the attacks on September 11. The government was able to detain these men with little public protest at least in part because the September 11 attacks were seen as the product of a foreign culture and religion and the men who were detained were believed to be part of that other culture.

Another example of the American tendency to perceive the criminal actions of immigrants as representative of their culture occurred shortly after an Egyptian immigrant shot and killed two people while waiting in line at the El Al Airlines ticket counter at the Los Angeles International Airport on July 4, 2002. After the incident, Governor Gray Davis told Maher Hathout, senior adviser to the Muslim Public Affairs Council, that he was concerned that members of the Muslim community were not clearly condemning the Egyptian man's actions.[80] The Muslim Public Affairs Council quickly sent a letter to Israel's consul general, calling the shooting heinous and offering condolences to the families of the victims.[81]

When Caucasian Americans commit criminal acts, predominantly White organizations are not called upon to issue words of condemnation and apology, because the actions of White criminals are not attributed to all Whites.[82]

## INTEREST CONVERGENCE THEORY

Given the general resistance to the use of cultural evidence in criminal cases, how can we explain the exceptional cases in which immigrant defendants and nonimmigrant defendants of color have been able to use culture to their benefit? One possibility is that immigrant and minority defendant claims which serve the dominant culture are more likely to succeed than claims that do not serve dominant interests.[83]

Derrick Bell first announced the principle of interest convergence in a *Harvard Law Review* article published in 1980. In that article, Bell responded to Herbert Wechsler's criticism of the Supreme Court's *Brown v. Board of Education* decision to end racial segregation in the public schools.[84] Wechsler complained that the *Brown* decision lacked a neutral and principled basis.[85]

Bell provided two responses to Wechsler's assertion that the *Brown* decision lacked a neutral and principled basis. First, Bell noted that racial equality provided "the neutral principle which underlay the *Brown* opinion," at least on a normative level (i.e., as a description of the way the world *ought* to be).[86] At the time *Brown* was decided, however, racial equality was not yet viewed as a legitimate principle by large segments of the American people. Therefore, racial equality could not be the real reason why the Court acted the way it did. Bell posited that interest convergence was the actual driving force behind the *Brown* decision. Interest convergence provided a neutral, positivist (i.e., how the world actually *is*), explanation for the Supreme Court's generosity.

According to Bell, the principle of interest convergence is the notion that "the interest of blacks in achieving racial equality will be accommodated only when it converges with the interests of whites."[87] Bell argued that *Brown* is best understood as a decision which served the interests of powerful Whites in America. It did so in three ways. First, the decision helped the United States in its foreign relations by providing it with almost immediate credibility regarding America's commitment to racial equality.[88] Segregation had damaged the reputation and prestige of the United States as a nation truly committed to the principle of equality and undermined its efforts to convince communist countries to convert to democracy. By ending racial segregation in the public schools, the Supreme Court gave a much needed boost to America's flagging reputation in the world community. Second, the *Brown* decision served to convince Blacks at home that America was a place where they were welcome. Blacks who had fought in World War II on behalf of the United States were returning home and encountering widespread racial discrimination and violence. Powerful elites worried that if there was another war, pervasive racial discrimination might discourage Blacks from again volunteering to fight for America. The *Brown* decision helped majority interests by conveying to Blacks the message that America was committed to treating them equally.[89] Finally, Bell argued, ending segregation served the interests of White Southerners trying to industrialize the South.[90]

## ASIAN IMMIGRANT MEN WHO KILL THEIR FEMALE PARTNERS

Just as interest convergence helps us understand the *Brown v. Board of Education* decision, it may also help us understand why some cultural claims are more successful than others.[91] A good number of the cases in which cultural evidence is used successfully involve Asian immigrant men who kill their Asian immigrant wives for some kind of infidelity, whether actual or merely imagined. Dong Lu Chen, for example, killed his Chinese wife after she rebuffed his sexual advances and confessed to seeing another man. Chen was permitted to introduce evidence that cultural factors caused him to react the way he did, and received a light sentence of probation and time served.

It is interesting that Chen's attorneys advanced a temporary insanity defense, a defense that requires a finding that the defendant was suffering from a mental disease or defect at the time of the act that caused him not to be able to tell right from wrong or to control his actions. No evidence was presented suggesting that Chen didn't know it was wrong to kill his wife, and the argument that family members would have stopped him if this had happened while he was in China, suggesting a lack of ability to control his actions, borders on the ludicrous. The presence of family members in the home (his wife's two sisters) certainly didn't stop another Asian immigrant defendant, May Aphaylath, from stabbing his wife to death for talking on the telephone with a former boyfriend,[92] and it is doubtful that family members present somewhere in the Chen house would have been able to stop Chen, who killed his wife in the privacy of their bedroom.

The evidence presented by Chen's attorneys, and on which the judge relied, is much more supportive of a claim of reasonable provocation. Chen's attorneys essentially argued that any ordinary Chinese man would have cracked from the strain of learning that his wife had been unfaithful. According to the defense, Chen's reaction was reasonable because a wife's adultery is a stain on the Chinese husband's honor. As James Sing notes, "[a]lthough neither the defense nor the court made any mention of the provocation doctrine, this crucial element of cultural sameness [that Chen acted the way other reasonable men in China would have acted] reveals that the court in essence ruled that Dong Lu Chen was provoked into killing his wife and that the crime was therefore excusable."[93]

Chen's claim of reasonableness is very similar to claims of reasonableness made by American men charged with murdering their wives.[94] American men who kill their wives, like Chen, often base their claim of reasonableness on the threat to masculine honor and identity posed by a wife's sexual infidelity. Recall Albert Joseph Berry's argument that he was reasonably provoked into a heat of passion by his wife Rachel's sexual infidelity. Like Chen, Berry's emotional upset was triggered by his wife's confession to adultery and her subsequent rejection of his sexual advances.

Consider another case in which an Asian immigrant man successfully invoked culture to support a claim of reasonable provocation.

January 20, 1998. 1:00 P.M. Chanh Van Duong, a former Vietnamese military officer, was waiting outside a divorce courtroom in Colorado when he saw his estranged wife, Huong "Rosie" Nguyen, with a man, Robert Jencks, whom Duong suspected was Rosie's lover and the reason she wanted to divorce him. Duong, who had brought a gun with him to the courthouse, fired at Jencks, hitting him in the wrist. Duong then fired at his wife, killing her.[95]

Duong was charged with murder in the death of his estranged wife and second-degree assault in the shooting of Jencks. At trial, Duong argued he should be found not guilty of murder or assault because he was provoked into a sudden heat of passion when he saw his estranged wife with the man he thought was her lover. According to Duong's attorney, the average or ordinary Vietnamese man would have been similarly provoked because divorce in Vietnam is a serious taboo.

Provocation ordinarily does not serve as a defense to any crime other than murder. Even in murder cases, it serves only as a partial, not a complete, defense. Nonetheless, the jury acquitted Duong of assault in the shooting of Robert Jencks, permitting Duong's provocation to be used as a complete defense to assault. The jury also returned a verdict of manslaughter, rather than murder, for Duong's killing of his estranged wife, even though Duong's claim that he was provoked into a *sudden* heat of passion was undermined by his having brought a loaded gun with him to the courthouse where he knew he would see his wife.[96]

Duong may not have needed to introduce cultural evidence to receive the mitigation to manslaughter. His argument was similar to that made by Jimmy Watkins, the Texan whose wife kicked him out of the family home after a female relative accused him of sexual assault, and then invited her boyfriend to live there with her.[97] Watkins was so upset at his wife's flagrant rejection of him that he called her repeatedly from his cell phone the day he killed her. When he was just outside her house, he asked her which room she was in. When she told him that she was in the kitchen, he burst into that room and shot her once in the head in front of his ten-year-old son. He then turned on her boyfriend and shot him twice. When his gun jammed, Watkins left, fixed the jam, then came back and pumped five more bullets into his wife's head as she was on the telephone, pleading for help from 911. The only reason Watkins did not receive a manslaughter conviction is because Texas law no longer recognizes provocation as a partial defense to murder. The jury had no choice but to convict Watkins of murder in the death of his wife. The jurors, however, showed how they really felt about what Watkins did when they recommended that he be sentenced to probation and serve no jail time for murder. Duong, in contrast, was convicted of the lesser offense of manslaughter, but sentenced to sixteen years in prison.

When the claim of cultural reasonableness is far removed from American cultural norms, legal decision makers are more likely to disagree about the propriety of admitting such evidence at trial. In May Aphaylath's case, conflicting views about the relevance of cultural evidence and the propriety of admitting such evidence were reflected in the trial and appellate courts.

> December 1982. Rochester, New York. May Aphaylath, a Laotian man in his twenties, came to the United States and settled in upstate New York in 1981. In November 1982, he and Lati Souvannavong, also from Laos, got married. Soon after the wedding, the couple began to quarrel over a man named Nunh, who was Lati's former boyfriend. Lati taunted May by using Nunh as an example of what a husband should be like. Lati even told May she wished she were married to Nunh. One day, May came into the kitchen and found his wife talking on the telephone with Nunh. Even though Lati's two sisters were in another room in the house at the time, May grabbed a kitchen knife and stabbed his wife sixteen times.[98]

Charged with murder for the slaying of his wife, May Aphaylath maintained he was suffering from extreme emotional distress (the Model Penal Code equivalent to the provocation defense) caused by the stress of being a Laotian refugee, his shame over his wife's display of affection for another man, and her receiving telephone calls from this man.[99] This shame, Aphaylath claimed, led to his loss of self-control. Aphaylath's attorney requested permission to call expert witnesses to the stand who would testify that in Laos the shame of having a wife receive calls from a single man is so great that a husband can be expected to lose his control. In other words, the Laotian husband who kills his wife for talking on the telephone with a single man acts reasonably or at least the way any ordinary Laotian husband would act. The judge, however, refused to allow this testimony and Aphaylath was convicted of murder.

Aphaylath appealed his conviction, arguing that the trial court erred in refusing to admit the expert witnesses who would have confirmed his claim of cultural reasonableness. The Court of Appeals of New York (the highest court in New York) agreed with Aphaylath, and overturned his conviction on the ground that the trial court erred in refusing to allow the expert testimony on Laotian culture. Following his successful appeal, Aphaylath pled guilty to the less serious offense of first-degree manslaughter, and was sentenced to eight years in prison. Had his murder conviction been affirmed, Aphaylath would have served fifteen years to life in prison.[100]

## HMONG MARRIAGE-BY-CAPTURE

The Asian immigrant female infidelity cases are the strongest evidence of interest convergence at work in cases involving claims of cultural reasonableness. A second example of interest convergence involves the Hmong practice of marriage-by-capture.[101] Consider how a Hmong man's claim of reasonableness in a case involving nonconsensual sexual intercourse was treated by prosecutors and a judge in Fresno, California.

In 1985, Kong Moua, a twenty-three-year-old Hmong man from Laos, abducted Seng Xiong, a nineteen-year-old woman, also a Hmong from Laos, from her dormitory room at Fresno City College in Central California, brought her back to his family's home, and had sexual relations with her without her consent. When charged with rape and kidnapping, Moua defended his actions as part of the Hmong cultural practice of zij paj niam or "marriage by capture." Under this custom, a Hmong man will take a woman he wants to marry from her home, bring her to his family home, and then have sexual intercourse with her to consummate the marriage. The woman may scream, cry, and say no, but her protests will be understood by all involved as demonstrating her virtue. Moua argued that in light of his cultural background, he honestly and reasonably believed his female friend was consenting to sexual intercourse, and therefore he was not guilty of rape. Prosecutors allowed Moua to plead guilty to false imprisonment, a lesser offense than either rape or kidnapping. Moua was then sentenced to only one hundred and twenty days (approximately three months) in jail and a $1,000 fine.

In an attempt to better understand what happened from both the defendant's and the victim's perspectives, Deirdre Evans-Pritchard and

Alison Dundes Renteln reviewed statements Kong Moua and Seng Xiong gave to the police and court records. They first describe what happened from the defendant Kong Moua's perspective:

## A. Kong Moua's Version

Kong first met Seng in 1982 while visiting relatives in Fresno, California. He then returned to Colorado to study, but came back to California in December 1983 to celebrate the Hmong New Year. At this time he reestablished contact with Seng:

> Me and my friend Phong Yang went back to see Seng almost every day. Me and Seng have a commitment that we really love each other. So we were going to marry on February 12, 1984. We make a statement that we were adult we should keep our commitment. This moment Seng gave me two pictures with her signature. I went back to Colorado. When I was in Colorado, I wrote a letter to Seng with some pictures of mine and Seng to her. We also talked on the phone three times. We were always saying that we were going to get married on February 12, 1984.

> Kong subsequently moved to Stockton and visited Seng every weekend. During this period Kong felt that he had a strong relationship with Seng. She had shown all the signs of wanting to marry him. Indeed, he claimed that she had already indicated that she was prepared to elope with him. The first attempt had failed because her father intervened. They exchanged watches and Kong also gave her a necklace—"to prove that I'm going to marry her for sure."

> On April 24, 1984 Seng asked him to pick her up at City College at noon. Taking a male friend, Yang Hue, with him, he met her and had a half-hour conversation about marriage. They left together in the car and, according to Kong, Seng was happy and fully aware that she was eloping with him. Kong took Seng to a close relative's home.

> At the house, his male relatives collected four hundred and fifty dollars to give to Seng's father and uncle to finalize the marriage. "They took the money, that means they were agreed and give Seng to be my wife." Seng's father phoned Seng at Kong's home and she told him that she had married Kong and not to worry about her. At that point Kong's sister, Blay, helped Seng change into clothes Kong had bought her the week before. Kong returned, and they had sexual intercourse several times that night.

> The next morning Seng talked to her mother on the phone. Following

that conversation she informed Kong that her mother did not agree for her to marry Kong. "I asked her if that was so, why she came over to marry me and had sexual intercourse with me. Seng said because she loves me and she wants to make me happy."[102]

Evans-Pritchard and Renteln then describe the facts from the victim Seng Xiong's perspective:

## B. Seng Xiong's Version

Seng stated that she met Kong at the New Year's Festival in 1984 and that while they became friends, there was no romantic involvement. On the day in question, when she left work at City College, she met Kong and Yang Hue who told her they were kidnapping her. Yang informed her that she was to marry Kong, to which she replied that she never would. She was then physically forced into the car. "During the struggle getting into the vehicle she . . . called out to Irene [an American college friend] who came up to the vehicle to look inside, but [Kong] Moua covered her mouth when she tried to ask for help."

While at Kong's house, she was prevented from communicating with her parents. She was convinced to change her clothes by Yang's wife who assured her that it was she who would be sleeping with her. Seng refused Kong's sexual advances, but he forced her onto the bed.

When the police met Seng outside [Kong] Moua's house the next day, she said that she had not been sexually molested and that she did not wish to report the kidnapping because she did not want to get the boys (Kong and Yang) into trouble. She also said that she did not report anything to the police because they "would not take her where she wanted to go." Thus, she chose to stay with [Kong] Moua instead of going with the police in order not to miss an important appointment with a lawyer concerning another matter.

Kong drove her to the appointment at the Lao Community Center where she implored her brother to rescue her from her kidnappers, saying she "wanted to come home and would die if she stayed." She subsequently returned with Kong to her family to resolve the situation in a Hmong fashion. The two families met to discuss how to settle the dispute but reached no agreement.

Seng eventually notified the police because Kong and Yang said they would kidnap her again. Her explanation for why she had not contacted the police previously was that her reputation in the Hmong community was at stake. If it became known that she was no longer a virgin, she might not be able to find a husband.[103]

The *Moua* case highlights the difficulty of ascertaining the facts when the defendant and victim's accounts differ dramatically. The prosecutors who allowed Moua to plead guilty to false imprisonment and the judge who sentenced him to one hundred and twenty days in jail apparently found credible and reasonable Moua's belief that Seng Xiong had consented to the sexual intercourse.

One way to understand the result in *Moua* is to compare the case to date rape cases involving American men charged with raping female friends or women they were dating. Prosecutors are often reluctant to prosecute date rape cases because they fear jurors will sympathize with the male defendant who claims he honestly and reasonably believed his female friend consented to having sexual intercourse.[104] In America, an honest and reasonable belief in consent to sexual intercourse is a complete defense to a charge of rape. In he-said/she-said cases, prosecutors will often plea bargain with the defendant, permitting him to plead guilty to a lesser offense in order to secure some kind of conviction rather than risk a complete acquittal. In light of the way date rape cases involving American men and women are often handled, the result in the *Moua* case does not seem so extraordinary.

## BLACK RAGE

A third example of interest convergence is the successful use of a Black Rage and mob contagion argument by attorneys representing Damian Williams and Henry Keith Watson, two of the young Black men charged with attempted murder in the beating of Reginald Denny. Since a description of this case appears earlier in this chapter, I will not repeat that discussion here.

At first glance, it is hard to understand how the use of a deviance defense like Black Rage or mob contagion supports Bell's interest convergence theory. Young White males charged with crimes of violence generally do not argue that their acts are a result of White rage or mob contagion. The result in the *Williams and Watkins* case, however, does serve the interests of the dominant culture, although in a different way than the Asian immigrant female infidelity and the Hmong marriage-by-capture rape cases do. The dominant culture has an interest in perpetuating stereotypes about young Black males as deviant criminals. Such stereotypes keep the masses from questioning the large numbers of young Black men in prison and on death row. They keep the masses from questioning verdicts of acquittal and prosecutorial decisions not to charge police officers when they shoot and kill unarmed young Black men. The Black-as-Criminal stereotype reinforces the belief that Black men in prison are there because they committed a crime. It reinforces the belief that an officer who shoots a Black man *reasonably* believes the Black man poses an imminent threat of death or serious bodily injury.

### Oya-ko Shinju

Interest convergence theory provides an explanation for the successful use of culture by Asian immigrant men who kill their female partners, Hmong men who have nonconsensual sexual intercourse with women they desire, and African American men who assert deviance defenses. Can it also explain the apparently successful use of culture in *People v. Kimura*, the case in which a Japanese woman walked into the Pacific Ocean from a beach in Santa Monica, California with her two young children, fully intending to kill them and then herself? Deborah Woo notes that Fumiko Kimura, a thirty-two-year-old immigrant from Japan, had lived in the United States for sixteen years, but had never really assimilated into American society.[105] Even though she lived in Los Angeles, a city where most people drive because the public transportation there is so poor, Kimura did not drive and had few friends or interests outside the home. She was a very traditional Japanese wife, "waiting up each night to bathe her husband's feet upon his return home from work."[106] In November 1984, she learned that "her husband had been supporting a mistress during a good part of their marriage, a waitress at the restaurant where he worked."[107] "Nine days before the drowning incident, the mistress had called [Kimura], herself distressed over the husband's being 'deceitful.'"[108]

On January 29, 1985, Kimura walked into the Pacific Ocean with her infant daughter and four-year-old son.[109] Two college students spotted Kimura and pulled her and the two children out of the surf.[110] Kimura survived, but her children did not. Kimura was charged with two

counts of first-degree murder and two counts of felony child endangerment. The Japanese American community found out about her case,
and gathered over twenty-five thousand signatures for a petition for leniency on her behalf.[111] Kimura was permitted to plead guilty to
manslaughter and was sentenced to five years of probation and one
year in jail. Since Kimura had already served fifteen months in jail by
the time she came up for sentencing, she received credit for time served
and was released the same day.[112]

Kimura is often cited as an example of the successful use of culture
by an immigrant defendant because her actions were in accord with the
Japanese practice of *oya-ko shinju* (parent-child suicide). Alison Matsumoto explains that *oya-ko* means parent- child.[113] *Shinju* means "any
suicide involving more than one person."[114] *Oya-ko shinju* may be committed for a number of reasons by either parent, but in most cases it is
the mother who commits *oya-ko shinju* in response to the father's infidelity or neglect.[115] Matsumoto notes that the wife/mother may commit
*oya-ko shinju* for a number of reasons. First, she may wish to punish her
husband, hoping that his social position will be destroyed and that he
will lose his job. Second, she may feel obligated to kill her children so as
not to leave them motherless and subject to social stigma and prejudice.[116] Had Kimura done what she did in Japan, her acts would still
have been criminal, but she would have been looked upon with extreme sympathy. Most likely, she would have received a short jail sentence or probation.[117]

Deborah Woo notes that, contrary to popular belief, Kimura's attorneys actually sought to downplay the influence of culture. "[A]ny
cultural factors, such as the custom of *oyako-shinju*, could have been
useful as 'incriminating' evidence, helping to establish an intent to
kill."[118] Instead of arguing that Kimura acted reasonably within her cultural upbringing, her attorneys argued she was temporarily insane
when she walked into the Pacific Ocean. In other words, in order to
achieve a favorable result for their client, the attorneys argued Kimura
acted abnormally, not the way an ordinary Japanese woman would
have acted.

Critics of the use of culture have compared Kimura to Susan Smith,
the American woman who drowned her two young sons by strapping
them into their car seats and then pushing her car into a lake.[119] Smith
initially claimed a Black carjacker had kidnapped her sons. When police
discovered this was a lie, Smith was arrested and charged with two

counts of first-degree murder.[120] On July 23, 1995, Smith was convicted of first-degree murder.[121] Six days later, she was sentenced to life in prison with the possibility of parole.[122]

Smith may have received some leniency as a result of her race and gender. Initially, when the public believed her claim that a Black man had kidnapped the children, there were loud cries for the death penalty. When the public found out that Smith herself had killed the two young boys, the cries for the death penalty subsided and were replaced with pleas to spare the life of the troubled young White mother.

The *Smith* case, while superficially similar, is not truly analogous to the *Kimura* case. First, Smith never intended nor tried to kill herself. She strapped her two young boys into their car seats and pushed the car they were in into a lake, never once putting herself in any danger. Second, the reason Smith killed her children was in order to please her boyfriend, who had made it clear that he was not interested in continuing a relationship with a single mother burdened with two young children. In contrast, Kimura not only intended to kill herself, but her primary intent was to kill herself. It was only because she thought she would be dead that she decided to kill her children. In Japan, the mother is primarily responsible for child rearing. Children who grow up without a mother are viewed with distrust. Kimura felt a tremendous responsibility not to leave her children in this world without a mother. Deborah Woo explains, "Without the natural mother, then, offspring are essentially subjected to the strong social prejudices against orphans: 'Orphans are regarded as unreliable because of a lack of parental protection, supervision, and disciplining. Banks usually do not hire them.'"[123]

The manslaughter conviction Kimura received is actually similar to the manslaughter convictions received by the bulk of women who kill their young children. Most women who kill their children are initially charged with murder, but end up pleading guilty to manslaughter.[124] In most of these cases involving child homicide, the mother kills her children without also trying to kill herself, yet she still receives a manslaughter conviction. In the one case I was able to find involving a mother who shot and killed her daughter and also shot herself, the woman was found not guilty by reason of insanity and committed to a mental institution.[125] Susan Smith and Andrea Yates, the woman who drowned her five young children in the bathtub of her home, are rather exceptional in the amount of attention their cases garnered and the results obtained. Both women were convicted of murder and received life sentences.[126]

## CONCLUSION

In this chapter, I have sought to use the lens of the immigrant male defendant to demonstrate the false neutrality of our own objectivity. Opponents of the so-called cultural defense argue that admitting cultural evidence in the criminal courtroom gives immigrants and other minority defendants special treatment, which is unfair to majority defendants. These critics view the admission of cultural evidence as a kind of reverse discrimination against White American defendants. These critics, however, overlook the fact that majority culture defendants already receive the benefit of cultural norms, those of American culture, every time they walk into the courtroom. American defendants don't need to bring in experts to testify about why their beliefs and actions are reasonable in light of existing norms because judges and jurors are already familiar with those norms. Dominant social norms bolster these defendants' claims of reasonableness without any special effort on their part.

# PART II

# CRIMES OF FEAR
# (THE DOCTRINE OF SELF-DEFENSE)

# 5

# An Overview of the Doctrine of Self-Defense

UNDER TRADITIONAL SELF-DEFENSE DOCTRINE, also known as perfect self-defense, a defendant is justified in using a reasonable amount of force against another person if she honestly and reasonably believes that (1) she is in imminent or immediate danger of unlawful bodily harm from her aggressor, and (2) the use of such force is necessary to avoid the danger.[1] Traditional self-defense doctrine requires necessity, imminence, and proportionality. Additionally, the threatened attack must be unlawful and the defendant must not have been the aggressor.

## THE NECESSITY REQUIREMENT

The first requirement is necessity. The defendant must honestly and reasonably believe that it is necessary to use force to protect against a threatened attack. This requirement seeks to ensure that people not use force against others unless and until it is really necessary to do so. The term necessity suggests that one has no choice but to use force to protect oneself. If less drastic alternatives are available, then the use of force to repel an attack is not truly necessary.

In keeping with the necessity requirement, early English common law required one who was being attacked to retreat until the wall was at his back before using deadly force in self-defense.[2] In the United States, however, a person threatened with attack is not required to retreat before using *nondeadly* force to repel an attacker. In most states, a person is not even required to retreat before using *deadly* force to repel a threatened attack, *even if a safe retreat is available*.[3] This no-retreat rule runs counter to the necessity requirement. If a safe retreat is available and known to the defendant, then the use of force is not truly necessary. Nonetheless, the law does not require retreat because it is thought unreasonable to require an innocent person whose life or limb is being threatened to bow to his attacker.

A small handful of jurisdictions require persons threatened with harm to retreat before using deadly force.[4] However, even in these jurisdictions, a person who is attacked in his own home may use deadly force without first retreating. This exception to the minority rule is called the "castle" exception, reflecting the old saying that "a man's home is his castle." Some jurisdictions have expanded the castle exception to include the curtilage of a person's home (the area immediately surrounding the home) and his or her place of work.

Some states direct the jury to consider whether a safe retreat was available to the defendant as one factor in the necessity calculus.[5] In these states, the defendant is not required by law to retreat before using force in self-defense, but his failure to do so may be held against him if he tries to claim self-defense at trial. In other words, the jury has the discretion to decide what weight it wishes to give the defendant's failure to retreat before using force.

## THE IMMINENCE REQUIREMENT

A second requirement is imminence. The defendant must honestly and reasonably believe that death or serious bodily injury is imminent or about to happen. It is not sufficient for the defendant to honestly and reasonably believe that an attack will happen sometime in the future. The threatened attack must be impending.

The imminence requirement has come under attack from feminist scholars and others concerned with the way battered women who kill their abusers are treated by the criminal justice system. Judges often refuse to permit battered women who kill their abusers in nonconfrontational situations, such as when the abusive partner is sleeping, to argue self-defense. This refusal is based on the view that no reasonable person could believe that an attack from a sleeping partner is imminent.

Several different views have emerged on the question of how to deal with the imminence requirement in cases involving battered women. Some, such as Richard Rosen, have argued that the imminence requirement should be relaxed when a battered woman kills her abuser in a nonconfrontational situation. Rosen argues that a strict imminence requirement fails to adequately address cases in which death or serious bodily injury is inevitable, though perhaps not impending.[6] In Rosen's view, the imminence requirement acts as a proxy for the necessity requirement. Accordingly, the requirement should be relaxed or eliminated in cases in which necessity and imminence conflict.[7] If a battered woman reasonably believes that it is necessary to kill her abuser in order to save her own life, the fact that he was not just about to kill should not preclude her from claiming self-defense.

Others take the position that the imminence requirement does not have to be relaxed for battered women defendants.[8] Holly Maguigan, for example, argues that judges and juries just need to apply the usual rules in a fair and even-handed manner when dealing with battered women's self-defense claims.[9] Some argue that the imminence requirement should be applied strictly in battered women's self-defense cases, because any relaxation of the requirement would encourage self-help or vigilantism.[10]

A strict imminence requirement negatively impacts others besides battered women. Paul Robinson illustrates how, using a hostage hypothetical:

> Suppose A kidnaps and confines D with the announced intention of killing him one week later. D has an opportunity to kill A and escape each morning as A brings him his daily ration. Taken literally, the *imminent* requirement would prevent D from using deadly force in self-defense until A is standing over him with a knife, but that outcome seems inappropriate. If the concern of the limitation is to exclude threats of harm that are too remote to require a response, the problem is adequately handled by requiring simply that the response be "necessary." The proper inquiry is not the immediacy of the threat but the immediacy of the response necessary in defense. If a threatened harm is such that it cannot be avoided if the intended victim waits until the last moment, the principle of self-defense must permit him to act earlier—as early as is required to defend himself effectively.[11]

The hostage hypothetical illustrates the difference between harm that is imminent and harm that is inevitable. Inevitable harm can be just as threatening as that which is imminent. A strict imminence requirement, however, precludes a self-defense claim in cases involving inevitable, but not imminent, harm.

One way to deal with problems caused by a strict imminence requirement is to combine the imminence and necessity elements and require the defendant to have honestly and reasonably believed that his use of force was "immediately necessary." This is the approach taken by the drafters of the Model Penal Code. Under the Model Penal Code, "the use of force upon or toward another person is justifiable when the actor believes that such force is *immediately necessary* for the purpose of protecting himself against the use of unlawful force by such other person on the present occasion."[12]

## THE PROPORTIONALITY REQUIREMENT

A third requirement is proportionality. A person who acts in self-defense must only use an amount of force that is not excessive in relation to the force or harm threatened. If an attacker threatens the defendant with nondeadly force, the defendant may not respond with deadly force. Deadly force, defined as force likely to cause death or serious bodily injury, generally may only be used against deadly force. This does not mean that one can never use a weapon against an unarmed assailant. For example, if a small person is threatened by a large, but unarmed, person, the small person may use a gun (deadly force) against an unarmed attacker if the threatened attack is likely to cause death or serious bodily injury. Use of deadly force in such a case meets the proportionality requirement because the smaller person is using deadly force to combat deadly force.

The proportionality requirement is often viewed as part of the necessity requirement. However, force that may be necessary to avoid a threatened attack is not necessarily proportionate. For example, imagine D and V on a crowded platform standing next to the subway tracks.[13] Suddenly, V raises his arm above his head and threatens to slap D. Because of the crowd surrounding D and V, D cannot simply move out of the way to avoid V's slap. The only way D can avoid V's slap is by pushing V onto the tracks just as an oncoming train is passing through. Although pushing V onto the tracks might be *necessary* to avoid the threatened harm, it certainly is not proportionate to the harm threatened. The proportionality requirement ensures that individuals who use excessive force are held accountable for their actions.

## AN UNLAWFUL OR UNJUSTIFIED ATTACK

Fourth, the threatened attack must be (or at least the defendant must reasonably believe it to be) unlawful or unjustified.[14] A defendant has no right to use force in self-defense against lawful force. Thus, if a police officer lawfully attempts to arrest a suspect, the suspect is not justified in using deadly force to resist the arrest.[15] If, however, the officer exceeds the scope of his lawful authority by using excessive force to effectuate the arrest, the suspect may be entitled to use deadly force if necessary to protect himself from death or grievous bodily injury.[16] If, however, the arrest is unlawful only because the arresting officer lacks probable cause, most jurisdictions will not permit the arrestee to use deadly force in self- defense.[17]

## NOT THE INITIAL AGGRESSOR

Finally, the defendant must not be the initial aggressor, the one who started the affray.[18] If the defendant was the initial aggressor, he may be required to retreat before using deadly force even if the incident occurred in a jurisdiction that does not normally require retreat.[19]

## REASONABLENESS

The first three elements of self-defense, namely, necessity, imminence, and proportionality, are not absolute requirements.[20] All three elements are qualified by a reasonableness requirement. The law does not insist that the defendant be correct about the justifying circumstances leading her to use force in self-defense. All it requires is that the defendant honestly and reasonably believed it was necessary to act in self-defense to protect against an imminent threatened attack and that the defendant honestly and reasonably believed the force she used was proportionate to the force threatened. The law does not require actual necessity because individuals in situations of danger cannot know with 100 percent certainty whether the threatened attack is actually going to occur. It is thought to be unfair to treat such individuals as having had the benefit of hindsight.

Similarly, the law does not require actual imminence because sometimes the defendant might reasonably perceive that an attack is imminent when it is not actually imminent. Johnny points a gun at Danny and threatens to shoot. Even though Johnny has no intention of shooting Danny at that moment, Danny honestly and reasonably believes he is about to be shot. The imminence requirement has been met.

The proportionality requirement is also concerned with the defendant's honest and reasonable perception of the force needed to protect against the threatened force. Imagine that Danny comes across a boy waving something that looks like a gun at him.[21] Danny honestly and reasonably believes that he is being threatened with deadly force when in fact the boy is waving a toy gun. Danny may respond by shooting the boy even though his use of deadly force is not in fact proportionate to the actual force threatened. Imagine now that the toy gun is pink. In this case, Danny's belief that he is being threatened with deadly force is not reasonable and his use of a real gun (deadly force) to respond to the boy's pink toy gun (nondeadly force or no force at all) would fail the proportionality requirement because it was not reasonable to think the pink gun was real.

Because the necessity, imminence, and proportionality requirements turn on the reasonableness of the defendant's perceptions, the reasonableness or unreasonableness of the defendant's beliefs and actions becomes the key to whether or not the defendant is acquitted. Reasonableness, however, is a standard capable of different meanings.[22] I discuss these different meanings in chapter 8.

## DEEDS VERSUS REASONS

While the basic elements of self-defense are quite straightforward, there is considerable disagreement over what elements ought to be required for self-defense as a justification defense, as opposed to self-defense as an excuse defense. In criminal law, affirmative defenses are divided into two main categories: justification defenses and excuse defenses. A justification defense is one that exculpates the defendant, despite the fact that he is in violation of a criminal statute, because he did the right thing under the circumstances. An excuse defense, in contrast, recognizes that what the defendant did was wrong, but exculpates the defendant or mitigates the charges on the ground that the defendant was not culpable or blameworthy for some reason personal to the defendant, such as his impaired mental condition (insanity) or the situation he was in (duress).

At one time, the justification-excuse distinction made a difference. A justified felony defendant received a complete acquittal, while an excused felony defendant was subject to the same punishment as a convicted felon—the death penalty and forfeiture of his property.[23] An excused defendant, however, could petition for a pardon and for restitution of his property. Today, both justified and excused defendants are treated similarly. Both are acquitted if the defense at issue is a complete defense.

Self-defense is generally considered a justification defense.[24] When an individual is threatened with imminent unlawful force, we want that individual to protect himself. Because the defendant who uses force in self-defense acts the way society wants him to act, the defendant is considered justified rather than merely excused.

Current self-defense doctrine focuses on the reasonableness of the defendant's beliefs or reasons for acting. Paul Robinson calls this approach the "reasons" theory of justification.[25] Under the "reasons" theory, a defendant is justified in using deadly force in self-defense as long as he honestly and reasonably believes such force is necessary to protect himself from imminent death or grievous bodily injury. A defendant who is mistaken about the threat of harm is still justified as long as his belief in the need to use force in self-defense is reasonable.

Robinson argues that current doctrinal focus on beliefs or reasons is misplaced. Robinson advocates what he calls a "deeds" theory of justification under which a defendant is justified in using force in self-defense if and only if he is correct about the circumstances justifying his use of force.[26] Under Robinson's view, the defendant's beliefs are irrelevant to the question of justification. In other words, D is justified in using deadly force against V, who appears to be a jogger minding his own business, if it turns out V is actually a would-be assailant who is about to attack D. This is so even if D doesn't believe that V is about to attack him.

George Fletcher agrees with Robinson that a defendant is justified in using force in self-defense only if he is correct about the justifying circumstances. In contrast to Robinson, Fletcher believes the defendant's reasons for acting are also important. Fletcher therefore argues that individuals who use force in self-defense are justified if and only if they honestly and reasonably believe it is necessary to use such force *and* they are correct in their beliefs.[27]

Requiring the defendant to be right or correct about the existence of justifying circumstances is extremely problematic. First, in most cases it is impossible to know, after the fact, whether the victim was going to attack the defendant. One can only know the facts and circumstances that led the defendant to believe, reasonably or unreasonably, that he was being threatened with an imminent attack. Second, as a practical matter, requiring the defendant to be right would just about eviscerate self-defense as we know it. The defense would only be available to those defendants lucky enough to kill or assault individuals who were actually going to kill or attack them. In chapter 10, I propose a different way of thinking about self-defense as a justification. I agree with Fletcher that the law should look at both deeds (or acts) and reasons (or beliefs). However, requiring a reasonable act does not have to mean that the defendant is right about the existence of justifying circumstances. I suggest that reasonableness in action can be satisfied by using force which is proportional to the force threatened.

## IMPERFECT SELF-DEFENSE

Recognizing that an individual might honestly but unreasonably believe in the need to act in self-defense, some jurisdictions permit murder defendants to argue the defense of "imperfect" self-defense.[28] "Perfect" self-defense refers to a situation in which all the elements of self-defense have been met. An individual, not the initial aggressor, who honestly and reasonably believes in the necessity of using deadly force to protect against an imminent unlawful threat of death or grievous bodily injury is entitled to an acquittal. "Imperfect" self- defense refers to the murder defendant who honestly *but unreasonably* believes in the need to use deadly force in self-defense.[29] This defendant receives a conviction on the lesser offense of manslaughter. In some jurisdictions, imperfect self-defense refers to the situation in which the defendant was a nondeadly aggressor who failed to retreat before using deadly force in self-defense.[30]

One example of how an imperfect self-defense argument can have a significant influence on the outcome of a trial is reflected in the double murder trial of the Menendez brothers, who used shotguns to kill their parents while they were in their living room watching television. At their first trial, the brothers were permitted to argue imperfect self-defense. They claimed they honestly believed their parents posed an imminent threat of death or serious bodily injury because of physical and sexual abuse that had occurred years earlier. That trial ended in a mistrial when jurors couldn't agree on whether to convict the brothers of murder or manslaughter. When the brothers were tried the second time, Judge Stanley Weisberg refused to allow an imperfect self-defense argument and both brothers were convicted of first-degree murder.

## THE MODEL PENAL CODE

The Model Penal Code, drafted in 1962, permits the complete acquittal of a defendant charged with an intentional crime of violence who *honestly* believed the use of force was immediately necessary to protect against an unlawful attack.[31] The Code does not require a defendant claiming self-defense to show that his belief was reasonable as well as honest. If, however, the defendant was reckless or negligent in believing that the use of force was necessary, that defendant may be found guilty of an offense for which recklessness or negligence suffices to establish culpability.[32] In other words, if a murder defendant's belief in the need to use force in self-defense was honest but unreasonable (due to his recklessness or negligence), then the defendant could be found guilty of involuntary manslaughter or negligent homicide.

The Model Penal Code approach is praised for addressing the failure of traditional self-defense doctrine to recognize differing levels of culpability. The defendant who honestly and reasonably believes in the need to act in self-defense is not as culpable as the defendant who honestly but unreasonably believes in the need to act in self-defense. The defendant who honestly but unreasonably believes in the need to act in self-defense is not as culpable as the intentional killer. The Model Penal Code approach, however, is also criticized for being too limited. The approach works only if there is a lesser offense with a reckless or negligent state of mind requirement. The Model Penal Code is also subject to criticism because of its complexity.

In the end, it may not matter which approach is taken if the jurors who decide the validity of a defendant's self-defense claim confound the sincerity of a defendant's belief in the need to act in self-defense with the reasonableness of this belief. The next few chapters take a closer look at claims of reasonableness in self-defense cases with a racial component.

# 6

# Race and Self-Defense

ANOTHER CULTURAL NORM—the racial stereotype*—is pervasive in this society. Like masculinity and heterosexuality norms, racial stereotypes are a feature of contemporary American culture. Like other norms, race norms work beneath the surface, helping certain claims of reasonableness appear more credible than others.[1]

What is a stereotype? Jody Armour explains that stereotypes are well-learned sets of associations that result in automatic, gut-level responses.[2] Stereotypes are correlational constructs based on an individual's membership in an identifiable group, such as the idea that most Blacks are good athletes, most Mexicans are poor, and most Asians are smart. All of us are influenced by stereotypes, even the most egalitarian-minded of us.

In self-defense cases, racial stereotypes can influence the reasonableness determination in a myriad of ways. If the victim belongs to a racial group whose members are perceived as violent or hot-blooded, jurors may perceive ambiguous actions by the victim as more hostile than they actually are. Conversely, if the defendant belongs to a racial group whose members are perceived as violent and dangerous but the victim belongs to a racial group whose members are not marked by stereotypes of violence and dangerousness, jurors may be less willing to believe the defendant's claim of self-defense.

Race norms can also affect the reasonableness determination in other, less obvious, ways. According to social cognition theory, people tend to emphasize the positive attributes of those who are perceived to be like them and the negative traits of those who are perceived to be different or other.[3] We have all seen examples of this in real life. If you

* When I use the term "racial stereotype," I refer to both racial and ethnic stereotypes.

meet a person for the first time, you are more likely to think positively of that person if you find you have common interests and mutual friends. In a homicide case in which the victim belongs to a racial or ethnic minority group whose members are perceived as foreigners or immigrants, jurors may subconsciously minimize the harm suffered by the victim and be more willing to view the defendant's use of force as reasonable.

## THE BLACK-AS-CRIMINAL STEREOTYPE

Despite the abolition of slavery, passage of the Civil Rights Act, and other positive changes in the law, Blacks in America today still suffer from race-based discrimination. While overt racial prejudice appears to have declined, negative stereotypes about African Americans still persist. One stereotype about African Americans in general, and young Black men in particular, is that they are more likely to be dangerous, prone to violence, and involved in criminal activity than other members of society.[4] When people talk about high-crime neighborhoods, it is understood that these neighborhoods are predominantly Black. When a young Black male is seen in a predominantly White[5] neighborhood, residents often call the police, worried that the youth is going to commit a burglary or some other crime. According to Adeno Addis, crime has "become a metaphor to describe young black men."[6]

Leonard Baynes reports that media images reinforce the Black-as-Criminal stereotype by "emphasizing black-on-white crime even though it is a small percentage of the actual crimes reported."[7] One study found that Blacks and Latinos "are twice as likely to be shown in local crime stories than in human interest stories."[8] The same study also found that persons of color "are more often shown as perpetrators than as victims" and that "stories with non-white offenders and white victims are given more emphasis than stories with same-race perpetrators and victims."[9]

The fear of Black-on-White violence is reinforced by incidents such as the beating of Reginald Denny, a White truck driver who was pulled from his truck and brutally beaten by several Black men during the 1992 Los Angeles riots following the acquittal of the four police officers who brutally beat Rodney King.

April 29, 1992. Los Angeles, California. About 6:30 P.M. Reginald Denny, a $16.70 per hour White truck driver, was in the process of delivering twenty-seven tons of sand to an Inglewood cement-mixing plant. He drove west down the San Bernadino Freeway, then took the Harbor Freeway south, and got off at Florence. Hours earlier, the jury in the state trial of the four White Los Angeles police officers who brutally beat African American Rodney King had announced not guilty verdicts on all but one count. Unbeknownst to Denny, who rarely watched television and did not even subscribe to a newspaper, people in the neighborhood he was about to enter had reacted violently to the verdicts, overturning trash cans, throwing rocks and bottles at cars and buildings, and looting stores. Denny pulled up to the intersection of Florence and Normandie streets where an angry mob filled the streets. As Denny slowed his truck to accommodate the crowd, five Black men surrounded his truck. One man yanked open the door of Denny's truck and dragged Denny out into the street. Several Black men began beating and kicking Denny, knocking him down to the ground. They continued to kick and beat Denny after he was on the ground. One man grabbed a fire extinguisher from Denny's truck and smashed it against Denny's head. Another hit Denny on the head with a brick. While Denny lay bleeding and helpless, another man rifled through his pockets and ran away after he found Denny's wallet.[10]

Many people saw the beating of Reginald Denny, rather than the beating of Rodney King, as a typical criminal event. Young Black males kicking and beating an innocent White man reinforced the already present White fear of the violent young Black male criminal. The incident, however, was atypical in terms of offenders and victims. As Samuel Walker points out, racial minorities are more likely than Whites to be the victims of crime.[11] Moreover, if typical means average, the typical criminal offender is actually White. In 1999, over two-thirds (69 percent) of those arrested were White, while less than one-third (28.6 percent) were Black.[12]

In self-defense cases, the Black-as-Criminal stereotype can influence the jury in several ways. When the accused is African American, jurors may discount his claim of self-defense, believing that the defendant provoked the confrontation. When the victim is African American, jurors may more readily believe the defendant's claim that he honestly and reasonably believed he needed to act in self-defense.

It is important to remember that the Black-as-Criminal stereotype is not simply a manifestation of White racism. White taxicab drivers are not the only ones who drive past waiting Black men. Non-White taxicab drivers also refuse to pick up Black men. White police officers are not the only ones who engage in racial profiling.[13] Black, Latino, and Asian American police officers also stop and harass Black and Brown drivers. Whites are not the only ones who fear Black men. Even Black men fear other Black men. The Reverend Jesse Jackson, a leader in the African American community, once admitted, "There is nothing more painful to me at this stage in my life than to walk down the street and hear footsteps and start thinking about robbery . . . [t]hen look around and see somebody white and feel relieved."[14] All individuals in this society, including African Americans, Asian Americans, Latinos, and other racial minorities, are influenced by the Black-as-Criminal stereotype.

According to the General Social Science Survey, an institution associated with the University of Chicago, 52.8 percent of individuals representing all different races polled in 1990 viewed violence as a trait characteristic of African Americans and 42.8 percent viewed violence as a trait characteristic of Latinos.[15] In contrast, only 18.8 percent of the individuals polled attributed violence to Whites.[16]

Negative stereotypes about Blacks and fear of Black-on-White crime may be one reason for the disproportionate number of Black men on death row. Numerous studies have found that prosecutors are more likely to seek the death penalty and juries are more likely to recommend a death sentence over life in prison without the possibility of parole when the defendant is Black and the victim is White.[17] David Baldus, for example, examined over two thousand capital murder cases and found that juries imposed the death penalty in 22 percent of the cases involving Black defendants and White victims; 8 percent of the cases involving White defendants and White victims; 3 percent of the cases involving White defendants and Black victims; and only 1 percent of the cases involving Black defendants and Black victims.[18] In recent years, DNA tests have proven that many Black men sentenced to death did not commit the crimes which put them on death row.[19]

Social science studies verify the existence and influence of the Black-as-Criminal stereotype. Birt Duncan found that White undergraduate students at the University of California (U.C.) at Irvine perceived ambiguously hostile acts (acts that could be perceived as either violent or nonviolent) as violent when a Black person engaged in these acts and as nonviolent when a White person engaged in the same behavior.[20] Students participating in Duncan's study observed two people involved in a heated argument that ended with one party shoving the other. Immediately after observing the shove, the subjects were asked to characterize the behavior of the person who shoved the other person. Duncan found that when the person shoving was Black and the person being shoved was White, 75 percent of the students tested characterized the Black person's behavior as "violent." Only 6 percent of the students characterized the Black person's behavior as "playing around." When the person shoving was White and the person being shoved was Black, only 17 percent of the students characterized the White person's act as "violent," while 42 percent characterized the White's person's act as "playing around."[21]

H. Andrew Sagar and Janet Ward Schofield conducted a similar study on forty Black and forty White male sixth graders, and found that both the Black and the White sixth graders tended to perceive ambiguously hostile behavior by Blacks as more threatening than similar behavior by Whites.[22] The students also perceived clearly nonaggressive behavior by Blacks as more hostile than similar behavior by Whites.[23]

Charles Bond, Clarisse DiCandia, and John MacKinnon found similar patterns at the Altobello Youth Center in Connecticut.[24] Bond, DiCandia, and MacKinnon studied 453 incidents involving juvenile patients who engaged in violent behavior at a Connecticut state youth psychiatric facility. Patients who acted violently could receive one of two negative sanctions. A patient could either be secluded (a nonphysical restraint) or forcibly restrained by being placed in a straitjacket or tied to a bed with sheets. A patient who was forcibly restrained would then be injected with a strong tranquilizer that would induce unconsciousness.

Bond, DiCandia, and MacKinnon found no difference in the mean number of violent offenses by Black and White patients. In other words, Black and White patients acted violently at about the same rate. However, the researchers found a substantial racial difference in the sanctions given to violent patients by the predominantly White staff workers. Black patients who acted up were forcibly restrained four times as often as White patients who committed similar transgressions.

The Black-as-Criminal stereotype is so deeply entrenched in our culture that Whites are able to use the stereotype to manufacture believable, but patently false, claims of Black criminal activity. In *The Color of Crime*, Katheryn Russell discusses the prevalence of "racial hoaxes," false claims of criminality by an individual of one race who blames someone of another race for his or her own crimes.[25] For example, in 1994, Susan Smith told police that a Black man had kidnapped her two sons at gunpoint and taken her car. Initially, many voiced the belief that the wrongdoer, whoever *he* was, should be punished with the death penalty. Later, Smith confessed to pushing her car into a lake and watching it sink with her two sons inside. Once it was discovered that a Black man was not responsible for the disappearance of the two boys, calls for the death penalty subsided. By the time Smith was tried and convicted of first-degree murder, pleas for sympathy and mercy had replaced the initial public outcry for the death penalty. Smith was sentenced to life imprisonment.[26]

In 1989, Carol Stuart was shot and killed in an inner-city neighborhood in Boston, Massachusetts. Charles Stuart, Carol's husband, told police that a Black man had abducted the two of them at gunpoint, robbed the couple, then shot both of them. Police combed the city of Boston, stopping and searching more than one hundred and fifty young Black men each day. Finally, police arrested William Bennett, a Black man who had been in trouble with the law and served two terms in prison for threatening and shooting police officers. It was not until Charles Stuart's brother came forward and admitted that he helped Charles hide the murder weapon that Charles confessed to killing his wife. Joe Feagin and Hernan Vera note, "Charles Stuart counted on the strong presumption among powerful Whites that a White businessperson would be telling the truth in his account of a black male attacking a White woman, even though his story was full of obvious inconsistencies."[27] Had police been more skeptical of Charles Stuart's claim, they might have found out earlier that Charles was having an affair with another woman, had taken out several large life insurance policies on his wife, and had previously plotted to kill her.

The Black-as-Criminal stereotype can also influence prosecutorial charging decisions.

August 23, 1995. San Francisco, California. Patrick Hourican, a thirty-three-year-old Irish-American construction worker, rode his bicycle past a car driven by Louis Waldron, a twenty-two-year-old Black college student. For no apparent reason, Hourican hit and then broke the side view mirror of

Waldron's car, then sped off on his bicycle. Angered by the unprovoked vandalism of his car, Waldron drove after Hourican. When Waldron caught up with Hourican, he got out of his car. Hourican, ready for a confrontation, punched Waldron, then got back on his bike and rode away. Waldron gave chase again. When he caught up with Hourican the second time, Waldron demanded that Hourican pay for the side view car mirror. Hourican refused. Waldron then punched Hourican in the face. Hourican fell, hit his head on the pavement, and died two days later.[28]

Former San Francisco District Attorney Arlo Smith charged Waldron, never before arrested or convicted, with first-degree murder, a crime for which the punishment in California is twenty-five years to life imprisonment. First-degree murder generally requires proof of premeditation and deliberation. In this case, there was little evidence that Waldron had thought about killing Hourican in advance. Indeed, there was evidence of provocation, since Hourican, a man with twenty-eight prior misdemeanor convictions and three felony contacts with police,[29] was the one who initiated the confrontation by breaking Waldron's car side view mirror and throwing the first punch. Many believed race influenced the decision to charge Waldron with the most serious type of homicide apart from capital murder. There was some support for this view. Just two months before Hourican's death, a White man punched another White man outside a bar. Even though the second man died as a result of the punch, the same District Attorney who filed first-degree murder charges against Waldron declined to file any charges against this White man.[30]

While the Black-as-Criminal stereotype is triggered most often by the sight of a young Black male in baggy pants worn low around the hips, even Black men who do not fit this profile are treated as suspect. In *Race Matters,* Harvard professor Cornel West describes the all-too-common experience for Black men of not being able to hail a taxicab.

> This past September my wife, Elleni, and I made our biweekly trek to New York City from Princeton. I was in good spirits. My morning lecture on the first half of Plato's *Republic* in my European Cultural Studies course had gone well. And my afternoon lecture on W. E. B. Du Bois's *The Souls of Black Folk* in my Afro-American Cultural Studies course had left me exhausted yet exhilarated. . . .
>
> I dropped my wife off for an appointment on 60th Street between Lexington and Park avenues. I left my car—a rather elegant one—in a safe

parking lot and stood on the corner of 60$^{th}$ Street and Park Avenue to catch a taxi. I felt quite relaxed since I had an hour until my next engagement. At 5:00 P.M. I had to meet a photographer who would take the picture for the cover of this book on the roof of an apartment building in East Harlem on 115th Street and 1$^{st}$ Avenue. I waited and waited and waited. After the ninth taxi refused me, my blood began to boil. The tenth taxi refused me and stopped for a kind, well-dressed, smiling female fellow citizen of European descent. As she stepped in the cab, she said, "This is really ridiculous, is it not?"

Ugly racial memories of the past flashed through my mind. Years ago, while driving from New York to teach at Williams College, I was stopped on fake charges of trafficking cocaine. When I told the police officer I was a professor of religion, he replied "Yeh, and I'm the Flying Nun. Let's go, nigger!" I was stopped three times in my first ten days in Princeton for driving too slowly on a residential street with a speed limit of twenty-five miles per hour. (And my son, Clifton, already has similar memories at the tender age of fifteen.) Needless to say, these incidents are dwarfed by those like Rodney King's beating or the abuse of black targets of the FBI's COINTEL-PRO efforts in the 1960s and 1970s. Yet the memories cut like a merciless knife at my soul as I waited on the godforsaken corner. Finally I decided to take the subway. I walked three long avenues, arrived late, and had to catch my moral breath as I approached the white male photographer and white female cover designer. I chose not to dwell on this everyday experience of black New Yorkers.[31]

Black women are also subject to the Black-as-Criminal stereotype. Poor Black women on the street are often seen as potential thieves or con artists scamming for a free dollar. Sometimes, even Black women dressed in business suits inspire racialized fear. Taunya Banks, a law professor at the University of Maryland, recounts one incident in which several White women refused to get on an elevator in a luxury condominium with her and four other well-dressed Black women law professors in Philadelphia.

One Saturday afternoon I entered an elevator in a luxury condominium in downtown Philadelphia with four other Black women law professors. We were leaving the apartment of another Black woman law professor. The elevator was large and spacious. A few minutes later, the door opened and a White woman in her late fifties peered in, let out a muffled cry of surprise, stepped back and let the door close without getting on. Several floors later the elevator stopped again, and the doors opened to reveal yet another White middle-aged woman, who also decided not to get on.

Following the first incident we looked at each other somewhat puzzled. After the second incident we laughed in disbelief, belatedly realizing that the two women seemed afraid to get on an elevator in a luxury condominium with five well-dressed Black women in their thirties and forties. Our laughter, the nervous laugh Blacks often express when faced with the blatant or unconscious racism of White America, masked our shock and hurt.

The elevator incident is yet another reminder that no matter how well-educated, well-dressed, or financially secure, we are Black first and thus still undesirable "others" to many White Americans. It reminds me that no matter what my accomplishments, I am still perceived as less than equal and *even dangerous!*[32]

Patricia Williams, a Black female law professor who teaches at Columbia University, recounts the humiliating experience of not being buzzed into a Benetton store in New York City while other White patrons were happily shopping within:

Buzzers are big in New York City. Favored particularly by smaller stores and boutiques, merchants throughout the city have installed them as screening devices to reduce the incidence of robbery. When the buzzer sounds, if the face at the door looks "desirable," the door is unlocked. If the face is that of an "undesirable," the door stays locked. Predictably, the issue of undesirability has revealed itself to be primarily a racial determination. Although the buzzer system was controversial at first, even civil rights organizations have backed down in the face of arguments that the system is a "necessary evil," that it is a "mere inconvenience" compared to the risks of being murdered, that discrimination is not as bad as assault, and that in any event, it is not *all* blacks who are barred, just "seventeen-year-old black males wearing running shoes and hooded sweatshirts."

Two Saturdays before Christmas, I saw a sweater that I wanted to purchase for my mother. I pressed my brown face to the store window and my finger to the buzzer, seeking admittance. A narrow-eyed white youth who looked barely seventeen, wearing tennis sneakers and feasting on bubble gum, glared at me, evaluating me for signs that would pit me against the limits of his social understanding. After about five seconds, he mouthed,

"We're closed," and blew pink rubber at me. It was one o'clock in the afternoon. There were several white people in the store who appeared to be shopping for things for *their* mothers. . . . [That salesperson] *saw me only as one who would take his money* and therefore could not conceive that I was there to give him money.[33]

These incidents happened to Black professors who, by all accounts, have been successful in their careers. Yet, despite their professional successes, they still were viewed by others—who knew nothing about them other than the way they looked—with race-based suspicion and fear.

## STATISTICAL ARGUMENTS SUPPORTING RACIALIZED FEAR OF BLACK MEN

In self-defense cases, a defendant's claim that he feared his Black victim may be perceived as more credible because of statistics that show that Blacks are arrested and convicted of crimes far more often than Whites.[34] In 1990, Marc Mauer with the Sentencing Project published a report entitled *Young Black Men and the Criminal Justice System: A Growing National Problem*.[35] In this report, Mauer reported that on any given day in 1989, 23 percent of Black men between the ages of twenty to twenty-nine were in prison, on probation, on parole, or in some way connected with the criminal justice system.[36] Five years later, Mauer updated his study with a new report entitled *The Sentencing Project, Young Black Americans and the Criminal Justice System: Five Years Later*.[37] This time, Mauer and coauthor Tracy Huling reported that "30.2% of African American males in the age group 20–29 were under criminal justice control—prison, jail, probation, or parole—on any given day."[38]

At first glance, these statistics seem powerful evidence that it is eminently reasonable to fear a Black man even if one would not fear a White man under the same circumstances. The Mauer and Huling report, however, cautions its readers not to jump to such conclusions. As Mauer and Huling are careful to note, "The typical African American male in the criminal justice system is *not a violent offender*."[39] The vast majority of Black men in prison are convicted of nonviolent drug offenses.[40]

Mauer and Huling also report that contrary to common expectations, "the majority of arrestees for violent offenses are white."[41] The Federal Bureau of Investigation's Uniform Crime Reports confirms this. In 2000, 59.9 percent of those arrested for violent crime were White.[42] Only 37.8 percent were Black.[43]

Because Whites constitute approximately 83 percent of the population in the United States, it is not surprising that Whites would constitute a majority of those arrested for violent crime. Blacks, in contrast, constitute only 12 percent of the population, yet account for almost 45 percent of those arrested for violent crime. Some would argue that these statistics therefore support the position that it is reasonable to fear Blacks in general because Blacks constitute a disproportionate number of persons arrested for violent crime.

The problem with saying it is reasonable to fear Blacks because they constitute a disproportionate number of violent crime arrestees is that this attributes the criminality of some Blacks to the entire Black population. When the total number of Blacks arrested for violent offenses is compared to the total number of Blacks in the United States, those arrested make up only a small percentage of the total Black population. In 2000, for example, Blacks arrested for violent crime comprised less than 1 percent of the total Black population.[44] Even this figure could be of doubtful reliability if racial stereotypes influenced those police decisions to arrest.[45]

Ellis Cose points out that if we relied upon statistics to justify everything, it would be reasonable to fear all men. Men are arrested for violent crime far more often than women,[46] yet no one argues that it is reasonable to fear all men because of their propensity for violence. Cose elaborates:

> According to the FBI Uniform Crime Report, in 1990, men, regardless of age, were arrested for violent crimes at levels that dwarfed the numbers for women. Men twenty-five to thirty-four years old were seven times as likely as women in the same age bracket to be arrested for murder, forcible rape, robbery, and aggravated assault. Those from thirty-five to forty-four were seven to eight times more likely to land in jail, and those over sixty-five were nearly fifteen times as likely.
>
> If one applies [the argument that it is reasonable to fear Blacks over Whites because Blacks are arrested for violent crimes at rates greater than Whites] to those statistics, one would expect discrimination

against men to be much more prevalent than discrimination against women. One would expect that until such time as the male crime rate is made to equal the female crime rate, society would treat men as objects of fear and terror.[47]

It is dangerous to rely heavily upon statistics because statistics can be used to support almost any proposition. For example, according to government statistics, a White person is more than four times as likely to be killed by another White person than by a Black person.[48] Approximately 80 percent of all crimes of violence occur between and among persons of the same race.[49] If one relied upon these statistics, one could argue that it is reasonable for Whites to fear other Whites. Statistics, however, are not used to support race-based fear of Whites because no White-as-Criminal stereotype exists to give social legitimacy to such fear. The average person on the street who finds himself or herself in a situation of perceived danger probably does not know what percentage of crimes of violence are committed by Whites and what percentage are committed by Blacks. Statistics or no statistics, Whites fear being attacked by a Black person much more than they fear being attacked by a fellow White person.

Ultimately, the use of statistics to justify race-based fear is unhelpful. Fear inspired by race will exist with or without statistics. The question in self-defense cases is usually not whether that fear is genuine, but whether that fear is reasonable. And whether or not that fear is considered reasonable depends in large part upon who is making that determination. Consider a well-known case involving a claim of self-defense by a White man who shot four Black youths on a New York subway.

## BERNHARD GOETZ: RACIST VIGILANTE OR SUBWAY HERO?

December 22, 1984. 1:00 p.m. Troy Canty, Darryl Cabey, James Ramseur, and Barry Allen, four Black youths, boarded an express subway train in the Bronx. The four teenagers rode together in the rear portion of one of the cars of the train. Bernhard Goetz, a White man, boarded the same car a little later and sat down on a bench in the rear section. Goetz was carrying an unlicensed .38 caliber pistol loaded with five rounds of ammunition, concealed in a waistband holster. Canty and Allen walked up to Goetz. Canty smiled at Goetz and said, "Give me five dollars." Without a word, Goetz stood up, pulled out his gun, and started firing rapidly at Canty, Allen, Cabey, and Ramseur. The youths scattered, trying to avoid the bullets. Noticing that Cabey appeared to be unhurt, Goetz walked up to him and said, "You seem to be all right, here's another." He then fired his last bullet into Cabey's spinal cord.

After the shooting, Goetz fled. Even though flight is usually considered evidence of a guilty conscience, Goetz's flight did not affect his popularity. Complete strangers called Goetz a subway hero and applauded his actions.

Subsequently, Goetz surrendered himself to police. He admitted that when he shot his gun, he was certain none of the Black youths had a gun. Nonetheless, he told police, "My intention was to do anything I could do to hurt them. My intention . . . I know this sounds horrible, but my intention was to murder them, to hurt them, to make them suffer as much as possible."[50]

Goetz was charged with assault, attempted murder, reckless endangerment, and illegal possession of a weapon. At trial, Goetz claimed he shot at the youths in self-defense. His jury[51] returned a verdict of not guilty on all the charges except Goetz's illegal possession of a weapon.

As a textbook criminal law hypothetical, Goetz's claim of self-defense should have been rejected out of hand. First, under New York law, a defendant is justified in using defensive physical force if and only if he honestly and reasonably believes two things: (1) that his assailant is attacking or about to attack him, and (2) that the use of physical force is necessary to defend himself. Moreover, deadly force can only be used if one is protecting oneself against an imminent threat of death or serious bodily injury.[52] Even if Goetz honestly believed the Black youths were about to attack him, it is a stretch to say this belief was reasonable. Neither of the two youths who approached Goetz displayed a weapon; neither made any menacing movement toward Goetz suggesting an imminent threat of death or grievous bodily injury.[53]

Second, it was not necessary for Goetz to shoot the youths. Goetz could have simply responded to the youths' demand for money with a polite "no." He could have moved to another section of the subway. He could have warned the youths not to bother him by showing them his gun and then walking away. Instead, Goetz's immediate response was to fire upon the youths, endangering their lives and the lives of everyone else in that subway car.

Some may think it unreasonable to expect Goetz, an "innocent" citizen minding his own business in the subway car, to move to another section of the subway car. The law of self-defense recognizes this sentiment in its "no duty to retreat" rule. The necessity requirement of self-defense doctrine means one should not use force, particularly deadly force, unless it is reasonably necessary to do so. If one can avoid using deadly force, but chooses to use such force anyway, then one is responsible for the often fatal consequences of one's actions. Most jurisdictions, however, do not require individuals to retreat before using deadly force even though the no duty to retreat rule is contrary to the necessity requirement. Even if Goetz had no duty to retreat to another subway car, several less lethal alternatives were available to him and should have been pursued prior to his shooting a deadly weapon in a crowded subway. The availability of these alternatives suggest it was not necessary for Goetz to have acted the way he did.

Calling Goetz an "innocent" suggests that the young Black men who were shot at were "wrongdoers" who deserved whatever they got. When a White defendant is charged with killing or assaulting a Black victim, defense attorneys and commentators often refer to the victim as the attacker and call the actual wrongdoer (the defendant) the victim. This is problematic because it shifts the focus of attention away from the appropriateness of the defendant's use of deadly force to the conduct of the victim.

One might also object to requiring Goetz to warn the youths by showing them his gun because such action could have been interpreted by the Black youths as a challenge and might have encouraged them to attack Goetz. Perhaps this is true, but the law is clear that one should not use deadly force unless it is reasonably necessary to do so. If one of the youths had actually started to attack, Goetz might have had a legitimate reason to fear imminent death or serious bodily injury. Until that time, Goetz should have held his fire.

Goetz's self-defense claim should have been rejected for a third reason. His use of a loaded gun was not proportionate to the threatened harm. Deadly force generally is not an appropriate response to non-deadly force. Goetz responded with deadly force to a verbal request ("give me five dollars"), one unaccompanied by any show of force, movement, or other indication of an imminent attack. Goetz admitted that he was certain none of the youths had a gun, yet he chose to shoot them.

Some scholars, known as rights-based deontologists, object to the proportionality requirement on the ground that one whose rights are threatened by another has an unqualified right to fight back. George Fletcher, for example, argues that the right of self-defense is based on the right to protect one's autonomy.[54] Under this view, a homeowner would have the right to use deadly force even if he were merely threatened with loss of property.[55]

The proportionality requirement exists for a good reason. As a society, we value human life over property. Therefore, if a person is only threatened with loss of property, the property owner should not be entitled to use deadly force to defend his property. If a person is threatened with nondeadly force (e.g., a kiss or unwanted sexual touching), that person is expected to resist the advance with nondeadly force. One cannot claim self- defense if one shoots another person to stop an unwanted kiss.

Fourth, one who introduces deadly force into a situation of conflict can be viewed as a deadly aggressor. A deadly aggressor is unable to assert the defense of self-defense unless he first withdraws from the encounter and effectively communicates his withdrawal to the other person.[56] When Goetz pulled out his loaded gun in response to the boys' verbal demand for money, he became a deadly aggressor and lost his right to claim self- defense. Since Goetz never withdrew from the conflict, he did not have a right to act in self-defense.

Finally, Goetz admitted to police that his intention was to murder the youths, to hurt them, and make them suffer as much as possible. Far from constituting self-defense, Goetz's act of shooting the youths with an intent to kill them fits the textbook definition of attempted murder. Goetz had the specific intent to kill the youths and took a substantial step toward accomplishing this objective by pulling the trigger of his gun more than once.

If Goetz's claim of self-defense was so patently unreasonable, why did the jury acquit him of all but the illegal possession of a firearm charge? After the trial was over, some of the jurors explained that they didn't feel the prosecution had met its burden of proving its case beyond a reasonable doubt.[57] One of the jurors opined, "We felt that Mr. Goetz had no chance to retreat in that situation."[58] Another juror insisted that race had no effect on the jury's decision to acquit, stating, "It didn't matter if he was a white man or a black man. Crime doesn't know color."[59]

The appeal to racial stereotypes in self-defense cases is less obvious than the appeal to norms of masculinity and heterosexuality in female infidelity killings and gay panic killings. An overt race-based appeal is likely to meet with objection from all but those with a White supremacist mentality. Therefore, the clever attorney who wants jurors to rely on racial stereotypes rarely addresses the racial component of a case directly. Instead he uses the jurors' own fears to create a backdrop of sympathy for his client's situation.

Goetz's attorney knew that a jury of New Yorkers would likely sympathize with a lone White subway rider confronted by a group of Black teens not merely *asking* for spare change, but *demanding* five dollars. Nonetheless, Barry Slotnick never once explicitly mentioned race as a factor contributing to Goetz's fear of the youths. Instead, his appeal to race norms was more subtle. Slotnick referred to the Black teens as "savages," "predators," and "vultures," language that conveyed the message that these Black youths were not law-abiding citizens, but gang members or criminals who preyed on innocent law-abiding New York subway riders.[60] In other words, these boys were wrongdoers and predators who had to be shot before they harmed Goetz.

George Fletcher, who observed Goetz's criminal trial, explains how Goetz's attorney cleverly played the race card by using four young Black men from the Guardian Angels to re-create the subway shooting scene:

> The covert appeal to racial bias came out most dramatically in the re-creation of the shooting, played out while Joseph Quirk was testifying. The defendant called in four props to stand in for the four victims Canty, Allen, Ramseur, and Cabey. The nominal purpose of the demonstration was to show the way in which each bullet entered the body of each victim. The defense's real purpose, however, was to re-create for the jury, as dramatically as possible, the scene that Goetz encountered when four young black passengers began to surround him. For that reason (defense attorney) Barry Slotnick asked the Guardian Angels to send him the four young black men to act as the props in the demonstration. In came the four young black Guardian Angels, fit and muscular, dressed in T-shirts, to play the parts of the four victims in a courtroom minidrama.[61]

A study by Paul Robinson and John Darley provides a nonracial explanation for the outcome in *Goetz*. In 1995, Robinson and Darley published the results of a study comparing community views regarding the assignment of criminal liability and punishment in various cases to the legal rules expressed in criminal codes such as the Model Penal Code.[62] Robinson and Darley found that the average person tends to have considerably looser standards regarding what constitutes acceptable use of force in self-defense than the criminal law normally permits. For example, subjects were asked to consider the criminal culpability of a person who shoots and kills a beggar who persists in requesting money even after the person turns the beggar down. Most subjects felt the person who used deadly force against the unarmed beggar deserved some punishment, but they also thought the person who used deadly force against an unarmed beggar was not as culpable as the individual who used deadly force in a no threat situation.[63] Lay intuitions about the culpability of the person who kills an unarmed beggar are at odds with modern self-defense doctrine and the Model Penal Code, both of which assign murder liability to an individual who uses deadly force against another individual who does not threaten death or serious bodily injury.

Theorizing about the reasons for the discrepancy between community views and the criminal codes, Robinson and Darley suggest that criminal codes are drafted with the presupposition that people who commit crimes have a high likelihood of being caught, convicted, and punished. The average person, not involved in the drafting of such legislation, may believe the criminal justice system inadequately protects innocent citizens. If the system is perceived as ineffective at providing protection, the average person may be more willing to let individuals take the law into their own hands even if this means permitting the use of deadly force against a nondeadly threat, in violation of the proportionality principle.

In the 1980s, when the Goetz shooting took place, New York subways were places where gang members terrorized riders by demanding money, covering cars with graffiti, and stealing tokens. These crimes often went unpunished. Perhaps the members of Goetz's criminal jury (six of whom had been victimized by crime; three by subway crime)[64] felt Goetz had a right to use deadly force against the four Black youths who demanded that he give them five dollars, because the New York City police and Transit police were not adequately protecting New Yorkers who rode the subway. As James Levine explains:

In New York, the subway symbolizes the perilous state of the city. It is on the subways that people often find themselves shoulder to shoulder and eye to eye with unsavory characters whom they can often avoid in the normal course of their lives. And it is in the subway that they feel at the mercy of the criminal element, with nowhere to flee and usually with no help around. The subway situation is so unnerving that many would rather endure the enormous cost and aggravation of commuting by bus or car than expose themselves to that terrifying situation.[65]

While it is tempting to write off the *Goetz* case as *not* involving race, the racial dimensions of the case should not be ignored. Reconsider the reasonableness of Goetz's actions if we imagine Goetz as a Black man and the four youths as White teenagers.

Four White teens board an express subway train in the Bronx at around 1:00 P.M. A Black man, carrying a concealed unlicensed pistol loaded with five rounds of ammunition, boards the same car a little later and sits down. Moments later, two of the White youths approach the Black man and one says, "Give me five dollars." Without any warning, the Black man stands up, pulls out his gun, and starts to fire it at the youths. The youths scramble to get out of the way. The Black man corners one of the youths and says, "You seem to be all right, here's another." Then he fires his last bullet into the youth's spinal cord.[66]

It is hard to imagine anyone thinking that shooting a loaded gun in a crowded subway is a reasonable response to a request for money. Yet the predominantly White jury that acquitted Goetz of all but the illegal possession charge obviously felt he acted reasonably when he shot the youths in response to a request for money. If Goetz had been a Black man and the four youths had been White, the jury might have seen things differently.[67] Likewise, if the jury had been constituted differently, they might have reached a different verdict.[68] Nine years later, an all-minority six-person civil jury, composed of four Blacks and two Hispanics, found Goetz liable to Darryl Cabey, the boy who was paralyzed after Goetz shot him in the spine, and ordered him to pay Cabey $43 million in damages.[69]

## STEREOTYPES ABOUT MEXICAN AMERICANS
## AND OTHER LATINOS

Stereotypes about Mexican Americans and Latinos are varied and complex. Not all persons with Mexican or Latin American ancestry suffer from the same stereotypes because not all Latinos look alike. Some Latinos are fair and can pass as non-Latino Whites, while others are darker skinned.

Stereotypes about Mexican Americans and Latinos have received relatively little attention in legal scholarship.[70] Moreover, very little social science research has been conducted on Latino stereotypes. Despite the dearth of scholarship in this area, it is commonly known that Mexican Americans and other Latinos are often perceived as foreigners or immigrants. Particularly in states bordering Mexico, such as California, New Mexico, and Texas, Mexican Americans are more often seen as Mexican than American. Even outside these southwestern states, the stereotype persists.

The foreigner stereotype may have influenced a Capitol Police security aide in Washington, D.C., who stopped U.S. Congressman Luis Gutierrez, a Puerto Rican American, and accused him of presenting false congressional credentials.[71] Gutierrez was passing through a metal detector security checkpoint in one of the Capitol buildings with his daughter and niece who were carrying two small Puerto Rican flags. The security aide stopped Congressman Gutierrez, and began screaming at him for allowing the flags to slightly unfurl. According to the Congressman, "She said she didn't want to see those flags, and I told her I would take care of them. Then she said, 'Who do you think you are?' When I told her I was Congressman Gutierrez, she said, 'I don't think so.'"[72] The aide then added insult to injury, telling the Congressman, who was born in Chicago, to go back to his country.[73] The confrontation lasted until a Capitol Police sergeant noticed what was happening, recognized the Congressman, and took the security aide away.

The Latino-as-Foreigner stereotype is particularly troublesome when it slides into the Latino-as-Illegal Immigrant stereotype because of negative associations linked to illegal immigration.[74] Immigrants from Mexico and other countries in Latin America are viewed by many as lawbreakers who sneak across the border and take jobs from more deserving Americans, even though not all immigrants from Mexico are here unlawfully and many of the jobs they hold are low-paying positions that most Americans are unwilling to perform, such as janitorial services, housecleaning, and gardening. Hostility against immigrants who illegally enter this country sparked a popular movement in California in the 1990s to deny publicly funded nonemergency medical care, public schooling, and other social services to undocumented immigrants and their children.[75] Major parts of Proposition 187 were later ruled unconstitutional.[76]

Linked to the image of poor, unemployed Mexicans crossing the border illegally to steal jobs from law-abiding American citizens is the idea that persons of Mexican descent are involved in criminal drug activity, either as distributors or as carriers. Mexican Americans are often stereotyped as drug users and drug dealers,[77] even though drug use is lower among Latinos than it is among Whites or Blacks.[78]

Stereotypes about the inherent criminality of Mexican Americans have a long history in this country. Former Chief of the Foreign Relations Bureau of the Los Angeles County Sheriff's Office, Captain Ed Duran Ayres, once presented a report to a grand jury in which he asserted that Mexican youths, unlike their Caucasian counterparts, were more inclined to use lethal force during fights because of their "desire to kill."[79] Mexican Americans have also been stereotyped as sly, treacherous, wily, and undependable knife carriers.[80] Embracing this stereotype, former FBI director J. Edgar Hoover once said, "You never have to bother about a President being shot by Puerto Ricans or Mexicans. They don't shoot very straight. But if they come at you with a knife, beware."[81]

Today, young Latino males who live in low-income high-crime neighborhoods and wear baggy pants and T-shirts are often seen as dangerous gang members.[82] The belief that young Latino men dressed in a certain way are likely to be gang members may have encouraged prosecutors to believe William Masters's claim that he acted reasonably in self-defense when he shot and killed Cesar Rene Arce, a young Mexican American teenager, after catching him spray painting with a friend under a freeway in Los Angeles.

> January 31, 1995. Around 1:00 A.M. Hollywood (Los Angeles), California. William Masters II, a White man, was out for a late-night walk. He spotted Cesar Rene Arce and David Hillo, two Mexican American teenagers, spray painting columns under a freeway. Masters was carrying a loaded gun in

his fanny pack. Masters picked up a piece of paper from the ground and wrote down the license plate number of the only car parked in the area, assuming the car belonged to the boys. He planned to report the boys to the proper authorities. He was tired of seeing gang-type graffiti all over the city.

One of the teens spotted Masters as he was writing. Cesar Arce approached Masters and demanded that he hand over the piece of paper. A scuffle ensued. Arce tried to rip the paper from Masters's hand while Masters tried to jam the paper into his pocket. Then Hillo came over and held up a screwdriver in a threatening manner. Masters gave up the paper and began walking away. Suddenly, Masters pulled his gun out of his fanny pack, swung around, and began firing at the teenagers. Masters hit Arce in the back and Hillo in the buttocks. Arce died as a result of this shooting.[83]

Masters told the first officers to arrive on the scene, "I shot him because he was spray painting." Later, Masters claimed he shot the boys in self-defense. In yet another explanation, Masters said he shot the boys because they tried to rob him. Hillo, the teen who survived the shooting, denied that the two had tried to rob Masters. Hillo told police that after Masters shot him in the buttocks, Masters walked up to Hillo, held the gun to Hillo's head while Hillo was lying on the ground, and said, "This all happened because you were tagging."

Although Masters was initially arrested and jailed on suspicion of murder, the Los Angeles County District Attorney's Office ultimately declined to prosecute Masters on the ground that he acted in self-defense when he shot the boys.[84] The determination that Masters reasonably believed he was about to be attacked by Arce is surprising in light of the fact that Masters shot Arce in the back. It is hard to believe that one is protecting oneself against an imminent threat of death or grievous bodily injury when one shoots one's victim as he is trying to run away.

Indeed, this was the primary reason why a claim of self-defense in another high-profile case that occurred two years earlier was rejected by the same Los Angeles District Attorney's Office that declined to file murder charges against William Masters. That office filed murder and manslaughter charges against two Black men, one of whom was the rap singer known as Snoop Doggy Dogg, rejecting the defendants' claim of self-defense primarily on the ground that the victim was shot in the back. The prosecutor in charge of the case summed up his view of the case when he remarked, "If the famous rapper and his bodyguard acted in self-defense, why was the victim shot in the back?"[85]

The decision not to file criminal homicide charges against Masters was probably motivated by the belief that the government would have a difficult time convincing a jury to return a guilty verdict. The local community voiced loud support for Masters. Telephone calls flooded into the police station where Masters was being held, offering Masters money and legal assistance. Sandi Webb, a Simi Valley councilwoman, expressed her support for Masters by declaring, "Kudos to William Masters for his vigilant anti-graffiti efforts and for his foresight in carrying a gun for self-protection. If [Los Angeles] refuses to honor Masters as a crime-fighting hero, then I invite him to relocate to our town."[86]

Masters's supporters were likely reacting to the fear of crime and gang violence. In Southern California, graffiti on freeway overpasses, public buildings, and even private property serves as a reminder that the threat of violent gang-related crime, including carjackings and drive-by shootings, is never too far away. One individual reflected these sentiments when he stated, "Whatever [Masters] did doesn't bother me. I'm not saying shooting people is the way to do it. . . . But [the graffiti is] just disgusting. It doesn't seem like anyone's doing anything about it."[87]

However legitimate the generalized fear of gang violence, such fear does not satisfy the requirement in self-defense doctrine that a person using deadly force in self-defense must have a reasonable belief that another individual poses an imminent threat of death or serious bodily injury. Moreover, defacing property through graffiti is not a capital offense. If the state is not permitted to execute a graffiti offender after a trial and conviction, a private citizen should not be permitted to kill such an offender.

Stereotypes about young Mexican Americans as gang bangers might also have influenced the lack of public concern for the victims in this case. Little research has been published on whether and to what extent presumptions about young Mexican American males as gang bangers influence perceptions of dangerousness, but such presumptions are common in cities like San Diego, which have large concentrations of lower-class and dark-complexioned Mexican Americans and Mexican nationals and in other cities close to the Mexican border.

The support generated in favor of William Masters for shooting two Mexican American teenagers engaged in spray painting is striking when compared to the condemnation of the Singapore government in response to its decision to cane Michael Fay, a non-Latino White teenager who was caught spray painting cars in Singapore less than a year earlier. In 1994, Fay pleaded guilty to two counts of mischief, admitting that he and others spray painted eighteen cars, threw eggs at other cars, and switched license plates on other cars.

A Singapore judge sentenced Fay to four months in prison, a $2,230 fine, and six lashes with a rattan cane. The outrage in America was immediate. Describing her son as "a *typical* teenager," Fay's mother appealed to U.S. government officials to intervene and insist on clemency for her son, explaining, "Caning is not something the *American* public would want *an American* to go through. It's barbaric."[88] U.S. Embassy officials and members of the American Chamber of Commerce responded by condemning the severity of the sentence. Even President Bill Clinton asked the Singapore government to reconsider the sentence.

When a White American shoots two Mexican Americans for spray painting columns supporting a freeway, killing one of the youths, he is called a crime-fighting hero. When a foreign government canes a White American youth for spray painting and egging cars, that punishment is denounced as inhumane and cruel. If a Singapore citizen had shot and killed Fay after catching him in the act of spray painting his car, then claimed that he acted in self-defense because he thought Fay was going to hurt him, it is unlikely that people in this country would believe that Singapore citizen's claim of self-defense. Yet many in this country saw Masters as a crime-fighting hero and were sympathetic to his claim of self-defense.

## STEREOTYPES ABOUT ASIAN AMERICANS

In 1995, David Magdael, President of the Asian American Advertising and Public Relations Alliance remarked, "Gone, it seems, are the days when Asian males were solely represented in the media as martial arts fighters, butlers, and laundry owners."[89] While Magdael's statement may be true, racialized and gendered stereotypes about Asian Americans in general and Asian American men in particular persist even today.

The ways in which Asian Americans have been socially constructed in American society are varied and contradictory. Some stereotypes about Asian Americans are considered "positive" stereotypes, or stereotypes that project a favorable image of Asian Americans, while other stereotypes are considered "negative." At least three stereotypes about Asian Americans may influence perceptions about the reasonableness of a violent act when the defendant or victim is Asian: (1) the Asian-as-Model-Minority stereotype, (2) the Asian-as-Foreigner stereotype, and (3) the Asian-as-Martial-Artist stereotype.

## THE ASIAN-AS-MODEL MINORITY

One of the most common stereotypes about Asian Americans is the model minority stereotype.[90] This stereotype depicts Asians as smart, hard-working, law-abiding, and respectful of authority.[91] Such positive images likely benefited a Korean American woman who claimed she acted in self-defense after she killed a fifteen-year-old African American girl by shooting her in the back of the head.

> March 16, 1991. Los Angeles. Soon Ja Du, a Korean American woman who owned and operated a liquor store was alone at the cash register. Latasha Harlins, a fifteen-year-old African American teenager came into the store, went to the section of the store where the orange juice was shelved, selected a bottle of orange juice and placed it in her backpack. Harlins approached the cash register with two dollars visible in her hand. The bottle of orange juice, which cost only $1.79, was also visible from Harlins's backpack. Du confronted Harlins and accused her of trying to steal the bottle of orange juice. Du called Harlins a "bitch" and pulled on Harlins's sweater. Harlins responded by hitting Du in the eye twice. Harlins put the orange juice down on the counter and turned to leave. Du reached under the counter and pulled out a .38 caliber revolver. From a distance of about three feet, Du shot Harlins in the back of the head, killing Harlins instantly.[92]

Du was charged with first-degree murder. At trial, Du argued that she should be acquitted of murder because she shot Harlins in self-defense. Alternatively, Du argued that she should be convicted of manslaughter rather than murder because she had an honest but unreasonable belief in the need to act in self-defense and acted in the heat of passion. Although the jury rejected Du's claim of perfect self-defense, it found her guilty of voluntary manslaughter rather than murder.

The sentencing judge was even more sympathetic to Du than the jury, and imposed an extraordinarily lenient sentence. Because Du used a firearm, she was presumptively ineligible for probation under California Penal Code section 1203(e)(2).[93] Nonetheless, Judge Joyce Karlin suspended execution of Du's prison sentence and placed Du on probation for five years. Du was not required to serve any jail time as a condition of probation.

In an insightful analysis of Judge Karlin's sentencing decision, Neil Gotanda notes that Judge Karlin relied upon positive stereotypes about Korean Americans and negative stereotypes about African Americans in deciding Du's sentence.[94] Judge Karlin described Du as a dutiful mother who was watching the store that day "to shield her son from repeated robberies."[95] In referencing repeated robberies, Judge Karlin's sympathy for the Korean storeowner defendant was clear. In contrast, Judge Karlin ignored several positive facts about Latasha Harlins. The court of appeals noted:

> The probation report also reveals that Latasha had suffered many painful experiences during her life, including the violent death of her mother. Latasha lived with her extended family (her grandmother, younger brother and sister, aunt, uncle and niece) in what the probation officer described as "a clean, attractively furnished three-bedroom apartment" in South Central Los Angeles. Latasha had been an honor student at Bret Hart Junior High School, from which she had graduated the previous spring. Although she was making only average grades in high school, she had promised that she would bring her grades up to her former standard. Latasha was involved in activities at a youth center as an assistant cheerleader, a member of the drill team and a summer junior camp counselor. She was a good athlete and an active church member.[96]

The *Soon Ja Du* case illustrates how the model minority stereotype can benefit Asian Americans. The stereotype, however, can also be harmful to Asian Americans. As Frank Wu observes, every positive attribute of the model minority stereotype is linked to a corresponding negative characteristic:

In the [model minority] stereotype, every positive element is matched
to a negative counterpart. To be intelligent is to *lack personality*. To be
hard-working is to be *unfairly competitive*. To be family-oriented is to be
*clannish, "too ethnic," and unwilling to assimilate*. To be law-abiding is to
be *rigidly rule-bound, tied to traditions in the homeland, unappreciative of
democracy and free expression*.[97]

For example, public reaction to the chaos and looting in Los Angeles
that followed the acquittal of four police officers who brutally beat Rodney King reflected conflicting feelings of sympathy for, as well as resentment against, the Korean Americans whose lives were caught up in
the destruction. Just as Asian Americans in general are often held up as
the "good" minority compared to the other "bad" minorities, Korean
American store owners were sympathetically portrayed as the unfortunate victims of "bad" African American and Latino looters. At the same
time, Korean Americans were negatively portrayed as property-loving,
gun-toting store owners who valued their material possessions over
human life.[98]

The model minority stereotype may have another harmful effect.
Rhoda Yen argues that it "may lead to an increased likelihood of criminal acquittals in cases involving Asian American victims."[99] This is because the stereotype encourages the belief that "Asian Americans are
unlikely targets for racially-motivated crimes."[100] Crimes involving
Asian American victims are rarely viewed as hate crimes. Instead they
are considered "crimes that merely happen to involve minority victims."[101] For example, the brutal beating of Vincent Chin, while perceived as a crime of hate by most in the Asian American community,
was largely seen by White Americans as "a drunken brawl between two
men, one of whom happened to be Asian."[102]

### Vincent Chin

Detroit, Michigan. June 19, 1982. Vincent Chin, a Chinese-American man,
and several of his friends had gone to the Fancy Pants strip bar to celebrate
Chin's upcoming marriage. Ronald Ebens and Michael Nitz, two White
men, were sitting directly across from Chin's group of friends. Ebens and
Nitz started calling Chin a "Nip," a derogatory name for a person of Japanese descent, derived from the word "Nippon" which is the Japanese word
for Japan. Referring to the growth of foreign car imports and rising unem-

ployment, Ebens yelled, "It's because of you little mother fuckers that we're out of work."[103] Chin got out of his chair and walked up to Ebens. Chin threw a punch, a scuffle ensued, and Chin, Ebens, and their friends were asked to leave the bar. Chin challenged Ebens to finish the fight outside. Ebens went to Nitz's car and retrieved a baseball bat. When Chin saw Ebens with a baseball bat, he fled. Ebens and Nitz chased Chin. When Ebens and Nitz finally caught up with Chin, Ebens struck Chin repeatedly with the baseball bat. Witnesses told investigators that Ebens swung the baseball bat at Chin's head as if he were hitting a home run. Chin's skull was fractured in several places and police officers on the scene said pieces of Chin's brain were splattered all over the sidewalk. Chin died four days later.[104]

Ebens and Nitz were charged with second-degree murder. They each pled no contest to manslaughter and were sentenced to three years of probation and a fine of $3,780. When asked why he did not impose any jail time on Ebens and Nitz, Judge Charles Kaufman responded, "*Had it been a brutal murder,* those fellows would be in jail now."[105] Judge Kaufman did not see the killing of Vincent Chin as a brutal murder, even though Ebens struck Chin's head so hard that pieces of his brain were splattered all over the sidewalk. Judge Kaufman explained further why he thought Ebens and Nitz did not deserve any jail time:

> These [aren't] the kind of men you send to jail. We're talking here about a man who's held down a responsible job with the same company for seventeen or eighteen years and his son who is employed and is a part-time student. . . . These men are not going to go out and harm somebody else. I just [don't] think that putting them in prison [will] do any good for them or for society.[106]

Expressing the sentiments of many Asian Americans, Chin's mother decried the judge's sentence, asking, "What kind of law is this? What kind of justice? This happened because my son is Chinese. If two Chinese killed a white person, they must go to jail, maybe for their whole lives."[107]

Most people who are familiar with the Vincent Chin story know it as a case of racial prejudice. Robert Chang explains how race, class, and gender converged to make the Vincent Chin story more complicated than it appeared in the press:

In order for Vincent Chin to become the focal point of organizing and politicizing people about anti-Asian violence, the unsavory parts of the narrative were suppressed. The standard narrative does not include the fact that the encounter between Vincent Chin and the two white autoworkers took place in a strip club where Chin was having a bachelor's party. In the standard narrative where Chin is a victim of racial violence, we are uncomfortable with Chin's participation in the objectification of women. The standard narrative also does not include the fact that it was Chin who threw the first punch, or the fact that . . . Chin said, "Come on, you chickenshits, let's fight some more." This is not to say that Chin was not a victim of racial violence—my point is that this is not a simple case of an aggressor and victim and mistaken racial/ethnic identification. Bringing in the suppressed details provides a richer story involving race, nation, class, and sexuality.[108]

Chang explains how Chin participated in the objectification of women.

There may have been other showgirls, but one stripper was black, the other white. Chin gave a large tip to the white dancer and a small tip to the black dancer. The black dancer didn't like the way Chin wanted to give her the tip, which we might presume was in her G-string, so she only received a small tip. We can imagine, then, that the white dancer permitted this way and got a larger tip. Furthermore, Ebens and Nitz were unhappy that Chin was enjoying the show. Why did Chin's enjoyment make them unhappy?[109]

Chang answers this question by explaining that Ebens and Nitz felt doubly displaced by Chin. First, they felt Chin and others like him were displacing them from their jobs. Second, because of Chin's economic security, they felt displaced by Chin as consumers of (the white dancer's) sexual attention. Chang explains:

My thesis is that Ebens and Nitz were suffering a double displacement. People like Chin were making people like Ebens and Nitz lose their jobs. Even though Ebens was still employed as a foreman in an automobile plant, he clearly identified with laid-off autoworkers. But there was more. Chin was displacing them as (the rightful) consumers of sexual attention. Here we have economics, race, gender, and sexuality coming together in interesting ways. Loss of jobs entails a loss of

masculinity. The loss of masculinity was caused by a racial and foreign Other, an Asian man who in many ways was just like them. The
bonding that might normally take place between men in a strip club is
disrupted by Chin's Asianness. Further, the Asian man may be improperly consuming the sexual attention of a white woman, which, in
part, he is able to do because he is doing well, economically, by displacing people like Ebens and Nitz from their jobs. We have, then, a
double displacement along with a threat to racial purity, a threat to the
very whiteness that provides their sense of place and entitlement in
America.[110]

## THE ASIAN-AS-FOREIGNER STEREOTYPE

Fear of the foreigner is sometimes a black streak that runs through
America's political culture. We see instances of [this] when it involves
hate crimes, not necessarily directed at black Americans, but at foreign
Americans.

—Mike McCurry, Former White House Press Secretary
to President Bill Clinton

Even though it is oxymoronic to speak of "foreign" "Americans," the
term "foreign Americans" conveys meaning. Asians and Latinos are
usually considered foreign Americans. A person who asks an Asian
American, "So, where are you from?" usually expects to hear, "I'm from
Japan," or "I'm from China," or "I'm from Vietnam." If one answers,
"I'm from Houston," or "I'm from New York," one is likely to be asked,
"No, I mean, where are your parents from?" Even if true, it won't do to
say, "My parents were also born in Houston," because the speaker is interested in finding out which foreign country the Asian person is from,
even if she isn't from a foreign country.

The focus on the Asian in Asian American is deep-rooted. During
World War II, when the United States was at war with Japan, hostility
toward Japan extended to all persons of Japanese ancestry, even Japanese Americans born and raised in the United States for several generations. From 1942 to 1945, all persons of Japanese descent were forced to
leave their homes and were incarcerated in internment camps because
the American government viewed them as a potential threat.[111]

In times of economic uncertainty, resentment and violence against

Asian Americans seem to increase as individuals vent their frustrations on model-minority Asian Americans who are perceived as stealing valuable job opportunities from "real" Americans. Because many individuals can't tell Americans of Asian descent apart from Asian nationals, Asian Americans are mistaken for Asian nationals and then blamed for foreign imports that threaten domestic goods, such as American cars. In the film, *Who Killed Vincent Chin?* filmmakers Renee Tajima and Christine Choy illustrate the association between Asians and foreign car imports by juxtaposing the image of angry White American autoworkers and their friends taking turns swinging a baseball bat as hard as possible at a Japanese economy car with the actual baseball bat beating of Vincent Chin, a Chinese American man who was mistaken for a Japanese.[112] Around the time of Chin's death, a Detroit radio station hosted "Toyota parties," encouraging people to demolish Japanese autos with a sledgehammer, and a car dealership in Detroit ran television commercials that showed a battle tank crushing a Japanese car.[113]

The Asian-as-Foreigner stereotype continues today, although it often takes more subtle forms. During the O. J. Simpson trial, for example, much of the racial joking that arose in connection with the case was directed at two prominent Asian Americans, the presiding judge, Lance Ito, and the criminalist, Dennis Fung. Ito and Fung, both of whom speak English without a noticeable accent, were portrayed by radio station disk jockeys, publishing houses, and even a United States senator as bumbling, heavily accented Asians who could barely speak English.[114] The 1996 campaign finance scandal involving Johnny Huang and the Democratic National Party and the December 1999 arrest of scientist Wen Ho Lee on charges of illegally downloading nuclear secrets raised the specter of the evil Asian foreigner again, prompting Neil Gotanda to opine that "The Wen Ho Lee case and the campaign finance scandals are the most serious threat to Asian Pacific Americans since the end of the Vietnam war."[115]

Another example of the Asian-as-Foreigner stereotype at work is reflected in crimes of violence against Asians and Asian Americans. Jerry Kang has noted that Asians and Asian Americans are often targeted by muggers who assume that all Asians carry a lot of cash.[116] The fact that some individuals from certain Asian countries do carry a lot of cash contributes to this type of targeting. A mugger who sees someone who looks Asian is not likely to know whether the person was born and raised in the United States or is from another country, and is not likely to ask. The problem is compounded by stereotypes about Asians as "physically weak and culturally adverse to defending themselves."[117]

The Asian-as-Foreigner stereotype is complicated by the fact that approximately two-thirds of all Asians in the United States are foreign-born. Frank Wu cautions us not to use this statistical information to "justify the assumption that everyone with an Asian name is a guest or a tourist," because such an assumption "leads to implications that the Asians are enjoying their sojourn and will ultimately return elsewhere."[118]

Because of the constant conflation of Asian nationals and Asian Americans, symptomatic of the Asian-as-Foreigner stereotype, the tragic shooting of Yoshihiro Hattori, a Japanese foreign exchange student, has special significance for Asian Americans. Hattori died after being shot by a Louisiana homeowner who claimed he shot the unarmed Japanese teenager in self- defense.

October 17, 1992. Two sixteen-year-old high school students, Webb Haymaker and Yoshihiro Hattori, were looking for a Halloween party in the suburbs of Baton Rouge, Louisiana, when they came across the home of Rodney and Bonnie Peairs. The home was decorated for Halloween, and was just a few doors away from the correct house. Hattori was a Japanese foreign exchange student, and Haymaker was a member of his host family. Haymaker was dressed as a car accident victim. Hattori was dressed as the character played by John Travolta in the movie "Saturday Night Fever." He wore a white tuxedo jacket and carried a small black camera. The boys rang the front doorbell. No one answered the door, but the boys heard the clinking of window blinds coming from the carport area. The boys walked around the house towards the carport, Haymaker leading the way. A moment later, Bonnie Peairs opened the back door leading out to the carport. She saw Haymaker, who started to say, "We're here for the party." Then Hattori came around the corner. When Bonnie Peairs saw Hattori, she emitted a scream, slammed the door, and called for her husband to "get the gun." Without asking any questions, Rodney Peairs ran to the bedroom and grabbed a laser-scoped .44-magnum Smith and Wesson, one of a number of guns he owned.

The two boys had walked away from the house and were on the sidewalk about ten yards from the house when Peairs rushed out of the house from the back door and into the carport area. The carport light and a street light in front of the house illuminated the carport and the sidewalk area.

Hattori turned and approached Peairs, smiling and explaining in his broken English, "We are here for the party." Rather than telling Hattori that he had the wrong house, Peairs pointed his laser-scoped gun at Hattori and shouted, "Freeze." Hattori, who was from Japan, a country where firearms are prohibited, had never learned the English word "Freeze," so he continued to approach Peairs. Without waiting a second longer, Peairs fired one shot at Hattori's chest. Hattori collapsed and died on the spot. The entire incident—from the time Peairs opened his back door to the time he fired his gun—took place in approximately three seconds.[119]

Peairs was charged with manslaughter. At trial, Peairs asserted that he shot Hattori in self-defense. He claimed that Hattori was skipping or walking very fast toward him and looked very scary. Peairs said Hattori, the slight teenage boy, looked like a crazy man. When Hattori did not stop after Peairs shouted at him to freeze, Peairs claimed he was terrified and thought his life was in danger. Although Hattori was carrying a camera, Peairs did not claim that he thought the camera was a gun. In fact, Peairs later admitted, during the course of the civil wrongful death action filed by Hattori's parents, that he did not see a gun, knife, stick, or club in Hattori's hand that night.[120]

The judge instructed the jury that in order to acquit Peairs, they had to find that Peairs *reasonably* believed he was in imminent danger of losing his life or receiving great bodily harm and that the killing was necessary to save Peairs from that danger. After little more than three hours of deliberation, the jury found Peairs not guilty of manslaughter. Spectators in the courtroom applauded the verdict. In contrast to the public outrage over the short deliberation process in the *O. J. Simpson* case, in which jurors reached a verdict of acquittal in less than four hours,[121] there was little public outrage over the shortness of deliberation time leading to Peairs's acquittal. In fact, residents of the town of Baton Rouge felt so strongly that Peairs was justified in shooting Hattori that they loudly objected to plans to erect a memorial in honor of Hattori.

The key question in the *Peairs* case was whether it was *reasonable* for Peairs to believe (1) that he was in imminent danger of death or great bodily harm, and (2) that it was necessary to shoot Hattori to protect himself from such imminent death or great bodily harm. Reasonable minds can certainly disagree on this question. On the one hand, Peairs had pointed a gun at Hattori and shouted at him to freeze. Hattori kept approaching. Arguably, the average Louisiana homeowner in Peairs's situation could have thought Hattori posed a very real threat of death or great bodily injury. If Hattori wouldn't stop after being warned to stop, there was nothing left to do but shoot. Additionally, this shooting took place in Louisiana. As discussed in chapter 1, place (i.e., geographic location) has some influence over whether the use of deadly force is seen as reasonable. Studies have shown that men in Southern states are more prone to perceive nonthreatening insults as a threat to their honor and more prone to respond violently to threats of a non-deadly nature.[122]

On the other hand, Peairs could have completely avoided the shooting tragedy by retreating into his house and locking the door. Once inside, Peairs could have called the police. There was little reason to think Hattori would try to follow Peairs inside the house and force the door open. Recall that by the time Peairs came outside with his gun, the two boys were already on the sidewalk, leaving the premises. They were not hanging around near the back door, waiting for someone to open it so they could enter. Moreover, Peairs did not have to go outside in the first place. When his wife screamed at him to get the gun, Peairs could have asked her why she was screaming. He could have quickly locked the doors and called the police. In fact, if Hattori and Haymaker had been robbers, it would have been much safer for Peairs to lock the doors right away (to prevent entry into the home), rather than rushing to get a gun. Any of these less fatal measures would have avoided the imagined danger posed by Hattori.

How did the Asian-as-Foreigner stereotype influence the verdict in this case? The fact that Hattori was in fact a foreigner, a Japanese citizen and not an American, simply made it easier for the Baton Rouge jury to empathize with Peairs. They could picture themselves in Peairs's shoes. If an Asian teenager came onto their property and refused to freeze even with a gun pointed at his chest, that teenager was asking to be shot. Bonnie Peairs's trial testimony is very revealing in this regard. When asked to describe Hattori, she responded, "I guess he appeared Oriental. He could have been Mexican or whatever."[123] Mrs. Peairs was unable to tell whether Hattori was Asian or Mexican or neither. All she knew was that Hattori was different. He wasn't White like her.

Because of Hattori's nationality, the jurors couldn't see Hattori as one of their own sons. If Webb Haymaker, the boy from the neighborhood, had been the victim in this case, Peairs would have found it difficult to persuade the jury that he was terrified for his life and thought the boy looked like a crazy man. It would have been difficult for the defense to paint a credible picture of the victim as the bad guy. If Haymaker had been shot and killed, it is unlikely that the spectators in the courtroom would have applauded the not guilty verdict. Haymaker's parents and his siblings would have been in the courtroom, reminding the other members of that Baton Rouge community that the dead boy could have been their son. But it was a teenager from Japan who was shot and killed, and the sight of his grieving parents in the courtroom only served to remind the jurors that the victim was not one of the community's own.

## THE ASIAN-AS-MARTIAL-ARTIST STEREOTYPE

Another stereotype that affects mostly the male half of the Asian population is what I call the Asian-as-Martial-Artist stereotype.[124] This stereotype seems to surface only when convenient. Not all Asian men are assumed to know kung-fu or karate. As far as Asian male stereotypes go, Asian men are either thought of as nerdy computer scientists or engineer types who lack basic social skills or martial arts jocks like Bruce Lee.[125]

The Asian-as-Martial-Artist stereotype links Asians to proficiency in karate, kung-fu, Tae-kwan-do, or some other martial art form from Asia. The image of the Asian male as martial artist became popular in the 1970s with a series of kung-fu films featuring the legendary Bruce Lee. The image has continued with a number of high-profile Asian martial arts actors such as Jackie Chan, Chow Yun Fat, and Jet Li. Even older Asian men such as Pat Morita (the elderly Japanese man in *The Karate Kid* who teaches his young pupil how to block, kick, and punch), are portrayed as possessing almost magical ability to defend themselves from attack and disable opponents.

The Asian-as-Martial-Artist stereotype has influenced some individuals to use deadly force against an Asian American they thought knew martial arts. Take, for example, Anthony Simon, who shot his next-door neighbor because he thought the Chinese American knew martial arts.

> Anthony Simon, an elderly White man, was afraid of his next-door neighbor, Steffen Wong, because Wong was Chinese and Simon assumed Wong

was an expert in the martial arts. The two men each owned half of the same duplex and had exchanged heated words in the past. The elderly Simon was also afraid of the changing demographics in the neighborhood. Many Asians were moving into the neighborhood. An Asian had even expressed interest in buying Simon's home. Simon was afraid of being surrounded by "Orientals." One day, as Wong was entering his own home, Simon pulled out a gun and, for no apparent reason, shot Wong.[126]

Simon was charged with two counts of aggravated assault. At trial, Simon argued that he shot Wong in self-defense. Simon explained that he thought Wong knew martial arts and posed an imminent threat of danger to Simon. The judge instructed the jury that "A person is justified in the use of force to defend himself against an aggressor's imminent use of unlawful force to the extent it appears reasonable to him under the circumstances then existing." Finding Simon's claim of self-defense credible, the jury acquitted Simon on both counts.

Although the verdict of acquittal can be explained by reference to the subjective standard of reasonableness used in the jury instruction,[127] it is shocking that a jury could conclude that Simon acted in self-defense when Wong did nothing to provoke the attack. It is all the more disturbing because Simon's self- defense claim was explicitly based on an incorrect assumption about Wong's proficiency in the martial arts.

The Asian-as-Martial-Artist stereotype may have also encouraged a police officer in Rohnert Park, California, to shoot and kill Kuan Chung Kao, a drunk Taiwanese American man who had no martial arts experience:

April 29, 1997. Kuan Chung Kao, a thirty-three-year-old Taiwan-born engineer, lived in Rohnert Park with his wife and three children. One evening, Kao went to the Cotati Yacht Club to celebrate a new job. Kao came to the club about twice a week, always in a suit and tie. Normally, he did not get drunk or act aggressively towards other patrons. That night, however, Kao did get drunk and also got into an altercation with another customer who referred to Kao as a Japanese person. Kao corrected him, saying that he was Chinese. The other customer responded, "You all look alike to me." The bartender separated the two men, seating them at opposite ends of the bar. A couple of hours later, the same customer who had upset Kao earlier said something else (which the bartender couldn't hear) that provoked Kao. According to customers, Kao became livid and began kicking and shouting, "I'm sick and tired of being put down because I'm Chinese. If you want to challenge me, now's the time to do it." A scuffle broke out and the Cotati police were called. By the time the police arrived, Kao had calmed down. The bartender talked the police out of taking Kao in. Kao was sent home in a taxi. There, Kao continued to shout from the driveway of his home. Neighbors called the police around 2:00 A.M., complaining that Kao was screaming and yelling in the street. By this time, Kao had taken off his shirt and was lying in the middle of the street, crying, "Oh my neighbors, help me." Kao then retrieved a six-foot long wooden stick from a motor home parked in his driveway and began waving it around.

Minutes later, Officer Mike Lynch arrived on the scene. Officer Lynch tried to scare Kao by shining the headlights of his patrol car on Kao, driving his car quickly towards Kao, then braking about three or four feet from Kao to avoid hitting him. Kao continued to yell and banged his stick on Officer Lynch's car.

Next, Officer Jack Shields pulled up to the scene. Officer Mike Lynch radioed to Officer Shields and advised him to stay in his car and wait for back-up. Instead, Shields got out of his patrol car and, without identifying himself as a police officer, ordered Kao to drop the stick. Kao, with a blood alcohol level of 0.23, kept hold of the stick, jabbing it towards Officer Shields and his patrol car. Kao's wife, Ayling Wu, came out of the house and tried to approach her husband to take the stick away from him, but Officer Shields ordered her to back off. Wu retreated and the next thing she knew, Shields had shot her husband in the chest. A mere thirty seconds had elapsed between the time Officer Shields got out of his car and his decision to shoot Kao. After Kao was shot, the officers handcuffed him and left him lying face down on the ground. Wu, a registered nurse, tried to give first aid to her husband, but the officers restrained her and threatened her with arrest. By the time paramedics arrived, it was too late to save Kao.[128]

After the shooting, the Sonoma County Sheriff's Office conducted an investigation into the homicide. The Office interviewed the two officers who were on the scene, neighbors, and others, and concluded that Officer Jack Shields shot Kao in self-defense.[129] Relying largely on the Sheriff's Office's report, the Sonoma County District Attorney's Office declined to press charges against Officer Shields, explaining that "the death of Kuan-Chung Kao was the result of Officer Shields' use of deadly force to protect himself from serious bodily harm or death."[130]

The U.S. Attorney's Office also declined to prosecute Officer Shields for lack of sufficient evidence.[131]

Officer Shields could have chosen less fatal means of resolving the situation. He could have either stayed in his police car as his partner advised or retreated there once he surveyed the situation. He could have called for backup or fired a warning shot. Instead, the officer fired within thirty seconds of getting out of his car. Despite these less deadly alternatives, Officer Shields's belief that he had to shoot Kao, an obviously drunk and overweight middle-aged man,[132] in order to protect himself from death or serious bodily injury, was considered reasonable.

In this case, like the *Simon* case, the shooting was precipitated by a false belief that the target, an Asian male, knew martial arts. In his interview with the Sheriff's Office, Officer Shields stated, "He was flipping it [in] what I would refer to as a martial arts-type of uh, moves. Things that I have seen in demonstrations and on T.V. . . . flipping it around, over, around his head . . . and around his back."[133] Officer Lynch told investigators that when he arrived on the scene, he saw an Asian male, about thirty to forty years old, carrying a pole which looked like a closet rod.[134] Lynch continued, "He was running around in a little circle and started spinning the pole around in his hands like you see a Ninja fighter do."[135] "I was real concerned about this guy on top of the fact that I didn't know if the guy had any other weapons aside from this staff he's, he's playing with, um, and you know, the, the thoughts that went in my mind when I saw him spinning the thing around, it was like the, the, um, the movies you see with martial arts guys, the, you know, the Ninja and stuff."[136] Some of Kao's neighbors also thought the drunk Asian man was acting "in a manner consistent with a Ninja fighter" and standing in a "Samurai warrior-type stance."[137]

In an effort to substantiate Officer Shields's claim of self-defense, the police obtained a search warrant immediately after the shooting to look for martial arts equipment and any evidence that Kao was a martial arts expert.[138] Normally, search warrants are sought to aid police in gathering evidence of a crime against a suspect. In this case, however, a search warrant was sought to search the home of a dead man who could not be charged with any crime relating to the incident. The search warrant, like the rest of the investigation into the shooting, seemed designed to help exonerate the officers.[139]

No evidence of martial arts equipment was found because Kao had no martial arts experience.[140] The lack of evidence to support Officer Shields's belief that Kao knew martial arts, however, did not preclude the Sheriff's Office from finding that his belief was reasonable. According to both the Sheriff's Office and the District Attorney, a drunk, overweight Asian man waving a stick posed a sufficient threat to justify shooting him to death.

# 7

# Race and Police Use of Deadly Force

In the old days, the cops simply shot their black victims and [planted] a weapon the officers carried for such emergencies. Nowadays, weapons need exist only in the mind of the policeman in [the] firing position.

—Les Payne, Journalist for *Newsday*[1]

February 4, 1999. About midnight. Amadou Diallo, a twenty- two-year-old immigrant from West Africa, had just come home to his South Bronx apartment at 1157 Wheeler Avenue after an evening of selling CDs, hats, gloves, and watches on Fourth Street. The front door of the apartment building, which was painted red, was propped open, giving the building a warm and inviting appearance, like an oasis in the middle of a desert.

Lingering for just a moment in the vestibule of his apartment building, Diallo suddenly heard the screeching of tires and saw four white men with guns pointed straight at him come pouring out of a car. One of the men yelled something at Diallo. Even though English was not his first language, Diallo's English was fairly good and usually he didn't have trouble understanding people. That night, however, the West African man couldn't understand what the man was shouting. The only thing he could think was that this was a hold-up and the men wanted his money.

Diallo reached into his back pants pocket and pulled out his wallet, offering it to the men in a desperate effort to be left alone. Instead, he heard someone shout, "Gun!" and the next thing he knew, the men were firing at him. Stunned, Diallo tried to remain standing for as long as he could, but the rain of bullets kept coming. Forty-one bullets in all. Nineteen of the forty-one bullets entered his body, searing him with unbelievable pain. One bullet perforated his aorta. Another struck his spinal cord. Another his lungs. Another his liver. Another his spleen. Another his kidney. Another his intestines. More than ten bullets struck his legs. Finally, he couldn't stand any more and collapsed. Even then the shooting didn't stop. Several minutes later, when it was apparent to all that Diallo would not be getting up again, the officers finally stopped shooting. But it was too late for apologies. Amadou Diallo was dead. And the men who killed him were not robbers, but "New York's finest"—police officers from the Street Crimes Unit.[2]

Police officers are rarely prosecuted for murder because most fatal police shootings are deemed justifiable by prosecutors who decline to prosecute or grand juries which decline to return indictments. The Diallo shooting, however, coming shortly on the heels of the brutal beating and sodomization of Abner Louima, a dark-skinned immigrant from Haiti, was too politically charged to be swept under the rug. The four officers who shot Amadou Diallo were charged with second-degree murder. A second-degree murder conviction would have resulted in a sentence of twenty-five years to life imprisonment. The charges were later broadened to give the jury the option of returning a guilty verdict on lesser charges, ranging from first-degree manslaughter (with a maximum twenty-five-year sentence) to criminally negligent homicide (which would have allowed a sentence of probation and no jail time).

At trial, the officers claimed Diallo's death was a justifiable homicide. The officers had been looking for a rape suspect. Diallo fit the description because he was Black and in the neighborhood where the rape occurred. According to the officers, Diallo brought the shooting upon himself because of his suspicious movements—peering up and down the street, retreating into the dimly lit vestibule, and not responding to the officers' demands that he stop and show his hands. When Diallo reached into his back pants pocket and pulled out a black object, the officers thought he had a gun. One officer started shooting. Hearing the bullets ricocheting around the vestibule, the other officers thought Diallo was shooting back. They were wrong. The black object was Diallo's wallet.

On February 25, 2000, a jury of four Black women, one White woman, and seven White men acquitted the four officers of all charges. Two of the jurors, one Black and one White, told reporters after the trial that their verdict had nothing to do with race.[3]

## RACE AND POLICE SHOOTINGS

It is undisputed that Blacks are disproportionately represented among the victims of police shootings. In a comprehensive review of the literature to date on police use of deadly force, James Fyfe reports that "every study that has examined this issue [has] found that blacks are represented disproportionately among those at the wrong end of police guns."[4] Although Blacks represent approximately 13 percent of the population in the United States, in parts of this country they constitute 60 to 85 percent of the victims of police shootings.[5] On average, Blacks are more than six times as likely as Whites to be shot by police,[6] and are killed by police at least three times more often than Whites.[7] Latinos (or Hispanics) are about twice as likely as Whites, but only half as likely as Blacks, to be shot and killed by police.[8] There is a noticeable lack of data regarding police use of force against other non-Black minorities, such as Asian Americans, Arab Americans, South Asian Americans, and Native Americans, which is why this chapter focuses on police use of deadly force against Blacks. However, reports by Amnesty International and Human Rights Watch suggest that these other minorities are also disproportionately on the receiving end of police force.[9]

While widespread consensus exists that racial minorities are disproportionately represented as victims of police shootings, the reason for this disproportion is hotly disputed. Most people who have an opinion on the subject fall within one of two camps, which John Goldkamp, in his study of race and police shootings, calls "Belief Perspective I" and "Belief Perspective II."[10] Proponents of "Belief Perspective I" believe that racism on the part of police officers and police departments results in one trigger finger for racial minorities and another for Whites.[11] According to this view, police officers intentionally single out racial minorities for harsher treatment. Proponents of "Belief Perspective II," in contrast, contend that race does not influence the average police officer's decision to use force. According to this perspective, Blacks and other non-Whites are disproportionately represented as victims of police shootings because they disproportionately commit armed robberies, carry firearms, and engage in behavior that police officers are likely to find threatening, such as resisting arrest.[12]

The bulk of the social science research on race and police use of deadly force supports the race-is-irrelevant position of "Belief Perspective II."[13] According to this research, a police officer's decision to shoot a suspect is influenced by nonracial factors, such as whether the suspect *appears* to be armed and whether he or she complies with police orders. However, as discussed in this chapter, racial stereotypes may influence officers to think certain persons are armed when they are actually unarmed.

In sharp contrast to the research suggesting that the race of the suspect does not affect the officer's decision to use force are the actual lived experiences of persons living in poor minority communities and the perception in these communities that race not only matters, but matters significantly. In the foreword to *Race and Criminal Justice*, Daniel Georges-Abeyie, an African-Puerto Rican/Virgin Islander professor of criminology, remarks, "Through my own real life experiences I know that the differential treatment of minorities occurs. I also know that it is more widespread than official statistics might indicate."[14] A few social science studies support the race-matters perspective of "Belief Perspective I."[15]

Those who are inclined to support Belief Perspective II might ask why we as a society should care about the beliefs of a minority of citizens, particularly if the bulk of social science research shows that officer decisions regarding the use of force are the result of nonracial considerations. We should care because actual or perceived unfairness and racial bias in law enforcement undermines police effectiveness. Simmering tensions between communities of color and the police, if unaddressed, can ignite into chaos like the rioting that erupted after the acquittals of the four Los Angeles police officers charged with the brutal beating of Rodney King. The post-verdict chaos was a wake-up call, serving as a reminder that just below the surface of apparent calm brews deep anger, resentment, and a feeling that the criminal justice system protects some folks better than others. As former Attorney General Janet Reno noted in an address at a conference on strengthening police-community relations in June 1999:

> Tensions between police and minority residents affect all aspects of the criminal justice system. When citizens do not trust their local police officer, they are less willing to report crime, and less willing to be witnesses in criminal cases. Jurors are less willing to accept as truthful the testimony of officers, and recruitment of officers from minority communities becomes that much more difficult.[16]

The problem with Goldkamp's two belief perspectives theory is that it explains the problem in an all or nothing way. Either police officers are bigots who intentionally target racial minorities (Belief Perspective I) or they are completely unbiased and color-blind (Belief Perspective II). The truth more likely lies somewhere between these two extremes.

Another way to explain the disproportion—a way that accommodates *both* the lived experiences of persons of color *and* the belief that police officers use force more often against persons of color because such individuals appear to be more threatening to the officer—is to acknowledge that racial stereotypes operate at a subconscious level to influence the police officer's decision to use deadly force.[17] The police officer does not consciously decide to use deadly force because of the suspect's race, but the suspect's race nonetheless influences the officer. Racial stereotypes may alter the officer's perception of danger, threat, and resistance to authority. A simple question, "Officer, why am I being stopped?" may be perceived as behavior challenging the officer's authority when asked by someone who is Black. Police officers may also "see" danger more readily when dealing with a person of color. Just as racial and ethnic stereotypes influence private citizen decisions to use force in self-defense, it is likely that such stereotypes also influence police officer decisions to use force.

I should note at the outset that I am not making any empirical claims regarding the extent to which racial stereotypes influence the police officer's decision to use force. I leave this to the social scientists who are trained in the methodologies of empirical and quantitative research. My purpose is merely to challenge the conventional wisdom that race does not influence the police officer's decision to use deadly force. Conventional wisdom suggests that police officers use deadly force only when necessary to protect themselves or others from death or serious bodily injury. We know this is the conventional wisdom because most fatal police shootings do not result in the filing of criminal charges or disciplinary action against the officer. In the rare case that is prosecuted, the officer is usually acquitted or, if convicted, given a sentence much lower than the penalty usually imposed on a private citizen who shoots and kills another person.

While there is substantial overlap between cases involving clear acts of police brutality without even the slightest suggestion of justification, such as the beating and sodomization of Abner Louima on

August 9, 1997, and cases in which police assert self-defense, such as the case concerning the beating of Rodney King, this chapter is *not* about clear acts of police brutality.[18] This chapter deals with the much more complicated subject of police use of force in claimed self-defense.

Claimed self-defense cases are troublesome because the officer may have sincerely believed in the need to use deadly force to protect himself or others from death or great bodily harm. It is hard to feel punitive toward someone who sincerely believed he was acting in self-defense. The law, however, requires that officers who claim self-defense must have more than just an honest belief in the need to act in self-defense. The officer's belief must also be reasonable or, as the courts have held, one that a reasonably prudent officer in the same situation would have held.

The reasonableness requirement can be helpful and problematic at the same time. On the one hand, the reasonableness requirement operates as a check on the officer's subjective beliefs. It ensures some objective standard against which the officer's personal beliefs are to be measured so that an officer's completely unfounded and irrational fears cannot justify actions that injure innocent citizens. On the other hand, the reasonableness requirement provides a way in which social attitudes and biases can influence the legal determination regarding the validity of police use of force. Racial stereotypes can make an officer's use of deadly force seem reasonable, when in the absence of such stereotypes the officer's actions would appear unjustified. If stereotypes encourage police officers to use deadly force against certain members of the community and not others, it is necessary to critically examine whether it is appropriate to call the officer's belief in the need to use force reasonable.

Addressing the problem of racial stereotypes influencing a police officer's perception of criminality and danger is a difficult task for several reasons. First, all police work requires some amount of stereotyping or generalizing about people based on external characteristics. Police officers in the field must quickly size up a suspect and make decisions about how to handle a situation. In making split-second decisions, officers often must rely on external cues, such as dress, demeanor, location, and race. Because some stereotyping is necessary, it is easy to think that any and all stereotyping is permissible.

The second problem lies in the deeply ingrained belief that the use of force is part and parcel of good police work. Police officers, as enforcers of the law, often need to use force in order to do their jobs. Most people feel police officers have a right to use force against uncooperative suspects. As Paul Chevigny notes, "We've all heard people say, 'Well, if the police have to kick a little butt in order to keep order, so be it.'"[19] Television shows like *NYPD Blue, America's Most Wanted, COPS,* and even *Law and Order* depict police officers as good guys who need to break the rules sometimes by roughing up suspects in order to get to the truth.

This chapter focuses on police use of force against Blacks because of the significant lack of published research on police use of force against other racial minorities. Although the focus here is on Black victims, it is important to remember that members of other minority groups also find themselves disproportionately at the receiving end of police force.[20]

## UNCONSCIOUS RACISM

At the entrance to the Museum of Tolerance in Los Angeles, California, one is presented with two doors. One door is labeled "prejudiced." The other is marked "unprejudiced." If one tries to enter the door marked "unprejudiced," one finds that the door is locked and one cannot enter the museum that way. The following message is then projected onto the door:

THINK . . . NOW USE OTHER DOOR.

We are all prejudiced—some to a greater degree, others to a lesser degree. Stereotypes, particularly those based on race, affect us all, influencing both the way we view others and the way we understand ourselves. Charles Lawrence comments on this shared experience:

> Americans share a common historical and cultural heritage in which racism has played and still plays a dominant role. Because of this shared experience, we also inevitably share many ideas, attitudes, and beliefs that attach significance to an individual's race and induce negative feelings and opinions about nonwhites. To the extent that this cultural belief system has influenced all of us, we are all racists. At the same time, most of us are unaware of our racism. We do not recognize the ways in which our cultural experience has influenced our beliefs

about race or the occasions on which those beliefs affect our actions. In other words, a large part of the behavior that produces racial discrimination is influenced by unconscious racial motivation.[21]

Americans attach significance to race. When a young Black male approaches and starts talking to us, we worry about getting robbed or conned. When we see an Asian woman, we think she is likely to be quiet and deferential to authority. When a Mexican man gets angry, we attribute his anger to machismo, something we believe Mexican men have as part of their cultural upbringing. Most of us are not aware that we make assumptions every day about people based on their race. We just do. We think of racism as the intentional acts and beliefs of a few, not something we all engage in. Yet, as Lawrence explains, "[r]acism is in large part a product of the unconscious."[22]

Lawrence offers two possible explanations for our unconscious racism. One explanation rests on psychoanalytic theory which suggests that the human mind defends against the discomfort of guilt by refusing to recognize beliefs that conflict with what the individual has learned is good or right. American society today embraces the principle of equality and rejects racism as immoral. When one experiences conflict between one's personal beliefs, which may be inegalitarian, and the principle of equality, the mind excludes racism from consideration.[23] The second explanation rests on cognitive psychology. Cognitive psychologists theorize that racism is transmitted by tacit cultural understandings. The media, one's parents, one's peers, and authority figures all communicate certain beliefs and preferences. A White child may never be told explicitly that Blacks are inferior but learn this lesson by observing the behavior of others.[24] For example, his parents may invite only White people to the house and not permit him to play with Black or Brown children. The child may infer from this behavior that non-Whites are unclean or untrustworthy.

When police officers shoot unarmed Black citizens, they may be responding to racial cues which link Blacks to criminality and violence. All of us are influenced by such racial cues, but police officers, more than private citizens, often find themselves in situations in which they have to respond quickly without thinking. Police officers often don't have time to evaluate whether or not they are responding to actual danger or assumptions based on a person's race.

Recent social science studies provide support for Lawrence's theory. These studies indicate that police shootings of unarmed Blacks are likely due to unconscious racism. In one recent study, Anthony Greenwald, Mark Oates, and Hunter Hoffman, psychology professors at the University of Washington in Seattle, sought to determine the extent to which police shootings of unarmed Black citizens "are due to reduced perceptual sensitivity (i.e., less ability to distinguish weapons from harmless objects when these objects are held by Blacks than by Whites) or increased response bias (i.e., increased tendency to respond to any object held by a Black as a weapon)."[25] Greenwald, Oakes, and Hoffman created a desktop virtual reality simulation in which subjects (University of Washington undergraduate students) were asked to play the role of a plainclothes police officer who has to rapidly respond to armed and unarmed persons. Subjects were given less than one second to respond to individuals from one of three categories of targets—criminals, fellow police officers, and citizens. All the targets appeared in street clothes, but criminals and police officers held guns while citizens held harmless objects, such as cameras, flashlights, and beer bottles. The only variable that distinguished police officers from criminals was their race.

Subjects played the simulation exercise twice. In one simulation, subjects were told that all the criminals were White and all the police officers were Black. In the second simulation, they were told that all the criminals were Black and all the police officers were White. Citizens could be either Black or White. Subjects were told to click the mouse button if they thought the target was a criminal with a gun, hit the space bar if they thought the target was a fellow officer with a gun, and do nothing if they thought the target was an innocent citizen with a harmless object in hand.

The researchers found that in both simulations, subjects had greater difficulty distinguishing weapons from harmless objects when dealing with Black targets than White targets.[26] Additionally, subjects shot at Black targets more often than White targets, "giving the weapon-appropriate response more readily to Black than to White targets."[27] Other recent studies have reached similar conclusions.[28]

## THE BLACK-AS-CRIMINAL STEREOTYPE

As discussed in chapter 6, one of the stereotypes most often applied to African Americans, particularly young Black males, is that they are more dangerous, more prone to violence, and more likely to be involved in criminal activity than other members of society.[29] Part of the reason why many people are fearful of Black men stems from statistics that show that Blacks are arrested and convicted at rates that greatly exceed their numbers in the general population.[30] Relying upon such statistics to support the argument that it is reasonable to fear a Black man when one would not necessarily fear a similarly situated White man is problematic. When the total number of Blacks arrested for violent crime is compared to the total number of Blacks in society, Blacks who are arrested for violent crime comprise less than 1 percent of the total Black population.[31] To assume that any Black person one runs into is likely to be a violent criminal attributes the criminality of a few Blacks to the entire Black population. Such generalization also overlooks the fact that most of the Blacks who are incarcerated are serving time for nonviolent drug offenses.[32] Despite the misleading nature of statistical information regarding Blacks and crime, the linkage between Blackness and criminality persists in the American imagination. As a number of social science studies have shown, people of all races tend to view Blacks as more dangerous and more threatening than Whites.[33]

Whites, in contrast, are not generally viewed as potential threats, even though there is no shortage of evidence that White people, particularly White men, have been responsible for a great deal of violence. Two White teenage boys were responsible for the deadly shooting at Columbine High School in Littleton, Colorado, in April 1999 that left thirteen dead and many more injured. The bombing of the Oklahoma City federal building in 1995 was the brainchild of a White man. Whites constitute more than two-thirds of all individuals arrested for criminal activity, and more than half of the individuals arrested for *violent* criminal activity.[34] Nonetheless, Whites generally are not feared because of their race. No White-as-Criminal stereotype exists in this society.

## CANDY BARS, KEYS, AND WALLETS: RACIALIZED FEAR AND THE IMAGINED GUN

The fear of Black individuals is so powerful that law enforcement officers often "see" guns in the hands of unarmed Black men and women. In 1997, a federal law enforcement officer shot a Black teenager because he thought the teen was carrying a gun. The teen was actually carrying a 3 Musketeers candy bar.

> November 6, 1997. Around 7:00 P.M. Queens, New York. Andre Burgess, a seventeen-year-old Black high school student, was walking to a friend's house with a 3 Musketeers candy bar in his right hand. Burgess was the goaltender and captain of the Hillcrest High School soccer team. At around 138th Avenue and 24th Street, Burgess passed an unmarked police car which contained undercover officers looking for a fugitive in a federal narcotics case. After passing the car, Burgess started to open the wrapper of his candy bar and lifted it to his mouth. Deputy Marshal William Cannon, a thirty-year-old White man who was sitting in the unmarked car, thought Burgess's silver foil-wrapped candy bar was a gun. Cannon jumped out of the car, pointed his gun at Burgess, and yelled, "Hey you. Hold on."[35] Burgess started to turn around to see who was yelling at him. Before Burgess could complete his turn, Cannon shot Burgess in the back of his left thigh. Burgess fell to the ground, bleeding. Cannon quickly handcuffed Burgess, then shook hands with other officers who had arrived on the scene. While Burgess was lying, handcuffed and bleeding, on the ground, he heard Deputy Marshal Cannon, completely oblivious to Burgess's pain, remark to one of the officers, "Don't I know you from some other case?"[36]

A Queens grand jury refused to return an indictment against Deputy Marshal Cannon, finding that the law enforcement officer *reasonably* believed the Black teenager posed an imminent threat of death or serious bodily injury to the officer or others. Responding to the grand jury's decision, Cannon's attorney, Lawrence Berger, said the grand jury did the right thing. "Our position is and has been that this was an unavoidable accident, one that Mr. Cannon felt horrible about. Nevertheless, if the matter occurred exactly the same way tomorrow, without the hindsight of knowing it was a candy bar in Mr. Burgess's hand, he [Cannon] would have reacted the same way."[37]

There are several disturbing aspects to this case. First, it is disturbing that a federal law enforcement officer could mistake a 3 Musketeers candy bar for a gun. If Deputy Marshal Cannon had watched Burgess a few seconds longer before initiating the confrontation, he might have realized the silver object in Burgess's right hand was a candy bar. Right before the shooting, Burgess had unwrapped the candy bar and was starting to take a bite out of it, hardly something he would do if the item in his hand was a gun. Second, given that Burgess had passed the un-marked police car and was walking away from it when Deputy Marshal Cannon jumped out of the car, it appears Burgess did not pose a threat to Cannon or any of the officers. Third, Burgess was shot in the back of his leg, undermining Cannon's claim that he shot Burgess in self-de-fense. The most disturbing thing about this incident was Cannon's at-torney's statement that if this same incident were to happen again, Cannon would react the same way.

This was not the first time that Deputy Marshal Cannon had been accused of using excessive force against a Black man. Three years before he shot Andre Burgess, Deputy Marshal Cannon was prosecuted for beating a handcuffed Black prisoner with a lead- filled leather pouch. At Cannon's trial, two former deputy marshals testified that he repeatedly struck the prisoner with an eight-inch leather pouch, known as a slap-jack, after the prisoner broke Cannon's nose while resisting an arrest. The two deputy marshals had firsthand knowledge of this attack be-cause they held the prisoner down so that Cannon could beat him. These two deputy marshals pleaded guilty to charges of conspiracy to obstruct justice, and were dismissed from their jobs. Cannon, in con-trast, was acquitted of all charges, and was never disciplined by the Marshal's Service for this beating.[38]

It would be easy to write off the shooting of Andre Burgess as an unfortunate but isolated incident caused by one bad cop. In fact, this is the reaction most people have when confronted with shocking exam-ples of excessive force by the police. When the beating of Rodney King was captured on home video and broadcast all across the nation, many Whites were shocked that such a beating by police officers, sworn to up-hold the law, could take place in America in the 1990s. The beating was seen as a horrible, tragic aberration. African Americans, by and large, were not shocked by the beating and saw it as just another example of the treatment they were used to receiving from the police. As others have noted, what was unique about the *Rodney King* case for Black America was not that the beating occurred, but that it was captured on home video. Now that more and more people have camcorders, the videotaping of police misconduct may become more common. In July 2002, for example, a White police officer in Inglewood, California, was caught on home video slamming a handcuffed African American teenager named Donovan Jackson into the trunk of a patrol car and beating him for no apparent reason.

Because so many incidents of police force against Blacks and other minorities go unreported, it is easy for those living comfortable lives in middle- or upper-class neighborhoods to believe that police abuse of force is uncommon. The U.S. Supreme Court reflects this type of ostrich-with-its-head-in-the-sand mentality when it treats acts of police brutality as aberrational or isolated incidents.[39] For example, in *City of Los Angeles v Lyons*,[40] the Supreme Court reversed a preliminary injunction issued by a lower federal court prohibiting Los Angeles police officers from using the chokehold unless threatened with death or serious bodily injury. The Court vacated the injunction on the ground that Adolph Lyons, a Black man who was stopped by Los Angeles police officers for a traffic violation and subjected to a chokehold which rendered him unconscious and damaged his larynx, lacked standing to sue since Lyons was not likely to be stopped again by the Los Angeles police and subjected to a chokehold. The Court's refusal to see Lyon's case as part of a pattern and practice by the Los Angeles police department was particularly disappointing in light of the fact that between 1975 and 1980, more than a dozen people, a significant number of whom were Black, died after being subjected to a chokehold by a Los Angeles police officer.[41]

Perhaps to the extent that a law enforcement officer mistook a candy bar for a gun, the Andre Burgess case is unique. However, to the extent that a law enforcement officer "saw" a weapon in an unarmed Black man's hand, it is not at all unique. Many unarmed Black men have been shot by law enforcement officers who thought, or claimed they thought, that the Black male suspect had a gun. Two months after Andre Burgess was shot, on Christmas day in 1997, another young Black man was shot and killed because a police officer thought he was armed. This Black man was "armed" with a set of keys.

December 25, 1997. About 1:00 P.M. Brooklyn, New York. Officer Michael Davitt was among a team of four police officers from the Brooklyn South Task Force responding to a report of a domestic dispute at the Glenwood House, a housing project in Carnegie, Brooklyn. As the officers neared the housing project, they heard what sounded like shots from the rooftop of one of the buildings and saw a Black man on a wall near the roof. As the police moved closer to the housing project, William Whitfield, a twenty-two-year-old black man, was leaving one of the apartments where his fiancée, Candy Williams, lived. Because Williams did not have a phone,

Whitfield was going to call his mother from a pay phone to tell her that he was bringing Williams and her children over for Christmas dinner. Whitfield had just given Williams a diamond ring and planned to marry her in 1998. As Whitfield came around the corner, he ran into Officers Davitt and Michael Dugan who ordered him to stop. Unbeknownst to the officers, Whitfield was wanted on three outstanding warrants for failing to appear in court on two misdemeanor assault charges and a marijuana possession charge. He also had some marijuana in his pocket that day. Whitfield knew that if he stopped, he would likely spend the rest of Christmas in jail rather than with his family, so he ran.

Officer Davitt shouted at Whitfield, "Stop!" to which Whitfield responded, "Not today." Whitfield raced into the Milky Way Supermarket at 1669 Ralph Avenue, and ran to the back of the store to hide behind an aisle of groceries. The officers followed quickly on Whitfield's heels with their guns drawn and ordered Whitfield to come out. When Whitfield did come out from behind the aisle with his hands up, Officer Davitt shot him once in the chest and killed him. Officer Davitt claimed that he saw a gleam of silver in Whitfield's hand and assumed Whitfield had a gun.[42]

Despite an exhaustive search, no gun was found at or anywhere near the scene of the police shooting. The only object found was a large ring of keys which Whitfield might have been clutching when he tried to surrender to police. Nonetheless, a grand jury found that Officer Davitt *reasonably* believed he or others were in imminent danger of death or serious bodily injury and refused to issue an indictment. Prior to shooting and killing William Whitfield, Officer Davitt had been involved in numerous police shootings.[43] He was named in twelve civilian complaints, seven of which alleged excessive force.[44] None of these complaints, however, resulted in disciplinary action.[45] In his personnel file, Officer Davitt had thirteen commendations for exceptional, meritorious, and excellent police duty.[46]

In July 1999, two San Jose police officers shot and killed a Black man named Odest Mitchell. The officers claimed they shot Mitchell because he suddenly stopped running and turned toward them with a metallic-looking object in his hand which they thought was a gun. Actually, he was carrying a pair of sunglasses and a set of keys.

July 1, 1999. Around 9:40 P.M. Salinas, California. San Jose Sergeant Thomas Murphy and Officer Anthony Mata were looking for a man named Odest

Mitchell who was wanted for a series of hotel and gas station robberies. Mitchell was nicknamed "The Leaper" by police because of his reputation for leaping over counters and quickly overpowering clerks. Acting on a tip, the officers tracked Mitchell to a gas station in Salinas where Mitchell was buying gas. The officers shouted at Mitchell to surrender, but instead he ran away from the officers towards a freeway off-ramp. The officers followed after him with their guns drawn. Suddenly, Mitchell stopped and turned towards the officers. The officers fired twelve shots at Mitchell. Six of these shots hit Mitchell and killed him.[47]

The officers explained that they fired at Mitchell because they saw a metallic object in his hand and thought it was a gun. A passing motorist who witnessed the shooting said he too thought Mitchell was carrying a metallic-looking object.[48] After an investigation into the shooting, the Monterey County District Attorney's Office concluded that the object in Mitchell's hand was a pair of sunglasses, but declined to file criminal charges against the officers.

The *Mitchell* case is a difficult one to judge because the officers were chasing a man who apparently had an extensive history of violent criminal activity. At the time of the shooting, Mitchell was suspected of being involved in fifteen armed robberies in the San Francisco Bay Area.[49] The two officers chasing Mitchell did not know whether Mitchell was carrying a weapon, but when he stopped running and turned toward them, they thought they saw something metallic that could have been a gun. That a passing motorist also thought he saw something metallic in Mitchell's hand bolsters the officers' claim that they reasonably believed Mitchell was armed and dangerous.

That Mitchell had an extensive criminal history was clearly a factor that influenced the officers' decision to shoot. However, even convicted felons have a right to life and a right to be tried by a jury of their peers.

It is always easy to criticize from the comfortable and safe position of an armchair long after an incident has taken place. Police officers on the street need to make quick decisions on a moment's notice. Many a police officer has been killed in the line of duty by a suspect who has not hesitated to shoot. The officers who shot Odest Mitchell no doubt were worried that Mitchell might try to shoot them in order to escape arrest. The point is simply that Mitchell's race and gender may have encouraged the officers to "see" something metallic in Mitchell's hand, rather than the pair of sunglasses he was actually carrying.

## RACIALIZED FEAR OF THE BLACK FEMALE

Young Black females have also been shot and killed by police officers who see them as a deadly threat. In June 1999, for example, a Chicago police officer shot and killed a young Black woman, thinking the woman was brandishing a gun. The woman was holding a black cellular phone in her hand when she was shot.

> June 4, 1999. Chicago, Illinois. LaTanya Haggerty, a twenty-six-year-old computer analyst at a downtown Chicago encyclopedia company and a graduate of Southern Illinois University, was the passenger in a 1986 Oldsmobile driven by Raymond Smith. Two officers noticed that the Oldsmobile was blocking traffic in the 8800 block of South Cottage Grove Avenue and asked Smith to move on. Smith backed up, almost hitting the officers, and then sped off. The officers fired shots at Smith's car and gave chase. Using his cellular telephone, Smith tried to reach his father. When he couldn't reach his father, Smith called his mother, who was hospitalized at Northwestern Memorial Hospital, to tell her that the police were chasing him. The police finally succeeded in blocking Smith's car in the 6400 block of King Drive. The officers ordered Smith and Haggerty to come out. Smith jumped out of the car and tried to run, while Haggerty, who was talking with Smith's mother on the cell phone, stayed in the vehicle. Officer Serena Daniels, also African American, was standing on the driver's side of the car near the rear door with her 9 millimeter Smith and Wesson aimed at Haggerty. Suddenly, Daniels fired. Haggerty screamed and cried out, "They shot me, Raymond." The bullet struck Haggerty's left shoulder, passed through her heart, lungs, and liver before stopping just beneath the skin under her right armpit. When officers opened the passenger side door, Haggerty tumbled face-first onto the sidewalk, the cell phone falling from her left hand. Officer Daniels knelt beside Haggerty, placed Haggerty's head on a leather coat, stroked Haggerty's bloody hair, and said, "I'm sorry. I didn't mean to shoot you. I thought you had a gun."[50]

Officer Daniels told investigators that she fired her weapon because she saw a shiny, silvery object in Haggerty's hand and thought Haggerty had a gun. According to an internal police report of the shooting, however, not one eyewitness corroborated Officer Daniels's contention that Haggerty was holding a shiny, silvery object in her hand that might have been mistaken for a gun.[51] All the eyewitnesses to the shooting, including a police officer standing on the passenger side of the car with his gun drawn and aimed at Haggerty, saw a black cell phone in Haggerty's hand, not a shiny object. One eyewitness said Haggerty had both hands in the air and was saying, "I'm getting out; I'm getting out," just before she was shot and killed.[52] Police did find a four-inch silver padlock, a device placed on a car's steering wheel to prevent theft, on the floor of the car on the passenger's side. However, no discernible fingerprints were on the lock, calling into question whether Haggerty was holding it when she was shot. It seems unlikely that Haggerty would have grabbed a car steering wheel lock while surrounded by police officers with guns drawn.

The *Haggerty* case is noteworthy for several reasons. First, it shows that the Black-as-Criminal stereotype is attributed to Black women as well as Black men. Second, it suggests that the stereotype can affect Black individuals' perceptions of other Blacks. Of course, just as in other cases, there is no way to prove that the stereotype influenced Officer Daniels to "see" a gun in LaTanya Haggerty's hand. As a Black woman herself, Officer Daniels should have been particularly sensitive to the fact that not all Black women are dangerous or violent. Nonetheless, in the heat of the moment, Officer Daniels thought a cell phone looked like a gun. Would she have "seen" a gun if the girl in the car had been a blond or a redhead?

That non-White police officers use force against non-White suspects just as much as their White police officer counterparts is used by some as support for the argument that the problem of police use of force against minorities is not a problem of racial discrimination or bias. Hubert Locke rejects this proposition, explaining that "the studies suggest that residential and deployment patterns in many jurisdictions place officers of color in exceptionally dangerous places—where they are, more than fellow white officers, likely to have to use deadly force *legitimately*, both on and off duty."[53] Others have offered the suggestion that "the overaggressive peer culture of policing in some agencies is so strong that it pressures Black officers, who might know better, into abusing minority-race citizens."[54]

In another case involving a Black female victim, an unconscious young Black woman with a gun on her lap in a car was shot and killed by Riverside police officers.

Monday, December 28, 1998. Riverside, California. After midnight. Tyisha Miller, a nineteen-year-old Black teenager, was returning home from a night out with friends when she discovered that the car she was driving, a White Nissan Sentra belonging to her aunt, had a flat tire. Miller was in the car with her best friend, Bug. A man stopped to help the two girls change the flat tire, but they discovered that the spare tire was also flat. The man followed Tyisha and Bug to a nearby gas station, then drove Bug to a friend's house so she could call for help. Uncomfortable with being left alone at a gas station at such a late hour, Tyisha got back into her car, locked the doors, and waited with an inoperable .38-caliber handgun on her lap to discourage potential attackers. She felt cold and a little dizzy. Tyisha turned on her emergency hazard blinkers and kept the engine running so she could keep the heater and radio on, then reclined the driver's seat and began to doze.

In the meantime, Bug safely made it to a friend's house and called Tyisha's home. She spoke with Antonette Joiner, Tyisha's cousin, and told Antonette that Tyisha was at a gas station on Brockton Avenue with a flat tire and needed help. Antonette and her friend, Chilean King, rushed to the gas station. When they arrived, they found Tyisha lying unconscious in the front driver's seat of her car with a gun on her lap. Tyisha appeared to be in some kind of medical distress as she was shaking, rolling her eyes, and drooling at the mouth. The girls tried to get Tyisha's attention by knocking on the car window, but when Tyisha failed to respond, Antonette called Tyisha's aunt and asked her to send someone with an extra set of car keys. Chilean called 911, explaining to the dispatcher that Tyisha seemed in need of medical attention.

Instead of sending an ambulance to the scene, the dispatcher sent four officers and a Sergeant from the Riverside County police department. The officers arrived at the gas station shortly before 2:00 A.M. Less than seven minutes later, they had unleashed more than twenty bullets into the car, killing Tyisha Miller.[55]

It is unclear exactly what happened just before Tyisha Miller was shot and killed. Initially, the officers claimed they started shooting because Tyisha fired the first shot. After an investigation failed to uncover any shell casings ejected from Tyisha's gun and an autopsy showed there was no gun residue on Tyisha's hands, the officers backed down from this initial claim and instead maintained they shot Tyisha when she reached for the gun on her lap.

The District Attorney's investigation into the shooting is very revealing.[56] According to the District Attorney's report, after the officers failed to wake Tyisha up by shouting at her and shaking her car, Officer Wayne Stuart tried to break the driver's side window by hitting it with his baton. This attempt too failed. However, the sound of Officer Stuart's baton hitting the car window roused Tyisha. She sat up in a daze, picked up her pager, and looked at it. One officer yelled at the others to hold their fire. The other officers backed away from the car. Tyisha then lay back down.

Officer Daniel Hotard, who was standing next to the driver's window, used his baton to break the window, then reached into the car in an attempt to retrieve Tyisha's gun. Suddenly, Officer Hotard heard a shot close to his ear. Believing he had been shot, Officer Hotard threw himself to the ground. Seeing Hotard hit the ground, the other officers assumed Tyisha had shot Hotard and began firing at Tyisha. Hotard too began firing. Actually, Officer Paul Bugar had fired the first shot. Although he couldn't see the gun on Tyisha's lap because of the shattered glass, Officer Bugar said he fired because he saw Tyisha's arm move and thought she was reaching for her gun.

Given the inoperability of Tyisha's gun, the absence of shell casings from that gun, and the lack of gun residue on Tyisha's hands, it is clear that she did not fire her gun at Officer Hotard or any other officer. Yet, Officer Hotard heard a shot and assumed Tyisha had shot him. Officer Hotard linked the shot from his fellow officer's gun with an imaginary shot from the unconscious, but nevertheless fear-inspiring, nineteen-year-old Black female teenager. It is worth nothing that Tyisha's hair was cropped very short at the time of the shooting, and the officers may have mistaken her for a young Black man. Officer Hotard never *saw* Tyisha reach for her gun. He *heard* a loud noise which he assumed was Tyisha shooting at him. The other officers, responding to Hotard's fear, assumed the young Black woman with a gun had fired it at their colleague. This is why the initial police explanation for the shooting was that Tyisha shot first. When the evidence to support this claim did not turn up, the explanation shifted and two officers began to claim they started shooting because they saw Tyisha reach for her gun.

We will never know whether Tyisha Miller in fact reached for her gun that night. Antonette Joiner, Tyisha's cousin, who was present throughout the entire shooting, claims Tyisha never moved. However, Joiner was thirty feet away from the car and if Tyisha was reclined in the driver's seat, it would have been difficult for Joiner to see movement below the driver's side window. Tyisha could have made a completely innocent move that the officers interpreted as a move for her gun.

In some ways, it doesn't really matter whether Tyisha reached for her gun. The officers could have handled the situation with more care and with an eye toward avoiding the use of deadly force. The officers might have foreseen that shattering the driver's side car window with an unconscious or sleeping person inside the car on the driver's seat might startle the person within. The officers had seen how the first unsuccessful attempt to break the window had roused Tyisha. It is unfortunate that the officers did not stop to consider other, less risky ways to handle the situation. They might have asked if anyone from Tyisha's family had an extra set of car keys and could bring them to the gas station. If they had done this, they would have learned that someone from the family was on the way with an extra set of car keys to open the car door. One wonders why the officers did not attempt to use a coat hanger or other device to get into the car without frightening Tyisha.

In May 1999, the Riverside County District Attorney's Office announced that no criminal charges would be filed against any of the officers involved in the shooting death of Tyisha Miller.[57] In announcing the decision not to file charges, Riverside County District Attorney Grover Trask said the officers made a "mistake in judgment," but were not criminally liable for their actions. Trask also stated, "There is no evidence whatsoever that these four officers killed Tyisha Miller because of her race."[58] The four officers involved in the shooting were fired on July 12, 1999.[59]

Compare this case to the way San Diego police and California Highway Patrol officers handled a potentially dangerous situation just six months later. This incident involved a White woman who led police on a lengthy car chase after she had threatened another motorist with a gun.

> July 1, 1999. 10:30 A.M. San Diego County, California. Janet Lucero, a fifty-eight-year-old White woman, was in a long line of cars heading down Valley Grade in Valley Center near Escondido. A truck in front of Lucero was moving very slowly, forcing Lucero to repeatedly hit the brakes on her dull blue 1983 Honda Civic coupe. Lucero tried to pass the truck, and in the process, cut in front of motorist Roberta Nielson. The thirty-three-year-old

Nielson followed Lucero's car until both cars pulled into the parking lot of a Burger King in Escondido. Nielson got out of her car and walked to the driver's side of Lucero's car to demand an explanation for Lucero's almost causing an accident. The argument escalated into a shouting match. Nielson backed off and called the police after Lucero pulled out a .38 caliber revolver and pointed it at her.

Escondido police and California Highway Patrol (CHP) officers caught up with Lucero who refused to obey police orders to pull over. Lucero led officers on a slow-speed chase down Interstate 15 to Kensington (part of the city of San Diego) and then back up to the North County. CHP officers tried to stop Lucero several times with a spike strip, hoping to deflate her tires, but each time she evaded the spike strip. Once she even swerved toward the officer laying the strip, but did not hit him.

About noon, Lucero collided with a police car on Highway 78 in San Marcos. A bomb squad robot dispatched by the San Diego County Sheriff's Office to stand beside Lucero's car confirmed that Lucero was armed. Law enforcement officers surrounded Lucero with patrol cars and a special armored vehicle. From a safe distance with their guns drawn, the officers ordered Lucero to surrender. Lucero, however, refused to leave her car for almost seven hours. Because Lucero came to a stop on a freeway which served to connect the two most well-traveled north-south freeways in San Diego, traffic on several major freeways was backed up and at a standstill for nearly six hours. At one point, Lucero lifted her handgun, without her finger on the trigger, to show the officers that she was armed. After that, she alternately flashed her gun at the officers, laid it on her lap, then gripped it with her finger on the trigger.

Finally, Lucero came out of her car and walked toward authorities, first with one hand in her front shorts pocket, then with both hands in the air. Lucero was taken into custody without incident.[60]

Lucero was charged with reckless driving, resisting arrest, evading police, assault on a peace officer, and brandishing a firearm.[61] On March 13, 2000, Lucero finally went to trial. The jury acquitted her of most of the criminal charges, but convicted her of refusing to surrender to police, a felony offense, and fleeing police during the chase, a misdemeanor.[62] One juror expressed sympathy for Lucero by describing her as "this little grandmother type."[63] The judge was less sympathetic and sentenced Lucero to three years in prison.[64]

It turns out that Lucero was not simply a kind, elderly, White woman with a gun used for self-protection. She had a history of threatening behavior. In 1995, she flashed a handgun at another motorist in Ramona. Several months later, in a confrontation with a California Highway Patrol officer, she threatened to "get a .357 Magnum and blow him away." She also wrote Ramona court officials a letter, threatening to come after them with a .357 Magnum.[65] On July 1, 1999, even though Lucero had driven her car toward an officer laying a spike strip, endangering his life, and then taunted officers by flashing her gun at them with her finger on the trigger, Lucero was not viewed as a deadly threat. Black men and women have been shot and killed for far less threatening behavior.

Because of the timing of the two incidents, it is difficult to know whether the San Diego officers held their fire when dealing with Janet Lucero because they did not want to receive the same kind of criticism leveled at the Riverside officers who had shot Tyisha Miller, or whether they held their fire because Lucero was a middle-aged White woman with a gun as opposed to a young Black woman with a gun. At least some people thought Lucero was treated differently because of her race. Recall that when Lucero came out of her car to surrender, she had one hand in her pocket. The officers held their fire rather than jumping to the conclusion that the hand in the pocket was ready to pull out the gun the officers knew existed. Timothy Winters, a former San Diego police officer, now pastor of the Bayview Baptist Church, commented, "Did you see her put her hands in her pockets when she came out of the car? If [she] had been an African-American, she would not have just been gently taken away. She would've either been ordered to hit the deck . . . or the guns would've been blazing."[66]

At one point during the standoff, Lucero leaned forward while sitting in her car and reached down. An officer ready to perceive a threat might have interpreted this movement as Lucero reaching for the gun police officers knew she had in her car. Rather than jumping to the conclusion that this forward and downward movement meant that Lucero was reaching for her gun, the officers held their fire long enough to see that Lucero was merely rolling down the car window to get some air. Had Lucero been Black, the officers might have handled the situation quite differently.

Aswon Watson, a Black man, reached down and below the driver's seat of his car while surrounded by officers, and was not as fortunate as

Lucero. Unlike the officers surrounding Lucero, who *knew* she had a gun, these officers did not know whether Watson had a gun in his car. But when they saw Watson lean forward, they assumed he was reaching for a gun and quickly started firing into the car. It turns out they were wrong.

> June 13, 1996. Undercover officers Keith Tierney and James Gentile from the Brooklyn 67th Precinct's anti-crime unit saw a White Honda they thought had been carjacked. The officers blocked the car with their unmarked patrol car and approached. Aswon Watson, a Black man, was in the driver's seat of the car. According to one witness, one of the officers shouted, "Freeze, nigger. You're dead!" Watson froze, both hands outstretched on his car steering wheel. Another officer yelled at Watson to come out of the car with his hands up. Instead, Watson started to reach down and under the driver's seat. The officers responded by firing twenty-four rounds into Watson's car. Eighteen bullets hit Watson, killing him.[67]

A subsequent investigation revealed that a car steering wheel lock, not a gun, was under the driver's seat. Nonetheless, a grand jury found that the officers were justified in shooting Watson because it was *reasonable* for the officers to have believed their lives were in danger.

### TIMOTHY THOMAS

When I started writing this book, Amadou Diallo had just been shot and killed by New York City police officers who thought his wallet was a gun. In the wake of the controversy that case engendered, I did not expect another police shooting of an unarmed Black man to happen so quickly. I suppose I hoped the shooting would lead police officers throughout the nation to take additional precautions against killing innocent Black men.

Perhaps it did. Nonetheless, on April 7, 2001, Cincinnati became the scene of another racially tinged police homicide.

> April 7, 2001. 2:00 A.M. Nineteen-year-old Timothy Thomas was visiting his girlfriend, Monique Wilcox, and their three-month-old son in Over-the-Rhine, a high-crime neighborhood near downtown Cincinnati. Thomas went out to get a pack of cigarettes at a nearby convenience store. On the

way back, Thomas passed a nightclub. One of the club's security guards, an off-duty police officer, recognized Thomas as the subject of fourteen arrest warrants, most for minor traffic offenses. For no apparent reason, Thomas began running from the guard. During the ensuing minutes, Thomas sprinted through a parking lot, scaled two chain-link fences, and dashed into an alley. Several officers, including Officer Stephen Roach, joined in the chase. Officer Roach entered the alley with his 9 millimeter Smith and Wesson drawn and his finger on the trigger. He called out, "Show me your hands!" but before Thomas could comply, Roach shot him in the chest.[68]

Officer Roach's initial explanation for the shooting was that it was an accident. When three fellow officers arrived on the scene, Roach told them, "It just went off. It just went off."[69] Later that day, when questioned by homicide investigators, Roach changed his story. Now his reason for shooting was self-defense. According to Roach, "Thomas had extended a clenched fist, he couldn't see what was in the fist, and he feared for his life."[70] Three days later, when homicide investigators confronted Roach with a videotape recorded by another police unit at the scene which indicated that Roach fired his weapon less than four seconds after entering the alley, Roach returned to his initial explanation that the shooting was accidental.[71] In the ensuing weeks, Roach went back to his claim of self-defense, telling friends and coworkers that he shot Thomas because he thought Thomas was reaching for a gun in his waistband.[72]

It is unclear why Thomas started running in the first place. His mother told one reporter that about a year before his death, Timothy, his cousin, and a few other men were standing in front of the building where they lived when they were suddenly accosted by several policemen. The officers slammed the young men against the wall and then threw them onto the ground. The officers then jammed their knees into the backs of the young men, pulled their arms back, cuffed them, and searched them. Finding nothing, the officers let the men go. A few months later, Timothy was walking to the grocery store when he, along with five or six other young men, was again accosted by police officers and forced to lie face down on the pavement. Timothy's mother told reporter Mark Singer, "My son had a fear of police officers. His thing was, 'Mom, if they could do this to me in broad daylight with everybody watching, what would they do in the dark?'"[73]

Thomas's death sparked three days and four nights of protests and violence in Cincinnati. Many in the African American community saw Thomas's death as part of a pattern and practice of police brutality against African American males. Thomas was the fifteenth Cincinnati police homicide victim in only six years. All fifteen of these Cincinnati police shooting victims were Black.[74]

On May 8, 2001, a grand jury returned an indictment, charging Roach with only two misdemeanors: negligent homicide (carrying a maximum possible sentence of six months in jail) and obstructing official business (carrying a maximum penalty of ninety days in jail).[75] The case went to trial in September. Roach waived his right to a jury trial, electing to have his fate determined by Municipal Judge Ralph Winkler. On September 26, 2001, Judge Winkler acquitted Roach of all charges, explaining that he believed the officer had acted reasonably in self-defense.[76] As for Roach changing his explanation for the shooting, the judge said the discrepancies in his story were not substantial.[77]

# PART III

# RETHINKING REASONABLENESS

# 8

# The Elusive Meaning of Reasonableness

AFTER THE SEPTEMBER 11 ATTACKS on the World Trade Center and the Pentagon, in an effort to tighten security, Congress passed legislation requiring that security screeners at U.S. airports be U.S. citizens employed by the federal government.[1] According to the *Washington Post,* seventeen hundred federal screeners were hired as of May 1, 2002.[2] The overwhelming majority of the newly hired employees were White, two-thirds were male, 58 percent had college degrees, and 60 percent had military backgrounds. Commenting on the new airport security personnel, John Magaw, former Undersecretary of Transportation for Security, told the *Washington Post,* "They look like America."[3]

Actually, the new screeners do not look like America. America is not a place where the overwhelming majority of people are White males with college degrees and military backgrounds. When jurors are instructed to compare the defendant's beliefs or actions to those of the Reasonable Person, they too may imagine the Reasonable Person as well-educated, White, heterosexual, middle-class, and male, even though this image may not be an accurate reflection of the average or ordinary person who lives in America.[4]

Even though we live in a heterogeneous society with peoples of different cultural and religious backgrounds, different income levels, and different outlooks on life, the law assumes the existence of a typical or average person whom it calls the Reasonable Person. One example of this is reflected in Guido Calebresi's description of the Reasonable Man in tort law as "the man who takes the magazines . . . home and in the evening pushes the lawn mower in his shirt sleeves."[5]

Nancy Ehrenreich deconstructs this image of the Reasonable Man, arguing that the man in his shirt sleeves conveys a message of mediation, but in fact excludes and renders invisible certain viewpoints.[6] Ehrenreich explains how the image conveys a message of mediation:

In socioeconomic terms, the reasonable person depicted in this image is a member of neither the elite nor the underclass. The T-shirted, grass-smattered, sweaty condition of a man mowing his lawn is not usually associated with a life of wealth and leisure. Nor, on the other hand, does the average service industry worker or welfare mother own a home with a lawn, or have an office at which to receive magazines (receiving them at home instead). The symbol's identification with the middle American thus conveys the idea of mediation and compromise between these two extremes.[7]

Ehrenreich explains why, despite this message of mediation and compromise, the image of the man in his shirt sleeves is problematic. The man in his shirt sleeves seems neutral and objective, but actually "ignor[es] the existence of people who have no lawn to mow and cannot read or afford to buy magazines—as well as the existence of those who hire someone else to mow the lawn for them."[8] The image "promotes the illusion that we are all the same, rendering invisible those who differ from the 'average' person it creates."[9]

Of course we are not all the same. Some people fit the mold of an ordinary American better than others. Whites fit the mold better than Blacks and other minorities. Men fit the mold better than women. Individuals born in the United States fit the mold better than foreign-born immigrants. Heterosexual men and women fit the mold better than gays and lesbians.

## WHO IS THE REASONABLE MAN ANYWAY?

When reasonableness standards first started appearing in criminal law cases, courts would instruct jurors to compare the defendant's beliefs and actions to those of the reasonable *man*.[10] The Reasonable Man was supposed to represent a completely objective standard against whom the defendant would be measured, and may have seemed appropriate at a time when most individuals charged with violent crime were male. Nonetheless, this gender-specific standard was also applied in cases involving female defendants.[11] Eventually, courts began to replace Reasonable Man language with gender-neutral Reasonable Person language.

The movement from Reasonable Man to Reasonable Person did not resolve many questions. Just who is the Reasonable Person? Is he (or she) the person who exercises good judgment and acts with good reason or is s/he just the ordinary or average person?[12] Should courts employ a completely objective standard of reasonableness, a completely subjective standard of reasonableness, or something in between?[13] Which, if any, of the defendant's characteristics should be incorporated into the Reasonable Person standard?

The question whether reasonableness standards ought to be objective or subjective is part of a larger debate over whether the criminal law should focus on the objective harm caused by the defendant or the defendant's subjective mental state or culpability.[14] Objectivists believe the most important factor in determining criminal liability is whether an individual has caused social harm, either by engaging in bad conduct or causing bad results. Under this view, a person who robs a bank and kills someone in the process is more culpable than one who robs a bank but doesn't kill. A person who bombs a building is more culpable than one who attempts to bomb a building, but doesn't carry out his plan. The objectivist position is reflected in the felony murder rule which holds a felon strictly liable for unintentional killings that occur during the commission or attempted commission of certain qualifying felonies. Under this rule, a bank robber whose gun goes off accidentally during the holdup, killing a customer, is guilty of murder while a bank robber who pulls off his robbery without killing anyone is only guilty of robbery. It is also reflected in sentencing schemes that punish completed crimes more severely than attempts.

Subjectivists, in contrast, believe that criminal liability should focus on what was going on inside the defendant's mind at the time of his wrongful act. A subjectivist would say that a defendant who intends to cause social harm is more culpable than one who acts recklessly, and a defendant who acts recklessly is more culpable than a defendant who acts negligently. Subjectivists believe that a person who plans to bomb a building, but is caught before he executes his plan, is just as culpable as someone who actually bombs the building.

The criminal law resolves this debate between objectivity and subjectivity by requiring, as a general matter, both objective social harm *and* subjective fault or culpability. In most cases, a defendant cannot be convicted of a crime unless he engages in a voluntary act that causes social harm (the actus reus requirement) and performs this act with a culpable state of mind (the mens rea requirement).

A similar compromise has taken place with respect to the narrower question of whether courts should employ an objective or a subjective standard of reasonableness. Most courts today employ what I call a hybrid subjectivized-objective standard of reasonableness. Under this hybrid standard, some but not all of the defendant's characteristics are taken into account when evaluating the reasonableness of the defendant's beliefs and actions. The only question is which of the defendant's characteristics and circumstances should be taken into account.

It is somewhat misleading to talk about objective and subjective standards of reasonableness, as if one must choose one standard or the other. It is more accurate to think of reasonableness in terms of gradations of objectivity.[15] Nonetheless, a discussion of what is generally meant by objective and subjective standards of reasonableness can help illuminate problems with both extremes.

A purely objective standard of reasonableness is one that excludes consideration of any of the defendant's particular characteristics. Under such a standard, the defendant is compared to the Reasonable Person devoid of gender, race, culture, religion, and any particular physical strengths or weaknesses. Of course, no person is devoid of identifying characteristics. The Reasonable Person as well is not devoid of identifying characteristics. The Reasonable Person in the American imagination has a race, class, sexual orientation, and gender—all presumed ordinary.

One danger that inheres when one attempts to utilize a purely objective standard is that such a standard is particularly susceptible to juror bias.[16] When the Reasonable Person is stripped of identifying characteristics, jurors, who see themselves as reasonable people, simply put themselves in the shoes of the defendant and decide whether they would have felt or acted the way the defendant did. The problem is that jurors come to the courtroom with their own particular biases and perspectives, usually unaware that they see the world through biased lenses. The more the defendant looks and acts like the juror, the more the juror is likely to see the defendant's beliefs and actions as reasonable. If the jury is predominantly heterosexual and White, the Reasonable Person in the jury's imagination will likely also be heterosexual and White.

At the other end of the reasonableness spectrum is another legal fiction—a purely subjective standard of reasonableness. Under such a standard, the Reasonable Person is imbued with the defendant's race, gender, class, level of education, and other personal characteristics. If, however, the Reasonable Person has all the defendant's characteristics, the reasonableness standard simply collapses. A standard that incorporates all the defendant's personal characteristics allows the defendant's perspective to control the reasonableness determination. Under such a standard, if the defendant thinks his beliefs and actions are reasonable, the Reasonable Person with all the defendant's characteristics will likely feel the same.

It seems oxymoronic to talk about a subjective standard of reasonableness, because reasonableness suggests some level of objectivity whereas subjectivity suggests a lack of objectivity. Nonetheless, subjective standards of reasonableness are employed in the criminal law.[17] For example, the Model Penal Code utilizes a subjective standard of reasonableness in its approach to provocation. In jurisdictions which have adopted the Code's extreme emotional disturbance defense, the defendant's emotional outrage need not be objectively reasonable in order for the defendant to receive the manslaughter mitigation. The defendant need only have actually (or subjectively) suffered from an extreme mental or emotional disturbance for which there is a reasonable explanation or excuse.[18] The inclusion of a reasonableness requirement gives the impression of an objective standard, but because the Code directs that reasonableness be determined from the viewpoint of a person in the defendant's situation under the circumstances as he (the defendant) believes them to be, the standard is basically subjective.[19]

Subjective standards are problematic because they provide no external check on the appropriateness of an individual's reasons for using deadly force. When reasonableness is determined from the defendant's perspective, the reasonableness requirement simply collapses into the honesty requirement and becomes superfluous. For example, in *State v. Simon,* discussed in chapter 6, an elderly White homeowner shot his Chinese American next-door neighbor as the neighbor was entering his own home because he thought the neighbor, solely because of his Asian heritage, knew martial arts. The trial court gave the jury an instruction on self-defense which included a subjective standard of reasonableness:

> A person is justified in the use of force to defend himself against an aggressor's imminent use of unlawful force to the extent it appears reasonable to him under the circumstances then existing.[20]

Even though it was completely unreasonable for Mr. Simon to believe that he was in any danger from his next-door neighbor as he was entering his own home, the jury acquitted him on all counts. The judge's instruction to the jury, telling them that Mr. Simon was justified in using force to defend himself *"to the extent it appear[ed] reasonable to him,"* almost directed the jury to find in Mr. Simon's favor. Mr. Simon thought it was reasonable to fear imminent harm from his neighbor, and therefore his fear was reasonable. Subsequently, the Kansas Supreme Court ruled that the trial court's use of a subjective standard of reasonableness was improper,[21] but because the double jeopardy clause of the U.S. Constitution prevents retrial following an acquittal, Mr. Simon's acquittal was left in place.

In the *Goetz* case, discussed at length in chapter 6, New York's highest court had to decide whether New York's standard of reasonableness in self-defense doctrine was a subjective or an objective standard. The court below had interpreted the term "he reasonably believes" as requiring only that the defendant's beliefs were reasonable to him. In reversing, the Court of Appeals of New York explained that the lower court's standard "would hardly be different from requiring only a genuine belief; in either case, the defendant's own perceptions could completely exonerate him from any criminal liability."[22] The court went on to explain why a subjective standard was problematic:

> We cannot lightly impute to the Legislature an intent to fundamentally alter the principles of justification to allow the perpetrator of a serious crime to go free simply because that person believed his actions were reasonable and necessary to prevent some perceived harm. To completely exonerate such an individual, no matter how aberrational or bizarre his thought patterns, would allow citizens to set their own standards for the permissible use of force. It would also allow a legally competent defendant suffering from delusions to kill or perform acts of violence with impunity, contrary to fundamental principles of justice and criminal law.[23]

Besides the states that follow the Model Penal Code's completely subjective test for self-defense, North Dakota seems to be the only state today that embraces a subjective standard of reasonableness in self-defense cases.[24] In North Dakota, a defendant who honestly believes in the need to act in self-defense may be completely acquitted even if his (or her) beliefs were not reasonable. In *State v. Leidholm*, the Supreme Court of North Dakota explained:

> [A] defendant's conduct is not to be judged by what a reasonably cautious person might or might not do or consider necessary to do under the like circumstances, but what he himself in good faith honestly believed and had *reasonable* ground to believe was necessary for him to do to protect himself from apprehended death or great bodily injury.[25]

## WHICH CHARACTERISTICS OF THE DEFENDANT SHOULD BE INCORPORATED?

Since most jurisdictions utilize a hybrid subjectivized-objective standard, a critical question is which of the defendant's characteristics are or should be incorporated into the Reasonable Person standard? If the defendant is a forty-year-old man, should he be compared to the average forty-year-old adult male or just the average adult male? Are forty-year-old adult men likely to think and act differently than fifty-five-year-old adult men? Are they likely to think and act differently than twenty-five-year-old adult men? If the defendant was intoxicated at the time of the criminal act, should he be compared to the average intoxicated individual or the average sober individual? If the defendant is a woman who was physically and emotionally abused by her spouse, should she be compared to the average man, the average woman, or the average battered woman? Is it even possible to reduce people into averages and say that there exists an average man, woman, or person?

A cursory review of the cases suggests that courts draw a distinction between physical and mental attributes,[26] incorporating the defendant's physical attributes, such as gender, age, physical ability and/or disability, but not his or her mental attributes.[27] A fifteen-year-old boy will be compared to the average fifteen-year-old boy. A woman with a broken leg who feels threatened by a large unarmed man will be compared to the average woman with a broken leg, not the average woman with full use of both legs.[28] A blind man will be compared to the average blind man, not the average man who can see. An individual with paranoid schizophrenia, however, generally will not be compared to the average paranoid schizophrenic because paranoid schizophrenia is a mental rather than a physical attribute.[29]

Despite its apparent ease of application, the physical-mental distinction is of limited utility because it does not provide adequate guidance in hard cases. Many things do not fall neatly on one side or the other of the physical-mental divide. For example, most lay people and a fair number of judges and lawyers think of race as a physical or biological attribute.[30] Under the physical-mental distinction, physical attributes of the defendant are supposed to be incorporated into the Reasonable Person standard, yet when the defendant is a racial minority, the defendant's race is rarely considered as part of the reasonableness inquiry. The jury deciding the fate of a young Black male defendant charged with murdering a White man who called him the N word generally is not instructed to compare the defendant to the reasonable young Black male.

Another example of an attribute that sits at the border between physical and mental is the battered woman who kills her abusive male partner. Should the fact that a woman has been physically abused be incorporated into the reasonableness inquiry? On the one hand, one could argue that bruises and scars on the body of the abused victim are physical attributes and thus, the fact of physical abuse which caused these injuries should be incorporated. On the other hand, abuse is not so much a physical attribute of the female defendant as something she has experienced. Expert testimony on battered woman syndrome is often presented to suggest that the abused woman suffers from something akin to post-traumatic stress disorder, a mental condition. Even though the physical-mental distinction suggests that mental characteristics should not be incorporated into the Reasonable Person standard, many courts today permit juries to consider battered woman syndrome evidence when evaluating the reasonableness, not simply the honesty, of the defendant's beliefs and actions. Some courts will even instruct jurors to compare the female defendant who asserts a history of being battered to the Reasonable Battered Woman.[31]

Another way of deciding which attributes of the defendant ought to be incorporated into the Reasonable Person standard is to ask whether the provoking words or acts relate to that attribute. Attributes of the accused that are not common to most people might nonetheless be relevant to the reasonableness inquiry if the provocation relates to that attribute. Camille Nelson explains:

[T]he potentially provocative impact of the desecration of a crucifix might only be understood if the ordinary person is Catholic, whereas the same event for an agnostic or an atheist may be a matter of indifference. Similarly, it may be pointless to ask what the effect on an ordinary person would be of the desecration of the Koran, if the ordinary person was not a Muslim.[32]

In *Regina v. Hill*,[33] a sixteen-year-old boy killed a man after the man made an unwanted homosexual advance. Chief Justice Dickson, writing for the court, explained how a jury might determine whether a particular attribute of the defendant is or is not relevant to the reasonableness determination:

> For example, if the provocation is a racial slur, the jury will think of an ordinary person with the racial background that forms the substance of the insult. To this extent, particular characteristics will be ascribed to the ordinary person. Indeed, it would be impossible to conceptualize a sexless or ageless ordinary person. Features such as sex, age or race do not detract from a person's characterization as ordinary.
>
> . . . It is important to note that, in some instances, certain characteristics will be irrelevant. For example, the race of a person will be irrelevant if the provocation involves an insult regarding a physical disability. Similarly, the sex of an accused will be irrelevant if the provocation relates to a racial insult. Thus the central criterion is the relevance of the particular feature to the provocation in question.[34]

Interestingly, even though the alleged provocation in *Hill* was an unwanted sexual advance, Chief Justice Dickson did not think it necessary for the trial judge to instruct the jury that they should incorporate the defendant's gender and sexual orientation into the reasonableness inquiry. He explained, "I should also add that my conclusion that certain attributes can be ascribed to the ordinary person is not meant to suggest that a trial judge must in each case tell the jury what specific attributes it is to ascribe to the ordinary person. The point I wish to emphasize is simply that in applying their common sense to the factual determination of the objective test, jury members will quite naturally and properly ascribe certain characteristics to the 'ordinary person.'"[35]

Making a similar point, the English House of Lords, in *Director of Public Prosecutions v. Camplin*, noted, "To taunt a person because of his race, his physical infirmities or some shameful incident in his past may well be considered by the jury to be more offensive to the person addressed, however equable his temperament, if the facts on which the taunt is founded are true than it would be if they are not."[36]

## SAMENESS VERSUS DIFFERENCE: SHOULD THE LAW BE GENDER-BLIND OR GENDER-CONSCIOUS?

In order to better understand why courts incorporate certain characteristics of the defendant into the reasonableness requirement and not others, it is useful to consider the debate in feminist circles over whether the law should be gender-blind or gender-conscious. Feminist scholars generally agree that the law ought to take into account the experiences and values typical of women.[37] As Katharine Bartlett explains:

> Feminists across many disciplines regularly ask a question— a set of questions, really—known as "the woman question," which is designed to identify the gender implications of rules and practices which might otherwise appear to be neutral or objective. . . . The woman question asks about the gender implications of a social practice or rule: have women been left out of consideration? If so, in what way; how might that omission be corrected? What difference would it make to do so? In law, asking the woman question means examining how the law fails to take into account the experiences and values that seem more typical of women than of men, for whatever reason, or how existing legal standards and concepts might disadvantage women. The question assumes that some features of the law may be not only nonneutral in a general sense, but also "male" in a specific sense. The purpose of the woman question is to expose those features and how they operate, and to suggest how they might be corrected.[38]

Feminist scholars, however, disagree about the extent to which legal standards ought to recognize or reflect gender difference.[39] Traditional or moderate feminists tend to embrace what has been called the sameness or formal equality approach. Sameness feminists, also known as assimilationists, argue that men and women are basically the same, and therefore women should be treated just like men. Under this view, the best way to achieve equality is through gender-neutral standards. Sameness feminists tend to support the Reasonable Person standard because it looks like a gender-neutral standard that treats men and women the same.

Difference feminists, in contrast, focus on the ways in which men and women are different. For example, Carol Gilligan suggests that men and women engage in different processes of moral reasoning.[40] According to Gilligan, women tend to place a heavy emphasis on the importance of relationships. When confronted with a moral dilemma, women seek a resolution that maintains good relations between the parties involved. Men, in contrast, tend to see moral dilemmas as math problems that can be resolved simply by applying analytical reasoning from abstract principles.

Difference feminists argue that the law should embrace gender-conscious standards, at least in cases where gender matters. For example, gender-conscious laws providing pregnant women with maternity leave recognize the fact that women and men are not similarly situated in the area of pregnancy. Without laws recognizing this difference, pregnant women may be fired for taking time off to care for their newborn children. Martha Chamallas explains why treating men and women equally (for example, by treating pregnancy as a disability and saying that both men and women have the right to take disability leave) is an inadequate remedy:

> The equal treatment approach to pregnancy discrimination, however, had its drawbacks. Under the PDA [the Pregnancy Discrimination Act of 1978], employers were required only to treat pregnant workers as well as they treated others with temporary disabilities. Many employers, particularly those in highly competitive industries such as retail sales, employed a high percentage of women and tended to offer few benefits to any of their employees when it came to sick and disability leaves, guaranteed rights of reinstatement, and other fringe benefits. For the huge class of predominantly female temporary and part-time workers, moreover, there were often no fringe benefit programs of any kind. Thus, as a practical matter, the PDA left large numbers of women employees unprotected. For women in these marginalized jobs in the "secondary labor market," equality with men was an empty benefit.[41]

Difference feminists find the Reasonable Person standard problematic for several reasons. First, the Reasonable Person standard assumes that men and women are alike when they are not. Second, the standard is not really neutral. Because men are associated with reason while women are associated with emotion,[42] the Reasonable Person is really the Reasonable Man dressed up in gender-neutral clothing, and masculine values are in fact the mark by which all persons are measured. To ensure that women are not placed at a disadvantage, difference feminists advocate use of a gender-specific Reasonable Woman standard in cases involving female defendants.

Some courts have embraced such gender specificity.[43] For example, in *State v. Wanrow*, the Washington Supreme Court held that it was an error for the trial court to have given the jury a self-defense instruction using only the male pronoun when the defendant was a woman on crutches.[44] The trial court had given the following instruction:

> However, when there is no reasonable ground for the person attacked to believe that *his* person is in imminent danger of death or great bodily harm, and it appears to *him* that only an ordinary battery is all that is intended, and all that *he* has reasonable grounds to fear from *his* assailant, *he* has a right to stand *his* ground and repel such threatened assault, yet *he* has no right to repel a threatened assault with naked hands, by the use of a deadly weapon in a deadly manner, unless *he* believes, *and has reasonable grounds* to believe, that *he* is in imminent danger of death or great bodily harm.[45]

The Washington Supreme Court explained that this jury instruction was problematic because it told the jury to compare the defendant, a short woman with a cast on her leg, to the average man with no physical disability:

> [I]nstruction No. 10 not only establishes an objective standard, but through the persistent use of the masculine gender leaves the jury with the impression the objective standard to be applied is that applicable to an altercation between two men. The impression created—that a 5'4" woman with a cast on her leg and using a crutch must, under the law, somehow repel an assault by a 6'2" intoxicated man without employing weapons in her defense, unless the jury finds her determination of the degree of danger to be objectively reasonable—constitutes

a separate and distinct misstatement of the law and, in the context of this case, violates the respondent's right to equal protection of the law.[46]

In *A Law of Her Own: A Reasonable Woman as a Measure of Man*, Caroline Forell and Donna Matthews argue that a Reasonable Woman standard should be adopted in all cases "where men's and women's life experiences and views on sex and aggression diverge and women are overwhelmingly the injured parties."[47] Under Forell and Matthews's proposal, a Reasonable Woman standard would apply not only in cases involving female defendants, but also in cases involving male defendants. For example, if a man were to kill his wife and argue that he was provoked into a heat of passion by his wife's infidelity, jurors would be instructed to determine whether a reasonable woman would be provoked if she found out that her husband was being unfaithful. Forell and Matthews explain:

> Under our standard, decision makers would judge the killer in terms of whether a reasonable woman would have lost control and killed in the circumstances. Only secondarily would they consider the victim's "provocatory" conduct, and then only in terms of whether it would have provoked a reasonable woman to lose control and kill. Thus, for example, the decision maker would be asked whether a reasonable woman, on discovering her husband was unfaithful, or knowing that her ex-husband was seeing someone new, would react with deadly violence. The decision maker would also consider whether a husband's unfaithfulness or an ex-husband's dating behavior would provoke a reasonable woman to be violent. As a result of applying our reasonable woman standard, provocation would most likely disappear as a mitigating factor except in response to threatened or actual violence.[48]

According to Forell and Matthews, a Reasonable Woman standard would "make currently acceptable or excusable conduct unacceptable and inexcusable by focusing on respect for bodily integrity, agency, and autonomy."[49]

A third group of feminists, known as radical feminists or dominance feminists, reject both the sameness and difference approaches, and by implication all reasonableness standards. Catharine MacKinnon, the leading spokeswoman for this group, critiques sameness and difference feminism because both use man as the measure of all things. She explains:

> [T]o treat issues of sex equality as issues of sameness and difference *is to take a particular approach*. I call this the difference approach because it is obsessed with the sex difference. The main theme in the fugue is "we're the same, we're the same, we're the same." The counterpoint theme (in a higher register) is "but we're different, but we're different, but we're different." . . . There is a politics to this. Concealed is the substantive way in which man has become the measure of all things. Under the sameness standard, women are measured according to our correspondence with man, our equality judged by our proximity to his measure. Under the difference standard, we are measured according to our lack of correspondence with him, our womanhood judged by our distance from his measure. Gender neutrality is thus simply the male standard, and the special protection rule is simply the female standard, but do not be deceived: masculinity, or maleness, is the referent for both.[50]

The problem with the sameness and difference approaches, according to MacKinnon, is that both avoid confronting issues of male power, hierarchy and dominance. She explains, "the alternating and simultaneous rejection and embrace of sex as a difference has evaded the issues of power and left the hierarchy that is gender right in place."[51] Dominance feminists believe that efforts to attain equality must focus on the structures of patriarchy and male dominance that keep women subordinate to men, rather than on whether men and women are being treated the same or differently.

A fourth group of feminists, known as critical feminists because of their association with Critical Race Theory and their concern over axes of discrimination and bias beyond gender, have argued that replacing the Reasonable Person with the Reasonable Woman is an inadequate reform because it does not resolve problems inherent in the reasonableness requirement itself. Whenever the law embraces a reasonableness standard, it presumes that a universal standard of objectivity is attainable. When the law adopts a Reasonable Woman standard, it presumes that an average or typical woman exists. Critical feminists observe that the average or typical woman in the American imagination is White and heterosexual. The perspectives of women of color and lesbian women are not included in this vision of the Reasonable Woman.[52] Some critical feminists have argued that reasonableness standards should incorporate gender, race, ethnicity, and sexual orientation.[53] According to this view, the Black lesbian female defendant should be compared to the Reasonable Black Lesbian, not simply the Reasonable Woman, because the Reasonable Woman in the imagination is White and heterosexual.

Critical feminist Stephanie Wildman, who has written extensively on the Reasonable Man standard and the invisibility of White male privilege,[54] argues that a Reasonable Woman standard does not adequately address problems of equality and essentialism "because [such a standard] fails to name the power dynamic that initially creates the problems."[55] In a persuasive critique of Forell and Matthews's Reasonable Woman standard, Wildman posits that a Reasonable Woman standard "implicitly accepts the fundamental notion of legal liberalism that all members of society are equally-situated, autonomous actors, albeit with different perspectives. By failing to address the systems of privilege that maintain the sex-based, gendered status quo, the reasonable woman standard cannot go far enough to ensure that the legal system will recognize women's harms."[56]

I agree with Wildman that merely substituting a Reasonable Woman standard in place of a Reasonable Man standard in cases with female defendants, as some courts have done, does little to change fundamental problems with the reasonableness requirement. Forell and Matthews's proposal, however, goes further than mere substitution. Their proposal would require legal decision makers to use a Reasonable Woman standard in all cases implicating gender, including cases in which the defendant is a man. By forcing the legal decision maker to think about the reasonableness of the male defendant's beliefs and actions from the perspective of a woman, Forell and Matthews's proposal does expose (or at least helps to expose) the power dynamic and systems of privilege that make male violence seem reasonable or at least understandable.

## GENDER-SWITCHING

Although Forell and Matthews do not explicitly propose giving a gender-switching jury instruction, gender-switching is an implied consequence of their Reasonable Woman standard, at least in cases involving male defendants. Under Forell and Matthews's proposal, if the defendant is a man who claims he was provoked into a heat of passion when he caught his female partner in an act of infidelity, jurors would assess the reasonableness of the male defendant's outrage in light of what the average woman would do if she came home and found her male partner in bed with another woman. Most women in this situation would be upset, but few would become so violent as to kill. The exercise of imagining how a woman in the same situation would respond helps jurors understand the unreasonableness of the male defendant's use of deadly force.

Gender-switching can be criticized for not adequately acknowledging real differences between men and women. For example, if gender-switching were applied to a case involving an abused woman who killed her abusive male partner, jurors told to gender-switch would be told to imagine the average man in the abused woman's shoes. One problem with gender-switching in this type of case is that jurors may have difficulty imagining a man who has been physically abused by his female partner. Another problem is that gender stereotypes about men being physically stronger than women could lead jurors to conclude that because the average man would not be justified in using deadly force against his abusive female partner, the abused female defendant was not justified. Forell and Matthews avoid this particular problem by applying the Reasonable Woman standard to both male and female defendants. Under their proposal, gender-switching is required only when the defendant is a man. If the defendant is a woman, she is compared to the Reasonable Woman.

Applying gender-switching in a one-directional manner raises equal protection concerns. If gender-switching is to be used in the criminal courtroom, it should be available to both defendants and prosecutors regardless of the gender of the defendant, as long as switching is appropriate. Forell and Matthews presume that gender bias only benefits men, but this is not always the case. As noted in chapter 1, female defendants charged with murdering their husbands are more likely than male defendants charged with murdering their wives to be acquitted.[57] If convicted, these female defendants are more likely than their male counterparts to receive lighter sentences.[58] The high rate of acquittals may be due to the fact that many women who kill their intimate partners are victims of domestic violence and use deadly force in self-defense during a confrontation. However, not all female murder defendants are victims of domestic violence and not all kill in clear cases of self-defense. In these cases, stereotypes about women as the weaker sex, generally nonviolent and passive, may influence judges to impose lenient sentences and jurors to acquit.[59]

Gender-switching may be necessary to highlight the unreasonableness of a female defendant's claim of self-defense. For example, when she was a Deputy District Attorney, Hofstra law professor Alafair Burke tried a case against a young White female defendant who had thrown a cup of boiling tea on her live-in boyfriend, also White. The young woman claimed she acted in self-defense, but never alleged that her boyfriend had attacked her or threatened her with any physical violence. Instead, she testified that they were fighting about some money he had spent from the household budget and she threw the boiling tea on him to get him away from her. At the start of the case, Burke felt certain the young woman would be acquitted despite the lack of an imminent threat of physical force because she was an attractive, likable, upper-middle-class young woman. In contrast, the defendant's boyfriend, who didn't bother to show up at trial, came across as a whining loser. The defendant testified that her boyfriend was a drug user with a history of mental illness and anger problems. As Burke predicted, the judge (a woman) granted a judgment of acquittal on the assault charge. The judge was openly sympathetic toward the defendant, at one point apologizing to her that she had to miss so much time from work because of the trial.

The judge did permit the jury to decide the charge of harassment, which required offensive physical contact with the intent to harass or annoy. To address possible gender bias favoring the female defendant, Burke told the jury during her closing argument to imagine a man yelling at his wife about buying a scarf at Nordstrom that the couple couldn't afford, and then throwing a cup of boiling hot soup on his wife to get her away from him. Burke asked the jury to think about whether that man would have a valid self-defense claim. The jury came back with a conviction.[60]

Allowing gender-switching in a bidirectional manner (available to both prosecutors and defense attorneys) does not mean it will be appropriate in all cases. For example, gender-switching might not be appropriate in a case involving a battered woman who kills her abuser during a confrontation. A jury instructed to gender-switch in such a case might simply apply the usual standard—that of the reasonable or ordinary man. Battered women's advocates have worked hard to show how and why such a comparison is inappropriate. The solution, however, is not to bar gender-switching in all battered women's self-defense cases. Rather, the attorney representing the battered woman defendant can file a motion in limine, before the trial begins, explaining to the judge why the comparison to the ordinary man, who isn't likely to have suffered a history of physical and psychological abuse, is inappropriate. If this fails, the defense attorney can remind jurors that gender is the only attribute of the defendant they should switch. The defendant and victim's respective heights and weights stay the same and all other facts stay the same.

Another problem with gender-switching is the risk of essentialism.[61] If jurors are asked to imagine what a "reasonable woman" in the male defendant's situation would have done, jurors may engage in the same type of gender-stereotyping that I've been arguing is so problematic. Who is the Reasonable Woman? Is she White? Is she middle-class? Is she educated? Is she heterosexual?

Essentialism is a problem that inheres anytime one utilizes a reasonableness requirement, even a hybrid subjectivized-objective standard of reasonableness. However, unless one is willing to abandon reasonableness requirements altogether, the only thing that can ameliorate the problem is to try to educate the jury about gender bias and encourage them to be as fair as possible when making determinations of reasonableness. This is something the attorneys involved in the case can do during opening and closing arguments. Attorneys can also present expert testimony on gender bias.

Gender-switching in a provocation case, for example, avoids the essentialism problem, at least in part, by having jurors decide whether they would think a woman in the male defendant's situation would have been reasonably provoked into a heat of passion. In other words, jurors are not to imagine whether the hypothetical average or ordinary woman would have been provoked. Instead, they must imagine whether a woman like the defendant (e.g., a woman of the same height and weight as the defendant) who encounters whatever the defendant encountered would be provoked into a heat of passion.

## SEXUAL ORIENTATION–SWITCHING

Under Forell and Matthews's proposal, a Reasonable Woman standard would apply only in cases implicating gender. I would go further and encourage jurors to engage in gender- and sexual orientation–switching in cases where masculinity and heterosexuality norms interact to encourage juror bias either for or against the defendant. For example, if a heterosexual male defendant charged with murdering a gay man claims he was reasonably provoked into a heat of passion by a nonviolent homosexual advance, switching would involve imagining a heterosexual woman in the defendant's situation and deciding whether she would be considered reasonable if she used deadly force in response to an unwanted lesbian sexual advance. Sexual orientation–switching would involve imagining a gay man in the defendant's shoes and deciding whether he would be considered reasonable if he used deadly force in response to an unwanted nonviolent heterosexual advance (i.e., a sexual advance by a heterosexual woman who didn't realize the man was gay).

Christina Pei-Lin Chen advances a somewhat similar proposal.[62] Chen calls for a "counterfactual inquiry" in which "the respective roles of the victim and offender are transposed or reversed so that, in this counterfactual world, the actual victim (counterfactual offender) allegedly kill(s) the actual offender-defendant (counterfactual victim)."[63] With all other factors held constant, the judge "would assess whether the actual victim (counterfactual offender) in this hypothetical world would be able to invoke the USA [unwanted sexual advance] defense for his or her killing of the counterfactual victim (actual accused offender-defendant)."[64] In other words, in a case where a heterosexual male defendant killed a gay man in response to a nonviolent homosexual advance and claimed he was reasonably provoked, the judge would decide whether a gay man would be able to assert a provocation defense if he killed a heterosexual man in response to an unwanted sexual advance. If a gay man would be able to assert the defense, then the heterosexual defendant would not be precluded from arguing provocation. If, however, a gay man would not be able to argue provocation, then Chen would deny the heterosexual man the opportunity to argue provocation to the jury. Chen argues that because an unwanted sexual advance by a heterosexual man toward a gay man is in fact impossible (because a heterosexual man would never make a sexual advance upon another man), heterosexual men who claim gay panic should be precluded from asserting the provocation defense.[65]

It is not clear, however, that an unwanted sexual advance by a heterosexual man toward a gay man is impossible, as Chen claims. A heterosexual man might make a sexual advance upon a gay man—indeed, heterosexual men in prison often make sexual advances toward other male inmates[66]—and a gay man might not welcome such an advance. Just because a man is gay doesn't mean he welcomes any and all sexual advances from other men. A better counterfactual would ask whether it would be reasonable if a gay man became upset to the point of violent outrage if a heterosexual woman made an unwanted sexual advance upon him.

Rather than completely bar a heterosexual male defendant from arguing that he was reasonably provoked into a heat of passion by a nonviolent homosexual advance,[67] I would allow the defendant to make the argument and leave the decision as to reasonableness with the jury. The prosecutor could request a gender- and sexual orientation–switching jury instruction. She could also incorporate switching into her opening or closing argument to help jurors see the unreasonableness of the defendant's claim.


## COLOR-BLINDNESS VERSUS COLOR-CONSCIOUSNESS

Similar to the debate in feminist circles over whether the law ought to be gender-blind or gender-conscious, a debate over whether the law ought to be color-blind or color-conscious has raged in academic circles.[68] On the one hand are the traditionalists, including conservatives, neoconservatives, and White liberals, who believe race does not and should not matter, and that the law should be color-blind. On the other hand are Critical Race Scholars (or race crits) who argue that because we live in a society in which race does make a difference, the law ought to acknowledge this reality by embracing race-conscious or color-conscious standards.

The most visible arena in which color-blindness versus color-consciousness is fought is in the affirmative action debates.[69] Traditionalists argue that affirmative action unfairly gives special treatment to Blacks, Latinos, and other racial and ethnic groups, disadvantaging Whites who are denied jobs, promotions, and admission to elite schools. Waving the banner of color blindness, which was used during the civil rights movement in support of desegregation, traditionalists contend that affirmative action is bad because it stigmatizes minorities and harms Whites by denying them jobs and other opportunities. Traditionalists believe race is, and should be, irrelevant.

Race crits argue that while race should be irrelevant, it isn't.[70] Men and women of color in this country have been and continue to be discriminated against. The principle of color blindness is problematic because it denies the significance of race. It pretends that race doesn't matter and that everyone is equally situated, when in fact persons of color are still presumed incompetent or less competent than Whites. In order to remedy racial discrimination, some race crits argue that affirmative measures must be taken to even the scales, especially in the areas of education and employment.[71]

Traditionalists have successfully turned the tide of public opinion against race-consciousness in general and affirmative action in particular. In the 1990s, they spearheaded the movement in California to make unlawful the consideration of race, sex, color, ethnicity, or national origin in public employment, public education, and public contracting. In 1996, California voters passed an anti-affirmative action initiative, Proposition 209, misleadingly named the "California Civil Rights Initiative."[72] Proposition 209 inspired a similar initiative in the state of Washington.[73]

Just as traditionalists have won the day in terms of the current popular embrace of color blindness, they have also convinced courts that race should not be incorporated into the Reasonable Person standard. Most courts reject a Reasonable Man standard that incorporates the defendant's race or ethnicity.[74] Generally speaking, the jury deciding whether a Black man who responds to a racial epithet with fatal violence was reasonably provoked is not told to compare the defendant to the reasonable or ordinary Black man. Similarly, the jury deciding whether a Native American who shoots a White law enforcement officer out of fear for his life had an honest and reasonable belief in the need to act in self-defense is not told to compare the defendant to the reasonable Native American. In both cases, the jury is simply told to compare the defendant to the Reasonable (raceless) Man. Color blindness, however, is not race-neutral, because the average man in the American imagination is White.

## RACE-SWITCHING

Rather than run the risk of oversubjectivizing the reasonableness requirement by incorporating most or all of the defendant's characteristics into the Reasonable Person test, I propose a race-switching jury instruction in cases involving a risk that racial stereotyping will influence the jury's determination of reasonableness. For example, if a White male defendant has killed a Black man and claims he acted in self-defense, there is a danger that the Black-as-Criminal stereotype will bias the jury in favor of the defendant. Encouraging jurors to think about whether they would feel the defendant acted reasonably in self-defense if he was Black and his victim White, all other facts the same, would help illuminate the role of race and racial stereotypes. Race-switching avoids the problem of essentialism that inheres in a subjectivized Reasonable Black Man standard because the jury doesn't have to imagine what the average or ordinary Black man would have believed or done. All they have to do is consider what a Black man *in the defendant's shoes* would have felt and done. This means that if the defendant is 5'4" and weighs 150 lbs, so is the Black man in the defendant's shoes. If the Black male victim was dressed in baggy pants and a tank top, then so is the White male victim in the race-switch. If the incident took place at night in a dark alley, this circumstance stays the same. The only thing that changes in the race-switch is race. All other factors remain constant. Of course, it will be difficult (some might say impossible) for a White juror to know what a Black person in the defendant's situation would think, but the race-switch will achieve its purpose if it reveals an inconsistency in the juror's opinion of the facts and encourages the juror to rethink his or her original interpretation of the case.

The usefulness of race-switching is not limited to cases involving White defendants who have used deadly force against victims of color. Race-switching can also help expose racial bias in cases involving defendants of color and White victims. In such cases, racial stereotypes about Black men as prone to violence and criminality may bias the jury against the defendant. Race-switching forces jurors to focus less on the defendant's race and more on the objective circumstances of the case.

Race-switching may not be appropriate in all cases. When a Black man kills in response to a racial insult, what is needed is juror education about the history of discrimination against Blacks in America and the use of the N word to denigrate Blacks and put them in their place. As

Camille Nelson notes, "in order to consider the insulting effect of racial abuses on a person of color, for example, the legacy of such racist abuse is relevant, otherwise the assessment of the provocation is taken in a vacuum—devoid of any societal underpinnings and context."[75] Race-switching in such cases is inappropriate for a simple reason. It doesn't make sense to ask whether a White man would be reasonably provoked into a heat of passion if he were called the N word because that word is not generally used to insult Whites. Even if jurors were to do more than simply switch the races of the parties, such as replacing the N word with the word "honky," race-switching might still be inappropriate. Nelson explains, "If it strains credulity to imagine what the 'ordinary white man' would do in the position of a black man bombarded with racial slurs, it is probably because white men do not typically find themselves in that situation."[76]

# 9

# Toward a Normative Conception of Reasonableness

It is of the very nature of a free society to advance in its standards of what is deemed reasonable and right.[1]

—U.S. Supreme Court Justice Felix Frankfurter

FOR A DEFENDANT to receive the provocation mitigation, the jury (or some other legal decision maker) must find that a reasonable person in the defendant's shoes would have been provoked into a heat of passion. For a defendant to receive an acquittal based on self-defense, the jury must find that a reasonable person in the defendant's shoes would have believed he was in imminent danger of death or grievous bodily injury. The reasonableness determination in both types of cases turns on juror beliefs and attitudes, which are a reflection of prevailing social norms.

The reasonableness requirement is not the only thing linking these two important defenses. The doctrines are interrelated in several less obvious ways. For example, while provocation is generally considered a partial excuse and self-defense a justification, both doctrines contain elements of excuse and justification. Second, the emotions at issue in provocation and self-defense cases—anger, outrage, and fear—reflect normative judgments of evaluation. These commonalities are significant because they inform the question of reform. The justificatory elements in provocation and self-defense and the evaluative nature of the emotions at issue in both types of cases support a normative conception of reasonableness.

## THE JUSTIFICATION-EXCUSE DISTINCTION

Criminal law defenses are generally divided into two categories: justification defenses and excuse defenses. Justification defenses focus upon the actions of the defendant and exculpate if he did the right thing under the circumstances.[2] Under the residual justification defense of necessity, a defendant is justified in committing a crime if he avoids a greater harm than would have come about had he refrained from acting unlawfully. For example, an individual is justified in trespassing upon private property if he does so to save a drowning child. Excuse defenses, in contrast, focus upon the actor-defendant, rather than the act or crime. An excuse defense acknowledges that what the defendant did was wrongful, but says we ought to exculpate (or mitigate) because he is not really blameworthy. He is excused because he couldn't help himself or did not know that what he was doing was wrong. For example, we excuse the insane actor because he did not know he was breaking the law or could not restrain himself from acting unlawfully.

The defense of provocation is generally considered an excuse defense rather than a justification because it focuses on the blameworthiness of the actor-defendant, rather than the wrongfulness of his or her acts. The reason we allow the mitigation from murder to manslaughter is not because we think the *act* (of stabbing or shooting or beating) is right or correct action, but because we feel the *actor* is not entirely to blame for what happened.[3] Self-defense, in contrast, is widely viewed as a justification defense. The defendant who successfully argues self-defense is acquitted because his or her *act* (of stabbing or shooting or beating) is considered the right thing to do. By acting to protect against a wrongful aggressor, the defendant does what society would want him to do. In general, it is correct to think of provocation as a partial excuse and self-defense as a justification.

The justification-excuse distinction serves to outline the major differences between the doctrines of provocation and self-defense. Neither doctrine, however, can be adequately explained by such narrow categorization.[4] If all that were required was a showing that the defendant lost his self-control, provocation might rightfully be considered solely an excuse defense. The modern test for provocation, however, also cares about the reasons why the defendant acted the way he did.[5] The observation of a wife's adultery is usually considered a good enough reason; a racial insult is not. The requirement that the provocation be legally adequate or such that a reasonable person would have been provoked into a heat of passion seems to speak more to justification than excuse.

The misdirected retaliation rule is another example of the justificatory nature of the provocation defense. In many jurisdictions, the provocation defense can only be asserted if the defendant kills the person who provoked him into a heat of passion. If the defendant's passion is misdirected and he ends up killing an innocent party, the defendant will be found guilty of murder. In lectures on the defense of provocation, Joshua Dressler uses a hypothetical based on *Rex v. Scriva*,[6] an Australian case in which a father kills an innocent bystander after observing a reckless driver run into his young child, to illustrate the misdirected retaliation rule. Father happens to see a reckless driver crash his car, hitting Father's son. Outraged, Father picks up a knife and heads toward Reckless Driver with the intention of killing him. Innocent Bystander intervenes, trying to stop Father from killing Reckless Driver. Father is so angry that he lashes out at Innocent Bystander, killing him. Jurisdictions which embrace the misdirected retaliation rule would deny Father the provocation defense because Reckless Driver, not Innocent Bystander, was the one who provoked Father into a heat of passion. But if the defense of provocation were solely an excuse-based defense, as claimed by defenders of the traditional view, it wouldn't matter who was killed as a result of the defendant's passion. The only thing that would matter would be whether the defendant lost control of his senses and couldn't help himself at the time of the killing, not the reason why.

The mere words rule also reflects the justificatory nature of the provocation defense. In most jurisdictions, mere words can never constitute legally adequate provocation. Even if words uttered by the victim actually incited the defendant to violence, the defendant cannot receive the provocation mitigation. Like the misdirected retaliation rule, the mere words rule suggests the law cares about more than just whether or not the defendant could control himself or herself. If provocation were solely an excuse, it wouldn't matter what triggered the defendant's emotional upset. As long as it could be satisfactorily proven that the defendant was actually provoked into a heat of passion, he or she would be eligible for the mitigation.[7]

One last example illustrates the justificatory nature of the provocation defense. Underlying many provocation claims is the idea that the victim got what he or she deserved. In female infidelity cases, the heterosexual male defendant argues that his female partner's wrongful act of engaging in sexual intercourse with someone else caused him to lose his self-control. In gay panic cases, the heterosexual male defendant suggests, either directly or by implication, that the victim's wrongful homosexual advance caused his violent outburst. In essence, the defendant blames the victim for his own acts. He argues that the victim deserved, at least in part, to die. The notion of desert, even partial, sounds in justification, rather than excuse.

Joshua Dressler, who has written extensively on the provocation defense, argues that thinking of provocation as a partial justification is misguided. According to Dressler, "[e]ither a person has a right to act in a certain manner or he does not."[8] While this may be true as a matter of theory, the defense of provocation in practice is not applied in such all-or-nothing terms. When Aaron McKinney, for example, testified that Matthew Shepard was sexually aggressive toward him, he was trying to suggest that Shepard was at least partially at fault for his own death. When Albert Joseph Berry introduced evidence that his wife, Rachel Pessah, was sexually unfaithful and taunted him with her infidelity, he was trying to suggest that she was partially to blame for her own death. I agree with those who find such justificatory reasoning morally objectionable,[9] but my personal objection to such reasoning does not eliminate the existence of such reasoning. Provocation is best understood as a partial excuse, but its justificatory elements should not be ignored.

Like the doctrine of provocation, the doctrine of self-defense contains elements of justification and excuse. Normally, one who acts in self-defense is considered justified because, in acting to protect himself against a wrongful aggressor, he does what society wants him to do. As between a wrongful aggressor and his innocent victim, society wants the innocent victim to protect himself. In putative self-defense cases, that is, in cases in which the defendant reasonably but incorrectly believes an innocent person poses a threat of imminent death or grievous bodily injury, it is not so clear that the act of killing is correct action. Several traditional criminal law scholars have argued that putative self-defense cases are better regarded as cases of excuse, rather than as cases of justification.[10] According to these scholars, a defendant who honestly and reasonably, albeit incorrectly, fears another enough to kill is acquitted not because he did the right thing (it is never just to kill an innocent person), but because he is not as morally blameworthy as one who acts without such fear. Despite the appeal of this argument, putative self-defense cases are correctly categorized as cases of justification rather than excuse. A defendant who honestly and reasonably believes in the need to act in self-defense acts the way society would have wanted him to act at the moment he acted.

Contrasting *ex ante* versus *post hoc* judgments of the appropriateness of the actor's choice illustrates why putative self-defense is appropriately viewed as a justification rather than as an excuse.[11] Only when we look back after the fact at the putative self-defender's acts—after we know what he didn't know at the time he acted (i.e., that his victim was *not* going to attack him or was *not* in fact threatening him with imminent death or serious bodily injury)—can we say that he chose the unpreferred course or action. When we view the putative self- defender's acts prospectively or at the time when he was faced with the decision, we come to quite a different conclusion. The putative self-defender chooses to act in the way society wants him to act in light of what he reasonably, albeit mistakenly, believes at the time he acts. Because it is unfair to expect individuals to be able to predict the future, we assess the reasonableness of the putative self-defender's acts in light of the circumstances at the time he acted.

In imperfect self-defense cases, cases in which the defendant's belief in the need to act in self-defense was honest but not reasonable, the defendant is granted leniency not because he did the right thing, but because society feels he is not as culpable as someone who intentionally kills another without such an honest belief. Imperfect self-defense is therefore characterized as a partial excuse rather than a partial justification. The person who has an honest but unreasonable belief in the need to act in self-defense does not act the way society would want him to act.

## MECHANISTIC VERSUS
## EVALUATIVE CONCEPTIONS OF EMOTION

In large part, the reasonableness requirement in provocation and self-defense seems anomalous. Reasonableness suggests some measure of reason or deliberation leading to correct or appropriate action, yet it is often said that the doctrines of provocation and self-defense are based on the theory that the provoked killer's or the self-defender's emotions overcame his (or her) ability to reason.[12] In provocation cases, the emotion at issue is anger, outrage, a sense of betrayal, or disgust. In self-defense cases, the emotion at issue is fear. The traditional view of provoked defendants is that they are excused because their emotions took over their senses, causing a partial loss of self-control. Similarly, the traditional view of self-defense is that the individual who is threatened with imminent death or grievous bodily injury acts upon reflex.[13] This sentiment is reflected in Justice Oliver Wendell Holmes's famous words, "Detached reflection . . . cannot be demanded in the presence of an uplifted knife."[14] Self-preservation as a basic instinct takes over and overpowers all other senses. According to this view, the reason we exculpate the self-defender and mitigate the charges for a provoked killer is because these defendants have not freely and voluntarily chosen to act.

The idea that strong emotions overcome the ability to reason can be placed in a broader context. Thinking about emotions as impulses or forces without cognitive content that impel individuals to action is what Dan Kahan and Martha Nussbaum call the "mechanistic" conception of emotion.[15] Kahan and Nussbaum explain:

> The mechanistic conception has force because it appears to capture well some prominent features of emotional experience. First, it captures a connection between emotion and passivity that occurs in much of our talk and experience. Emotions feel like things that sweep over us, or sweep us away, or invade us, often without our consent or control—and this intuitive idea is well preserved in the view that they really are impulses or drives that go their own way without embodying reasons or beliefs. Second, the view captures a sense we have that emotions are external to the self, forces that do something to "us" without being (or at least without clearly being) parts of what we think of as ourselves. Anger, for example, can seem to come boiling up from nowhere, in ways of which "we" strongly disapprove. Finally, the view appears to capture the urgency and "heat" of the emotions, the sense we have that they do have enormous force—for if we think of them as drives or forces similar to currents of an ocean, we can imagine these natural forces as extremely strong without being troubled by questions about how our own thoughts could have such force.[16]

Traditional criminal law scholars by and large seem to embrace the mechanistic view of emotions, especially when discussing the defense of provocation. For example, Michael Moore contends that the doctrine of provocation "excuses persons whose reasoning is temporarily 'unhinged' by their extreme emotional state."[17] Moore explains that "in these instances the incapacity to engage in practical reasoning, though not so extreme as to put the individual's personhood in jeopardy, is sufficient for excuse."[18] Similarly, Joshua Dressler contends that "when A kills P because his reason is 'disturbed or obscured by passion to an extent which might render ordinary men, of fair average disposition, liable to act rashly or without due deliberation or reflection, and from passion, rather than judgment,' he is less to blame than if he killed P while he is calm. This is because it is harder for A to control his actions when he is angry than when he is calm."[19] In short, under the mechanistic view, emotions such as anger and rage cannot be controlled. Such emotions simply take over, impairing the provoked individual's ability to think, reason, or control his actions.

American courts also tend to view heat of passion in mechanistic terms. This is most apparent in opinions which take the view that the provoked killer acts without malice aforethought. "Malice aforethought" is a legal term of art which refers to the mental state needed to be found guilty of murder. Most jurisdictions permit a finding of malice aforethought if any one of the following four conditions is satisfied: (1) the defendant intended to kill, (2) the defendant intended to commit grievous bodily injury, (3) the defendant acted with extremely reckless disregard for the value of human life, or (4) the defendant or one of his cofelons killed during the commission of a felony. Because malice aforethought is satisfied by any one of the above conditions, it is incorrect to assume that all provoked killers act without malice aforethought. The provoked defendant's anger or rage may actually create in him or her an intent to kill or at least commit grievous bodily injury against the provoker. Nonetheless, some courts assume the provoked killer is overcome by a passion which eliminates his ability to reason or form an intent to kill. For example, in *Lynn v. Commonwealth*,[20] a Virginia Court of Appeals opined, "Heat of passion excludes malice when the heat of passion arises from provocation that reasonably produces an emotional state of mind such as hot blood, rage, anger, resentment, terror or fear so as to demonstrate *an absence of deliberate design to kill*, or to cause one to act on impulse without conscious reflection."[21] Similarly, in *Febre v.*

*State,*[22] the Florida Supreme Court explained that the law reduces the charge from murder to manslaughter in a provocation case because passion aroused in the provoked killer takes away his ability to reason. "The law reduces the killing of a person in the heat of passion from murder to manslaughter out of a recognition of the frailty of human nature, of the temporary suspension or overthrow of the reason or judgment of the defendant by the sudden access of passion and because in such case there is *an absence of malice.*"[23]

Similarly, "the classic account of self-defense doctrine assumes a mechanistic conception of emotion."[24] According to Blackstone, the law of self-defense permits the man confronted with violence "to do himself that immediate justice, to which he is prompted by nature, and which no prudential motives are strong enough to restrain."[25]

In contrast to the mechanistic conception of emotion is what Kahan and Nussbaum call the evaluative conception of emotion. Under the evaluative conception, emotions include or express cognitive judgments that can be evaluated as reasonable or unreasonable, correct or incorrect. Under this view, emotions are not simply impulses or forces beyond our control. Moreover, the presence of emotions does not eliminate the possibility of reason or reflection. Kahan and Nussbaum explain how emotions express cognitive or evaluative judgments:

> We do not get angry over slights we think trivial. . . . In most cases, anger is associated with the high evaluation of things that matter to us, such as honor, status, the security of our possessions, or the safety and happiness of people we love. It appears that the emotions themselves *contain* an evaluation or appraisal of the object—that is, the appraisal is part of the belief-set in terms of which the emotion will be defined, and these ways of seeing the world are a part of what the emotional experience includes. Grief sees the lost one as of enormous significance; so too, in a happier way, does love. Disgust usually sees the object as one that threatens or contaminates, one that needs to be kept at a distance from the self. Fear perceives the impending harm as significant; anger sees the wrong as pretty large—whether or not this is the way these things really are.[26]

Kahan and Nussbaum argue that although the doctrine of provocation is usually viewed in mechanistic terms, it is better viewed as a reflection of the evaluative conception of emotion.[27] Provocation doctrine excuses only certain losses of self-control and not others. Evaluation plays a big part in deciding which losses of self-control ought to be excused. Evaluation is also at work in determining which types of provocation are considered legally adequate.

The evaluative conception of emotion also informs the self-defense doctrine.[28] A defendant claiming self-defense ordinarily must show that he honestly and reasonably believed in the *necessity* of using force to protect against imminent unlawful force. Most American jurisdictions, however, do not require individuals confronted with violence to retreat, especially if one is attacked in the home, even if a safe retreat is available. The "no duty to retreat" rule surely does not reflect "a mechanistic presumption that persons are incapable of voluntarily choosing flight when attacked [in the home]."[29] Rather, the rule reflects the normative judgment (or evaluation) that it is more important to allow individuals to stand their ground, particularly if they are attacked in their own home.

Evaluation is also found in the reasonableness requirement. Only certain types of provocation are legally adequate—those which would have provoked a reasonable person in the defendant's shoes. Only certain acts in claimed self-defense are justified—those in which the defendant's fear of imminent harm is deemed reasonable. Rather than being completely swept away by their emotions, both provoked killers and self-defenders retain some degree of control over their actions. As Finbarr McAuley points out, "the provocation exception covers cases in which [the defendant] merely *loses* control in circumstances in which it is difficult but not impossible to retain it."[30] The provoked killer *chooses* to act with violence rather than restrain himself, which is why he is only partially excused. If he truly lacked the ability to control his actions, it would not be just to impose any punishment at all. Likewise, the self-defender *chooses* to protect himself (or herself). Granted, the self-defender's actions may be motivated by fear, but this fear does not take away the voluntariness of the self-defender's use of force. The decision to shoot a perceived aggressor rather than run away is in fact a matter of choice. The self-defender *chooses* to protect himself rather than be harmed by another, and the law of self-defense presumes this element of choice. Exculpating the self-defender is a way of expressing our approval for his decision to act and of encouraging others who find themselves in similar situations to (choose to) do the same.

Given the presence of choice in both provocation and self- defense cases, it is simply incorrect to say that these doctrines exculpate the defendant or mitigate the crime because the defendant acted involuntarily. Rather, in both types of cases the reason the law gives the defendant a break is because it views the defendant's actions as appropriate or reasonable under the circumstances. Whether an individual's actions ought to be considered reasonable involves a normative judgment.

## POSITIVIST VERSUS NORMATIVE REASONABLENESS

If the purpose of utilizing a reasonableness standard is to bring some measure of uniformity and fairness to the inquiry, then it is important to interrogate what type of standard ought to be promoted. The debate might be framed in terms of reasonableness as a normative standard versus reasonableness as a positivist standard. What I mean by normative reasonableness is a conception of reasonableness that focuses on the beliefs and actions society *ought* to recognize as reasonable. A positivist (or empirical) conception of reasonableness, in contrast, focuses on what most individuals would actually feel, think, or do if they were in the defendant's situation. Under a positivist approach, legal decision makers take an imaginary poll of American attitudes, and whatever *is* the majority view is deemed reasonable.[31]

If anything can be said with certainty about the reasonableness requirement in provocation and self-defense doctrines, it is that courts tend to utilize a positivist conception of reasonableness. Since actual beliefs and feelings cannot be measured, reasonableness under a positivist approach is equated with typicality.

The positivist approach is problematic for many reasons. First, it is not possible to gauge the sentiments of "the community" with any accuracy. Many different communities exist in the United States. Even within these different communities, differences of opinion about what is reasonable abound. As Norman Finkel observes, "[community] sentiment, like winds, shift in direction and strength with time and circumstance, weather vane readings may be picking up momentary gusts, having a meaning confined only to the moment."[32]

Second, just because most people think something is fair and reasonable doesn't mean that the practice is just. As Ronald Dworkin observes, there is a difference between what the majority may think is fair and what is actually just.[33] Dworkin explains, "We might think that majority rule is the fairest workable decision procedure in politics, but we know that the majority will sometimes, perhaps often, make unjust decisions about the rights of individuals."[34] Most Americans at one time thought slavery was a reasonable and acceptable way of treating African Americans because the dominant belief was that African Americans were inferior to Anglo Americans. Some people still adhere to the belief that slavery was not a racist institution,[35] but the vast majority of Americans today condemn slavery. Most Americans in the 1940s thought it was reasonable, or at least unobjectionable, for the government to intern more than a hundred and twenty thousand Japanese Americans who were suspected of disloyalty after the bombing of Pearl Harbor.[36] Today, most Americans, though certainly not all, believe the internment of Japanese Americans during World War II was immoral. As a normative matter, most people believe we should not have incarcerated a group of individuals on the basis of their race.

It is always easier to look back and see the errors of past ways of thinking. It is much harder to turn the critical gaze on one's own attitudes and beliefs which always seem reasonable at the time. This is particularly true when these attitudes and beliefs are held by most of one's peers. The proponents of slavery felt strongly that their views were reasonable and correct, and could feel righteous in their viewpoint because most people around them felt the same way. As I write these words in May 2002, many (if not most) Americans think it is reasonable in the wake of the attacks on the World Trade Center and the Pentagon on September 11, 2001, for the government to have incarcerated more than a thousand men, most of whom are of Arab or South Asian descent, on little or no evidence of criminal activity, deny these men counsel, and refuse to disclose their identities and locations to the public. When the *Washington Post* reported that the Department of Justice was considering the use of torture or truth serums to extract information from these men,[37] few objected, even though such methods would likely be deemed a violation of due process if applied under any other circumstances. Only time will tell whether future generations will agree that the post 9/11 secret detentions were reasonable.

Another problem with the positivist approach is that social attitudes about what is reasonable change over time. Deciding that a belief or action is reasonable simply because most people think it is reasonable ignores the shifting and contingent nature of social norms. As Joanne St. Lewis and Sheila Galloway note:

> Social attitudes towards what is wrongful and insulting do change over time: what might have been offensive 100 years ago may be tolerated today. Thus, wrongful acts or insults are essentially fluid and open-ended in character. It is our challenge to consider how to incorporate an understanding of the experiences of all members of society, including members of equality-seeking communities, to ensure that legal rules operate without reinforcing systemic or historically discriminatory perpectives.[38]

One might question the wisdom of equating reasonableness with typicality if one thinks about why reasonableness standards are used in the first place. One reason the law embraces reasonableness standards is to ensure that "no defendant may set up his own standard of conduct and justify or excuse himself because *in fact* his passions were aroused."[39] Moreover, the criminal law tries to encourage certain behavior and discourage other behavior through the threat of penal sanctions. A normative conception of reasonableness does a better job than a positivist one of encouraging people to act in ways that society deems appropriate. It precludes a defendant from arguing that he ought to be excused because he was simply doing what most people would have done. A parent trying to teach a child to behave reasonably is not likely to excuse a child's rude behavior if the child's only excuse is that all the other children he knows act the same way. Similarly, the criminal law ought not to excuse an individual simply because most people would have felt or acted the way the defendant did. Moreover, as a matter of empiricism, it probably isn't true that most people would become so outraged as to kill in response to partner infidelity or an unwanted sexual advance. Most people, especially if we include women, the elderly, and young children, probably would not kill if faced with a threat of death or serious bodily injury. An ordinary person might freeze, attempt some nonfatal defensive action, or try to run away. It is the rare individual who would actually kill or even attempt to kill someone else in self-defense.

Equating reasonableness with typicality is particularly problematic in light of current doctrinal focus on emotion reasonableness.[40] When the question is simply whether the defendant's emotions were reasonable, legal decision makers will be inclined to ask whether they, as reasonable people, would have felt the way the defendant did if they were in the defendant's shoes. If they would have been outraged by the victim's conduct or would have been afraid of the victim, they are likely to conclude that the defendant acted as a reasonable person would have acted. A more difficult inquiry, but one which better addresses the question of reasonableness as something more than whatever happens to be popular, is whether the judge or jury ought to give society's stamp of approval to the defendant's actions. In other words, perhaps the law should embrace a normative conception of reasonableness, one that asks the "ought" question rather than just the "is" question.

A normative conception of reasonableness may seem novel, but it is not a completely unfamiliar concept in American law. For example, the U.S. Supreme Court has expressed some support for a normative conception of reasonableness in its Fourth Amendment search jurisprudence. Unlike reasonableness in the criminal law doctrines of self-defense and provocation, reasonableness in the Fourth Amendment context is not based solely on the average or ordinary person's actual views. Here, the Court seems to embrace both positivist and normative reasonableness.[41]

According to the Court, a search within the meaning of the Fourth Amendment is defined in terms of the individual citizen's expectations of privacy. Under the two-pronged *Katz* test, expressed in Justice Harlan's concurring opinion in *Katz v. United States*, first, the aggrieved individual must have "exhibited an actual (subjective) expectation of privacy, and second . . . the expectation [must be] one that society is prepared to recognize as *reasonable*."[42] Justice Stewart, writing for the majority in *Katz*, used the term "justifiable" to describe the expectation of privacy Mr. Katz had with respect to his telephone conversation.[43] In subsequent opinions, the Court has used the terms "reasonable," "justifiable," and "legitimate" interchangeably to describe the objective portion of the *Katz* test.

The fact that the Court uses the words "justifiable" and "legitimate" in place of "reasonable" in the Fourth Amendment context is significant. As Joshua Dressler notes,

> To say that a person's belief is "reasonable" ordinarily means that it is one that a reasonable [or ordinary] person in D's situation would hold. In the privacy context, this would mean that an expectation of privacy is "reasonable" when a reasonable person would not expect her pri-

vacy to be invaded. . . . In contrast, to say that D has a "legitimate" or "justifiable" expectation of privacy is to draw a normative conclusion that she has a right to that expectation. Or, as one court has put it, the privacy protected by the Fourth Amendment under this view "is not the privacy that one reasonably expects but the privacy to which one has a *right.*"[44]

Dressler then presents a hypothetical to illustrate the difference between positivist and normative conceptions of reasonableness:

> For example, suppose that D commits a crime in a secluded spot in a park during the middle of the night after carefully ascertaining that the area is virtually never frequented at that hour. Based on this information, D expects that her actions will not be observed. That expectation might be "reasonable" in the sense that a reasonable person would expect to be free from observation.
>
> Nonetheless, if a police officer happens by and observes the criminal conduct, most commentators agree that D's subjective privacy expectation will not be protected. If this is so, it is because D's expectation, although perhaps "reasonable," was "unjustifiable" or "illegitimate." That is, as a *normative* matter, people have no right to expect privacy if they conduct crime in the open, no matter how unlikely it is that they will be discovered.[45]

When a court says that a police officer's observation of D's criminal conduct is not a search because it is not reasonable for D to expect privacy in a park, it rests its legal conclusion upon a normative conception of reasonableness. Even if D actually believed he wouldn't be observed and even if most people in D's shoes would have felt the same way, D's expectation of privacy is not reasonable because it is not one that society (or, more accurately, the court) is willing to accept as legitimate or justifiable.

The criminal in the public park hypothetical may not be the best illustration of the difference between positivist and normative reasonableness. A secluded spot in a park during the middle of the night is still a spot in a public park, open to anyone who wishes to frequent it. Most people probably would not expect privacy in a public park even during the middle of the night, and therefore D's expectation of privacy is not reasonable even from a positivist perspective.

Another hypothetical perhaps better reflects the difference between positivist and normative reasonableness. D lives in a multilevel apartment in a low-income high crime neighborhood. The walls separating the apartments are paper thin. It is a hot summer night. Most people have their windows open. Because of the paper-thin walls and the open windows, anyone in the apartment building can hear what everyone else in the apartment building is doing or saying. Moreover, apartments are broken into on a regular basis by burglars. As a positivist matter, it just isn't reasonable to expect any privacy in that apartment building. Nonetheless, the government could not use D's empirical lack of a reasonable expectation of privacy as a reason to go in and search D's apartment without a warrant. This is because D has a normatively reasonable expectation of privacy in his home.

A few Supreme Court cases illustrate the positivist- normative distinction. For example, in *California v. Greenwood*,[46] the Court held that an individual has no reasonable expectation of privacy in the contents of a closed, opaque trash bag left on the curb for the trash collector. Even though most people would be pretty upset if they found out that the police were snooping through their trash for evidence of criminal activity, the Court found the Greenwoods' expectation of privacy in their trash to be unreasonable. The Court reasoned that by leaving their trash out on the curb to be picked up by the trash collector, the Greenwoods assumed the risk that scavengers, children, and nosy neighbors might rummage through it.

There are two problems with the Court's reasoning if one applies a positivist conception of reasonableness. First, how many people actually expect children and nosy neighbors to rummage through their trash? Of course the answer to this question will vary depending upon the neighborhood, but I would suspect that most people do not expect others to go through their trash.[47] Second, even if one did expect some persons, such as homeless individuals looking for food or would-be identity thieves looking for credit card stubs, to go through one's trash, this doesn't mean one expects the police to do so. The Court's conclusion that the Greenwoods did not have a reasonable expectation of privacy in their trash was a normative judgment about whether people *ought to* expect privacy from police snooping in their trash, rather than whether they *actually* do expect such privacy.

In *The Unwanted Gaze: The Destruction of Privacy in America*, Jeffrey Rosen offers additional examples which reflect the Court's embrace of a normative conception of reasonableness. Rosen notes that "[w]hen Americans reveal information to a bank, they don't, in fact, believe that the bank will turn their deposit information over to the government, as Congress recognized when it passed a law . . . prohibiting banks from turning over records to federal agencies."[48] Yet in *United States v. Miller*,[49] the Supreme Court held that an individual's expectation of privacy in his bank records is not reasonable. As it did in *Greenwood*, the Court reasoned that whenever an individual turns over information to a third party, such as a bank, the individual assumes the risk that the third party may reveal the information to the government. Accordingly, when the government demands that a bank turn over the personal financial records of a particular customer, it has not engaged in a "search" within the meaning of the Fourth Amendment because the customer's expectation of privacy in his bank records is not one that American society (as imagined by the Supreme Court) would respect as reasonable. A 1993 study by Christopher Slobogin and Joseph Schumacher, however, indicates that most people would view governmental perusal of an individual's personal bank records as extremely intrusive.[50]

The Court has also made normative judgments about the reasonableness of an individual's expectations of privacy in conversations with a trusted confidante.[51] According to the Court, whenever one talks to another person one assumes the risk that the person might be a government informant, and therefore it is normatively unreasonable to expect privacy in one's conversations with anyone. Slobogin and Schumacher's study, however, found that most people would feel that the government's use of a chauffeur or secretary as an undercover informant is very intrusive of privacy.

The debate over whether the criminal law ought to adopt a positivist or normative conception of reasonableness is reflected in an exchange between Robert Mison and Joshua Dressler, who take different positions on how the law ought to deal with a male murder defendant's claim that he was reasonably provoked by a nonviolent homosexual advance.

Mison argues that a positivist conception of reasonableness is problematic because the typical or ordinary man in the American imagination is heterosexist (biased in favor of heterosexual orientation) and homophobic (hostile to homosexual orientation). The average heterosexual man is therefore likely to sympathize with the heterosexual male defendant's claim that a nonviolent homosexual advance posed a significant threat to his bodily integrity and sense of masculinity. Mison argues that the law should not excuse the killing of gay men simply because the average heterosexual man would be outraged by a nonviolent homosexual advance. As a normative matter, such homicides are problematic and ought to be condemned.[52] Mison explains why the Reasonable Man standard should be understood as aspirational or normative:

> The reasonable man is an ideal, reflecting the standard to which society wants its citizens and system of justice to aspire. It is an "entity whose life is said to be the public embodiment of rational behavior." If the reasonable man is the embodiment of both rational behavior and the idealized citizen, a killing based simply on a homosexual advance reflects neither rational nor exemplary behavior. The argument is not that the ordinary person *would not* be provoked by a homosexual advance, but rather that a reasonable person *should not* be provoked to kill by such an advance.[53]

Mison's argument that the Reasonable Man is, or ought to be, construed as an ideal or aspirational construct finds limited support in English case law. In *Holmes v. Director of Public Prosecutions*,[54] the House of Lords ruled that a wife's confession of adultery to her husband did not constitute legally adequate provocation. Even though earlier courts had suggested an exception to the mere words rule for wifely confessions of adultery, the *Holmes* court refused to follow this precedent, arguing that "as society advances, it *ought* to call for a higher measure of self-control in all cases."[55] Speaking the language of aspiration, the court pronounced that "the law *expects* a reasonable man to endure [verbal] abuse without resorting to fatal violence."[56] Elaborating on this idea, the court explained:

> the application of common law principles in matters such as this must to some extent be controlled by the evolution of society. For example, the instance given by Blackstone . . . that if a man's nose was pulled and he thereupon struck his aggressor so as to kill him, this was only manslaughter, may very well represent the natural feelings of a past time, but I should doubt very much whether such a view should necessarily be taken nowadays.[57]

At least some judges in Canada embrace normative reasonableness. In *R. v. S. (R.D.)*,[58] Justices L'Heureux-Dube and McLachlin acknowledged that the average Canadian citizen was either a racist or one who subconsciously operated on the basis of negative racial stereotypes:

> Racism, and in particular anti-black racism, is a part of our community's psyche. A significant segment of our community holds overtly racist views. A much larger segment subconsciously operates on the basis of negative racial stereotypes. Furthermore, our institutions, including the criminal justice system, reflect and perpetuate those negative stereotypes.[59]

Nonetheless, they concluded that the Reasonable Person "is an informed and right-minded member of the community, a community which, in Canada, supports the fundamental principles entrenched in the Constitution by the Canadian Charter of Rights and Freedoms. Those fundamental principles include the principles of equality."[60]

Despite good reasons for thinking of reasonableness in normative terms, the Reasonable Man in modern America generally is *not* viewed as an ideal or aspirational construct. The Reasonable Man is simply the ordinary or typical man in the defendant's shoes. Joshua Dressler argues that this positivist conception of the Reasonable Man, at least in the provocation context, is correct:

> In the provocation area, the law does not deal with an idealized human being, because an ideal Reasonable Man, by definition, would never become angry enough that he would lose his self-control and kill solely on the basis of passion, rather than reason. Instead, the provocation defense is based on the principle that the defendant is, unfortunately, just like other *ordinary* human beings.[61]

It is true that an ideal person would never become so angry as to kill, but then jurors in provocation cases generally are not required to find that a reasonable man would have killed. In most jurisdictions, they need only find that a reasonable person would have lost his self-control or become as impassioned as the defendant.[62]

In response to Mison's concern that the average person is homophobic and heterosexist, Dressler argues that the Reasonable Man standard has a normative component[63] which eliminates extreme character flaws such as homophobia and racism:

> If the Ordinary Man standard is to maintain a normative component, it is also important that the law assume this person to be devoid of other extreme character flaws relevant to the defense. Specifically, the Ordinary Man may not possess "idiosyncratic moral values" that manifest the actor's moral depravity and which render the person abnormally likely to take affront and lose self-control. This means that, for purposes of determining whether a person is justified in becoming indignant by an otherwise harmless act, *the Ordinary Man is not racist, anti-Semitic, or prejudiced against any class of persons. Thus, too, the Ordinary Man is not homophobic.*[64]

It would be great if courts and juries made a nuanced distinction between positivist and normative reasonableness as Dressler does, but they don't. Only positivist reasonableness, the Ordinary Man with all his ordinary character flaws, is recognized in the criminal courtroom. Jurors debate whether an ordinary person in the defendant's situation *would have* lost his self-control, not whether it was reasonable or appropriate for him to have done so.

If reasonableness standards are to be used, the law ought to recognize both positivist and normative reasonableness. Jurors in cases involving claims of provocation or self-defense should first consider whether the defendant's emotions or beliefs were reasonable as a positivist matter (emotion reasonableness as a function of typicality). Jurors should then decide whether the defendant's actions ought to be deemed reasonable (act reasonableness as a normative matter). In other words, jurors should draw a distinction between act reasonableness and emotion reasonableness, which I discuss more fully in chapter 10. They should also recognize both positivist and normative reasonableness.[65]

In arguing for a normative conception of reasonableness, I do not mean to suggest that there is one normative truth or a single correct way to deal with all claims of provocation or self-defense. Each case that finds its way into the criminal justice system is unique and the defendant's culpability will turn on many factors. For this reason, I feel the jury is the best institutional actor to resolve questions of reasonableness and to decide whether the defendant should be convicted of murder, manslaughter, or nothing at all.[66]

A normative conception of reasonableness in self-defense cases makes sense because self-defense is generally recognized as a justification rather than an excuse. Justification defenses focus on the act rather than the actor. A justification defense exculpates the defendant if he or she did the right thing under the circumstances. A defendant who uses deadly force in self-defense does the right thing because the law prefers that an actor threatened with death or grievous bodily injury kill rather than be killed.

A normative conception of reasonableness in provocation cases is not as easily defended because the defense of provocation is generally understood as a partial excuse, rather than a partial justification. Excuse defenses focus on the actor, not the act. An excuse defense recognizes that what the defendant did (the defendant's act) was wrongful, but exculpates him (or mitigates the offense) on the ground that the defendant was not morally blameworthy. The provocation defense recognizes that killing in response to something less than a threat of death or serious bodily injury is wrong. This is why a provoked killer never receives a complete acquittal. The provoked killer is given a manslaughter mitigation largely because it is felt that he lost his self-control and therefore is less blameworthy than other intentional killers.

While the doctrine of provocation rests primarily on grounds of excuse, the defense also contains elements of justification. As discussed earlier in this chapter, the focus on the victim's wrongdoing, the misdirected retaliation rule, and the requirement of legally adequate provocation all suggest a normative concern over whether the defendant's acts were appropriate in relation to the circumstances. As George Fletcher, one of the leading criminal law theorists in the academy, notes, "The issue [in provocation cases] is *plainly normative* in the sense that the homicide is not mitigated to manslaughter by a mere factual showing that the slayer was provoked. He must be provoked under circumstances and to such a degree that he is not expected completely to control himself. The standard of adequate provocation is obviously shaped by social convention."[67]

Once one recognizes that the doctrine of provocation contains elements of excuse and justification, then adding a normative conception of reasonableness to the mix makes sense. In addition to asking whether an ordinary person in the defendant's shoes would have lost self-control, jurors should also ask whether the defendant's response ought to be recognized as reasonable.[68]

One potential problem with using a normative standard of reasonableness is that jurors might assume that a defendant whose *emotions* or beliefs are reasonable also *acted* reasonably. In other words, jurors might conflate emotion reasonableness with act reasonableness.[69] Such misdirection can be remedied by a jury instruction explaining the difference between the two.[70] Another conflation problem is possible. Jurors who think the ordinary person *would have* felt and acted the way the defendant did may conclude that the defendant acted the way he *should have* acted. In other words, the jury may conflate positivist reasonableness with normative reasonableness.

To minimize the risk of conflation, I recommend that we put into effect what Alan Michaels calls "judgmental descriptivism."[71] Michaels argues that rules of criminal liability should combine descriptive standards with judgmental standards. Michaels defines "judgmental standards" as normative assessments about the moral blameworthiness of an individual. Under Michaels's definition, judgmental standards are indeterminate, announcing broad goals but providing little guidance. In contrast, descriptive standards delineate more precisely what is required or expected. In describing in detail what is required, descriptive standards advance the goals of consistency, predictability, and reduced opportunity for bias.[72]

The reasonableness requirement as used in the doctrines of provocation and self-defense is a judgmental standard. It announces a broad principle (provoked killers must be reasonably provoked and self-defenders must reasonably believe in the need to act in self-defense) according to which jurors are asked to assess the moral blameworthiness of the defendant. Because reasonableness is left undefined, jurors have little guidance regarding what is or should be considered reasonable.

One way of implementing Michaels's judgmental descriptivism in provocation cases would be to describe very clearly the acts or events which would not qualify as legally adequate provocation. For example, the legislature could pass legislation precluding murder defendants from claiming spousal infidelity as legally adequate provocation. In 1997, the Maryland legislature took such a step when it added section 387A to the Maryland Penal Code, announcing that the observation of a spouse in the act of adultery does not constitute legally adequate

provocation.[73] Legislatures could also pass legislation precluding murder defendants from claiming that a nonviolent homosexual advance
constitutes legally adequate provocation.[74] In 1998, the government of
New South Wales considered implementing such a proposal after the
New South Wales Homosexual Advance Defence Working Party, com-
missioned by the New South Wales Attorney General to study the problem, recommended "the exclusion of a non-violent homosexual advance from forming the basis of the defence of provocation."[75]

While I agree that legislative action sends a clear message to both
jurors and would-be defendants regarding what types of actions are
considered unreasonable as a matter of law, I find legislative preclusion
problematic for several reasons. First, legislative preclusion takes decision making away from the jury. It literally precludes jurors from considering whether something is or is not legally adequate provocation.
Jurors should be encouraged to deliberate explicitly about social norms,
stereotypes, and bias when deciding what constitutes reasonable
provocation, not barred from deciding such issues.

Juries serve an extremely important function in our criminal justice
system. Jurors deliver what Norman Finkel calls commonsense justice.[76] They serve as a bulwark against overzealous government prosecutors and cynical judges.[77] A jury of twelve is more likely than a single
judge to consider a wide range of factors bearing on the question of culpability, simply because twelve individuals are likely to remember and
interpret the evidence in twelve different ways. Because of the jury's
special role, the Supreme Court has held that juries rather than judges
must decide facts which might affect the ultimate sentence.[78]

Juries are also better situated than legislatures to deliver individualized justice, which is what the criminal justice system is supposed to
be about. No two criminal cases are exactly the same. When the legislature passes a law, it makes a broad pronouncement that affects a large
number of individuals. The legislature cannot foresee every single individual who might be affected by that law. Juries, in contrast, do not
make broad pronouncements. They pass judgment on only one individual, the defendant who is being tried.

Questions such as whether the defendant was reasonably provoked
into a heat of passion and whether the defendant reasonably believed
in the need to use force in self-defense are value judgments best left to
the jury. Legislative preclusion, however, bars the jury from considering
the full context of the case in assessing the defendant's culpability. It

lumps all infidelity and all gay panic claims together, ignoring the specific facts and circumstances of an individual case, and says that all such
claims are unreasonable.

In *A Feminist Approach to Social Scientific Evidence*, Andrew Taslitz
discusses the importance of giving jurors as much information as possible so they can engage in contextualized decision making.[79] Taslitz
notes that when jurors decide questions about what was going on in the
defendant's mind, such as whether the defendant was provoked into a
heat of passion or had a reasonable belief that he needed to act in self-
defense, they craft "an interpretation that partly embodies their own assumptions, attitudes, and beliefs."[80] To reach a just decision, jurors need
to recognize that their assumptions, attitudes, and beliefs will influence
the way they decide the case. The ideal juror, however, acts as a "judi-
cious spectator," one who is "simultaneously emotionally empathetic,
detached, and judgmental."[81] Taslitz explains:

> The judicious spectator is not personally involved in what he wit-
> nesses, so his emotions and thoughts do not relate to his well-being.
> He is thus unbiased and somewhat detached. He may, however, draw
> on his own personal history. But in doing so, "[T]he spectator must . . .
> endeavor, as much as he can to put himself in the situation of the other,
> and to bring home to himself every little circumstance of distress
> which can possibly occur to the sufferer."[82]

For the jury to exercise such empathetic yet detached judgment, it needs
to hear both sides of the story. It needs to hear both the dominant narrative and the outsider's view of what happened.[83]

In racialized self-defense cases, for example, the dominant narrative presumes that Blackness equals dangerousness and Whiteness is
neutral. When the defendant is White and the victim is Black, the dominant narrative bolsters the defendant's claim of reasonableness. Race-
switching allows a different narrative to be told. Race-switching can
call into question claims of reasonableness that rest on racial stereotypes without precluding defendants from presenting their cases to the
jury.

The view that the jury can and should be both detached and empathetic has its critics. Judge Richard Posner, for example, is opposed to
attempts to make the jury more empathetic. According to Posner, "the
internal perspective—the putting oneself in the other person's shoes—

that is achieved by the exercise of empathetic imagination lacks normative significance."[84] Posner explains, "when we succeed in looking at the world through another's eyes, we lose the perspective necessary for judgment."[85]

Posner's argument is unpersuasive because jurors in criminal cases are asked to put themselves in the defendant's shoes all the time. In self-defense cases, jurors have to decide whether the defendant reasonably believed he was facing an imminent unlawful attack, and they make this determination by thinking about what they would have done if they had been in the defendant's shoes. In provocation cases, jurors have to decide whether the defendant was reasonably provoked into a heat of passion. In duress cases, jurors must decide whether a person of reasonable firmness would have succumbed to the coercive pressures faced by the defendant. In cases involving a defendant charged with a general intent crime who claims a mistake of fact, jurors must decide whether the defendant's mistaken belief was reasonable. In rape cases in which the defendant claims he thought the victim was consenting, jurors must decide whether a reasonable person in the defendant's shoes would have made the same assumption. In all these cases, jurors decide whether the defendant acted reasonably by putting themselves in his or her shoes.

The problem is not that jurors are insufficiently empathetic to defendants. Rather they may be all too likely to empathize with the defendant, particularly if dominant norms bolster the defendant's claim of reasonableness. Race-switching, gender-switching, and/or sexual orientation–switching may be necessary to shake up the dominant narrative. Switching forces jurors to think about what objective circumstances contribute to a finding of reasonableness.

A second problem with legislative preclusion is that it turns back the clock on advances made in provocation doctrine. Precluding defendants from arguing provocation in all cases involving spousal infidelity and nonviolent homosexual advances hearkens a return to the early common law categorical approach to provocation. The only difference is that under the early common law approach to provocation, the law specified a short list of things that could constitute legally adequate provocation. Legislative preclusion creates a short list of things that *cannot* constitute legally adequate provocation. As discussed above, this is problematic because it takes decision making away from the jury and gives it to the legislature.

A third and related concern is that legislative preclusion limits the types of arguments and evidence that a criminal defendant can present at trial. Despite the presumption of innocence and the protections of the Bill of Rights, a criminal defendant is at a huge disadvantage from the moment he walks into the courtroom. Jurors often presume the defendant is guilty, simply by virtue of the fact that he has been charged with a crime, notwithstanding the constitutional requirement that a defendant must be presumed innocent until proven guilty beyond a reasonable doubt. Judges often exercise their discretion in ways that favor the prosecution. As if the deck weren't already stacked against defendants, the Supreme Court has retreated from the long-standing principle that an accused has a due process right to present relevant evidence in his defense.[86]

One might argue that if the law is committed to ending racism, sexism, and heterosexism, then it should preclude defendants from taking advantage of such -isms. While I agree that defendants should not profit from arguments that play on such negative social attitudes and beliefs, the solution, in my opinion, is not to broadly preclude all defendants from claiming provocation or self-defense in certain limited circumstances. The solution is for prosecutors to do a better job of educating jurors about the dangers of such -isms.

One reason the legislature might seek to preclude certain provocation arguments might be a fear of divisiveness.[87] Legislators might believe that the best way to handle cases involving racial conflict is to ignore race. Likewise, they may believe that disallowing claims of gay panic and female infidelity will encourage juror unanimity in favor of conviction. The problem with this kind of reasoning is that it invites jurors to rely on dominant social norms in an unthinking fashion. I believe it is better for jurors to engage in reasoned debate about whether a nonviolent homosexual advance or a female partner's sexual infidelity should constitute legally adequate provocation or whether the fact that the victim was a young Black male should support the defendant's claim of reasonable fear, rather than pretend that there is consensus on these questions.

Legislative preclusion is problematic for another reason. When a legislature rules that a particular type of action can never constitute legally adequate provocation, it represents itself as the voice of the community although its action might only represent the voice of a particular segment of that community. For example, I happen to think sexual infidelity is inadequate reason to mitigate an intentional killing to manslaughter, and I know many others who feel the same way I do. I also know many people who feel quite strongly that sexual infidelity is a very good reason to mitigate. When the legislature chooses my view, it denies legitimacy to the opposite view. Moreover, if legislative preclusion is endorsed for certain types of cases, it will be difficult to oppose it for other cases. Conservative legislators could decide to preclude the argument that battering constitutes legally adequate provocation and prevent battered women from arguing that they were provoked into a heat of passion by their abuser's violent actions.

Several scholars have called for the abolition of the doctrine of provocation. Jeremy Horder, for example, argues that the doctrine should be abolished because historically it has been biased in favor of men who kill women.[88] Stephen Morse also thinks the doctrine should be abolished, but offers a different rationale.[89] Morse would abolish the defense because he thinks "actors who commit the same acts with the same mens rea should, on moral grounds, be convicted of the same crime and punished alike."[90]

In defense of his position, Morse argues, "Reasonable people do not kill no matter how much they are provoked and enraged people generally retain the capacity to control homicidal or any other kind of aggressive or antisocial desires."[91] It takes quite a lot to move from being outraged to killing another human being. "As virtually every human being knows because we all have been enraged, it is easy not to kill, even when one is enraged."[92] Morse continues:

> How hard is it not to offend the law? How hard is it not to kill, burgle, rob, rape, and steal? The ability to resist the temptation to violate the law is not akin to the ability required to be a fine athlete, artist, plumber, or doctor. The person is not being asked to exercise a difficult skill; rather, he or she is being asked simply to refrain from engaging in antisocial conduct. Think, too, of all the factors mitigating against such behavior: parental, religious, and school training; peer pressures and cultural expectations; internalized standards ("superego"); fear of capture and punishment; fear of shame; and a host of others. Not all such factors operate on all actors or with great strength. . . . Nonetheless, for all persons there are enormous forces arrayed against lawbreaking. It is one thing to yield to a desire to engage in undesirable conduct such as to gossip, brag, or treat one's fellows unfairly; it is

another to give in to a desire to engage in qualitatively more harmful conduct such as to kill, rape, burgle, rob, or burn.[93]

While I find the arguments for abolition very appealing, ultimately I would maintain the doctrine of provocation because it allows juries to return verdicts that reflect appropriate gradations of culpability. If the defense of provocation was abolished, jurors deciding the fate of provoked killers would have to choose between murder and complete acquittal. While Morse and others might hope that jurors would return a murder conviction if the defendant intentionally took the life of a fellow human being, jurors who feel sympathy for the defendant or who feel that murder is too harsh a penalty are just as likely to acquit.

Morse provides a hypothetical that illustrates my point. Imagine the parent who comes home to find that a man has just brutally attacked his child.[94] The perpetrator is running away, so the child is no longer in danger. The understandably enraged parent runs after, then shoots and kills the fleeing criminal. The parent would have a difficult time arguing he was justified in using deadly force in self-defense or in defense of others because the man was running away. If there were no provocation defense, the law would say the parent is guilty of murder. The jury would then be faced with the choice of finding the parent guilty of murder or guilty of nothing. Either choice is unsatisfactory. Murder seems too harsh a punishment for the understandably enraged parent and a complete acquittal seems too lenient for someone who has intentionally taken another person's life.

Many, like Jeremy Horder, support abolition because they see the doctrine of provocation as a deeply sexist doctrine which favors men who kill their female partners. The doctrine, however, also helps some women who kill their male partners. Battered women who kill their abusers during a lull in the violence are often denied the opportunity to argue self-defense because the judge feels there was no imminent threat. If the defense of provocation were abolished, these women would be unable to argue that they were provoked into a heat of passion by their abuser.[95]

To give descriptive content to normative reasonableness, I propose that judges instruct jurors that while it is completely normal to be influenced by dominant social norms, including masculinity norms, heterosexuality norms, and race norms, they should try not to let such norms bias their decision making. If they are uncertain as to whether such norms have influenced them, jurors may engage in gender-, race-, and/or sexual orientation–switching. If jurors come to one conclusion without switching and a different conclusion with switching, this would be an indication that they have been influenced by such norms.

For example, in a case in which a male defendant asserts that he was provoked by his female partner's actual or perceived infidelity, jurors would assess the reasonableness of the defendant's emotions and actions from the perspective of a woman in the defendant's situation. If the case involved a female defendant who killed her male partner after catching him in bed with another woman, jurors would think about whether they would grant the provocation mitigation if the female defendant was a man. In cases in which a heterosexual male defendant employs a gay panic argument, the jury could assess the reasonableness of the defendant's emotions and actions from the perspective of a gay man faced with an unwanted nonviolent heterosexual advance from a woman. In cases in which a White male defendant claims he acted in self-defense against a young Black male, jurors could think about whether the defendant's actions would be considered reasonable if the defendant was a Black man using deadly force against a young White male.[96] If a Black man is charged with murdering a White man, jurors could think about whether they would more readily believe his claim of self-defense if he was White.

Switching is not a completely novel idea, although its use has largely been explored in literature and film. In his novel, *A Time to Kill,* John Grisham tells the story of an African American man whose ten-year-old daughter is abducted and raped by two White rednecks in Clanton, Mississippi. The men take the little girl to a remote place and proceed to brutally beat and rape her. The two men are arrested and charged with rape, kidnapping, and aggravated assault. Because of rampant racial discrimination, the African American father doubts that the jury will convict the White men. He decides to take matters into his own hands. When the two men are brought out of the courthouse after their bail hearing, the father shoots and kills them.

The father is arrested and charged with two counts of capital murder. After the case is tried, the jury retires to deliberate. During jury deliberations, the jury is hopelessly deadlocked until a female juror asks her colleagues to indulge her in an exercise:

Wanda Womack stood at the end of the table and nervously cleared her throat. She asked for attention. "I have a proposal," she said slowly, "that just might settle this thing." . . .

"I thought of something last night when I couldn't sleep, and I want you to consider it. It may be painful. It may cause you to search your heart and take a long look at your soul. But I'll ask you to do it anyway. And if each of you will be honest with yourself, I think we can wrap this up before noon."

. . . "Right now we are evenly divided, give or take a vote. We could tell Judge Noose that we are hopelessly deadlocked. He would declare a mistrial, and we would go home. Then in a few months this entire spectacle would be repeated. Mr. Hailey would be tried again in this same courtroom, with the same judge, but with a different jury, a jury drawn from this county, a jury of our friends, husbands, wives, and parents. . . . That jury will be confronted with the same issues before us now, and those people will not be any smarter than we are."

"The time to decide this case is now. It would be morally wrong to shirk our responsibilities and pass the buck to the next jury. Can we all agree on that?"

They silently agreed.

"Good. This is what I want you to do. I want you to pretend with me for a moment. I want you to use your imaginations. I want you to close your eyes and listen to nothing but my voice."

They obediently closed their eyes. Anything was worth a try.[97]

A short time later, the jury reached a unanimous verdict. They acquitted the father of all charges. Only later does the reader learn what Wanda Womack had asked her colleagues to do. Grisham writes:

She made them all close their eyes and listen to her. She told them to pretend that the little girl had blond hair and blue eyes, that the two rapists were black, that they tied her right foot to a tree and her left foot to a fence post, that they raped her repeatedly and cussed her because she was white. She told them to picture the little girl layin' there beggin' for her daddy while they kicked her in the mouth and knocked out her teeth, broke both jaws, broke her nose. She said to imagine two drunk blacks pouring beer on her and pissing in her face, and laughing like idiots. And then she told them to imagine that the little girl belonged to them—their daughter. She told them to be honest with themselves and to write on a piece of paper whether or not they would kill those black bastards if they got the chance. And they voted, by secret ballot. All twelve said they would do the killing. The foreman counted the votes. Twelve to zero.[98]

Race-switching was also the theme of Desmond Nakano's film *White Man's Burden*. That film, produced in 1995, depicts an imaginary American society in which Blacks hold all the positions of wealth and power. Whites in this imaginary society serve in the positions usually occupied by Blacks and other minorities in contemporary American society. They are the maids, butlers, and blue-collar workers. Most Whites in this imaginary society are poor. Blacks think of Whites as genetically inferior or culturally deprived.

John Travolta plays a White blue-collar worker in a chocolate factory. Thinking that he will be perceived as a hard worker, Travolta volunteers to deliver a package to the home of his Black boss, played by Harry Belafonte. When Travolta arrives, Belafonte is upstairs with his wife, who is standing in front of an open window, dressed only in a bath towel. Belafonte's wife removes the towel, and at that moment, Belafonte looks down and sees Travolta standing on the grounds below, looking for someone to receive the package. Belafonte thinks that Travolta, who is staring off into space, is peeping at his naked wife. Belafonte later tells his assistant not to send Travolta to the house again because Belafonte doesn't like peeping toms. The assistant takes it upon himself to fire Travolta. Travolta tries to find employment elsewhere, but is unsuccessful. When Travolta cannot make the rent payments, he is evicted from his home.

In frustration, Travolta goes to Belafonte's house to explain the injustice of the situation but is turned away. In desperation, he kidnaps Belafonte so he can show Belafonte that he was wrong to think Travolta was peeping at his wife.

In the concluding scene, Belafonte is very ill. Travolta tries to take Belafonte to a hospital, but his pickup truck breaks down. Travolta takes Belafonte out of the car and places him on the street where he lies in obvious pain. Travolta tries to flag down a passing motorist to help get Belafonte to a hospital, but after agreeing to help, the motorist speeds away. Since they are in a predominantly White, low-income, and high- crime neighborhood, Travolta knows that the police, who are predominantly Black, will not come to the neighborhood unless they think a crime has been committed. Travolta uses his gun to shoot out the windows of a nearby car and store, triggering security alarms in order to summon police to the rescue. When two Black police officers arrive, they see Belafonte, a Black man, on the ground and Travolta, an obviously distraught White man, standing next to him. Immediately suspicious of the White man, the officers yell at Travolta to put his hands up. Travolta, still holding his gun, starts to put his hands up in the air. Since White men in the film's imaginary society are stereotyped as violent and dangerous criminals, the officers see the gun and assume Travolta is about to shoot them. Responding to this imaginary threat, they shoot and kill Travolta.

One might object that gender-switching, sexual orientation–switching, and race-switching could end up being simply an exercise in futility. Jurors who see the jealous husband, the heterosexual man who is outraged by a homosexual advance, and the man who thinks his life is threatened by a Black man or other person of color as reasonable could simply rationalize their judgments as gender-neutral, sexual orientation-neutral and race-neutral. Examples from real life, however, suggest that switching can be an effective way to minimize bias in the courtroom.

In 1997, Jim McComas and Cynthia Strout, criminal defense attorneys in Alaska, were representing an African American teenager charged as an adult with first-degree assault for striking an older White student in the head with a hammer during a construction electricity class at a vocational high school. The White student was the initial aggressor, but because he was not armed, the prosecutor argued the Black teen used excessive force. McComas and Strout were worried that the mostly White jury (nine Whites, two Alaskan natives, and one African American) would be inclined to convict their client because of racial stereotypes about young Black men being violent aggressors, and that the legal principle of excessive force would provide a facially race- neutral means to render such a conviction. As McComas explained, "Our case analysis identified the race difference as the single biggest problem we would have—that is, the prosecution claim of excessive force would be more easily bought since our client was a black teen—presumably prone to pointless violence—and the "victim" was white—presumably non-aggressive."[99]

McComas and Strout devised a five-part plan for addressing the racial dynamics of the case.[100] First, they presented their case to mock jurors. Second, they drafted a written jury questionnaire. Third, they devised a strategy for dealing with race during voir dire. The attorneys wanted to talk to prospective jurors about race and racial bias without causing them to feel defensive. During voir dire, Strout told the prospective jurors about an incident that happened to her a few weeks before the trial. She saw a young Black male driving an expensive BMW, and her first thought was that he was a drug dealer, rather than a doctor's son. The defense attorney's revelation about her own racially biased feelings gave prospective jurors permission to admit their own stereotyped thinking. It also prompted the jurors to start thinking and talking about racial stereotypes right away. During voir dire, the attorneys also made a point of distinguishing between playing the "race card" (or using race as an excuse) and legitimate ways in which race might be deployed in the courtroom, such as "explaining the complainant's motive to initiate aggression, as evidenced by his use of racial slurs, and the influences which might affect witness perception of the events."[101] Fourth, the attorneys retained a research psychologist to testify about the effects of racial stereotypes on memory and perception. Finally, they asked the judge to give a race-switching jury instruction, modeled after a jury instruction I proposed in a 1996 *Minnesota Law Review* article.[102] The only modification they made to my proposed instruction was to make race-switching mandatory rather than simply discretionary. In agreeing to the defense request, the Honorable Milton M. Souter gave the following instruction:

Instruction No. 36
It is natural for human beings to make assumptions about the parties and witnesses in any case based on stereotypes. "Stereotypes" constitute well-learned sets of associations or expectations connecting particular behaviors or traits with members of a particular social group. Often, we may rely on stereotypes without even being aware that we are doing so. As a juror, you must not make assumptions about the parties and witnesses based on their membership in a particular racial group. You must not assume that a particular interpretation of a person's behavior is more or less likely because the individual belongs to any particular racial group. Reliance on stereotypes in deciding real cases is prohibited both because every accused is entitled to equal protection of law, and because racial stereotypes are historically, and notoriously, inaccurate when applied to any particular member of a race.

> To ensure that you have not made any unfair assessments based on racial stereotypes, you should apply a race- switching exercise to test whether stereotypes have affected your evaluation of the case. "Race-switching" involves imagining the same events, the same circumstances, the same people, but switching the races of the parties and witnesses. For example, if the accused is African-American and the accuser is White, you should imagine a White accused and an African-American accuser.
>
> If your evaluation of the case is different after engaging in race-switching, this suggests a subconscious reliance on stereotypes. You must then reevaluate the case from a neutral, unbiased perspective.[103]

After two hours of deliberation, the jury acquitted the defendant of all charges. Later, a White female juror called McComas and thanked the defense team for the wonderful job they did, stating, "You restored my faith in the justice system."[104]

Switching is one way to implement what Mari Matsuda calls "looking to the bottom" or adopting the perspective of those who have experienced discrimination.[105] Matsuda, however, warns against "abstract consideration of the position of the least advantaged" because "the technique of imagining oneself black and poor in some hypothetical world is less effective than studying the actual experience of black poverty and listening to those who have done so."[106] For this reason, attorneys engaging in switching should call expert witnesses and introduce social science studies to help jurors understand the effects of stereotypes on memory and perception.[107]

By making gender, race, and sexual orientation salient, individuals who might otherwise rely on deeply rooted biases are encouraged to think critically about those biases. As Jody Armour has pointed out, social science studies have shown that making race salient encourages egalitarian-minded individuals to suppress their natural instinct toward racial prejudice.[108] The same is likely true for other types of bias. Moreover, when jurors are informed about the ways in which their cognitive biases can influence the way they "see" the evidence, they are more likely to exercise their decision-making power in a less biased way.

Role reversal through gender-, race-, and sexual orientation–switching is a useful way of exposing bias and privilege. Switching helps expose the fact that heterosexual male violence is often presumed reasonable when similar violence by heterosexual females, gay men, and men of color would not be seen as reasonable. Switching is also likely to spark debate and discussion in the jury room about whether violence in response to female infidelity, gay panic, or racialized fear ought to be considered reasonable.

# 10

# The Act-Emotion Distinction

ALL OF US can empathize with the individual who has just found out that his or her intimate partner has been sexually unfaithful. Anger, outrage, sadness, a feeling of worthlessness, depression—all these are understandable emotional responses to the betrayal of trust that comes with infidelity. It is eminently reasonable to feel these strong emotions. Provoked killers, however, go beyond *feeling* outraged. They *act* on their emotions in the most extreme way—by taking a human life. Most of us would not kill, even if we were extremely angry. Yet the provocation doctrine partially excuses an act of killing if the defendant's emotional response is considered reasonable. If a reasonable person in the defendant's shoes would have been provoked into a heat of passion, then the provoked killer is acquitted of murder and convicted of the lesser offense of voluntary manslaughter. The provoked killer receives this mitigation even if the reasonable person would not have killed, because provocation doctrine does not require act reasonableness.

We can also empathize with the individual who is afraid of being physically harmed by another person. An individual can have differing degrees of fear depending on the situation. In *The Gift of Fear*, Gavin de Becker describes a woman with a gut feeling that the stranger who has offered to carry her groceries has an ulterior motive for being so nice.[1] It would be foolish if that woman ignored her gut feeling. Ignoring one's intuition can place one in harm's way. There is, however, a big difference between preventive action, such as refusing the suspicious offer of assistance, and preemptive action, such as shooting the man. It would hardly be reasonable for the woman with a gut feeling that the stranger offering to carry her groceries is really a criminal-in-waiting to take out a gun and shoot that stranger before he did anything to confirm her gut feeling.

Now let's pretend the woman pushes her gut feeling aside and accepts the offer of assistance from the stranger who seems so kind. He carries her heavy groceries all the way up five flights of stairs, then asks her for a drink of water or asks to use her telephone to make a local call. The woman feels uneasy about letting this man she doesn't really know into her apartment, but he has been kind enough to carry her groceries. The least she can do, she rationalizes, is give him a glass of water or allow him to use her phone. Once inside the apartment, the man who was all charm just seconds ago turns into a sexual predator. He pins the woman against the wall. He presses himself against her, and starts to grope at her breasts. At this point, the woman knows the man is up to no good. She can't break loose from his grip because he is much bigger and stronger than her. If this woman were to grab a nearby instrument—say a pair of scissors or a kitchen knife—and stab her attacker once, twice, maybe even three times, just enough to get him off her, then run for help, most of us would feel she had acted reasonably in self-defense.

Now let's change the facts once again. This time, the woman stabs her attacker twice. He falls to the floor, and is temporarily immobilized. If the woman were to continue stabbing the man repeatedly and fatally after he no longer posed a threat to her, her actions would seem less reasonable.

In each of these scenarios, the woman's *fear* of bodily harm was reasonable. The reasonableness of her *actions,* however, varies depending on the situation. As these examples suggest, there is a big difference between reasonable emotions (fear, anger, outrage) and reasonable action. Even if a particular *emotion* is reasonable under the circumstances, this does not mean that acting on that emotion by using deadly force is also reasonable.[2] It may be reasonable to feel anger at one's unfaithful partner, but not reasonable to act on that anger by killing the partner. It may be reasonable to fear an attack, but if that attack is not imminent or if one can avoid it by running away or disabling the attacker, then killing may not be a reasonable response.

It makes sense to engage in separate inquiries regarding the reasonableness of a given action and the reasonableness of the emotions leading to that action. Yet most legal decision makers considering provocation and self-defense cases focus almost exclusively upon the reasonableness of the defendant's emotions (or beliefs), and pay scant attention to the reasonableness of the defendant's acts.

## THE ACT-EMOTION DISTINCTION IN PROVOCATION CASES

In modern jurisdictions, the key issue is whether legally adequate provocation was present. Legally adequate provocation is said to exist if the defendant was *reasonably* provoked into a heat of passion. One could interpret this ambiguous language as requiring what I call "act reasonableness," a finding that a reasonable person in the defendant's shoes would have responded or *acted* as violently as the defendant did.[3] An unscientific survey of model jury instructions used in the fifty states indicates that only two states take this approach. These two states ask jurors to decide whether a reasonable man in the defendant's shoes would have been so provoked as to kill or inflict serious bodily harm. Maryland, for example, tells its jurors that legally adequate provocation is "something that would cause a reasonable person to become enraged enough *to kill or inflict serious bodily harm.*"[4] Jurors in West Virginia are told that "[t]he term 'provocation' as it is used to reduce murder to voluntary manslaughter, consists of certain types of acts committed against the defendant which *would cause a reasonable man to kill.*"[5]

The reluctance of most states to require "act reasonableness" probably stems from the belief that the ultimate act of killing in the heat of passion is never reasonable. The provoked killer's actions are wrongful as a matter of law, which is why he does not receive a complete acquittal. We do not want others to emulate the behavior. We mitigate the charges only because we feel sympathy for the provoked killer. As Wayne LaFave and Austin Scott, Jr., explain:

> It is sometimes stated that, in order to reduce an intentional killing to voluntary manslaughter, the provocation involved must be such as to cause a reasonable man to kill. *Yet the reasonable man, however greatly provoked he may be, does not kill.* The law recognizes this fact, by holding that the one who thus kills is guilty of the crime of voluntary manslaughter, while at the same time, the law considers that one who really acts reasonably in killing another (as in proper self-defense) is guilty of no crime. What is really meant by "reasonable provocation" is provocation which causes a reasonable man to lose his normal self-control; and, although a reasonable man who has thus lost control over himself would not kill, yet his homicidal reaction to the provocation is at least understandable.[6]

Most states which follow the modern test seem to require what I call "emotion reasonableness," a finding that the defendant's *emotional* outrage or *passion* was reasonable.[7] Passion is generally considered an emotional state. As the Florida Supreme Court explained, passion "is one of the emotions of the mind known as anger, rage, sudden resentment, or terror."[8] A Tennessee court describes passion as "the deepest and most powerful emotion."[9]

An example of "emotion reasonableness" is found in the model jury instructions in Illinois. Illinois tells its jurors that legally adequate provocation is "conduct sufficient to excite an intense *passion* in a reasonable person."[10] Similarly, Alaska defines "serious provocation" as "conduct which is sufficient to excite an *intense passion* in a reasonable person in the defendant's situation."[11] That many states focus on the reasonableness of the defendant's passion or emotion is not surprising. After all, the doctrine of provocation is also known as the heat of passion defense.

A handful of states focus on loss of control as a result of intense passion, instructing jurors in provocation cases that legally adequate provocation exists if an ordinary person in the defendant's shoes would have lost his or her self-control.[12] Even though jurors in these states are told to scrutinize the reasonableness of the defendant's loss of control as opposed to the reasonableness of his or her passion, which suggests some concern with the reasonableness of the defendant's acts, focusing on the reasonableness of the defendant's loss of self-control may still be thought of as an evaluation of "emotion reasonableness" as opposed to "act reasonableness." Language from a Kansas Supreme Court case highlights the link between passion and loss of control:

> The passion aroused by the provocation must be so violent as to dethrone the reason of the accused for the time being; it must prevent thought and reflection, and the formation of a deliberate purpose. . . . Mere anger, in and of itself, is not sufficient, but must be of such a character as to prevent the individual from cool reflection and a control of his actions.[13]

Finally, a few states require both "act reasonableness" and "emotion reasonableness."[14] This, in my opinion, is the best of the three approaches. New Jersey, for example, first tells its jurors that "[p]rovocation in law must be of a type and degree that in the jury's opinion probably would throw the mind of an average person of ordinary self-control into a state of uncontrolled *rage or anger*."[15] This particular instruction focuses upon the reasonableness of the defendant's *emotions*. New Jersey, however, also directs its jurors to examine the reasonableness of the defendant's *acts*, instructing jurors that "[t]he provocation must be so gross as to cause the ordinary reasonable person to lose his or her self-control and *to use violence with fatal results*."[16] Ohio too looks at the reasonableness of the defendant's acts and emotions, first instructing jurors that "[t]he defendant is 'under the influence of a sudden passion or in [a] sudden fit of rage' when there is serious provocation occasioned by the victim that is reasonably sufficient to incite a person into *using deadly force*."[17] Jurors in Ohio are also instructed, "For provocation to be reasonably sufficient to bring on sudden passion or a sudden fit of rage, you must determine that the provocation was sufficient to arouse *the passions of an ordinary person* beyond the power of his/her control."[18]

Requiring the jury to focus on the reasonableness of the defendant's actions does not mean they must find it was reasonable for the defendant to kill. Rather, act reasonableness can be satisfied if the provoking incident would have provoked an ordinary person to violence. Joshua Dressler explains why the focus should be on whether the ordinary person would have been provoked to violence:

> The ultimate issue should not be whether "the provocation was enough to make a reasonable man do as he did," because "reasonable men" do not kill others when provoked, least of all in the ultra-violent way provoked killers often do it. Instead, the issue should be articulated as follows: whether the provocation "might render ordinary [persons], of fair average disposition, liable to act rashly or without due deliberation or reflection, and from passion, rather than judgment."[19]

In his 1992 book entitled *Provocation and Responsibility*, Jeremy Horder provides a detailed history of English provocation doctrine. Horder also provides a useful explanation of the difference between reasonable feelings of anger (reasonable emotions) and reasonable action in anger (reasonable acts). According to Horder, a reasonable *feeling* of anger means "being angered for the right reason, at the right time, to the right extent, and so on."[20] In other words, one's emotional response is considered reasonable if one has the right amount of anger and outrage relative to the provoking incident. For example, if someone kidnaps your family and tortures them, a reasonable emotional response is to be very angry. If you are only moderately angry, your emotional response is not reasonable because it is too mild. If, on the other hand, you feel outraged at a baby's persistent crying, your emotional response would probably be perceived as unreasonable and excessive.[21]

In contrast, reasonable *action* in anger means proportional retaliation against the person who has wronged you. Horder explains, "For men of honour, therefore, to *act* justly in the face of an affront or other injustice is to inflict proportional requital, retaliation of the correct amount, on the perpetrator of the injustice."[22] In other words, reasonable action in provocation means action which is proportionate to the provocation. For example, if V slaps D for no reason at all and D responds by hitting V once or perhaps even twice, one can say that D's response is proportionate to the initial wrong, and therefore reasonable. If D were to instead take out a knife and stab V to death, his response would likely be deemed unreasonable because a fatal stabbing is grossly disproportionate to a slap.

Under a proportionality principle, the reasonableness of the provoked defendant's action depends upon the type of force and degree of force he uses in relation to the triggering provocation. Proportionality, however, does not mean the provoked defendant must respond with force equal to the force used by the provoker. Horder explains:

> [W]hen a man provokes another, as by insulting, assaulting, or forcibly confining him, or committing adultery with his wife, he commits injustice through taking an unfair advantage. This unfair advantage consists of an unwarranted gain to the provoker (lack of self-restraint or liberty to do as one pleases) acquired through inflicting an unwarranted loss on the victim (wrongful loss of self-esteem, bodily integrity, property, liberty, or whatever). . . . As far as the degree of rectification or retaliation is concerned, in order to remedy the injustice and restore the *status quo ante*, the perpetrator of the injustice must be deprived of his unmerited gain *and* the wronged victim must have his loss restored or compensated for. . . . The important thing to note about the concept of rectificatory justice is that it is neither the mere compensation of the victim nor solely doing to the perpetrator what he did to the victim. The former leaves the perpetrator's gain and the latter

leaves the victim's loss out of the moral account. True retributive justice, "proportional requital" (as Aristotle called it), is a punishment
that represents the value of both the gain and the loss together. It is
thus a symbolic restoration of the *status quo ante*, negating the effect of
*both* the unwarranted gain acquired and the unwarranted loss inflicted. The administering of such punishment is the display of justice
in accordance with the mean.[23]

Under this view, "only a greater injury than that actually inflicted by the
perpetrator of the injustice would be punishment enough to restore the
*status quo ante*."[24]

In England, provocation doctrine has included a proportionality
component since at least the nineteenth century.[25] As the English Criminal Law Commissioners of 1839 explained, a provoked killing was
murder rather than manslaughter if the defendant's response was "so
excessive and disproportionate to the cause of provocation that the
killing [could not] be attributed to mere heat of blood arising from the
provocation given."[26] For a while, English courts treated proportionality as a strict requirement.[27] As expressed by Viscount Simon in *Mancini
v. Director of Public Prosecutions*, "the mode of resentment *must* bear a
reasonable relationship to the provocation if the offence is to be reduced
to manslaughter."[28] After passage of the Homicide Act of 1957, however, English courts came to view proportionality as just one factor for
the jury to consider in determining whether a reasonable man would
have reacted the way the defendant did, rather than a strict requirement.[29] Proportionality continues to be viewed as an important factor in
English provocation cases. In the 2001 case of *Regina v. Smith*,[30] an English court reiterated the importance of proportionality, stating that "the
critical question is that of the proportionality between the provocation
and the response."[31]

Provocation doctrine in Ireland also includes a proportionality requirement.[32] An Irish defendant's actions are scrutinized to determine
whether the method and degree of force used was reasonable under the
circumstances. Strict proportionality or an eye for an eye is not required. If the provoking incident is a punch to the nose and the defendant's response is to punch the victim in the face three times, this response could still be considered reasonable because a loose proportionality exists between the provoking incident and the defendant's
response. Even if the victim punched the defendant only once, a re-

sponse of three punches in return might still be considered reasonable. The means used (fists) and degree of force (three punches as opposed to a hundred punches) is loosely proportionate to the provocation. If, however, the defendant were to take out a gun and shoot the victim, his act of shooting (deadly force) might be deemed unreasonable in relation to the punch (nondeadly force) because the means and the degree of force used were grossly excessive.

Even in America, some courts have explicitly recognized a proportionality requirement in provocation cases. In *People v. Matthews*,[33] for example, an Illinois court affirmed the trial court's refusal to give an instruction on voluntary manslaughter in a case in which the defendant shot and killed a man after an argument over whether the defendant would pay the man $5 or $10 for having given him a ride to his car. The defendant claimed that when the victim hollered and waved his hand in front of the defendant's face, he lost his self-control and shot the victim. The court rejected the defendant's claim of provocation, explaining:

> A slight provocation will not be adequate since the provocation must be *proportionate* to the manner in which the accused retaliated and therefore if accused on a slight provocation attacked deceased with violence out of all *proportion* to the provocation and killed him the crime is murder.[34]

Similarly, in *U.S. v. Sielaff*,[35] the Seventh Circuit recognized a proportionality requirement in provocation doctrine:

> The requirement that the response be proportional is clear in *People v. Simpson* [cites omitted], where denial of a voluntary manslaughter instruction was upheld because "(i)t is an extravagant suggestion that scratches by the wife could serve as provocation for a malice-free but ferocious attack by the defendant with a deadly instrument.[36]

Some would reject a proportionality requirement in provocation doctrine on the ground that once a person has been provoked into a heat of passion, he cannot control the mode or degree of force he uses to retaliate against his provoker. This criticism might be persuasive if the presence of passion completely obliterated the ability to control one's actions. The law, however, assumes that there are degrees of loss of self-control.[37] If the provoked killer completely lacked the capacity to control his acts, it would not be just to punish him at all. However, we do punish provoked killers, albeit less severely than murderers. The treatment of provocation as only a partial defense reflects the assumption that the provoked killer's loss of self-control is not complete.

Norman Finkel argues that requiring proportionality is unwise because such a requirement would limit the provocation defense to those who respond to physical violence or threat of physical violence.[38] Act reasonableness, however, does not mean the defendant's response must be strictly proportionate to the alleged provocation. Proportionality is merely suggested as a tool to help jurors think about whether the defendant's acts should be deemed reasonable.

To implement the act-emotion distinction in provocation doctrine, states could adopt the following sample jury instruction which requires both emotion reasonableness and act reasonableness:

> Voluntary Manslaughter. An individual who kills in response to legally adequate provocation is guilty of voluntary manslaughter rather than murder. Legally adequate provocation is defined as provocation which would provoke the reasonable person in the defendant's shoes into a state of uncontrolled passion. Before you may return a verdict of voluntary manslaughter, you must be satisfied that the following three requirements are met:
>
> Actual Heat of Passion. The defendant was actually provoked into a heat of passion.
>
> Emotion Reasonableness. The defendant's emotions were reasonable. A defendant's emotions may be considered reasonable if the reasonable (i.e. ordinary) person in the defendant's shoes would have been provoked into a heat of passion.
>
> Act Reasonableness. The defendant's acts were also normatively reasonable. A defendant's acts may be considered normatively reasonable if the defendant's response bears a reasonable relationship to the provoking act or incident.[39]

In requiring both emotion reasonableness and act reasonableness, the proposed reform is not a radical departure from modern provocation doctrine. It merely encourages jurors to think about the defendant's provocation claim more fully. Like the modern test, it requires jurors to find that the defendant was actually provoked into a heat of passion. It also keeps the second element of the modern test (whether the reasonable person would have been provoked), but clarifies that the focus here is on emotion reasonableness. Act reasonableness is the only new requirement. Additionally, the proposed reform eliminates the no-cooling-off period required in many modern statutes in recognition of the fact that one can be provoked into a state of uncontrolled rage by a series of events occurring over a period of time.

## THE ACT-EMOTION DISTINCTION IN SELF-DEFENSE CASES

A similar distinction between emotion reasonableness and act reasonableness exists in the self-defense arena.[40] Even though act reasonableness is implied in self-defense doctrine's proportionality requirement, jury instructions on self-defense tend to focus only on emotion (or belief) reasonableness.[41] Jurors are instructed to find that the defendant reasonably *believed* (or reasonably feared) that deadly force was necessary to counter an imminent threat of death or grievous bodily injury. Jurors are not instructed to separately find that the defendant's *act* of shooting or stabbing or beating the victim was reasonable. This focus on reasonable beliefs reflects the presumption that a defendant who reasonably fears imminent harm acts reasonably as well. In most cases, a correlation between reasonable fears and reasonable acts will exist. However, just because someone has a reasonable belief that another poses an imminent threat of death or serious bodily injury does not necessarily mean a particular action leading to death is reasonable.[42]

For example, in *State v. Dill*,[43] two men in the parking lot of a bar a little before midnight were having trouble getting their truck to start because of a low battery. One of the men, Terry Greenwood, walked over to another car in the lot and asked the three occupants whether they could give him a jump. One of the passengers in that car offered to give Greenwood a jump for $5. Offended that the men would not help him for free, Greenwood began to argue loudly with the passenger and then walked toward the driver's side of the car. Defendant Dill was sitting in the driver's seat with the window down. Suddenly, Dill saw Greenwood lunge toward the open car window with a knife. Dill responded by reaching for a loaded gun from between the seats of the car. He opened the car door, and shot Greenwood in the head. Greenwood died a short time later.

Dill was charged with murder. At trial, Dill argued that he shot Greenwood in self-defense. Like most self-defense statutes, the Louisiana statute on self-defense focused exclusively on the reasonableness of the defendant's beliefs, providing that a homicide is justifiable "[w]hen committed in self-defense by one who *reasonably believes* that he is in imminent danger of losing his life or receiving great bodily harm and that the killing is necessary to save himself from that danger."[44] Rejecting Dill's claim of self-defense, the jury found Dill guilty of manslaughter. Dill's conviction was affirmed on appeal.

In affirming Dill's conviction, the Louisiana Court of Appeals found that even though Dill's *belief* in the need to act in self-defense was reasonable, his *act* of shooting Greenwood was not. The court explains why Dill's fear was reasonable in the following passage:

> There is no question that the two men were engaged in a heated argument at the time of the shooting. The victim approached the car during the encounter to continue the altercation. From the relative sizes of the two men it appears that Dill (5'4", 145 lbs.) would have received the worst end in a fight, even if the victim (6'0", 200 lbs.) had been unarmed. *Accordingly, [Dill's] apprehension of receiving great bodily harm could be deemed reasonable.*[45]

Even though Dill's *fear* of bodily harm was reasonable, the appellate court affirmed Dill's conviction because Dill's *act* of shooting Greenwood in the head at close range was not reasonable. In drawing this conclusion, the court pointed to several less fatal alternatives Dill might have employed to avoid the threatened harm.

> In the present case, it would appear that the trier of fact could readily conclude that the defendant possessed the ability to retreat or withdraw from the impending conflict. He was in an automobile. It was possible to have driven off or at the very least, rolled up the window to prevent any attack by the victim. . . . [I]t was likewise evident that deadly force was not mandated by the situation. By the defendant's own admission he issued no warning to the victim. Nor, apparently

when firing at a close range did he aim for a less vital area than the head.[46]

Another self-defense case illustrates the difference between reasonable fear of great bodily harm and reasonable action in self-defense. In *State v. Garrison*,[47] Jessie Garrison went to visit his sister at her apartment. Jeremiah Sharp, his sister's former boyfriend, showed up drunk and belligerent and began arguing with Garrison's sister. Garrison intervened, and his sister left the room. During the argument, Sharp reached for a pistol in his waistband. Because of Sharp's intoxicated state, Garrison was able to remove the pistol from Sharp's waistband. Sharp then grabbed a steak knife and advanced toward Garrison with the knife raised high. Garrison backed up and, using the pistol he'd just retrieved from Sharp, fired at Sharp's left ankle. Garrison then fired one more shot which killed Sharp.

Garrison was charged with manslaughter in the first degree with a firearm. At trial, Garrison argued he acted in self-defense. Even though Garrison's *fear* of grievous bodily harm may have been reasonable since Sharp was advancing toward him with a knife, the court rejected Garrison's self-defense argument on the ground that Garrison's *act* of shooting Sharp was unreasonable. According to the trial court, Garrison's act of shooting was unreasonable because less drastic alternatives were available to avoid the threatened harm. Garrison could have retreated or he could have again disarmed Sharp, especially after Sharp was shot in the left ankle.[48]

A person who honestly and reasonably *fears* imminent death or great bodily harm does not necessarily *act* reasonably if he uses deadly force in self-defense. The type and degree of force used by the defendant to ward off the threat may or may not be reasonable depending upon the gravity of the threatened harm and whether less deadly alternatives are available to deal with the threatened harm. Recognizing the distinction between reasonable beliefs and reasonable acts would go a long way toward ensuring that outcomes in self-defense cases reflect appropriate judgments about the use of deadly force.

I suggest that the following language be adopted to clarify the distinction between reasonable beliefs and reasonable action in self-defense:

A person is justified in the use of force against an aggressor if:

1) S/he honestly and reasonably *believes* that his/her use of [deadly] force is immediately necessary to defend against a threat of unlawful [deadly] force, i.e., force for which there is no justification, and

2) His/her *actions* are also reasonable. The defendant's use of force is reasonable if:

   A) it is reasonably proportionate to the perceived threat; or

   B) it is the least drastic means reasonably available to avoid the threatened attack

3) The finder of fact may consider the following factors in deciding whether the defendant's use of force was reasonable:

   A) whether the defendant could have retreated to a place of complete safety,

   B) whether the defendant could have given up property to avoid the threatened harm,

   C) whether the defendant could have given a warning before resorting to the use of force,

   D) if the defendant used a gun, whether s/he could have shot at a less vital part of the body,

   E) whether the defendant could have complied with a demand to do something s/he was not legally obligated to do,

   F) where the threat took place (in the defendant's home or place of business or another place where the defendant had a right to be)

4) Definitions and Explanations

   A) A "reasonable belief" is one which an ordinary person in the defendant's shoes would have held.

   B) In assessing whether the defendant's acts were reasonable, the jury should think about whether the defendant's acts were appropriate under the circumstances.[49]

The above reformulation is largely a clarification, rather than a revision, of existing self-defense doctrine. However, it differs from current doctrine in a few important ways. First, the reformulation adopts language from the Model Penal Code which asks the jury to consider whether the defendant's use of force was immediately necessary rather than whether the threatened force was imminent or impending. Second, the reformulation specifies that in addition to finding that the defendant's belief in the need to act in self-defense was honest and reasonable, the jury must also find that the defendant's actions were reasonable. To guide the jury, the reformulation states explicitly that the defendant's act is not reasonable if it is disproportionate or if less deadly alternatives were available. It then lists a number of other factors the jury can consider in deciding whether the defendant's use of force was reasonable.

## CONCLUSION

One might question how the act-emotion distinction I am proposing addresses the problem of dominant social norms affecting juror determinations of reasonableness. Requiring a finding of reasonable emotion (or reasonable belief) and reasonable action is not a gender-specific, race-specific, or sexual orientation-specific reform. The requirement would apply across the board in all provocation and self-defense cases, not simply those involving race, gender, and sexual orientation. How does this universal reform address the specific problem of bias influencing determinations of reasonableness? The reform addresses the problem of invisible bias by heightening juror scrutiny of all claims of reasonableness, making it more difficult for defendants claiming they were provoked to receive the mitigation from murder to manslaughter. Similarly, it makes it more difficult for those who claim they acted in self-defense to receive a complete acquittal.

There are at least two reasons to support this proposal. First, a reform that applies across the board to all defendants is more politically feasible and more likely than a gender-specific, race-specific, or sexual orientation-specific reform to be adopted by both conservative and liberal legislators who tend today to be wary of proposals that appear to give special treatment to women, racial minorities, and/or gays and lesbians. The liberal mantra of color blindness in the arena of race and sameness equality in the arena of gender encourages lawmakers to adopt race-neutral and gender-neutral language, even when such language often is anything but.

Second, requiring both act reasonableness and emotion reasonableness is likely to lead to more just results in cases involving claims of female infidelity, gay panic, and racialized self-defense. In these three types of cases, the defendant relies on dominant social norms to bolster his claim of reasonableness. When the focus is on the reasonableness of the defendant's beliefs or emotions, it is easy for jurors to overlook the fact that social norms support the defendant's claim of reasonableness because the defendant's beliefs and emotions seem familiar. It is easy for jurors to sympathize with a defendant when they feel they too would have felt angry or fearful if they had been in the defendant's shoes. If jurors must take the additional step of deciding whether the defendant *acted* reasonably, they will be forced to think about whether the defendant's actions were appropriate under the circumstances. While the two inquiries (whether the defendant's emotions were reasonable and whether his acts were reasonable) will often overlap, this will not always be the case. As the *Garrison* and *Dill* cases illustrated, one can have a reasonable belief in the need to act in self-defense, yet act unreasonably by using disproportionate force or killing when less fatal alternatives are available. Similarly, one can be reasonably provoked into a heat of passion (one can understandably feel outraged and impassioned if one, for example, finds out that one's beloved has been unfaithful), yet act unreasonably by using force completely out of proportion to the provoking incident.

In many respects, what I am proposing is not a radical reform of current doctrine. Self-defense doctrine already includes a reasonable act requirement. The defendant's response has to be reasonably necessary and it has to be proportionate to the threatened harm. Implicit in both the proportionality and necessity requirements is the notion that the defendant's acts must be reasonable in light of the threat. The problem is that most model jury instructions on self-defense fail to tell jurors that they must scrutinize the reasonableness of the defendant's actions. My proposal would simply make explicit that which is implicit in current self-defense doctrine.

With respect to provocation, however, only a few jurisdictions currently require jurors to consider the reasonableness of the defendant's acts. Therefore, unlike self-defense doctrine which already includes a reasonable act requirement, requiring act reasonableness in provocation doctrine would constitute a departure from current practice in most jurisdictions. Does act reasonableness effectively abolish the doctrine? On the surface, one might think it does because no provoked defendant could ever show that his act of killing was reasonable. Act reasonableness, however, does not mean the act of killing itself has to be reasonable. Act reasonableness simply means that the defendant's conduct has to be normatively reasonable. Act reasonableness exists if the mode and degree of force used by the defendant was relatively proportionate to the provoking act. Requiring act reasonableness in the form of relative proportionality serves to remind jurors that one who takes a human life and claims he was reasonably provoked should expect some heightened scrutiny of his or her claim of reasonableness.

# Conclusion

THE REASONABLENESS REQUIREMENT is by no means perfect. We've seen how it allows dominant culture defendants, namely White heterosexual males, to get away with murder. We've also seen how it disadvantages others whose beliefs and actions are not considered reasonable in the eyes of the average American. One concerned about fairness in the criminal justice system might legitimately ask, Why bother to retain the requirement? Why not, as some feminists and critical race scholars have proposed, abandon the pretense of neutrality and objectivity, which is all that the reasonableness requirement seems to offer?

While I am just as harsh a critic of the reasonableness requirement as others, I believe we should retain it, warts and all, because the alternative—a completely subjective standard—would be worse. If we were to abolish the reasonableness requirement, then all a murder defendant would have to do to receive an acquittal is say, "I honestly believed my life was in danger and that's why I shot the victim." Even if the victim made no threatening move and said nothing to indicate any hostility prior to being killed, the jury would have to acquit as long as they believed the defendant was telling the truth. Likewise, a murder defendant who claimed he was actually provoked into a heat of passion would almost automatically receive the mitigation to manslaughter, no matter how ridiculous his claim of provocation. Without a reasonableness requirement, no objective limits would restrict the ability of a defendant claiming provocation or self-defense to obtain the outcome he or she desired.

The problem with the reasonableness requirement is not that it exists, but the way it is applied. As discussed in chapter 9, legal decision makers in self-defense and provocation cases apply a positivist conception of reasonableness, equating reasonableness with typicality. The problem is that what is typical is not always that which is just. For ex-

276

ample, all of us are influenced by racial stereotypes. Racial stereotypes about Blacks and Latinos as dangerous and violent criminals can make us "see" a weapon in the hands of an unarmed Black or Latino person. Even though such beliefs may be typical, they are not necessarily reasonable. A better way of thinking about reasonableness is to apply what I call normative reasonableness. Normative reasonableness focuses on whether the defendant believed or acted the way the reasonable person *ought* to have believed or acted.

A second problem with the reasonableness requirement, discussed in chapter 10, is the tendency of judges and juries to focus on emotion (or belief) reasonableness instead of act reasonableness. In self-defense cases, model jury instructions tell jurors to focus on whether the defendant's fear of the victim was reasonable, not whether the defendant's use of deadly force was reasonable. In provocation cases, most jurisdictions tell jurors to focus on whether the defendant's emotional upset was reasonable, rather than whether his response was appropriate under the circumstances. The tendency to focus on emotion reasonableness rather than act reasonableness allows individuals who have intentionally taken a life to easily escape liability for murder. To address this problem, I suggest that jurors be required to find both act reasonableness and emotion reasonableness.

The biggest problem, however, is that certain defendants, namely, majority culture defendants, are able to rely on dominant social norms of masculinity, race, and sexual orientation to bolster their claims of reasonableness while others cannot. The solution to this problem is not to abolish the reasonableness requirement, but to attempt to make it less susceptible to this type of bias. I propose using switching as a vehicle to expose jurors to the largely invisible social norms that influence their reasonableness determinations. Switching gives descriptive meaning to normative reasonableness and helps even the scales between majority culture defendants and others.

Whenever inequities exist in the criminal justice system, one can either ratchet up the scrutiny so that everyone is scrutinized as carefully as the most carefully scrutinized defendant or ratchet down the scrutiny to the level of scrutiny enjoyed by the least scrutinized defendant. Adopting my proposed reforms—a normative conception of reasonableness, switching, and requiring both act and emotion reasonableness—represents a choice to ratchet up the scales, so that majority culture defendants' claims of reasonableness are subjected to the same kind of scrutiny accorded others. Ratcheting up may not be appropriate in all cases, but it makes particular sense when the defendant has taken another human being's life.

By offering three proposals for legal reform (one theoretical, one practical, and one doctrinal), I do not mean to suggest that the law can solve all problems. As this book has illustrated, the beliefs and attitudes of specific legal decision makers and those of society in general play a significant role in determining outcomes. While the law can encourage attitudinal change, people's attitudes are more likely to be influenced by what their friends and colleagues think. My hope is that this book will encourage people to think more critically about what constitutes reasonable violence and the notion of reasonableness as it is used in the criminal law.

# Notes

## NOTES TO THE INTRODUCTION

1. Oliver Wendell Holmes, *The Path of the Law,* 10 HARV. L. REV. 457, 476 (1897).

2. *See, e.g.,* ELIZABETH SCHNEIDER, BATTERED WOMEN AND FEMINIST LAWMAKING (2000); ANGELA BROWNE, WHEN BATTERED WOMEN KILL (1987); CHARLES P. EWING, BATTERED WOMEN WHO KILL (1987); LENORE WALKER, THE BATTERED WOMAN (1979); Holly Maguigan, *Battered Women and Self-Defense: Myths and Misconceptions in Current Reform Proposals,* 140 U. PA. L. REV. 379 (1991); Martha R. Mahoney, *Legal Images of Battered Women: Redefining the Issue of Separation,* 90 MICH. L. REV. 1 (1991); Joshua Dressler, *Battered Women Who Kill Their Sleeping Tormenters: Reflections on Maintaining Respect for Human Life While Killing Moral Monsters,* in CRIMINAL LAW THEORY: DOCTRINES OF THE GENERAL PART 259 (2002); Laurie J. Taylor, *Provoked Reason in Men and Women: Heat of Passion Manslaughter and Imperfect Self- Defense,* 33 UCLA L. REV. 1679 (1986); Robert F. Schopp, Barbara J. Sturgis, & Megan Sullivan, *Battered Woman's Syndrome, Expert Testimony, and the Distinction between Justification and Excuse,* 1994 U. ILL. L. REV. 45; Richard A. Rosen, *On Self-Defense, Imminence, and Women Who Kill Their Batterers,* 71 N.C. L. REV. 371 (1993); Charles Ewing, *Psychological Self-Defense: A Proposed Justification for Battered Women Who Kill,* 14 LAW AND HUMAN BEHAV. 579 (1990); Cathryn Jo Rosen, *The Excuse of Self-Defense: Correcting a Historical Accident on Behalf of Battered Women Who Kill,* 36 AM. U. L. REV. 11 (1986); David L. Faigman, Note, *The Battered Woman Syndrome and Self-Defense: A Legal and Empirical Dissent,* 72 VA. L. REV. 619 (1986); Elizabeth Schneider, *Equal Rights to Trial for Women: Sex Bias in the Law of Self-Defense,* 15 HARV. C.R.–C.L. L. REV. 623 (1980). *See also* Donna K. Coker, *Heat of Passion and Wife Killing: Men Who Batter/Men Who Kill,* 2 S. CAL. REV. L. & WOMEN'S STUD. 71 (1992); Elizabeth Rapaport, *Capital Murder and the Domestic Discount: A Study of Capital Domestic Murder in the Post-Furman Era,* 49 SMU L. REV. 1507 (1996).

3. There is considerable disagreement over whether dominant social norms help or hurt battered women who kill their abusers. Advocates for

battered women argue that dominant social beliefs and attitudes tend to undermine claims of reasonableness by battered women defendants. They point out that the ordinary lay person, unassisted by expert witness testimony on battered woman syndrome, is likely to think the battered woman could have (and should have) left the abusive relationship, and conclude that it was not necessary for her to kill her abuser in order to escape the abuse. Additionally, popular misconceptions about battered women, such as the belief that such women intentionally provoke their husbands, may lead jurors to discount battered women's claims of reasonableness. Others argue that social attitudes about domestic violence have changed significantly over the last two decades, resulting in sympathy for battered women. *See, e.g.,* Alafair S. Burke, *Rational Actors, Self-Defense, and Duress: Making Sense, Not Syndromes, Out of the Battered Woman,* 81 N.C. L. Rev. 211 (2002); James P. Levine, Juries and Politics 85 (1992).

## NOTES TO CHAPTER I

1. People v. Berry, 18 Cal.3d 509 (1976). I wish to thank Donna Coker for allowing me to review the trial transcripts in this case.

2. A complete defense is one which completely exonerates the defendant. A partial defense exonerates the defendant of the offense with which he is charged, but holds the defendant liable for a lesser offense.

3. In forty-eight of the fifty states, provocation mitigates a killing which would otherwise be murder down to manslaughter. In Washington and Texas, a provoked killing is second-degree murder. *See* State v. Van Zante, 614 P.2d 217 (Wash. App. 1980); Texas Criminal Jury Charges § 5:30 (2000).

4. Cal. Penal Code § 193 (West 1999).

5. Cal. Penal Code § 190(a) (West 1999).

6. *Id.*

7. Joshua Dressler, Understanding Criminal Law § 31.07[B][2][a], at 491 (2d ed. 1995). In England, category three was described more narrowly as the discovery by a father of someone committing sodomy upon his son. Dir. of Pub. Prosecutions v. Camplin [1978] 2 All E.R. 168, 171.

8. Under English common law rules, only unlawful acts could constitute legally adequate provocation. Moreover, if the defendant provoked the provoker, he was not entitled to assert the defense of provocation. A. J. Ashworth, *The Doctrine of Provocation,* 35 Cambridge L.J. 292, 295 (1976).

9. State v. Starr, 38 Mo. 270, 277 (1886).

10. That is, the rationale seems to fit the first four categories if a "serious crime against a relative" means a crime of violence and if an "illegal arrest" means an arrest which is executed with excessive force.

11. In England, category three was more narrowly described as a father

discovering someone committing sodomy on his son. Dir. of Pub. Prosecutions v. Camplin [1978] 2 All E.R. 168, 171. Defined in this way, category three only protected male defendants acting on behalf of male victims (fathers defending their sons), not female defendants acting on behalf of female victims (mothers defending their daughters against a child molester).

12. Donna K. Coker, *Heat of Passion and Wife Killing: Men Who Batter/Men Who Kill*, 2 S. CAL. REV. L. & WOMEN'S STUD. 71, 72 (1992).

13. Laurie J. Taylor, *Provoked Reason in Men and Women: Heat of Passion Manslaughter and Imperfect Self-Defense*, 33 UCLA L. REV. 1679, 1694 (1986). See also Henderson v. State, 221 S.E.2d 633, 636 (Ga. 1975); State v. Greenlee, 269 P. 331, 333 (N.M. 1928); Shaw v. State, 510 S.W.2d 926, 927 n. 1 (Tex. 1974); State v. Williams, 163 P. 1104, 1108 (Utah 1917).

14. State v. Greenlee, 269 P. 331, 333 (N.M. 1928) (emphasis added).

15. Henderson v. State, 221 S.E.2d 633, 636 (Ga. Ct. App. 1975).

16. JEREMY HORDER, PROVOCATION AND RESPONSIBILITY 39 (1992) (noting it was commonly believed that "adultery is the highest invasion of property").

17. DRESSLER, UNDERSTANDING CRIMINAL LAW, *supra* note 7, § 33.06, at 547. Additionally, under what was known as the marital coercion defense, a married woman who committed a crime in her husband's presence was presumed to have been coerced by her husband into doing so, and therefore could not be held personally accountable for her criminal acts. Anne M. Coughlin, *Excusing Women*, 82 CAL. L. REV. 1, 31 (1994).

18. Reva B. Siegel, *The Rule of Love: Wife Beating as Prerogative and Privacy*, 105 YALE L.J. 2117, 2122–23 (1996).

19. Bram P. Buunk et al., *Sex Differences in Jealousy in Evolutionary and Cultural Perspective*, 7 PSYCHOL. SCI. 359 (1996).

20. Reed v. State, 59 S.W.2d 122 (Tex. Crim. App. 1933).

21. *Id.* at 123 (emphasis added).

22. *Id.* at 124.

23. *See, e.g.,* Reed v. Reed, 404 U.S. 71 (1971) (holding that statutory provision in probate code giving a mandatory preference for appointment as administrator of a decedent's estate to male applicants over equally qualified female applicants violated the equal protection clause of the Fourteenth Amendment); Craig v. Boren, 429 U.S. 190 (1976) (striking down Oklahoma statute prohibiting the sale of nonintoxicating 3.2 percent beer to males under the age of twenty-one and to females under the age of eighteen on the ground that the gender-based differential constituted a denial of equal protection to males between the ages of eighteen and twenty-one); Miss. Univ. for Women v. Hogan, 458 U.S. 718 (1982) (holding that state-supported university policy excluding males from enrolling violated the equal protection clause).

24. Elizabeth Rapaport, *Capital Murder and the Domestic Discount: A Study*

*of Capital Domestic Murder in the Post-Furman Era*, 49 SMU L. REV. 1507, 1546 (1996).

25. Joshua Dressler, *Rethinking Heat of Passion: A Defense in Search of a Rationale*, 73 J. CRIM. L. AND CRIMINOLOGY 421, 440 (1982).

26. *See, e.g.*, People v. Chevalier, 544 N.E.2d 942 (Ill. 1989) (holding that a wife's confession of adultery to her husband was not sufficient for a voluntary manslaughter instruction because it did not fit within any of the distinct categories of legally adequate provocation recognized under Illinois law at the time).

27. One of the first American cases to utilize the reasonable man standard was the 1862 case of Maher v. People, 10 Mich. 212 (1862). It appears that at least one state continued to use the early common law categorical approach until as late as 1989. *See* People v. Chevalier, 544 N.E.2d 942 (Ill. 1989).

28. WAYNE R. LaFAVE & AUSTIN W. SCOTT, JR., CRIMINAL LAW § 7.10, at 654 (2d ed. 1986); WHARTON'S CRIMINAL LAW § 165, 262 (1979).

29. Mullaney v. Wilbur, 421 U.S. 684 (1975) (holding that the prosecution bears the burden of proving the absence of heat of passion or provocation). However, in Patterson v. New York, 432 U.S. 197 (1977), the U.S. Supreme Court held that while the prosecution bears the burden of proving every element of a criminal offense, the legislature may allocate to the defendant the burden of persuasion regarding non-elements, including affirmative defenses to crimes.

30. DRESSLER, UNDERSTANDING CRIMINAL LAW, *supra* note 7, at 491 ("The rigid common law categories of 'adequate provocation' have given way in many states to the view that the issue of what constitutes adequate provocation should be left to the jury to decide").

31. In other areas of the law, such as the law of accidental personal injury or negligence in tort law, the ostensibly gender-neutral reasonable man standard is applied in gender-differentiated ways. *See, e.g.*, Barbara Y. Welke, *Unreasonable Women: Gender and the Law of Accidental Injury*, 19 LAW AND SOC. INQUIRY 369 (1994).

32. LAWRENCE A. GREENFIELD ET AL., U.S. DEP'T OF JUSTICE, VIOLENCE BY INTIMATES 6 (March 1998). Approximately nine percent of all homicides in the United States are murders attributable to intimates or a killing committed by a current or former spouse, boyfriend, or girlfriend. *Id.* at 1.

33. *Id.* at 5–6.

34. *Id.* at 1.

35. *Id.;* CALLIE MARIE RENNISON & SARAH WELCHANS, U.S. DEP'T. OF JUSTICE, BUREAU OF JUSTICE STATISTICS SPECIAL REPORT, INTIMATE PARTNER VIOLENCE 2 (May 2000). According to Marina Angel, women are five to six times more likely than men to be victims of a violent crime committed by an intimate. Marina Angel, *Abusive Boys Kill Girls Just Like Abusive Men Kill Women: Explaining the Obvious*, 8 TEMP. POL. & CIV. RTS. L. REV. 283, 296 (1999), citing SENATE

JUDICIARY COMM., VIOLENCE AGAINST WOMEN: A WEEK IN THE LIFE OF AMER-
ICA, S. REP. NO. 118, 102D CONG., 2D SESS. 2 (1992). Some studies estimate that
between 2,000 to 4,000 women die each year as a result of domestic abuse.
United States v. Morrison, 529 U.S. 598, 632 (2000), citing S. Rep. No. 101-545, at
36 (1990). *But see* Glenn Sacks, *Myths of Domestic Violence Put Men at a Disadvantage,* L.A. DAILY J., Aug. 8, 2002, at 6 (reporting that men are nearly 40 percent of
all domestic violence victims).

36. PATRICK A. LANGAN AND JOHN M. DAWSON, U.S. DEP'T OF JUSTICE,
SPOUSE MURDER DEFENDANTS IN LARGE URBAN COUNTIES 21 (1995).

37. *Id.*

38. *Id.*

39. CHARLES P. EWING, BATTERED WOMEN WHO KILL 23–31 (1987) (discussing numerous studies which suggest that many of the women who kill their
male partners do so in response to physical and psychological abuse); ANGELA
BROWNE, WHEN BATTERED WOMEN KILL 144–46 (1987) (noting several studies
finding that the vast majority of women charged with killing their male partners did so in response to physical abuse). See also Susan Edwards, *Battered
Women Who Kill,* 140 NEW. L.J. 1380 (1990) (noting that three-quarters of the five
hundred or so women who kill their husbands each year have been battered by
their male spouses). *But cf.* Rapaport, *Capital Murder and the Domestic Discount,*
*supra* note 24, at 1517 (noting that two-thirds of the women on death row for
killing an intimate partner did so for pecuniary gain).

40. Approximately 60 percent of the men who kill their wives claim they
did so because she was unfaithful. Coker, *Heat of Passion and Wife Killing, supra*
note 12, at 91.

41. LANGAN AND DAWSON, SPOUSE MURDER DEFENDANTS IN LARGE URBAN
COUNTIES, *supra* note 36, at 21 (1995). *See also* KATHARINE T. BARTLETT & AN-
GELA P. HARRIS, GENDER AND LAW: THEORY, DOCTRINE, COMMENTARY (1998);
Rapaport, *Capital Murder and the Domestic Discount, supra* note 24, at 1546 (argu-
ing that a domestic discount operates to exclude domestic murder from capital
liability).

42. Rapaport, *Capital Murder and the Domestic Discount, supra* note 24.

43. *See* Carolyn Ramsey, *The Discretionary Power of "Public" Prosecutors in
Historical Perspective,* 39 AM. CRIM. L. REV. 1309 (2002).

44. Coker, *Heat of Passion and Wife Killing, supra* note 12, at 89.

45. *Id.*

46. *Id.* at 95.

47. *Id.*

48. *Id.*

49. *Id.* at 96.

50. SUSAN FALUDI, STIFFED: THE BETRAYAL OF THE AMERICAN MAN 8–9
(1999).

51. Wendy Keller, *Disparate Treatment of Spouse Murder Defendants*, 6 S. CAL. REV. L. & WOMEN'S STUD. 255, 263 (1996).

52. ELEANOR EMMONS MACCOBY & CAROL NAGY JACKLIN, THE PSYCHOLOGY OF SEX DIFFERENCES 352 (1974) ("The sex difference in aggression has been observed in all cultures in which the relevant behavior has been observed."); Stephen Goldberg, THE INEVITABILITY OF PATRIARCHY 104 (1973) ("[T]here are no differences between men and women except in a hormonal system that renders the man more aggressive."); Aaron Kipnis, *Men, Movies and Monsters: Heroic Masculinity as a Crucible of Male Violence*, 29 PSYCHOL. PERSP. 38, 49 (1994) ("Higher levels of testosterone endow men with a biological potential to be more aggressive than women, but this does not mean they are destined to be more violent").

53. GREGORY L. WHITE & PAUL E. MULLEN, JEALOUSY: THEORY, RESEARCH AND CLINICAL STRATEGIES 113 (1989).

54. Buunk, *Sex Differences in Jealousy in Evolutionary and Cultural Perspective*, *supra* note 19, at 359.

55. Emily L. Miller, *(Wo)manslaughter: Voluntary Manslaughter, Gender, and the Model Penal Code*, 50 EMORY L.J. 665, 681 (2001), *citing* David M. Buss et al., *Sex Differences in Jealousy: Evolution, Physiology, and Psychology*, 3 PSYCHOL. SCI. 251 (1992).

56. *Id.*, *citing* Barbara Smuts, *Male Aggression against Women: An Evolutionary Perspective*, *in* SEX, POWER, CONFLICT: EVOLUTIONARY AND FEMINIST PERSPECTIVES 231 (David M. Buss & Neil M. Malamuth eds. 1996).

57. *Id.*

58. *Id.*

59. SHERE HITE, THE HITE REPORT ON MALE SEXUALITY 142 (1981) ("Seventy-two percent of men married two years or more had had sex outside of marriage"). Other studies report much lower figures. One study estimated that 37 percent of married men have had at least one extramarital affair. JUNE M. REINISCH, THE KINSEY INSTITUTE NEW REPORT ON SEX: WHAT YOU MUST KNOW TO BE SEXUALLY LITERATE 7 (1990). Another estimated that 25 percent of married men in America have been unfaithful. Bruce Handy, *How We Really Feel about Fidelity: A New Poll Suggests America Hates the Sin, Not the Sinner*, TIME, Aug. 31, 1998, at 52 (*citing* The Social Organization of Sexuality, a study conducted by the University of Chicago in 1994).

60. SHERE HITE, THE HITE REPORT: WOMEN AND LOVE: A CULTURAL REVOLUTION IN PROGRESS 395 (1987). Other studies report much lower figures. *See, e.g.*, Handy, *How We Really Feel about Fidelity*, *supra* note 59, at 52 (noting that The Social Organization of Sexuality reports that upward of 15 percent of wives have been unfaithful).

61. DRESSLER, UNDERSTANDING CRIMINAL LAW, *supra* note 7, § 31.07[B], at 492, *citing* Girouard v. State, 583 A.2d 718, 722 (Md. Ct. App. 1991).

62. Holmes v. Dir. of Pub. Prosecutions [1946] 2 All E.R. 124, 127 ("A blow may in some circumstances rouse a man of ordinary reason and control to a sudden retort in kind, but the proverb reminds us that hard words break no bones, and the law expects a reasonable man to endure abuse without resorting to fatal violence").

63. People v. Berry, 18 Cal.3d 509 (1976).

64. People v. Ambro, 505 N.E.2d 381 (Ill. 1987), *overruled by* People v. Chevalier, 544 N.E.2d 942 (Ill. 1989); Commonwealth v. Schnopps, 417 N.E.2d 1213 (Mass. 1981) (holding that the defendant was entitled to an instruction on voluntary manslaughter when, after begging his wife to let him keep the children, she responded, "No, I am going to court, you are going to give me all the furniture, you are going to have to get the Hell out of here, you won't have nothing," then pointed to her crotch and said, "You will never touch this again, because I have got something bigger and better for it"); Raines v. State, 277 S.E.2d 47 (Ga. 1981) (finding that trial court should have given jury instruction on voluntary manslaughter where wife admitted to adultery after husband found a letter she had written to another man and then made degrading comments about disabled husband's inability to satisfy her sexually). *See also* Annotation, *Spouse's Confession of Adultery as Affecting Degree of Homicide Involved in Killing Spouse or His or Her Paramour,* 93 A.L.R.3d 925 (1979 and Supp. 1991).

65. Dressler, Understanding Criminal Law, *supra* note 7, at § 31.07[B] 492 ("Some courts allow the defense [of provocation] to be raised in the case of informational, but not insulting, words").

66. *See* Ark. Code Ann. §§ 5-4-605(1), 5-10-104(a)(1) (Michie 1987); Conn. Gen. Stat. Ann. § 53a-54a (West 1994); Del. Code Ann. tit. 11, §§ 632(3), 641 (1953); Haw. Rev. Stat. Ann. § 707-702(2) (Michie 1987); Ind. Code Ann. § 35-50-2-9(c)(2) (Michie 1998); Pattern Instructions for Kansas (Criminal), No. 56.01-C(2), 56.05(A)(2) (3d ed. 1993 and Supp. 2000); Ky. Rev. Stat. Ann. §507.020 (Michie 1998); Kentucky Instructions to Juries (Criminal), § 3.22(C) (1999); La. Code Crim. Proc. Ann. art. 905.5(b) (West 1997); Missouri Approved Instructions (Criminal), No. 313.44B (3d ed. 1987); Mont. Code Ann. §45-5-103 (1997); Montana Criminal Jury Instructions, No. 5-103(2) (1990); Neb. Rev. Stat. Ann. § 29-2523(2)(c) (Michie 1973); Nev. Rev. Stat. Ann. 200.035(2) (Michie 1977); N.H. Rev. Stat. Ann. § 630:2(I)(a) (1971 and Supp. 2000); N.Y. Penal Law §§ 125.20(2), 125.25(1)(a) (McKinney 1997); N.D. Cent. Code §12.1-16 (1997); North Dakota Pattern Jury Instructions (Criminal), No. K-6.16 (1985); Uniform Jury Instructions (Criminal), No. 1307 (Oregon) (1994); Or. Rev. Stat. §163.135 (1997); Pa. Stat. Ann. tit. 42, § 9711(e)(2) (West 1998); S.C. Code Ann. § 16-3-20(b)(2) (Law, Co-op. 1962); Tennessee Pattern Jury Instructions (Criminal), No. 7.04(d)(2) (2000); Utah Code Ann. § 76-5-203(4)(a)(i) (1953); Wyo. Stat. Ann. § 6-2-102(j)(ii) (Michie 1977).

67. Model Penal Code § 210.3(1)(b) (1962).

68. *Id.*

69. Joshua Dressler, Understanding Criminal Law § 31.10[C][3][a], at 542 (3d ed. 2001). *See also* Patterson v. New York, 432 U.S. 197 (1977) (holding that placing the burden of proving the affirmative defense of extreme mental and emotional distress on the defendant does not violate due process).

70. Victoria Nourse, *Passion's Progress: Modern Law Reform and the Provocation Defense*, 106 Yale L.J. 1331, 1372 (1997) ("Ultimately, the Code offers an institutional solution: It tells us that the jury should decide whether the situation merits compassion").

71. Dressler, Understanding Criminal Law, *supra* note 69, § 31.10[C][3][b], at 504 ("First, a specific provocative act is not required to trigger the EMED defense").

72. *Id.* ("Fourth, there is no rigid cooling-off rule").

73. Courts in modern jurisdictions have also permitted defendants to argue that they did not have a reasonable opportunity to cool off, even when the killing took place several weeks after the triggering event.

74. Joshua Dressler, *Why Keep the Provocation Defense? Some Reflections on a Difficult Subject*, 86 Minn. L. Rev. 959, 986 (2002).

75. Model Penal Code § 210.3 cmt. at 49–50 (1962).

76. *Id.*

77. *See* text accompanying notes 20–23 in chapter 8 on the problems with subjective standards of reasonableness.

78. Nourse, *Passion's Progress, supra* note 70, at 1331 (1997).

79. Dixon v. State, 597 S.W.2d 77 (Ark. 1980).

80. Richard E. Nisbett and Dov Cohen, Culture of Honor: The Psychology of Violence in the South (1996).

81. *Id.* at 41.

82. *Id.*

83. State v. Martinez, 591 A.2d 155 (Conn. App. Ct. 1991); City of Bridgeport, Police Incident Report (on file with author); Statement of Hipolito Martinez taken June 21, 1987 (on file with author); State's Appellate Brief (on file with author).

84. State v. Chicano, 216 Conn. 699 (1990).

85. The three-judge panel also convicted Chicano of three counts of felony murder, one count of injury to a child, and burglary in the second degree. The Supreme Court of Connecticut later reversed the manslaughter convictions and remanded, holding that Chicano's convictions for felony murder and manslaughter in the first degree violated double jeopardy. That court remanded with instructions to the lower court to impose sentence only on the felony murder convictions.

86. Md. Code Ann., Crim. Law § 387A (1998) (stating that the observation of a spouse in the act of adultery does not constitute legally adequate provoca-

tion); Minn. Stat. Ann. § 609.20(1) (West 1987) (noting that the crying of a child does not constitute legally adequate provocation).

87. *See* Texas Criminal Jury Charges §§ 5:30 (2000) ("[T]he issue of sudden passion as a defense to murder no longer exists. Sudden passion is an issue now to be determined, if it is an issue, in the penalty phase. . . . If the jury finds sudden passion in the penalty phase, the homicide is still murder, but second degree, not first degree").

88. MD. CODE ANN., CRIM. LAW § 387A (1998) (emphasis added).

89. The problem with such blanket rules is that they return us to something like the early common law categorical approach to provocation in which certain acts constituted legally adequate provocation and other acts did not. The difference is that the early common law approach delineated categories of legally adequate provocation that would exculpate the defendant (at least partially), whereas statutory provisions like Maryland's recent amendment delineate categories of acts that cannot constitute legally adequate provocation. Rigid rules that prohibit defendants in a certain type of case from ever arguing provocation may result in unfairness to the individual defendant. Each case presents different facts and circumstances and the defendant should at least be allowed to argue to the jury that he or she was reasonably provoked. If the argument as to reasonableness is weak, then the prosecutor can explain to jurors why they should find that the defendant was not reasonably provoked. Despite all its problems, the modern approach to provocation at least lets the jury make the final decision as to whether there was legally adequate provocation.

90. Karl Vick, *Maryland Judge Taking Heat in Cuckolded Killer Case*, WASH. POST, Oct. 30, 1994, at A1.

91. The sentence was actually three years, but half the sentence was suspended, leaving an actual sentence of eighteen months. *Id.*

92. *Id.*

93. Deirdre M. Childress, *Maryland Judge Cleared of Bias in Remarks at Sentencing*, WASH. POST, May 4, 1996, at B3.

94. *Id.*

95. Associated Press, *18-Month Term for Wife-Killer Assailed*, S.D. UNION TRIB., Oct. 19, 1994, at A6.

96. MD. CODE ANN., CRIM. LAW § 387A (1998). In a similar attempt to carve out categories of things that do not constitute legally adequate provocation, the Minnesota legislature specifies that the crying of a child does not constitute legally adequate provocation. Minn. Stat. Ann. § 609.20(1) (West 1987).

97. Stephen Morse supports abolition of both the defense of provocation and the partial responsibility variant of the diminished capacity defense. *See* Stephen J. Morse, *Undiminished Confusion in Diminished Capacity*, 75 J. CRIM. L. & CRIMINOLOGY 1, 33 (1984). *See also* HORDER, PROVOCATION AND RESPONSIBILITY, *supra* note 16 (arguing for abolition of the defense of provocation).

98. *See* Tex. Penal Code Ann. § 19.02(d) (Vernon 1994) ("At the punishment stage of a trial, the defendant may raise the issue as to whether he caused the death under the immediate influence of sudden passion arising from adequate cause. If the defendant proves the issue in the affirmative by a preponderance of the evidence, the offense is a felony of the second degree"); Tex. Criminal Jury Charges §§ 5:30 (2000) ("[T]he issue of sudden passion as a defense to murder no longer exists. Sudden passion is an issue now to be determined, if it is an issue, in the penalty phase. . . . If the jury finds sudden passion in the penalty phase, the homicide is still murder, but second degree, not first degree").

99. *Id.* Similarly, the state of Washington allows provocation only as a partial defense to first-degree murder. *See* State v. Van Zante, 614 P.2d 217, 219 (Wash. App. 1980).

100. Gabrielle Crist, *Wife Killer's Witnesses Charged with Perjury*, Fort Worth Star-Telegram, June 28, 2000, at 1; Gabrielle Crist, *Appeal Delays 2nd Trial of Man Who Killed Wife*, Fort Worth Star-Telegram, Feb. 29, 2000, at 1; Michael Weissenstein, *Man, 33, Accused in Killing of His Wife*, Fort Worth Star-Telegram, Dec. 23, 1998, at 1; Linda P. Campbell, *Watkins Convicted of Wife's Murder*, Fort Worth Star-Telegram, Oct. 19, 1999, at 1; Debra Dennis, *Man Gets Probation in Slaying*, Dallas Morning News, Oct. 23, 1999, at 31A.

101. Associated Press, *Texas Man Gets 4 Months for Killing Wife*, L.A. Daily J., Oct. 25, 1999, at 4.

102. Coker, *Heat of Passion and Wife Killing, supra* note 12, at 119–20.

103. *Id.*

104. *Id.* at 121.

105. Caroline A. Forell & Donna M. Matthews, A Law of Her Own: The Reasonable Woman as a Measure of Man 188 (2000).

106. *Id.*

## NOTES TO CHAPTER 2

1. *See* Bella Stumbo, Until the Twelfth of Never: The Deadly Divorce of Dan and Betty Broderick (1992); Loretta Schwartz-Nobel, Forsaking All Others: The Real Betty Broderick Story (1992).

2. Broderick's attorney, Jack Earley, wanted to argue that Broderick was an emotionally battered woman who had killed in psychological self-defense, but the judge refused to allow this argument. Stumbo, Until the Twelfth of Never, *supra* note 1, at 495.

3. *Id.* at 17.

4. *See* cases discussed *supra* in chapter 1. *See also* cases discussed in Victoria Nourse, *Passion's Progress: Modern Law Reform and the Provocation Defense*, 106 Yale L.J. 1331 (1997).

5. In the other version of the story, Paltrow misses the train that would have taken her to the truth when the subway doors slide shut before she is safely inside the train. Paltrow catches a later train, arriving home after the boyfriend has finished his sexual tryst.

6. Lucinda Franks, *The Intimate Hillary*, TALK, Sept. 1999, at 174. *See also* Associated Press, *First Lady Calls Husband's Affair "Sin of Weakness" in "Good Man,"* S.D. UNION TRIB., Aug. 1, 1999, at A8.

7. Hillary Clinton may have also benefited from another man's extramarital activities. At the beginning of the race, the individual who posed the biggest challenge to her being elected was former Mayor Rudolph Giuliani. Giuliani pulled out of the Senate race after his wife of sixteen years, Donna Hanover, publicly accused him of having had an affair with a former aide. Giuliani denied this affair, but admitted to having an extramarital relationship with another woman. Giuliani explained that he was pulling out of the race due to health reasons, not his failing marriage. Dan Janison & Robert Polner, *Giuliani May Tell Today*, NEWSDAY, May 18, 2000, at A6; Dan Janison, Elaine Povich, & Ellen Yan, *New Turmoil in Senate Race*, NEWSDAY, May 11, 2000, at A5; Lara Jakes & Jay Jochnowitz, *Giuliani Leaves the Stage*, TIMES UNION, May 20, 2000, at A1.

8. People v. Williams, 576 N.E.2d 68 (Ill. App. Ct. 1991).

9. Self-defense was not asserted at trial because Robin stabbed George repeatedly in the back. Telephone conversation with Robin Williams's appellate attorney, Barbara Kamm, State Appellate Defender's Office, Chicago, Illinois. Memo of telephone conversation on file with author.

10. *Id.*

11. CAROLINE A. FORELL & DONNA M. MATTHEWS, A LAW OF HER OWN: THE REASONABLE WOMAN AS A MEASURE OF MAN 171–72 (2000).

12. People v. Washington, 58 Cal. App. 3d 620 (1976).

13. According to one dictionary, "servient" means "subject to some person or thing that dominates, rules, or controls." WEBSTER'S THIRD NEW INTERNATIONAL DICTIONARY 2076 (1993).

14. *See, e.g.,* Ellison v. Brady, 924 F.2d 872 (9th Cir. 1991).

15. FORELL & MATTHEWS, A LAW OF HER OWN, *supra* note 11.

16. *Lesbian Killed Male Love Rival*, THE HERALD (Glasgow), Jan. 6, 1996, at 9.

17. Her Majesty's Advocate v. McKean, 1996 SCCR 402 (1996).

18. According to the General Social Survey of three thousand households conducted in 1994 by the University of Chicago's National Opinion Research Center, a majority of Americans view homosexual sex as wrong. *General Social Survey*, at *http://icpsr.umich.edu/gss/about/gss/gssintro.html* (last visited Feb. 11, 2000), *cited in* Catherine Stengel, *Meals Instead of Men*, TAMPA TRIB., Sept. 23, 1996, at 2. The percentage of Americans who admit to having negative attitudes about homosexuality appears to have declined over the last forty years. During the 1960s, homosexuals were rated the third most dangerous people in the

United States after communists and atheists. Joseph E. Aguero et al., *The Relationships among Sexual Beliefs, Attitudes, Experience, and Homophobia*, 10 J. HOMO-SEXUALITY 95 (1984), *citing* STRONG S. WILSON ET AL., HUMAN SEXUALITY: A TEXT WITH READINGS (1977). In the mid-1980s, 78 percent of Americans polled by the Roper Center for Public Opinion admitted that they believed sexual relations between two adults of the same sex was wrong. In 1993, a NEW YORK TIMES poll reported that 55 percent of the Americans polled believed sexual relations between gays and lesbians was morally wrong. Annie L. Cotten-Huston and Bradley M. Waite, *Anti- Homosexual Attitudes in College Students: Predictors and Classroom Interventions,* 38 J. HOMOSEXUALITY 117, 118 (2000). Despite these somewhat encouraging figures, the fact remains that at least one out of every two Americans still views homosexual relations as wrong.

19. *See* 2000 Gallup Poll on Homosexual Relations, *http://www.gallup.com /poll/topics/homosexual.asp* (emphasis added).

20. Vermont is the only state that permits civil unions between gay men and lesbian women. Carey Goldberg, *Vermont Senate Votes for Gay Civil Unions,* N.Y. TIMES, Apr. 20, 2000, at A12. A same-sex civil union in Vermont, however, may not be given full recognition by other states. The Defense of Marriage Act, passed by Congress in 1996, provides that states are not required to recognize same-sex marriages from other states. Defense of Marriage Act of 1996, 28 U.S.C. § 1738C (2000). For a short time between 1996 and 1999, Hawaii appeared to recognize same-sex marriages after a circuit court judge ruled that denying marriage licenses to same-sex couples constituted a violation of the equal protection provisions of the Hawaii Constitution. Baehr v. Miike, Civ. No. 91-1394, 1996 WL 694235, at *1 (Hawaii Cir. Ct. Dec. 3, 1996). Subsequently, the Hawaii Legislature amended the State Constitution to define marriage as a union between a man and a woman. *See* Baehr v. Miike, 994 P.2d 566 (Haw. 1999) (holding that passage of the constitutional amendment validated the statutory provision and rendered the issue decided in Baehr moot).

21. Boy Scouts of America v. Dale, 120 S. Ct. 2446 (2000).

22. *Id.* at 2449.

23. *Id.* at 2452–53.

24. *Id.* Chief Justice Rehnquist, writing for the Court, denied that the Court was sanctioning the Boy Scouts' views on homosexual conduct. "We are not, as we must not be, guided by our views of whether the Boy Scouts' teachings with respect to homosexual conduct are right or wrong." *Id.* at 2458. Yet at every step of the analysis, the Court sided with the Boy Scouts and refused to recognize the state's interest in protecting gays and lesbians against discrimination on the basis of sexual orientation as a compelling state interest.

25. RHODE ISLAND TASK FORCE ON GAY, LESBIAN, BISEXUAL AND TRANS-GENDERED YOUTH, SCHOOL SHOULDN'T HURT: LIFTING THE BURDEN FROM GAY, LESBIAN, BISEXUAL AND TRANSGENDERED YOUTH (March 1996).

26. James Brooke, *Homophobia Often Found in Schools, Data Show*, N.Y. TIMES, Oct. 14, 1998, at A19.

27. *Id.*; Karen Franklin, *New Study Highlights Violence against Gay and Lesbian People*, BlackBoard on-line, The Website of the Gay, Lesbian, and Straight Education Network, at *http://www.glsen.org/pages/sections/library/reference/013 .article* ; Karen Franklin, *Psychosocial Motivations of Hate Crime Perpetrators: Implications for Prevention and Policy*, at *http://www.apa.org/ppo/pi/franklin.html*.

28. People v. Ambro, 505 N.E.2d 381 (Ill. 1987), *overruled by* People v. Chevalier, 544 N.E.2d 942 (Ill. 1989); Commonwealth v. Schnopps, 417 N.E.2d 1213 (Mass. 1981); Raines v. State, 277 S.E.2d 47 (Ga. 1981). *See also* Annotation, *Spouse's Confession of Adultery as Affecting Degree of Homicide Involved in Killing Spouse or His or Her Paramour*, 93 A.L.R.3d 925 (1979 and Supp. 1991).

29. State v. Erazo, 126 N.J. 112 (1991).

30. State v. Vigilante, 257 N.J. Super. 296, 303 (1992).

31. *See* State v. Jarrott, 23 N.C. 76 (1840); Nelson v. State, 29 Tenn. 518, 521–22 (1850) (repeating the trial court's charge to the jury: "For though among equals the general rule is, that words are not, but blows are sufficient provocation; yet there may be words of reproach so aggravating when uttered by a slave, as to excite in a white man the temporary fury which negatives the charge of malice.").

32. *Jarrott*, 23 N.C. at 82.

33. *Id.*

34. Nelson v. State, 29 Tenn. 518, 529 (1850).

35. People v. Green, 519 N.W.2d 853 (Mich. 1994).

36. *Id.*, as reported in JOSHUA DRESSLER, UNDERSTANDING CRIMINAL LAW § 31.07[B] at 492 (2d ed. 1995).

37. Because of the truncated way in which the opinion in *People v. Green* is written, it is unclear whether Green was permitted to argue provocation at trial. It appears, however, that he was not permitted to make the argument even though he may have actually been provoked by the neighbor's comments. According to the one dissenting judge who wrote an opinion, the fact that the neighbor told Green that he'd shot his dog coupled with the racial slur "might have been viewed by the trier of fact as sufficient provocation to have justified a finding of voluntary manslaughter." *Id.* at 857. Because this was the dissenting judge's opinion, the majority probably felt differently. My thanks to Joshua Dressler for this insight. *See also* Sims v. State, 573 A.2d 1317 (Md. 1990) (racial insults do not constitute legally adequate provocation); State v. Crisantos, 508 A.2d 167 (N.J. 1986) (holding that murder defendant who claimed the victim instigated the fight by calling him a "Mexican shit" and a "motherfucker" was not entitled to a manslaughter instruction).

38. State v. Watson, 214 S.E.2d 85 (N.C. 1975).

39. RANDALL KENNEDY, NIGGER 76 (2002).

40. *Watson*, 214 S.E.2d at 85.

41. *Id.*

42. *Id.* at 89.

43. Richard Delgado, *Words That Wound: A Tort Action for Racial Insults, Epithets, and Name-Calling*, 17 HARV. C.R.–C.L. L. REV. 133, 157 (1982).

44. Mari J. Matsuda, *Public Response to Racist Speech: Considering the Victim's Story*, 87 MICH. L. REV. 2320, 2327 (1989).

45. *Id.* at 2338.

46. KENNEDY, NIGGER, *supra* note 39, at 28.

47. Charles Lawrence, *The Id, the Ego, and Equal Protection: Reckoning with Unconscious Racism*, 39 STAN. L. REV. 317 (1987). *See also* Linda Hamilton Krieger, *The Content of Our Categories: A Cognitive Bias Approach to Discrimination and Equal Employment Opportunity*, 47 STAN. L. REV. 1161 (1995) (explaining human tendency to categorize).

48. See discussion in chapter 7.

49. Peggy Davis, *Law as Microaggression*, 98 YALE L.J. 1559, 1565 (1989).

50. Camille A. Nelson, *(En)raged or (En)gaged: The Implications of Racial Context to the Canadian Provocation Defence*, 35 U. RICH. L. REV. 1007, 1044 (2002). See also text accompanying notes 68–74 in chapter 8 (discussing the principle of color blindness and why the defendant's race generally is not incorporated into the Reasonable Person standard).

51. Randall Kennedy appears to favor such an approach. He writes, "I am persuaded that there should be no bright-line limits to the array of provocations that a jury is permitted to consider for the purposes of mitigation. It should be up to a jury to determine whether, in fact, a defendant lost control of himself or herself in the face of *nigger* or any other alleged provocation and whether society should soften its punishment in the event of such a loss of control." KENNEDY, NIGGER, *supra* note 39, at 80.

52. Paul Harris, *Black Rage* 7–10 (copy of article found on the Internet on file with author).

53. Report of Craig Haney, Ph.D, J.D., Professor and Chair of the Department of Psychology, U.C. Santa Cruz, Santa Cruz, California (report on file with author).

54. *Id.*

55. *Id.*

56. The provocation argument apparently had some influence on the jury's decision to spare Beverly's life. The jury could not unanimously agree upon the punishment, which required the trial judge to sentence Beverly to life without the possibility of parole. The capital verdict sheet indicated that all twelve of the jurors felt the racially hostile prison environment and the failure of the prison administration to properly respond to Beverly's complaints provoked Beverly into committing his offense. Jury Verdict Sheet (Penalty Phase) for the State of

New Jersey v. Steven Norman Beverley, Indictment No. SGJ389-97-4 (copy on file with author); Telephone conversation with Jorge Godoy, attorney for Stephen Beverly, on April 16, 2002. Beverly's defense might be characterized as an example of "imperfect" provocation. As Elizabeth Rapaport explains, "provocation insufficient to merit a reduction to manslaughter, may yet suffice to avoid capital responsibility for death eligible murder or reduce first degree to second degree murder." Elizabeth Rapaport, *Capital Murder and the Domestic Discount: A Study of Capital Domestic Murder in the Post-Furman Era*, 49 SMU L. Rev. 1507, 1538 (1996).

57. State v. Madden, 294 A.2d 609 (N.J. 1972).

58. See also U.S. *ex rel.* Merritt v. Hicks, 492 F. Supp. 99 (D.N.J. 1980).

59. Madden, 294 A.2d at 620–21 (emphasis added).

60. Reva B. Siegel, *The Rule of Love: Wife Beating as Prerogative and Privacy*, 105 Yale L.J. 2117 (1996).

61. Nourse, *Passion's Progress, supra* note 4.

62. *Id.* at 1332.

63. *Id.* at 1375–76.

64. Paul E. Mullen, *Jealousy: The Pathology of Passion*, 158 Brit. J. of Psychiatry 593, 594 (1991).

65. Peter N. Stearns, Jealousy: The Evolution of an Emotion in American History 21 (1989).

66. Lawrence A. Greenfield et al., U.S. Department of Justice, Office of Justice Programs Bureau of Justice Statistics, Violence by Intimates 5 (March 1998).

67. *Id.* at 1. Two thousand intimate partner homicides per year is two thousand too many. Of course, some of these homicides may have been accidental killings. Some probably represent the efforts of an abused partner to defend herself or himself. However, if studies indicating that as many as 60 percent of the men who kill their female partners admit to doing so because they believed she was unfaithful are correct, then many of these intimate partner homicides probably constitute female infidelity killings.

## NOTES TO CHAPTER 3

1. Donna Riley testified that Amedure left the note as a joke because Schmitz had a broken headlight on his car. Amedure told Schmitz to call him if he wanted the light properly installed. Apparently, Schmitz had asked Amedure to help him with mechanical repairs in the past. Bryan Robinson, *Mutual Friend of Amedure and Schmitz Admits Lying to Defendant* (Aug. 20, 1999), *available at* CourtTV Online, http://wysiwyg:///13/http://www.courttv.com/trials /schmitz/082099 _pm_ctv.html; *Talk-Show Retrial Closings to Portray Schmitz as*

*Victim and "Cold-Blooded" Murderer* (Aug. 24, 1999), *available at* CourtTV Online, http://www.courttv.com/trials/schmitz/082499_ctv.html; *Michigan v. Schmitz* (Aug. 25, 1999), *available at* CourtTV Online, http://www.courttv.com/verdicts/schmitz.html; *Airline Passenger Recalls Schmitz's Demeanor after "Jenny Jones" Appearance* (Aug. 20, 1999), *available at* Court TV Online, http://www.courttv.com/trials/schmitz/082099_am_ctv.html; *Airplane Passenger Recalls Schmitz's Demeanor after "Jenny Jones" Appearance* (Aug. 20, 1999), *available at* CourtTV Online, http://www.courttv.com/trials/schmitz/082099 _am_ctv.html; *Mutual Friend of Amedure and Schmitz Admits Lying to Defendant* (Aug. 20, 1999), *available at* CourtTV Online, http://www.courttv.com/trials /schmitz/082099_pm_ctv.html; *Schmitz's Supporters Tell of Defendant's Change after Appearance on "Jenny Jones"* (Aug. 23, 1999), *available at* CourtTV Online, http://www.courttv.com/trials/schmitz/082399_pm_ctv.html; *Schmitz Defense Says 'Jenny Jones' Guest Provoked His Own Slaying* (Aug. 19, 1999), *available at* CourtTV Online, http://www.courttv.com/trials/schmitz/081999_am_ctv .html; *Mutual Friend of Amedure and Schmitz Admits Lying to Defendant* (Aug. 20, 1999), *available at* CourtTV Online, http://www.courttv.com/trials/schmitz /082099_pm_ctv.html; *Talk- Show Retrial Closings to Portray Schmitz as Victim and "Cold- Blooded" Murderer* (Aug. 24, 1999), *available at* CourtTV Online, http://www.courttv.com/trials/schmitz/082499_ctv.html; *Prosecution Witnesses Challenge Schmitz's New Defense* (Aug. 19, 1999), *available at* CourtTV Online, http://www.courttv.com/trials/schmitz/081999_pm_ctv.html.

    2. Duncan Osborne, *The Homosexual Panic Defense: Are Juries Really Buying It?* LGNY News, Nov. 4, 1999, at 4. *See also* Robert Mison, *Homophobia in Manslaughter: The Homosexual Advance as Insufficient Provocation*, 80 Cal. L. Rev. 133 (1992); Joshua Dressler, *When "Heterosexual" Men Kill "Homosexual" Men: Reflections on Provocation Law, Sexual Advances, and the "Reasonable Man" Standard*, 85 J. Crim. L. & Criminology 726 (1995); *Developments in the Law—Sexual Orientation and the Law*, 102 Harv. L. Rev. 1519 (1989); Gary David Comstock, *Dismantling the Homosexual Panic Defense*, 2 L. & Sexuality 81 (1992); Martha C. Nussbaum, *"Secret Sewers of Vice": Disgust, Bodies, and the Law*, in The Passions of Law 30 (Susan Bandes ed. 1999); Kara S. Suffredini, *Pride and Prejudice: The Homosexual Panic Defense*, 21 B.C. Third World L.J. 279 (2001); Christina Pei-Lin Chen, *Provocation's Privileged Desire: The Provocation Doctrine, "Homosexual Panic," and the Non-Violent Unwanted Sexual Advance Defense*, 10 Cornell J. L. & Pub. Pol'y 95 (2000).

    3. Parisie v. Greer, 705 F.2d 882, 893 (7th Cir. 1983).

    4. At Schmitz's first trial, his attorneys argued that Schmitz's fear that his friends and relatives would think he was a homosexual shattered Schmitz's already fragile psyche and caused him to act with diminished mental capacity when he killed Amedure. Under Michigan law, diminished capacity is a partial defense to first-degree murder. If successful, the defense

mitigates a first-degree murder charge to second degree. Schmitz's attorneys further argued that Schmitz's shooting of Amedure was not an act of violence, but a declaration of his masculinity. In order to prove to others that he was not a homosexual, Schmitz felt he had to kill the man who was pursuing him. These arguments persuaded the jury to acquit Schmitz of first-degree murder, and find him guilty of the lesser offense of second-degree murder.

Schmitz appealed his second-degree murder conviction and was successful, winning a reversal of his conviction and a new trial. People v. Schmitz, 586 N.W. 2d 766 (Mich. 1998)(reversing on the ground that the trial judge erroneously refused to allow the defense to exercise a peremptory challenge against a prospective juror they had previously passed). Because diminished capacity is only permitted as a defense to first-degree murder under Michigan law, Schmitz could not again argue diminished capacity because he was only charged with second-degree murder at his second trial. Instead, Schmitz asserted the defense of provocation. Schmitz's attorneys argued that the revelation on the *Jenny Jones Show* that a man was his secret admirer pushed Schmitz over the edge and caused him to lose his self-control. This time, Schmitz's attempt to use a gay panic argument was not persuasive. Schmitz was convicted of second-degree murder.

In May 1999, a civil jury found the *Jenny Jones Show,* its parent company, and its production company liable for Jonathan Schmitz's 1995 killing of Scott Amedure, and awarded the Amedure family over $25 million in compensatory damages. Bryan Robertson, *Fieger Says $25M against "Jenny Jones" Verdict Sends Message to the Talk-Show Industry* (May 7, 1999), *available at* CourtTV online, file:///A/050799_fieger_ctv.html. This award was overturned on appeal.

5. Colleen R. Logan, *Homophobia? No, Homoprejudice*, 31 J. HOMOSEXUALITY 31 (1996).

6. *Id.* at 32.

7. Gregory M. Herek, *Beyond "Homophobia": A Social Psychological Perspective on Attitudes toward Lesbians and Gay Men*, 10 J. HOMOSEXUALITY 1, 2 (1984).

8. Stephanie A. Shields & Robert E. Harriman, *Fear of Male Homosexuality: Cardiac Responses of Low and High Homonegative Males*, 10 J. HOMOSEXUALITY 53, 66 (1984).

9. Comstock, *Dismantling the Homosexual Panic Defense, supra* note 2, at 81, 82 (1992), *citing* EDWARD J. KEMPF, PSYCHOPATHOLOGY (1920).

10. *Id.*

11. *Id.* at 84.

12. *Id.*

13. *Id.* at 83.

14. *Id.*

15. Henry E. Adams et al. *Is Homophobia Associated with Homosexual*

*Arousal?* 105 J. ABNORMAL PSYCHOL. 440 (1996). *See also* Michael Segell, *Homophobia Doesn't Lie*, ESQUIRE, Feb. 1, 1997, at 35.

16. SEXUAL ORIENTATION AND THE LAW 34 (HARV. L. REV. ed., 1990).

17. Thomas J. Ficarrotto, *Racism, Sexism, and Erotophobia: Attitudes of Heterosexuals towards Homosexuals*, 19 J. HOMOSEXUALITY 111 (1990). Negative attitudes about homosexuality also tend to arise from religious, social, or cultural factors, rather than psychological pressures. Adrian Howe, *More Folk Provoke Their Own Demise (Homophobic Violence and Sexed Excuses—Rejoining the Provocation Law Debate, Courtesy of the Homosexual Advance Defense)*, 19 SYDNEY L. REV. 336, 339 (1997).

18. Am. Psychiatric Assn., *Gay and Lesbian Issues* (1996), *available at* APA Online (Fact Sheet Series), http://www.psych.org/public_info/HOMOSE~1.HTM.

19. *Id.*

20. Am. Psychological Assn., *Policy Statements on Lesbian, Gay, and Bisexual Concerns, Discrimination against Homosexuals*, adopted by the Am. Psychological Assn. Council of Representatives on January 24–26, 1975, *available at* http://www.apa.org/pi/igbpolicy/against.html.

21. Erica Goode, *Being Gay Is Not Abnormal, Coalition Tells Educators*, S.F. CHRON., Nov. 23, 1999, at A1.

22. *Id.* at A12.

23. *Id.*

24. *See* 8 U.S.C. § 1182(a)(4) (1970) (naming as excludable "Aliens afflicted with psychopathic personality, or sexual deviation, or a mental defect"); Boutilier v. Immigration and Naturalization Service, 387 U.S. 118, 122 (1967) (holding that an alien who was a homosexual was afflicted with psychopathic personality); Rosenberg v. Fleuti, 374 U.S. 449, 461 (1963) (upholding Congress's power to exclude homosexuals and other "undesirable" aliens from the United States); Susan McRae, *Panel Discusses Restrictions on Gay Immigrants*, L.A. DAILY J., July 5, 2000, at 1.

25. Even though the Act was an assault on same-sex marriages, then President Bill Clinton signed the bill into law on September 21, 1996. *See* Patrick J. Shipley, *Constitutionality of the Defense of Marriage Act*, 11 J. OF CONTEMP. LEGAL ISSUES 117, 117 (2000).

26. GARY DAVID COMSTOCK, VIOLENCE AGAINST LESBIANS AND GAY MEN 82 (1991)(noting that none of the perpetrators of anti-gay/lesbian violence in his survey had a history of psychological problems).

27. *Id.* at 91–92.

28. *Id.* at 87.

29. Howe, *More Folk Provoke Their Own Demise, supra* note 17, at 336, 342.

30. Comstock, VIOLENCE AGAINST LESBIANS AND GAY MEN, *supra* note 26, at 89–90.

31. *Id.*

32. Osborne, *The Homosexual Panic Defense, supra* note 2, at 4.

33. According to Joshua Dressler, there are two variants of the diminished capacity defense. Under the mens rea variant, "evidence that the defendant suffered from a mental disease or defect at the time of his conduct is admissible if it is relevant to prove that he lacked a mental state that is an element of the charged offense." JOSHUA DRESSLER, UNDERSTANDING CRIMINAL LAW § 26.02[B][2] at 363 (3d ed. 2001). Under the partial responsibility variant, the charge is reduced from murder to manslaughter because the defendant is seen as "less blameworthy and therefore less deserving of punishment, than a killer who acts with a normal state of mind." *Id.* § 26.03[A][2] at 367.

34. Associated Press, "Gay Wyoming Student Dies, 5 Days after Brutal Beating," L.A. TIMES, Oct. 12, 1998; Julie Cart, "Wyoming Campus Mourns Slaying of Gay Student," L.A. TIMES, Oct. 13, 1998; Julie Cart, "Shepard Killer Pleads Guilty," S.J. MERCURY NEWS, April 6, 1999, at A1; "Second Suspect Goes on Trial in Killing of Gay Wyoming Man," S.F. CHRON., Oct. 25, 1999, at A7; Associated Press, "2d Trial Opens in Gay Killing," S.F. CHRON., Oct. 12, 1999, at A3; Associated Press, *Lawyer Cites Defendant's History of Sexual Trauma*, S.F. CHRON., Oct. 26, 1999, at A8; Associated Press, *Judge May Bar "Gay Panic" as Defense in Murder Trial*, S.F. CHRON., Oct. 28, 1999, at A3; Associated Press, *Wyoming Judge Bars "Gay Panic" Defense*, WASH. POST, Nov. 2, 1999, at A7; Michael Janofsky, *Gay-Panic Defense Ruled Out*, N.Y. TIMES, Nov. 2, 1999, at A3; Tom Kenworthy, *Murder Verdict in Slaying of Gay Student*, S.F. CHRON., Nov. 4, 1999, at A1; Thomas Fields et al., *Death in Wyoming*, PEOPLE MAG., November 2, 1998, at 52; Heather Gierhart, *Defense Claims "Gay Panic,"* BRANDING IRON (Oct. 26, 1999), *available at* http://bi.wyo.edu/news00/defense.htm; JoAnn Wypijewski, *A Boy's Life: For Matthew Shepard's Killers, What Does It Take to Pass as a Man?* HARPER'S MAG., Sept. 1999, at 61, 74. Additionally, I wish to thank Judge Barton Voigt, who presided over Aaron McKinney's trial, for reading a draft of my description of the case and providing helpful feedback.

35. BETH LOFFREDA, LOSING MATT SHEPARD: LIFE AND POLITICS IN THE AFTERMATH OF ANTI-GAY MURDER (2000).

36. Initially, McKinney told police that he had left the keys to his truck on the counter at a bar where he and Henderson were having a beer, that a stranger took his truck for a few hours, came back, returned his keys, and invited McKinney and Henderson to a party. *Id.* at 152–54.

37. Police were able to link McKinney and Henderson to Shepard's murder because McKinney used the same gun he'd used to beat Shepard to crack open the head of Emiliano Morales, a Latino youth, with whom he and Henderson picked a fight later that same night. Police called to investigate the altercation between McKinney and Morales found Shepard's shoes and credit card in McKinney's truck. On April 15, 1999, Henderson pled guilty to felony

murder and kidnapping. As part of his plea agreement, Henderson agreed to testify against Aaron McKinney in exchange for a promise from prosecutors not to seek the death penalty. Henderson was sentenced to two consecutive life sentences. *Surprise Plea Comes in Shepard Case* (Apr. 5, 1999), *available at* www.channel2000.com, wysiwyg://150/http://www.channel2000.com...ws/stories/news_99040 5-180604.html.

38. Judith Crosson, *Man Imprisoned for Murder of Gay Wyoming Student* (Apr. 5, 1999), *available at* Yahoo! News (also *available at* http://dailynews.yahoo.com/headlines/ts/html?s+v/nm/19990405/ts /crime_gays_5.html).

39. After the arrests, McKinney's girlfriend, Kristen Price, told reporters that McKinney became upset after Shepard "pushed himself onto" McKinney, embarrassing him in front of his friends. Price further stated that McKinney and Henderson decided to get back at Shepard by robbing him. According to Price, the two men did not intend to kill Shepard, but things simply got out of hand. Thomas Fields Meyer, Vickie Bane, & Elizabeth Leonard, *Death in Wyoming*, PEOPLE MAG., Nov. 2, 1998, at 52. Bartender Matt Galloway, who witnessed the interaction between Shepard, McKinney, and Henderson at the bar that night, said, "I refute 100 percent that Shepard approached them." *Id.*

40. Bryan Robinson, *Jury Selection Set to Begin for Wyoming Man Allegedly Responsible for Matthew Shepard's Fatal Beating* (Oct. 8, 1999), *available at* Court TV Online, http://www.courttv.com/trials/mckinney/100899_ctv.html.

41. Tom Kenworthy, *Wyo. Jury to Weigh Motives in Gay Killing*, WASH. POST, Nov. 3, 1999, at A3.

42. LOFFREDA, LOSING MATT SHEPARD, *supra* note 35, at 132.

43. Beth Loffreda, a University of Wyoming professor and author of *Losing Matt Shepard: Life and Politics in the Aftermath of Anti-Gay Murder*, reports that there was plenty of reason to doubt Tangeman's claim that McKinney was high on methamphetamine or alcohol the night he killed Shepard. The detective in charge of the case told Loffreda that:

> [N]o evidence of recent drug use was "found in the search of their residences. There was no evidence in the truck. From everything that we were able to investigate, the last time they would have done meth would have been up to two to three weeks previous to that night. What the defense attempted to do was a bluff." . . . "A meth crime is going to be a quick attack. . . . It's going to be a maniac attack. . . . No. This was a sustained event. And somebody that's going to be high on meth is not going to be targeting and zeroing in on a head, and deliver the blows that they did, the way they did" with such precision. "Consistently it was targeted, and even if you're drunk, you're going to have a tough time trying to keep your target. No. There's just absolutely no involvement with drugs."

*Id.* at 134. At trial, Kristen Price, McKinney's girlfriend, testified that as far as she could tell, McKinney was not high on methamphetamine the night of the murder. Price said McKinney often tidied up the house when high and usually seemed happier when he was drunk. Chastity Pasley, Henderson's girlfriend, echoed Price's assessment of McKinney. Matt Galloway, the bartender at the Fireside Lounge who served McKinney and Henderson, also testified that McKinney did not seem to be high or drunk when he left the bar that night. *Id.*

44. *Id.* at 132.

45. Decision Letter, State v. McKinney, Albany County Criminal Action No. 6381, Oct. 30, 1999, at page 4 (on file with author).

46. Decision Letter, State v. McKinney, Albany County Criminal Action No. 6381, Oct. 30, 1999 (on file with author); Associated Press, *Wyoming Judge Bars "Gay Panic" Defense*, WASH. POST, Nov. 2, 1999, at A7; Michael Janofsky, *Gay-Panic Defense Ruled Out*, S.F. CHRON., Nov. 2, 1999, at A3. *See also* Dean v. State, 668 P.2d 639 (Wyo. 1983) (stating, in dicta, that diminished capacity, like the irresistible impulse test, is not accepted as a defense in Wyoming).

47. Kevin T. Berril & Gregory M. Herek, *Primary and Secondary Victimization in Anti-Gay Hate Crimes: Official Response and Public Policy, in* HATE CRIMES: CONFRONTING VIOLENCE AGAINST LESBIANS AND GAY MEN 289, 295 (1992).

48. Bryan Robinson, *Final Ruling on So-Called "Gay Panic" Theory Hangs in Balance as Shepard Murder Defense Begins* (Oct. 29, 1999), *available at* Court TV Online, http://www.courttv.com/trials/mckinney/102999_pm_ctv.html.

49. LOFFREDA, LOSING MATT SHEPARD, supra note 35, at 135. Loffreda notes that this comment suggests the witness was more afraid of his own homosexuality than of Shepard. *Id.*

50. *Id.;* Bryan Robinson, *McKinney's Defense Rests in Shepard Murder Trial* (Nov. 1, 1999), *available at* Court TV Online, http://www.courttv.com/trials/mckinney/110199_pm_ctv.html.

51. LOFFREDA, LOSING MATT SHEPARD, *supra* note 35, at 40–41.

52. *Id.*

53. *Id.* at 141.

54. *Id.* at 27.

55. Deputy Laramie County Attorney Mark Voss, a prosecutor not associated with the Matthew Shepard case, remarked that the verdict was unusual because it sounded as if McKinney was convicted of murder three times for killing just one person, but explained that this was "just an illusion created by the nature of the verdict form." Becky Orr, *Guilty*, WYO. TRIB. EAGLE, Nov. 4, 1999, at A1.

56. Bryan Robinson, *Trial of Man Accused of Gay Hate Crime Slaying Begins with Defendant Blaming His Cohort* (Aug. 4, 1999), *available at* Court TV Online-TRIALS-Alabama v. Butler, http://www.courtv.com/trials/butler/080499_ctv.html.

57. Phillip Rawls, *Witness Describes Defendant in Gay Murder as Joking Afterwards*, ASSOCIATED PRESS NEWSWIRES, Aug. 6, 1999; Phillip Rawls, *Man Convicted of Capital Murder in Slaying of Homosexual*, ASSOCIATED PRESS NEWSWIRES, Aug. 5, 1999; Jay Reeves, *Suspects in Gaither Slaying Plead Innocent*, ASSOCIATED PRESS NEWSWIRES, May 20, 1999; Jay Reeves, *Prosecutor to Recommend Life Without Parole in Killing of Gay Man*, ASSOCIATED PRESS NEWSWIRES, June 25, 1999; Phillip Rawls, *Skinhead Describes Beating Death of Gay Man*, ASSOCIATED PRESS NEWSWIRES, Aug. 6, 1999.

58. Reeves, *Suspects in Gaither Slaying Plead Innocent, supra* at note 57.

59. Reeves, *Prosecutor to Recommend Life Without Parole in Killing of Gay Man, supra* at note 57.

60. Daniel Pedersen, *A Quiet Man's Tragic Rendezvous with Hate*, NEWSWEEK, Mar. 15, 1999.

61. Sue Anne Presley, *2 Accused of Killing, Burning Gay Man*, WASH. POST, Mar. 5, 1999, at A1.

62. Associated Press, *Cops: Men Plotted Gay Man's Grisly Slaying*, PHILA. DAILY NEWS, Mar. 5, 1999, at 26.

63. Excerpts of Steven Mullins's Testimony (Aug. 5, 1999), *available at* Frontline, Assault on Gay America, wysiwyg://5/http://www.pbs.org/wgbh/pages...tline/shows/assault/billyjack/mullet.html.

64. While McKinney and Schmitz were acquitted of first- degree murder, none of the high-profile defendants discussed in the preceding section succeeded in completely escaping a murder conviction. Charles Butler was found guilty of capital murder, Aaron McKinney was convicted of felony murder, and Jonathan Schmitz was convicted of second-degree murder.

65. JAMES P. LEVINE, JURIES AND POLITICS 89 (1992) (noting that "[o]ne study found that out of about 2 million criminal cases dealt with in American criminal courts in a single year, only 1,625 produced verdicts of not guilty on the basis of insanity.").

66. JOSHUA DRESSLER, UNDERSTANDING CRIMINAL LAW 330 (2d ed. 1995), *citing* IDAHO CODE §18-207 (1987), MONT. CODE ANN. §46-14-102 (1993), UTAH CODE ANN. §76-2-305(1) (1994). *But see* Finger v. State, 27 P.3d 66 (Nev. 2001) (holding that abolition of the insanity defense violates due process).

67. *But see* Miguel A. Mendez, *Diminished Capacity in California: Premature Reports of Its Demise*, 3 STAN. L. & POL'Y REV. 216 (1991) (arguing that even though Proposition 8, passed in 1982, declares that "[t]he defense of diminished capacity is hereby abolished," California still allows the use of diminished capacity in a modified form).

68. Dean v. State, 668 P.2d 639 (Wyo. 1983).

69. Because Michigan law does not permit diminished capacity as a defense to second-degree murder, Jonathan Schmitz had no choice but to argue provocation at his second trial, a fairly weak argument given Schmitz's actions

immediately following the revelation that Scott Amedure was his secret admirer (smiling and hugging Amedure and going out for drinks with him after the *Jenny Jones Show*) and the fact that Schmitz did not kill Amedure until three days after the show, ample time to cool off.

70. Mison, *Homophobia in Manslaughter, supra* note 2; Dressler, *When "Heterosexual" Men Kill "Homosexual" Men, supra* note 2.

71. Dir. of Pub. Prosecutions v. Camplin 2 All E.R. 168, 171 (1978).

72. Commonwealth v. Carr, 580 A.2d 1362 (Pa. Super. Ct. 1990).

73. Although Carr claimed the women were engaged in "nude" lovemaking, Brenner, the woman who survived, claims Wight was fully dressed and she was partially dressed when Carr shot them. CLAUDIA BRENNER, EIGHT BULLETS: ONE WOMAN'S STORY OF SURVIVING ANTI-GAY VIOLENCE (1995) ("we were having—not having oral sex with a capital O.S., but . . . we were . . . playing. . . . Why I mention that is that I was only partially dressed when the shooting happened. Rebecca was fully dressed. The image in the reports is that we were in the middle of a passionate sex act. I have always said 'making love' because I am paranoid they will discredit our relationship by saying, 'Oh, they were only playing around'").

74. Abbe Smith, *Criminal Responsibility, Social Irresponsibility, and Angry Young Men: Reflections of a Feminist Criminal Defense Lawyer*, 21 N.Y.U. REV. L. & SOC. CHANGE 433, 436 (1995) ("As victim's counsel, I convinced the prosecutor to move in limine to prevent the defense from arguing that the defendant was provoked by the women's sexual relationship").

75. *Carr*, 580 A.2d at 1364.

76. Deborah S. David and Robert Brannon, *The Male Sex Role: Our Culture's Blueprint of Manhood and What It's Done for Us Lately, in* THE FORTY-NINE PERCENT MAJORITY: THE MALE SEX ROLE 31 (Deborah S. David & Robert Brannon eds. 1976) ("Both men and women grow up in our culture thinking of male aggressiveness as natural and normal, and of men as the sexual aggressors").

77. Roy Scrivner, *Gay Men and Nonrelational Sex, in* MEN AND SEX: NEW PSYCHOLOGICAL PERSPECTIVES 229, 233 (Ronald L. Levant & Gary R. Brooks eds. 1997).

78. James Harrison, *Roles, Identities, and Sexual Orientation: Homosexuality, Heterosexuality, and Bisexuality, in* A NEW PSYCHOLOGY OF MEN 359, 378–79 (Ronald F. Levant & William S. Pollack eds. 1995). *See also* Francisco Valdes, *Queers, Sissies, Dykes, and Tomboys: Deconstructing the Conflation of "Sex," "Gender," and "Sexual Orientation" in Euro-American Law and Society*, 83 CAL. L. REV. 1 (1995) (noting the existence of judicial opinions that interpret male effeminacy as a sign of homosexuality).

79. *Id.*

80. Steve Tomsen, *Hatred, Murder and Male Honour: Gay Homicides and the "Homosexual Panic Defense,"* 6 CRIMINOLOGY AUSTL. 2, 5 (1994).

81. JoAnn Wypijewski, *A Boy's Life: For Matthew Shepard's Killers, What Does It Take to Pass as a Man?* HARPER'S MAG., Sept. 1999, at 61, 74.

82. Peter Johnson, *"More Than Ordinary Men Gone Wrong": Can the Law Know the Gay Subject?* 20 MELB. U. L. REV. 1152, 1178 (1996), citing Kendall Thomas, *Beyond the Privacy Principle,* 92 COLUM. L. REV. 1431, n. 188 (1992); *see also* Peter Frieberg, *Blaming the Victim: New Life for the "Gay Panic" Defense,* THE ADVOCATE, May 24, 1988, at 12. To be precise, the male defendant who claims that a nonviolent homosexual advance constitutes legally adequate provocation and is convicted of manslaughter rather than murder is not "right" or justified in having killed another person. Provocation is generally considered an excuse defense, which means that the act is still considered wrong.

83. Comstock, VIOLENCE AGAINST LESBIANS AND GAY MEN, *supra* note 26, at 90–91.

84. *Id.* at 91–92.

85. People v. Mangum, 260 Ill. App. 3d 631 (1994); Tracy Dell'Angela, *Murderous Intolerance,* CHI. TRIB., Oct. 25, 1998, at 1.

86. Dell'Angela, *Murderous Intolerance, supra* note 85, at 1.

87. Even though the prosecutor knew Eklund's sexual orientation would be a central issue in the case, he chose not to screen prospective jurors for anti-gay bias. The prosecutor explained that he didn't want to plant the idea that the victim was bad by questioning prospective jurors about their beliefs regarding homosexuality. The prosecutor thought that calling attention to the victim's sexual orientation would bias the jury against the victim. Rather than biasing the jury, highlighting the victim's sexual orientation and informing the jury that discrimination against gays and lesbians is wrong probably would have had the opposite effect. Questions posed during jury selection are often aimed at educating jurors about the inappropriateness of bias.

88. 86. Dell'Angela, *Murderous Intolerance, supra* note 85.

89. *Id.*

90. *Id.*

91. COMSTOCK, VIOLENCE AGAINST LESBIANS AND GAY MEN, *supra* note 26, at 82.

92. *Mangum,* 260 Ill. App. 3d at 635.

93. Schick v. Indiana, 570 N.E.2d 918 (Ind. Ct. App. 1991). Fran Jeffries, *Teen Convicted in Dugout Death,* COURIER-JOURNAL, Nov. 19, 1988, at 6A. In a posttrial statement, Schick provided another version of the events. In this version, Schick stated that initially, Lamie knocked him unconscious. When Schick awoke, Lamie was trying to force his penis into Schick's mouth. Schick had to fight Lamie off in order to avoid the sexual attack. Schick eventually broke free and while Lamie was stumbling toward him with his underwear around his ankles, Schick knocked Lamie down. As Lamie lay on the ground, Schick beat and kicked him to death. *Schick,* 570 N.E.2d. at 927.

94. Comstock, Violence against Lesbians and Gay Men, *supra* note 26, at 59–60.

95. Mills v. Shepard, 445 F. Supp. 1231 (W.D.N.C. 1978).

96. Tomsen, *Hatred, Murder and Male Honour, supra* note 80, at 2.

97. Star Bulletin Staff, *Defendant Says Brewer Grabbed Him, "Looked Evil"* (Sept. 29, 1998), *available at* Honolulu Star-Bulletin, http://starbulletin .com/98/09/29/news/briefs.html; Susan Kreifels, *Jury Tainted by Homophobia?* (Oct. 7, 1998), *available at* Honolulu Star-Bulletin, http://starbulletin.com /98/10/07news/story2.html; Susan Kreifels, *Blood in Jeans Evidence of Murder, Says Prosecutor* (Oct. 1, 1998), *available at* Honolulu Star-Bulletin, http://starbulletin.com/98/10/01/news/briefs.html; Star Bulletin Staff, *Killer Gets Community Service Hours* (July 7, 1999), *available at* Honolulu Star-Bulletin, http://starbulletin.com/1999/07/07/news/briefs.html.

98. Kreifels, *Jury Tainted by Homophobia? supra* note 97.

99. Star Bulletin Staff, *Killer Gets Community Service Hours, supra* note 97.

100. Stephanie M. Wildman, Privilege Revealed: How Invisible Preference Undermines America (1996).

101. Peter Kwan, *Complicity and Complexity: Cosynthesis and Praxis*, 49 De-Paul L. Rev. 673, 689 (2000) ("Cosynthesis allows us to move beyond a single axis or uni-dimensional view of identity to one that reconceives individuals as made up of many axes all supporting the others and together constituting the whole"); Peter Kwan, *Jeffrey Dahmer and the CoSynthesis of Categories*, 48 Hastings L.J. 1257, 1264 (1997) (arguing that "replacing assumptions of autonomic categories such as race, gender, and homosexuality with a notion that allows for their simultaneous implication may give us a richer understanding of both the production and consequences of categorical meanings"); Peter Kwan, *Invention, Inversion and Intervention: The Oriental Woman in the World of Suzie Wong, M. Butterfly, and the Adventures of Priscilla, Queen of the Desert*, 5 Asian L.J. 99 (1998) (arguing that certain stereotypes emerge out of a confluence of racial, sexual orientation, gender, and class identities which interact in a catalytic manner).

102. Darren Lenard Hutchinson, *Identity Crisis: "Intersectionality," "Multidimensionality," and the Development of an Adequate Theory of Subordination*, 6 Mich. J. Race & L. 285 (2001); Darren Lenard Hutchinson, *Ignoring the Sexualization of Race: Heteronormativity, Critical Race Theory and Anti-Racist Politics*, 47 Buff. L. Rev. 1 (1999). *See also* Francisco Valdes, *Afterword: Beyond Sexual Orientation in Queer Legal Theory: Majoritarianism, Multidimensionality, and Responsibility in Social Justice Scholarship or Legal Scholars as Cultural Warriors*, 75 Denver U. L. Rev. 1409 (1998) (discussing "ways in which legal scholarship devoted to social justice can be made more potent and relevant through multidimensional analysis").

103. To the extent possible, I have tried to include a multidimensional discussion of race, class, gender, and sexual orientation when discussing the cases

presented in this book. However, for most of the cases, a multidimensional analysis was not possible because of limited information.

104. David & Brannon, *The Male Sex Role, supra* note 76, at 12–35 (describing the four primary dimensions of the male sex role in America).

## NOTES TO CHAPTER 4

1. Leti Volpp, *(Mis)identifying Culture: Asian Women and the "Cultural Defense,"* 17 HARV. WOMEN'S L.J. 57, 65 (1994).

2. While Chen's defense attorney did not formally advance a provocation defense, arguing instead that Chen was suffering from insanity at the time he killed his wife, the cultural evidence that was presented indirectly suggested that Chen was reasonably provoked into killing his wife. James J. Sing, *Culture as Sameness: Toward a Synthetic View of Provocation and Culture in the Criminal Law,* 108 YALE L.J. 1845, 1876 (1999).

3. Volpp, *(Mis)identifying Culture, supra* note 1, at 73. *See also* Holly Maguigan, *Cultural Evidence and Male Violence: Are Feminist and Multiculturalist Reformers on a Collision Course in Criminal Courts?* 70 N.Y.U. L. REV. 36, 37 (1995).

4. Volpp, *(Mis)identifying Culture, supra* note 1, at 69.

5. *Id.* at 65 (emphasis added).

6. *Id.* at 66.

7. *Id.* at 70.

8. *Id.* at 73, *citing* Record at 301–2.

9. Daina C. Chiu, *The Cultural Defense: Beyond Exclusion, Assimilation, and Guilty Liberalism,* 82 CAL. L. REV. 1053, 1053 (1994), *citing* Nina Schuyler, *Cultural Defense: Equality of Anarchy?* S.F. WEEKLY, Sept. 25, 1991, at 1.

10. Madhavi Sunder, *Cultural Dissent,* 54 STAN. L. REV. 495, 511 (2001), *quoting* Edward B. Tylor, *Primitive Culture, in* HIGH POINTS IN ANTHROPOLOGY 6 (Paul Bohannan & Mark Glazer eds., 2d ed. 1988).

11. *Id.* at 507. Sunder argues against the current approach which views cultural identity as something that is imposed on members of a given community (she calls this approach "cultural survival") in favor of an approach which embraces "cultural dissent" and sees cultural identity as something individual members of a community choose.

12. *Id.*

13. *Id.* at 511.

14. *Id.* at 507.

15. *Id.* at 515.

16. Leti Volpp, *Blaming Culture for Bad Behavior,* 12 YALE J. OF L. AND HUMAN. 89, 89–90 (2000).

17. *Raise the Red Lantern* (Metro Goldwyn Mayer 1991).

18. Leti Volpp, *Talking "Culture": Gender, Race, Nation, and the Politics of Multiculturalism*, 90 COLUM. L. REV. 1573 (1996) (noting that Westerners believe non-European countries in Asia and Africa are patriarchal and oppressive, while America is viewed as progressive).

19. *See, e.g.,* State v. Girmay, 652 A.2d 150 (N.H. 1994) (refusing to allow Ethiopian murder defendant's expert witness to testify regarding Ethiopian social customs and gender relations in Ethiopia); State v. Haque, 726 A.2d 205 (Me. 1999) (excluding testimony of a cultural anthropologist who would have spoken about the defendant's Muslim upbringing and experience as an immigrant from India); People v. Odinga, 531 N.Y.S.2d 818 (App. Div. 1988) (rejecting defendant's argument that he had a reasonable belief, based on his experience as a member of a Black radical group, that police officers were trying to kill him when they twice rammed their vehicle into his). *See also* Maguigan, *Cultural Evidence and Male Violence, supra* note 3, at 86–87 (noting that "courts often fail to find cultural information either admissible or relevant to jury instructions requested by defendants").

20. Maguigan, *Cultural Evidence and Male Violence, supra* note 3, at 97.

21. *Id.* at 80–81; State v. Wanrow, 559 P.2d 548 (Wash. 1977).

22. *Id.*

23. *See infra* chapter 8 at text accompanying notes 44–46 for a brief discussion of this aspect of the case.

24. State v. Williams, 484 P.2d 1167 (Wash. 1971).

25. Indian Child Welfare Act of 1978, H.R. REP. No. 95-1386, at 7531 (1978).

26. *Id.*

27. *Id.*

28. *Id.*

29. *Id.* at 1171.

30. As discussed in chapter 10, in most cases courts focus on emotion reasonableness rather than act reasonableness. It is always easier to find emotion reasonableness than act reasonableness, so most defendants receive the benefit of this focus on emotion reasonableness. In the *Williams* case, however, the Native American defendants did not receive this benefit. Both the trial and appellate courts focused on act reasonableness.

31. My Evening Criminal Law class at George Washington University during the Fall of 2002 was an exception to this general trend. Several students in that class spoke critically of the appellate court's decision in *Williams*.

32. Chiu, *The Cultural Defense, supra* note 9, at 1101.

33. Patricia Hurtado, *Killer's Sentence Defended: "He's Not a Loose Cannon,"* NEWSDAY, Apr. 4, 1989, at 3 (emphasis added).

34. Volpp, *(Mis)identifying Culture, supra* note 1, at 76.

35. *Id.* at 74–75.

36. Volpp, *Blaming Culture for Bad Behavior, supra* note 16.

37. Lisa Piddington, *Fashion Style Laced Up*, BIRMINGHAM POST, Feb. 21, 2001, at 16–17.

38. Apparently, the corset is making a comeback in women's fashion. The new corsets, fortunately, are more comfortable than the corsets of old. *Id.*

39. Deborah S. David & Robert Brannon, *The Male Sex Role: Our Culture's Blueprint for Mankind and What It's Done for Us Lately, in* THE FORTY-NINE PERCENT MAJORITY: THE MALE SEX ROLE 12–35 (Deborah S. David and Robert Brannan eds. 1976).

40. Ronald F. Levant, *Toward the Reconstruction of Masculinity, in* A NEW PSYCHOLOGY OF MEN 232–33 (Ronald F. Levant & William S. Pollack eds., 1995).

41. *Id.*

42. *Id.*

43. SUSAN FALUDI, STIFFED: THE BETRAYAL OF THE AMERICAN MAN 10 (1999).

44. Volpp, *(Mis)identifying Culture, supra* note 1, at 66.

45. *See infra* text accompanying notes 90–99.

46. Anthony V. Alfieri, *Defending Racial Violence*, 95 COLUM. L. REV. 1301 (1995); Anthony V. Alfieri, *Race Trials*, 76 TEX. L. REV. 1293, 1354–55 (1998) (arguing that racialized narratives which are used to acquit young Black males of charges of interracial violence result in harm to the larger African American community). *But see* Eva S. Nilsen, *The Criminal Defense Lawyer's Reliance on Bias and Prejudice*, 8 GEO. J. LEGAL ETHICS 1 (1994).

47. Reginald Denny was the White truck driver who was pulled from his truck and beaten during the rioting in Los Angeles following the state court acquittal of the Los Angeles police officers who beat Rodney King.

48. Dawn Weber, *Videotape Evidence Key to Prosecution*, L.A. DAILY NEWS, July 26, 1993, at N14. According to Paul Harris, a "Black Rage" defense is an argument that an African American defendant should be excused from criminal liability because his (or her) rage was caused by widespread and persistent discrimination against Blacks. PAUL HARRIS, BLACK RAGE CONFRONTS THE LAW (1997). *See also* Judd F. Sneirson, *Black Rage and the Criminal Law: A Principled Approach to a Polarized Debate*, 143 U. PA. L. REV. 2251 (1995); Patricia J. Falk, *Novel Theories of Criminal Defense Based Upon the Toxicity of the Social Environment: Urban Psychosis, Television Intoxication, and Black Rage*, 74 N.C. L. REV. 731 (1996).

49. Edward J. Boyer & John L. Mitchell, *Attempted Murder Acquittal, Deadlock Wind Up Denny Trial*, L.A. TIMES, Oct. 21, 1993, at A1.

50. *Id.*

51. Abbe Smith, *Burdening the Least of Us: "Race Conscious" Ethics in Criminal Defense*, 77 TEX. L. REV. 1585, 1595 (1999).

52. *Id.* at 1596.

53. *Id.* at 1600, *quoting* Trial of Queen Caroline 8 (1821).

54. *See* Richard Delgado, *Making Pets: Social Workers, "Problem Groups," and*

*the Role of the SPCA—Getting a Little More Precise About Racialized Narratives,* 77 TEX. L. REV. 1571 (1999) (arguing that it is important to understand the role of racialized narratives so we can (1) appreciate the ways in which race determines outcomes in civil and criminal cases, (2) combat racialized narratives colored by racism, and (3) understand the limits of advocacy).

55. Maguigan, *Cultural Evidence and Male Violence, supra* note 3, at 36, 92.

56. *Id., quoting* Joan Morgan, *A Blackwoman's Guide to the Tyson Trial,* VILLAGE VOICE, Mar. 3, 1992, at 37, 39.

57. Morgan, *A Blackwoman's Guide to the Tyson Trial, supra* note 56, at 37, 39.

58. In reaching this verdict, the jury may have relied on other racialized stereotypes, such as the stereotype of the African American male as sexual predator.

59. Maguigan, *Cultural Evidence and Male Violence, supra* note 3.

60. Deirdre Evans-Pritchard & Alison Dundes Renteln, *The Interpretation and Distortion of Culture: A Hmong "Marriage by Capture" Case in Fresno, California,* 4 S. CAL. INTERDISC. L.J. 1, 36 (1994).

61. Cultural evidence can also cut against the defendant. Deborah Woo notes that in the Fumiko Kimura case, cultural evidence regarding the Japanese practice of *oya-ko-shinju,* under which a Japanese parent, usually the mother, kills her children and then tries to kill herself, was downplayed by the defense because it would have helped prosecutors prove that Mrs. Kimura had the requisite intent to kill her children, making her guilty of murder. Deborah Woo, *The People v. Fumiko Kimura: But Which People?* 17 INT'L J. SOC. L. 403 (1989).

62. Alison Dundes Renteln, *A Justification of the Cultural Defense as Partial Excuse,* 2 S. CAL. REV. L. & WOMEN'S STUD. 437, 444 n. 18 (1993).

63. Maguigan, *Cultural Evidence and Male Violence, supra* note 3.

64. Sing, *Culture as Sameness, supra* note 2, at 1845.

65. Maguigan, *Cultural Evidence and Male Violence, supra* note 3, at 36.

66. *Id.*

67. Doriane Lambelet Coleman, *Individualizing Justice Through Multiculturalism: The Liberals' Dilemma,* 96 COLUM. L. REV. 1093 (1996).

68. Maguigan, *Cultural Evidence and Male Violence, supra* note 3, at 53, *citing* Richard Delgado, *Shadowboxing: An Essay on Power,* 77 CORNELL L. REV. 813, 818 (1992); Charles R. Lawrence, III, *The Word and the River: Pedagogy as Scholarship and Struggle,* 65 S. CAL. L. REV. 2231, 2253 (1992); and Woo, *The People v. Fumiko Kimura: But Which People? supra* note 61.

69. Coleman, *Individualizing Justice, supra* note 67.

70. Volpp, *Talking Culture, supra* note 18, at 1576.

71. *Id.* at 1577.

72. *Id.* at 1576.

73. Andrew E. Taslitz, *What Feminism Has to Offer Evidence Law,* 28 SW. U. L. REV. 171, 206 (1999).

74. *Id.*

75. Volpp, *Blaming Culture for Bad Behavior, supra* note 16, at 90.

76. Leti Volpp, *Feminism and Multiculturalism*, 101 COLUM. L. REV. 1181, 1187 (2001).

77. *Id.* at 1189.

78. Richard A. Serrano, *Jury to Hear, See Oklahoma Blast Terror*, L.A. TIMES, Dec. 31, 1995, at A1; *see also* http://www.cnn.com/US/OKC/index.html (discussing the Oklahoma City bombing).

79. Laurie Goodstein, *Report Cites Harassment of Muslims*, WASH. POST, Apr. 20, 1996, at A3 (noting that "[i]n the days immediately following the Oklahoma City bombing, when public figures from news commentators to an Oklahoma congressman suggested that the perpetrators were Muslim extremists, there was a rash of attacks on mosques as well as harassment of Muslim citizens").

80. Charles J. Carter, *Muslims Condemn Airport Shooting, Offer Condolences*, S.D. UNION TRIB., July 10, 2002, at A4 (noting that Maher Hathout "wrote the letter after the governor told him of 'his concern some people of the Muslim community were not clear in condemnation'").

81. *Id.*

82. Richard Delgado points out that "white folks have a race too, although they rarely think about it or see themselves as racialized." Delgado, *Making Pets, supra* note 54, at 1579, *citing* CRITICAL WHITE STUDIES: LOOKING BEHIND THE MIRROR (Richard Delgado & Jean Stefancic eds., 1997).

83. I wish to thank my friend and colleague Burlette Carter for suggesting interest convergence theory as a possible explanation for this phenomena at a works-in-progress session at the 2002 North East People of Color Conference.

84. Brown v. Board of Education, 347 U.S. 483 (1954).

85. Herbert Wechsler, *Toward Neutral Principles of Constitutional Law*, 73 HARV. L. REV. 1 (1959).

86. Derrick A. Bell, Jr., *Brown v. Board of Education and the Interest Convergence Dilemma*, 93 HARV. L. REV. 518, 522 (1980).

87. *Id.* at 523.

88. *Id.* at 524.

89. *Id.* at 524–25.

90. *Id.* at 525.

91. *See also* Lamu Abu-Odeh, *Comparatively Speaking: The "Honor" of the "East" and the "Passion" of the "West,"* 2 UTAH L. REV. 287 (1997) (comparing and contrasting passion provocation killings in America and other Western societies with "honor" killings in the Arab world).

92. *See infra* text accompanying notes 98–100 (discussing May Aphaylath's case).

93. Sing, *Culture as Sameness, supra* note 2, at 1876.

94. *Id.* at 1877 ("In the end analysis, the judge fixated not on cultural dif-

ference, but rather on perceived symmetries between the American and Chinese cultural systems"), *citing* Chiu, *The Cultural Defense, supra* note, at 1113–14.

95. Associated Press, *Injured Court Bystander Loses Lawsuit*, COLO. SPRINGS GAZETTE TELEGRAPH, Mar. 1, 1991, at B3; Briefing, COLO. SPRINGS GAZETTE TELE-GRAPH, Aug. 12, 1988, at B7; Jenks v. Sullivan, 813 P.2d 800 (Col. 1991).

96. Briefing, COLO. SPRINGS GAZETTE TELEGRAPH, Aug. 12, 1998, at B7; Howard Pankratz, *Jury Rejects "Loss of Face" Insanity Plea*, DENVER POST, March 10, 1995, at B1. Duong was sentenced to sixteen years in prison.

97. *See* chapter 1 for a fuller description of the Jimmy Watkins case.

98. Robert Bellafiore, *Court Overturns Laotian Refugee's Murder Conviction*, U.P.I., Nov. 13, 1986; Associated Press, *Refugee to Get New Murder Trial*, N.Y. TIMES, Nov. 16, 1986, at 54; People v. Aphaylath, 510 N.Y.S.2d 83 (1986); People v. Aphaylath, 499 N.Y.S.2d 823 (1986); *New Trial in Killing*, NEWSDAY, Nov. 14, 1986; Dick Polman, *When Is Cultural Difference a Legal Defense? Immigrants' Native Traditions Clash with U.S. Law*, SEATTLE TIMES, July 12, 1989.

99. *Refugee to Get New Murder Trial, supra* note 98, at 54.

100. *Id.* at 54 (noting that the unanimous decision by the state's highest court vacated the second-degree murder conviction of May Aphaylath who was serving a sentence of fifteen years to life at Attica State Prison).

101. According to Deirdre Evans-Pritchard and Alison Dundes Renteln, "[n]umerous incidents of so-called 'marriage-by-capture' have occurred among the Hmong communities in the United States. To our knowledge, People v. Moua is the only one which has received national attention." Evans-Pritchard and Renteln, *A Hmong "Marriage by Capture" Case in Fresno, California, supra* note 60, at 8 n. 22.

102. *Id.* at 9–11.

103. *Id.* at 12–13.

104. For a fuller discussion of problems prosecutors face in date rape cases, *see* STEPHEN J. SCHULHOFER, UNWANTED SEX chap. 12 at 254–73 (1998) (discussing difficulties inherent in determining what counts as consent in dating situations); ANDREW E. TASLITZ, RAPE AND THE CULTURE OF THE COURTROOM (1999) (examining ways in which cultural narratives about gender and sexual violence shape outcomes in rape cases).

105. Woo, *The People v. Fumiko Kimura: But Which People? supra* note 61, at 404.

106. *Id.*

107. *Id.*

108. *Id.*

109. Alison Matsumoto, *A Place for Consideration of Culture in the American Criminal Justice System: Japanese Law and the Kimura Case*, 4 J. INT'L L. AND PRACTICE 507, 523 (1995).

110. *Id.*

111. Woo, *The People v. Fumiko Kimura: But Which People? supra* note 61, at 404.

112. Matsumoto, *A Place for Consideration of Culture, supra* note 109, at 524.

113. *Id.* at 510.

114. *Id.*

115. *Id.* at 511.

116. *Id.* at 512.

117. *Id.* at 514.

118. Woo, *The People v. Fumiko Kimura: But Which People? supra* note 61, at 416.

119. *See, e.g.,* Coleman, *Individualizing Justice, supra* note 67, at 1142 (opining that "Apart from the *doctrinally* inconsequential fact that Susan Smith drowned her two children by sending a car into lake water in South Carolina, rather than by holding them physically under ocean water in California, the facts of the *Smith* case were, in all relevant aspects other than culture, the same as those in *Kimura*").

120. *Jury Selection Finished in Susan Smith Case,* WASH. POST, July 16, 1995, at A23.

121. Tamara Jones, *Smith Found Guilty of Murdering Sons,* WASH. POST, July 23, 1995, at A1.

122. Gary Henderson & Clay Murphy, *Smith Verdict Met with Mixed Reaction in Union,* HERALD-JOURNAL (July 29, 1995), *available at* http://www.teleplex.net/SHJ/Smith/trial/judge11/html (noting that Smith will be eligible for parole in thirty years).

123. Woo, *The People v. Fumiko Kimura: But Which People? supra* note 60, at 411.

124. William Kleinknecht, *Experts Label Grossberg Guilty Plea Typical,* STAR-LEDGER, Apr. 24, 1998, at 25. *Cf.* Jason Wolfe, *Maine's Laws Show Leniency for Child Killers,* PORTLAND PRESS HERALD, July 12, 1998, at 1A (noting "The vast majority of the time, parents and caregivers who kill are charged with manslaughter, not murder").

125. Thirty-four-year-old Paula Pinckard shot herself, her eleven-year-old daughter Aubrey, and the family dog on March 29, 2000. *See Judge to Decide Woman's Fate Later,* BATON ROUGE ADVOCATE, Nov. 28, 2000, at 7B; *Mother Faces Sentencing in Slaying,* BATON ROUGE ADVOCATE, Feb. 6, 2001, at 4B; *Mother Suspected in Death of Girl, 11,* BATON ROUGE ADVOCATE, Mar. 31, 2000, at 5B; *Mom Suspected of Killing Girl,* BATON ROUGE ADVOCATE, Apr. 7, 2000, at 7B. After being found not guilty by reason of insanity, Pinckard was committed to a mental hospital for the criminally insane. *Woman Ordered to Mental Hospital,* BATON ROUGE ADVOCATE, Feb. 7, 2001, at 4B; Steve Bannister, *Accused Moms,* ALEXANDRIA DAILY TOWN TALK, May 6, 2002, at 8.

126. Attorneys for Andrea Yates claimed she was suffering from postpar-

tum depression and was insane at the time she killed her five children. The jury rejected Yates's insanity defense, finding her guilty of capital murder. Yates was sentenced to life in prison. Paul Burka, *It's Crazy*, Texas Monthly, July 2002, at 8.

## NOTES TO CHAPTER 5

1. This chapter is reprinted with permission from Cynthia K. Y. Lee, *The Act-Belief Distinction in Self-Defense Doctrine: A New Dual Requirement Theory of Justification*, 2 Buff. Crim. L. Rev. 191 (1998).

2. Richard Maxwell Brown, No Duty to Retreat: Violence and Values in American History and Society (1991); Garrett Epps, *Any Which Way But Loose: Interpretive Strategies and Attitudes Towards Violence in the Evolution of the Anglo-American "Retreat Rule,"* 55 Law & Contemp. Probs. 303 (1992).

3. Rollin M. Perkins, Criminal Law 1004–5 (2d ed. 1969).

4. *Id.* at 1009.

5. *See* Lee, *The Act-Belief Distinction in Self-Defense Doctrine, supra* note 1, at 202 n. 30.

6. Richard A. Rosen, *On Self-Defense, Imminence, and Women Who Kill Their Batterers*, 71 N.C. L. Rev. 371 (1993).

7. *Id.* at 405.

8. Holly Maguigan, *Battered Women and Self-Defense: Myths and Misconceptions in Current Reform Proposals*, 140 U. Pa. L. Rev. 379 (1991).

9. *Id.* at 459.

10. Cathryn J. Rosen, *The Excuse of Self-Defense: Correcting a Historical Accident on Behalf of Battered Women Who Kill*, 36 Am. U. L. Rev. 11, 31 (1986).

11. Paul H. Robinson, Criminal Law Defenses § 131(c)(1), at 78 (1984).

12. Model Penal Code §§ 3.04 and 3.09 (Proposed Official Draft 1962).

13. Cynthia Kwei Yung Lee, *Race and Self-Defense: Toward a Normative Conception of Reasonableness*, 81 Minn. L. Rev. 367, 477–78 (1996).

14. When the attacker is excused rather than justified, the defendant is permitted to resist the attack, because excused but unjustified conduct is nonetheless unlawful. The use of force to repel an attack by an innocent or excused aggressor, for example, an infant or a mentally insane individual, raises interesting philosophical issues. For discussion of such issues, *see* George P. Fletcher, *Proportionality and the Psychotic Aggressor: A Vignette in Comparative Criminal Theory*, 8 Isr. L. Rev. 367 (1973); Larry Alexander, *Self Defense, Justification, and Excuse*, 22 Phil. & Pub. Aff. 53 (1993); and Robert F. Schopp, *Self-Defense, in* In Harm's Way 255 (Jules Coleman ed. 1994).

15. Joshua Dressler, Understanding Criminal Law § 18.06[D] (2d ed. 1995).

16. *Id.*

17. *Id.*

18. *See* Lee, *The Act-Belief Distinction in Self-Defense Doctrine, supra* note 1, at 207–8 (discussing different rules for initial aggressors).

19. The treatment of deadly and nondeadly aggressors differs from jurisdiction to jurisdiction. Moreover, deadly aggressors, persons "whose acts are reasonably calculated to produce fatal consequences," are usually treated differently from nondeadly aggressors. Some jurisdictions require a deadly aggressor who meets with a deadly response to withdraw from the affray and successfully communicate his withdrawal before using deadly force in self-defense. In other jurisdictions, deadly aggressors completely forfeit the right to act in self-defense. As for nondeadly aggressors, some jurisdictions permit the nondeadly initial aggressor to use deadly force in self-defense once his victim responds to his nondeadly attack with deadly force. Other jurisdictions require the nondeadly aggressor to retreat, if a safe retreat is available, before using deadly force in self- defense. Failure to retreat might result in a manslaughter conviction rather than complete acquittal if the defendant meets all the other requirements of the defense of self-defense. DRESSLER, UNDERSTANDING CRIMINAL LAW, *supra* note 15, at § 18.03[B][2][a], at 202.

20. Some legal scholars have argued that the law should require actual necessity, a.k.a. necessity in fact, for a perfect self-defense acquittal. George Fletcher, for example, takes the position that necessity is, or at least should be, an absolute requirement. George P. Fletcher, *Domination in the Theory of Justification and Excuse*, 57 U. PITT. L. REV. 553, 561 (1996). Paul Robinson also takes this view. Paul H. Robinson, *Competing Theories of Justification: Deeds v. Reasons, in* HARM AND CULPABILITY (A. P. Simester & A. T. H. Smith eds. 1996).

21. Lee, *The Act-Belief Distinction in Self-Defense Doctrine, supra* note 1, at 205.

22. Richard Singer, *The Resurgence of Mens Rea: II—Honest But Unreasonable Mistake of Fact in Self Defense*, 28 B.C. L. REV. 459 (1987) (discussing different ways of viewing the reasonableness standard).

23. DRESSLER, UNDERSTANDING CRIMINAL LAW, *supra* note 15, at § 17.01.

24. Two versions of self-defense existed at common law in England. First, a homicide *se defendendo* could occur when "A and B, during a quarrel, became engaged in mutual combat and one of them escalated the level of the fight by beginning to use deadly force." Singer, *The Resurgence of Mens Rea, supra* note 22, at 472. If the accused retreated before using deadly force against his attacker, the homicide was excused as a *se defendendo* homicide. *Id.* The *se defendendo* killer would not suffer a conviction, but would have to forfeit his goods. *Id.* If the accused failed to retreat before using deadly force, the homicide was considered chance-medley manslaughter.

The second type of killing in self-defense was called felony prevention. If the defendant was the innocent victim of a violent crime, such as assault or robbery, and responded by killing his attacker, the killing was considered a justifiable homicide in prevention of a felony. Unlike the *se defendendo* killer, the person who killed to prevent a felony from occurring was not required to retreat before using deadly force. *Id. See also* NORMAN J. FINKEL, COMMONSENSE JUSTICE: JURORS' NOTIONS OF THE LAW 224–28 (1995) (explaining felony prevention, chance medley, and *se defendendo*).

25. Robinson, *Competing Theories of Justification, supra* note 20, at 46.

26. *Id.* at 47.

27. Fletcher, *Domination in the Theory of Justification and Excuse, supra* note 20.

28. Lee, *The Act-Belief Distinction in Self-Defense Doctrine, supra* note 1, at 240 n. 135.

29. *Id.*

30. *Id.* at 241.

31. MODEL PENAL CODE § 3.04(1).

32. MODEL PENAL CODE § 3.09.

## NOTES TO CHAPTER 6

1. This chapter is reprinted with permission from Cynthia Kwei Yung Lee, *Race and Self-Defense: Toward a Normative Conception of Reasonableness*, 81 MINN. L. REV. 367, (1996). For additional work on race and self-defense, *see* JODY DAVID ARMOUR, NEGROPHOBIA AND REASONABLE RACISM: THE HIDDEN COSTS OF BEING BLACK IN AMERICA (1997).

2. Jody Armour, *Stereotypes and Prejudice: Helping Legal Decision-Makers Break the Prejudice Habit*, 83 CAL. L. REV. 733, 741 (1995).

3. Linda Hamilton Krieger, *The Content of Our Categories: A Cognitive Bias Approach to Discrimination and Equal Employment Opportunity*, 47 STAN. L. REV. 1161 (1995).

4. *See* Lee, *Race and Self-Defense, supra* note 1. *See also* Dwight L. Greene, *Naughty by Nurture: Black Male Joyriding—Is Everything Gonna Be Alright?* 4 COLUM. J. GENDER & L. 73 (1994) (discussing media construction of the out-of-control young Black man who likes to steal cars). Many other stereotypes about African Americans exist, including those that depict Blacks as mentally inferior, lazy, good dancers, good athletes, and good musicians. Richard Delgado & Jean Stefancic, *Images of the Outsider in American Law and Culture: Can Free Expression Remedy Systemic Social Ills?* 77 CORNELL L. REV. 1258, 1261–67 (1992).

5. I capitalize the "B" in "Black" and the "W" in "White" to highlight the fact that Blackness and Whiteness are racial categories.

6. Adeno Addis, *"Hell Man, They Did Invent Us": The Mass Media, Law, and African Americans*, 41 BUFF. L. REV. 523, 555 (1993).

7. Leonard M. Baynes, *Paradoxes of Racial Stereotypes, Diversity and Past Discrimination in Establishing Affirmative Action in FCC Licensing*, 52 ADMIN. L. REV. 979, 985 (2000).

8. *Id.* at 984, *citing* Daniel Romer et al., *The Treatment of Persons of Color in Local Television News: Ethnic Blame Discourse or Realistic Group Conflict?* 25 COMM. RES. 286 (1998) (analyzing one thousand stories broadcast on the 11 P.M. newscasts for three major networks in Philadelphia from July 20 to October 22, 1994).

9. *Id.*

10. Laurie Becklund & Stephanie Chavez, *Beaten Driver a Searing Image of Mob Cruelty*, L.A. TIMES, May 1, 1992, at A1. Four Black strangers who saw Denny dragged from his truck and beaten emerged from the crowd to get Denny to the nearest hospital. *Id.*

11. SAMUEL WALKER ET AL., THE COLOR OF JUSTICE: RACE, ETHNICITY, AND CRIME IN AMERICA 25 (1996).

12. FEDERAL BUREAU OF INVESTIGATION, CRIME IN THE UNITED STATES: 1999: UNIFORM CRIME REPORTS 230 (1999).

13. For an excellent analysis of the problem of racial profiling, *see* Angela J. Davis, *Race, Cops and Traffic Stops*, 51 U. MIAMI L. REV. 425 (1997); David A. Sklansky, *Traffic Stops, Minority Motorists, and the Future of the Fourth Amendment*, 1997 SUP. CT. REV. 27; David A. Harris, *When Success Breeds Attack: The Coming Backlash Against Racial Profiling Studies*, 6 MICH. J. RACE & L. 237 (2001); David A. Harris, *The Stories, the Statistics, and the Law: Why "Driving While Black" Matters*, 84 MINN. L. REV. 265 (1999).

14. Mary A. Johnson, *Crime: New Frontier-Jesse Jackson Calls It Top Civil Rights Issue*, CHI. SUN TIMES, Nov. 29, 1993, at 4.

15. Baynes, *Paradoxes of Racial Stereotypes, supra* note 7, at 982, *citing* Robert M. Entman et al., *Mass Media and Reconciliation: A Report to the Advisory Board: The President's Initiative on Race*, chapter 1, *available at* http://www.raceandmedia.com/chp2.asp.

16. *Id.*

17. *See* DAVID C. BALDUS ET AL., EQUAL JUSTICE AND THE DEATH PENALTY: A LEGAL AND EMPIRICAL ANALYSIS (1990); David C. Baldus et al., *Comparative Review of Death Sentences: An Empirical Study of the Georgia Experience*, 74 J. CRIM. L. & CRIMINOLOGY 661 (1983). *See also* Cynthia K. Y. Lee, *Race and the Victim: An Examination of Capital Sentencing and Guilt Attribution Studies*, 73 CHICAGO-KENT L. REV. 533 (1998) (surveying capital sentencing studies indicating that race is a significant factor linked to imposition of the death penalty and social science studies examining the influence of juror-victim racial similarity on guilt attribution). Less research has been done outside the death penalty context, but

some studies suggest that the race of the victim impacts jury decisions in non-capital cases as well. *Id.*

18. Baldus, *Comparative Review of Death Sentences, supra* note 17.

19. JIM DWYER, PETER NEUFELD, & BARRY SCHECK, ACTUAL INNOCENCE: FIVE DAYS TO EXECUTION AND OTHER DISPATCHES FROM THE WRONGLY CONVICTED (2000).

20. Birt L. Duncan, *Differential Social Perception and Attribution of Intergroup Violence: Testing the Lower Limit of Stereotyping of Blacks,* 4 J. PERSONALITY & SOC. PSYCHOL. 590 (1976).

21. *Id.*

22. H. Andrew Sagar & Janet Ward Schofield, *Racial and Behavioral Cues in Black and White Children's Perceptions of Ambiguously Aggressive Acts,* 39 J. PERSONALITY & SOC. PSYCHOL. 590 (1980).

23. In Sagar and Schofield's experiment, each student met individually with an adult male experimenter of the student's own race. The experimenter provided the student with oral descriptions and accompanying pictures of four different interactions between two male students. In each scenario, one male student (the actor) did something that could be interpreted as hostile behavior to another male student (the target). All four interactions were fairly common interactions between male students in a school setting. For example, in one scenario, a male student pokes another male student who is trying to study in the back with the eraser end of his pencil. He continues to poke the other student for a while, and then stops. In another scenario, a male student approaches another male student in the student cafeteria, and demands the student's piece of cake. After listening to the description of the scenario and viewing the accompanying pictures which indicated the races of the parties, the students were asked how well each of several adjectives (e.g., playful, friendly, mean, threatening) described the actor's behavior. Sagar and Schofield found that both Black and White boys rated the actor's behavior as more threatening when the actor was Black than when the actor was White. Even relatively innocuous acts were considered more threatening when performed by Blacks than when performed by Whites. *Id.*

24. Charles F. Bond et al., *Responses to Violence in a Psychiatric Setting: The Role of Patient's Race,* 14 PERSONALITY & SOC. PSYCHOL. BULL. 448 (1988).

25. KATHERYN K. RUSSELL, THE COLOR OF CRIME: RACIAL HOAXES, WHITE FEAR, BLACK PROTECTIONISM, POLICE HARASSMENT, AND OTHER MACROAGGRESSIONS (1998); *see also* Katheryn K. Russell, *The Racial Hoax as Crime: The Law as Affirmation,* 71 IND. L.J. 593 (1996).

26. *See* Sherri L. Burr, *Scarlett's Code, Susan's Actions, in* CRITICAL RACE FEMINISM: A READER 255 (1997).

27. JOE R. FEAGIN & HERNAN VERA, WHITE RACISM 62–70 (1995).

28. Associated Press, *Charges Reduced in Deadly Fight of a Single Punch*, S.D. Union Trib., Feb. 3, 1996, at A3; Richard Cole, *Fatal S.F. Dispute Reflects Racial and Political Divisions*, S.D. Union Trib., Jan. 29, 1996, at A3; Nina Schuyler, *Hallinan Gets High Marks for Decision in High-Profile Case*, L.A. Daily J., Feb. 5, 1996, at 4.

29. Cole, *Fatal S.F. Dispute Reflects Racial and Political Divisions, supra* note 28, at A3.

30. Seth Rosenfeld & Dennis J. Opatrny, *2 Deaths Clouded by Race, Ties to Police, Fatal Fights in S.F.: White Man Walks, Black Man in Jail*, S.F. Examiner, Oct. 15, 1995, at A1.

31. Cornel West, Race Matters ix–xi (1993).

32. Taunya Lovell Banks, *Two Life Stories: Reflections of One Black Woman Law Professor*, 6 Berkeley Women's L.J. 46, 49–50 (1990–91).

33. Patricia Williams, *Spirit-Murdering the Messenger: The Discourse of Fingerpointing as the Law's Response to Racism*, 42 U. Miami L. Rev. 127, 127–28 (1987) (emphasis added).

34. Jody Armour calls the person who defends his fear of Blacks by pointing to such statistics an "intelligent Bayesian." Armour, Negrophobia and Reasonable Racism, *supra* note 1.

35. Marc Mauer, The Sentencing Project, Young Black Men and the Criminal Justice System: A Growing National Problem (1990).

36. *Id.* at 2–3.

37. Marc Mauer & Tracy Huling, The Sentencing Project, Young Black Americans and the Criminal Justice System: Five Years Later (1995).

38. *Id.* at 3.

39. *Id.* at 14 (emphasis in original).

40. *Id.* at 9.

41. *Id.* at 14.

42. Federal Bureau of Investigation, Crime in the United States: 1999: Uniform Crime Reports 234 (2000).

43. *Id.*

44. According to the Uniform Crime Reports for 2000, 236,299 African Americans were arrested for violent crime that year. Federal Bureau of Investigation, Crime in the United States, 2000, Uniform Crime Reports (200). According to the U.S. Census Bureau, the total Black population in the United States in 2000 was 32,147,382. *See* http://www.census.gov. 236,299 divided by 32,147,382 equals .0073504 (or .74 percent). *See also* Lee, *Race and Self-Defense, supra* note 1, at 412. *See also* Armour, Negrophobia and Reasonable Racism, *supra* note 1.

45. Angela J. Davis, *Benign Neglect of Racism in the Criminal Justice System*,

94 MICH. L. REV. 1660 (1996) (reviewing Michael Tonry, MALIGN NEGLECT: RACE, CRIME, AND PUNISHMENT IN AMERICA (1995)).

46. Eighty-three percent of the persons arrested for violent crime are male, while 17 percent are female. FEDERAL BUREAU OF INVESTIGATION, CRIME IN THE UNITED STATES: 1999: UNIFORM CRIME REPORTS 229 (1999).

47. ELLIS COSE, THE RAGE OF A PRIVILEGED CLASS 72 (1993).

48. Lee, *Race and Self-Defense, supra* note 1, at 413 n. 159.

49. Randall Kennedy, *The State, Criminal Law, and Racial Discrimination: A Comment*, 107 HARV. L. REV. 1255, 1255 n. 2 (1994).

50. *Id.*

51. The jury consisted of ten Whites and two Blacks. Joseph A. Kirby, *"Subway Vigilante" Case in Final Stage, Civil Suit Against Gunman Goetz Heads to All-Minority Jury*, CHI. TRIB., Apr. 23, 1996, at A4.

52. N.Y. PENAL LAW § 35.15(2)(a) (McKINNEY 1997) ("A person may not use deadly force upon another person under circumstances specified in subdivision one unless: (a) He reasonably believes that such other person is using or about to use deadly physical force").

53. Some newspaper accounts of the shooting erroneously reported that the youths had threatened Goetz with sharpened screwdrivers. None of the youths threatened Goetz with any screwdrivers. The two youths who did not ask Goetz for any money did have screwdrivers inside their jackets which they were planning to use to break into the coin boxes on some video machines. GEORGE P. FLETCHER, A CRIME OF SELF-DEFENSE: BERNHARD GOETZ AND THE LAW ON TRIAL (1988).

54. George P. Fletcher, *Proportionality and the Psychotic Aggressor: A Vignette in Comparative Criminal Theory*, 8 ISRAEL L. REV. 367 (1973).

55. *Id.; see also* George P. Fletcher, *The Right to Life*, 13 GA. L. REV. 1371, 1378 (1979) (Under the *absolute* theory of self-defense, "[k]illing an aggressor is permissible if it is the only means available to prevent the invasion of even a minor interest. Shooting an apple thief is rightful and proper if there is no other way to stop her").

56. JOSHUA DRESSLER, UNDERSTANDING CRIMINAL LAW § 18.02[B][2][a] (3d ed. 2001).

57. JAMES P. LEVINE, JURIES AND POLITICS 2 (1992).

58. *Id.* at 5.

59. *Id.* at 7.

60. FLETCHER, A CRIME OF SELF-DEFENSE, *supra* note 53, at 206.

61. *Id.* at 206–7.

62. PAUL H. ROBINSON & JOHN M. DARLEY, JUSTICE, LIABILITY, AND BLAME: COMMUNITY VIEWS AND THE CRIMINAL LAW (1995).

63. *Id.* at 55–57.

64. LEVINE, JURIES AND POLITICS, *supra* note 57, at 5.

65. *Id.*

66. Law professor Patricia Williams uses a race-switching vignette to illustrate this very point:

> A lone black man was riding in an elevator in a busy downtown department store. The elevator stopped on the third floor, and a crowd of noisy white high school students got on. The black man took out a gun, shot as many of them as he could before the doors opened on the first floor and the rest fled for their lives. The black man later explained to the police that he could tell from the "body language" of the students, from their "shiny eyes and big smiles," that they wanted to "play with him, like a cat plays with a mouse." Furthermore, the black man explained, one of the youths had tried to panhandle money from him and another asked him "how are you?" . . . His intention, he confessed, was to murder the high school students.

PATRICIA WILLIAMS, THE ALCHEMY OF RACE AND RIGHTS 76 (1991).

67. The most comprehensive study on race and capital sentencing, the Baldus study, found that a defendant charged with killing a White person is 8.3 times more likely to receive the death penalty than a defendant charged with killing a Black person. BALDUS, EQUAL JUSTICE AND THE DEATH PENALTY, *supra* note 17. For references to additional capital sentencing studies on the effect of race on the imposition of the death penalty, *see* Lee, *Race and the Victim, supra* note 17.

68. Several criminal law scholars have argued that affirmative steps should be taken to increase racial minority participation on juries. *See, e.g.*, Sheri Lynn Johnson, *Black Innocence and the White Jury*, 83 MICH. L. REV. 1611, 1698–99 (1985) (arguing that a defendant of color should be entitled to at least three racially similar jurors on his or her jury); Albert W. Alschuler, *Racial Quotas and the Jury*, 44 DUKE L.J. 704, 732 (1995) (advocating racial quotas in jury selection).

69. N.Y. L.J., Apr. 24, 1996, at 1. The civil jury that found Goetz liable consisted of four Blacks and six Hispanics. Joseph A. Kirby, *"Subway Vigilante" Case in Final Stage*, CHI. TRIB., Apr. 23, 1996, at 4.

70. *But see* Delgado & Stefancic, *Images of the Outsider in American Law and Culture, supra* note 4, at 1258, 1273–75 (discussing stereotypes about Mexican Americans); Kevin R. Johnson, *Public Benefits and Immigration: The Intersection of Immigration Status, Ethnicity, Gender, and Class*, 42 UCLA L. REV. 1509 (1995) (noting that undocumented immigrants are seen as criminals); Kevin R. Johnson, *"Aliens" and the U.S. Immigration Laws: The Social and Legal Construction of Nonpersons*, 28 U. MIAMI INTER-AM. L. REV 263, 282–84 (1997) (noting that Mexicans are stereotyped as illegal immigrants); Ediberto Roman, *Who Exactly Is Living La Vida Loca? The Legal and Political Consequences of Latino-Latina Ethnic and Racial*

*Stereotypes in Film and Other Media*, 4 J. GENDER RACE & JUST. 37 (2000) (noting that Latinos in major Hollywood films are almost always portrayed as hot-blooded lovers, gang members, entertainers, or immigrants); Shelan Y. Joseph, *Six Flags Magic Mountain: A Family Entertainment Park, but Only If You Wear the Right Clothes*, 16 LOY. L.A. ENT. L.J. 359 (1995) (discussing discriminatory effect of amusement park's policy of denying admittance to individuals, mostly young Latinos and African Americans, who appear to be gang members); Jenny Rivera, *Domestic Violence against Latinas by Latino Males: An Analysis of Race, National Origin, and Gender Differentials*, 14 B.C. THIRD WORLD L.J. 231, 240 (1994) (noting that "[h]istorically, Latinos have been stereotyped as violent and alien").

71. Kevin R. Johnson, *Some Thoughts on the Future of Latino Legal Scholarship*, 2 HARV. LATINO L. REV. 101 (1997).

72. Scott Bowles, *Lawmaker Says Capitol Security Aide Used Ethnic Insult*, WASH. POST, Apr. 18, 1996, at B1.

73. David Jackson & Paul de la Garza, *Rep. Gutierrez Uncommon Target of a Too Common Slur*, CHI. TRIB., Apr. 18, 1996, at 1.

74. Johnson, *"Aliens" and the U.S. Immigration Laws, supra* note 70.

75. Jeffrey R. Margolis, *Closing the Doors to the Land of Opportunity: The Constitutional Controversy Surrounding Proposition 187*, 26 U. MIAMI INTER-AM. L. REV. 363 (1994–95).

76. League of United Latin American Citizens v. Wilson, 997 F. Supp. 1244 (C.D. Cal. 1997); Todd S. Purdum, *Governor Seeks Compromise on Aid to Illegal Immigrants*, N.Y. TIMES, Apr. 16, 1999, at A14 (noting that "Proposition 187 has been blocked in the courts virtually since its passage . . . , and last year, Judge Mariana R. Pfaelzer . . . ruled that it unconstitutionally usurped the Federal Government's authority over immigration policy").

77. CORAMAE RICHEY MANN, UNEQUAL JUSTICE: A QUESTION OF COLOR 148 (1993).

78. WALKER, THE COLOR OF JUSTICE, *supra* note 11, at 100 (noting "the National Household Survey has found that drug use is only slightly higher among African Americans than among whites and lower among Hispanics than either of the other two groups").

79. Frankie Y. Bailey, *Law, Justice, and "Americans": An Historical Overview*, *in* RACE AND CRIMINAL JUSTICE 10, 19 (Michael J. Lynch & E. Britt Patterson eds. 1991).

80. MANN, UNEQUAL JUSTICE, *supra* note 77, at 144.

81. *Id.*

82. Roman, *Who Exactly Is Living La Vida Loca? supra* note 70; Joseph, *Six Flags Magic Mountain, supra* note 70.

83. Lee, *Race and Self-Defense, supra* note 1, at 445–46.

84. The City Attorney's Office prosecuted Masters for being in possession of a gun without a license. Julie Tamaki, *Valley Crime Rate Is Down, but Impact*

*Up*, L.A. TIMES, Dec. 22, 1995, at A1. Masters was convicted of a misdemeanor weapons charge, and was sentenced to three years of probation (i.e., no jail time) and thirty days of graffiti removal. David Bloom, *Latinos Urge DA to Examine Cases*, L.A. DAILY NEWS, Nov. 28, 1995, at N3. In contrast, David Hillo, the youth who survived the shooting, was sentenced to two-and-a-half years in prison for spray painting, grand theft, and probation violations. *Id.*

85. Tina Daunt, *Prosecution Calls Rappers' Contention "Not Logical,"* L.A. TIMES, Feb. 9, 1996, at B3; Michael White, *Rapper, Guard Acquitted of Gang Murder*, L.A. DAILY J., Feb. 21, 1996, at 2.

86. Hugh Dellios, *L.A. Vigilante Is Revered and Reviled*, HOUST. CHRON., Feb. 13, 1995, at A7.

87. Nicholas Riccardi & Julie Tamaki, *Pacoima Man Kills Tagger, but Police Hear 2 Versions, Graffiti*, L.A. TIMES, Feb. 1, 1995, at A1.

88. Franki V. Ransom, *"This Is Brutal": Clinton, Hall Vow to Aid Dayton Team in Singapore*, DAYTON DAILY NEWS, Mar. 5, 1994, at 1A (emphasis added).

89. *Panel to Discuss Images of Asian Men*, L.A. TIMES, Aug. 30, 1995, at B5.

90. For an excellent discussion of the model minority myth, *see* Frank H. Wu, *Neither Black Nor White: Asian Americans and Affirmative Action*, 15 B.C. THIRD WORLD L.J. 225 (1995).

91. Pat K. Chew, *Asian Americans: The "Reticent" Minority and Their Paradoxes*, 36 WM. & MARY L. REV. 1, 24 (1994).

92. People v. Superior Court (Soon Ja Du), 7 Cal. Rptr. 2d 177, 184 n. 7 (Cal. Ct. App. 1992); Reginald Leamon Robinson, *"The Other Against Itself": Deconstructing the Violent Discourse Between Korean and African Americans*, 67 S. CAL. L. REV. 15, 88 n. 364 (1993).

93. Section 1203(e) of the California Penal Code provides, "Except in unusual cases where the interests of justice would best be served if the person is granted probation, probation shall not be granted to any of the following persons: . . . (2) Any person who used, or attempted to use, a deadly weapon upon a human being in connection with the perpetration of the crime of which he or she has been convicted." Cal. Penal Code § 1203(e)(2) (West 1982).

94. Neil Gotanda, *Re-Producing the Model Minority Stereotype: Judge Joyce Karlin's Sentencing Colloquy in People v. Soon Ja Du, in* REVIEWING ASIAN AMERICA: LOCATING DIVERSITY 89 (Wendy L. Ng et al. eds. 1995).

95. *Id.*

96. People v. Superior Court (Soon Ja Du), 7 Cal. Rptr. 2d 177, 184 n. 7 (Cal. Ct. App. 1992).

97. Wu, *Neither Black Nor White, supra* note 90, at 240–41 (emphasis added).

98. The film *Sa-I-Gu*, directed by Christine Choy, illustrates that media images of Korean Americans during the Los Angeles riots focused on property-protecting Korean Americans atop store rooftops with guns, while ignoring the substantial numbers of Korean Americans who were killed during the riots. *See*

*also* Sumi K. Cho, *Korean Americans vs. African Americans: Conflict and Construction, in* READING RODNEY KING/READING URBAN UPRISING 196 (Robert Good-ing-Williams ed. 1993). *Compare* Lisa C. Ikemoto, *Traces of the Master Narrative in the Story of African American/Korean American Conflict: How We Constructed "Los Angeles,"* 66 S. CAL. L. REV. 1581, 1583 (1993) (noting that Korean American store owners were constructed as unfortunate victims in contrast to the African American and Latino looters).

99. Rhoda J. Yen, *Racial Stereotyping of Asians and Asian Americans and Its Effect on Criminal Justice: A Reflection on the Wayne Lo Case*, 7 ASIAN L.J. 1, 10 (2000).

100. *Id.* at 12. *But see* Jerry Kang, Note, *Racial Violence against Asian Americans*, 106 HARV. L. REV. 1926 (1993) (arguing that Asian Americans are often targeted by criminals who think Asians are weak, submissive, and loaded with cash).

101. Yen, *Racial Stereotyping of Asians and Asian Americans, supra* note 99, at 12.

102. *Id.* at 10.

103. United States v. Ebens, 800 F.2d 1422, 1427 (6th Cir. 1986).

104. *Id.;* Paula C. Johnson, *The Social Construction of Identity in Criminal Cases: Cinema Verité and the Pedagogy of Vincent Chin*, 1 MICH. J. RACE & L. 347 (1996); ROGER DANIELS, ASIAN AMERICA: CHINESE AND JAPANESE IN THE U.S. SINCE 1850 342 (1988); Robert S. Chang, *Toward an Asian American Legal Scholarship: Critical Race Theory, Post-Structuralism, and Narrative Space*, 81 CAL. L. REV. 1243, 1252 (1993); WHO KILLED VINCENT CHIN? (a film by Renee Tajima and Christine Choy); Lee, *Race and Self-Defense, supra* note 1.

105. Dana Sachs, *The Murderer Next Door*, MOTHER JONES, July–August 1989, at 54 (emphasis added).

106. Yen, *Racial Stereotyping of Asians and Asian Americans, supra* note 99, at 11, *citing* WHO KILLED VINCENT CHIN? (a film by Renee Tajima and Christine Choy).

107. *Id.*

108. ROBERT S. CHANG, DISORIENTED: ASIAN AMERICANS, LAW, AND THE NATION-STATE 23 (1999).

109. *Id.*

110. *Id.* at 24–25.

111. ERIC K. YAMAMOTO, MARGARET CHON, CAROL L. IZUMI, JERRY KANG, & FRANK H. WU, RACE, RIGHTS AND REPARATION: LAW AND THE JAPANESE AMERICAN INTERNMENT (2001); Eric K. Yamamoto, *Korematsu Revisited—Correcting the Injustice of Extraordinary Government Excess and Lax Judicial Review: Time for a Better Accommodation of National Security Concerns and Civil Liberties*, 26 SANTA CLARA L. REV. 1 (1986).

112. WHO KILLED VINCENT CHIN? (a film by Renee Tajima and Christine Choy).

113. *Bashing of Japan Dwindles: Awareness of Global Economy Replacing Fear, Hate, and Racism of 80's in Motor City*, DETROIT NEWS, July 26, 1998, at C1.

114. Cynthia Kwei Yung Lee, *Beyond Black and White: Racializing Asian Americans in a Society Obsessed with O. J.*, 6 HASTINGS WOMEN'S L.J. 165 (1995).

115. Neil Gotanda, presenter, *African American and Asian American Racialization: or Why Wen Ho Lee Should Hire Johnny Cochran*, Race and the Law at the Turn of the Century Symposium, UCLA School of Law, Feb. 25, 2000, Los Angeles, Calif.

116. Kang, *Racial Violence against Asian Americans, supra* note 100, at 1929–30 (noting that "Asian Americans appear to promise a larger than average benefit because they are seen as members of a merchant-entrepreneurial class or as rich tourists, who tend to carry and use cash instead of less convertible forms of money").

117. *Id.* at 1930.

118. Conversation with Professor Frank Wu, Howard University Law School (March 19, 2002).

119. Lee, *Race and Self-Defense, supra* note 1, at 432–43.

120. Hattori v. Peairs, 662 So. 2d 509, 515 (La. Ct. App. 1995).

121. *See, e.g., Jury Acquits O. J. Simpson*, L.A. TIMES, Oct. 4, 1995, at B8 (reporting one citizen's angry reaction to the verdict: "the jury obviously was thumbing their nose at justice with little or no deliberation. A very sick jury, probably anxious to get to the money watering-trough of the tabloids").

122. RICHARD E. NISBETT AND DOV COHEN, CULTURE OF HONOR: THE PSYCHOLOGY OF VIOLENCE IN THE SOUTH (1996).

123. Testimony of Bonnie Peairs at 22, State v. Peairs (May 22, 1993) (on file with author).

124. Oliver Wang, *New Faces, Old Scripts*, ASIAN WEEK, Aug. 6–12, 1998, at 12 (discussing the Asian as martial arts master stereotype).

125. "As Hollywood portrayed them, Asian American males were either nerds, sneaky criminals without remorse, or mysterious sages. Then came Bruce Lee, who was strong and violent, yes, but still oddly asexual. In *Enter the Dragon*, Lee and his white comrades fell an army of enemies. As reward, each is offered a girl. The Caucasian fighters go off with their prizes, but Bruce refuses." Candy Kit Har Chan, *Redefining APA Masculinity*, ASIAN WEEK, Jan. 26, 1996, at 13.

126. State v. Simon, 646 P.2d 1119 (Kan. 1982).

127. Although the government could not appeal the verdict of acquittal due to the constitutional prohibition against double jeopardy, it did appeal the trial court's jury instruction on self-defense on the ground that the trial court erroneously used a subjective standard of reasonableness in explaining the defense of self-defense to the jury. The court of appeals agreed with the government that the trial court used the wrong standard. *Id.*

128. Julie Chao, *Asian Man's Shooting by Police Spurs Three Probes*, S.F. EX-AMINER, May 25, 1997, at C1; Julie Chao, *Cop Won't Face Charges for Killing Drunken Man*, S.F. EXAMINER, June 19, 1997, at A16; Julie Chao, *Outrage at Killing by Cop in North Bay*, S.F. EXAMINER, May 21, 1997, at A1; Bill Wallace, *Widow Sues Rohnert Park over Killing by Officer*, S.F. CHRONICLE, Feb. 3, 1998, at A11.

129. Bert Eljera, *S.F. Rally Spotlights Kao Killing*, ASIAN WEEK, Aug. 22, 1997, at 12–13.

130. George Snyder, *Officer Will Not Face Charges, Rohnert Park Cop Shot Man He Says Threatened Him*, S.F. CHRON., June 19, 1997, at A15.

131. Julie Chao, *U.S. Won't Charge Cop in Death; Asians Upset*, S.F. EXAMINER, Jan. 29, 1998, at A7.

132. Conversation with Victor Hwang, staff attorney with the Asian Law Caucus and attorney for the Kao family (August 1997).

133. Transcript of Sonoma County Sheriff's Department's Interview with Officer Jack Shields, conducted by Detective Lorenzo Duenas on Apr. 29, 1997, at page 5 of thirteen pages (CR 97-0429-06).

134. Transcript of Sonoma County Sheriff's Department's Interview with Officer Michael Lynch, conducted by Detective Lorenzo Duenas on Apr. 29, 1997, at page 3 of eleven pages (CR 97-0429-06).

135. *Id.*

136. *Id.* at 6.

137. Chao, *Cop Won't Face Charges for Killing Drunken Man, supra* note 128, at A16.

138. Wiley A. Hall, III, *A Death by Stereotype*, CITY PAPER (Urban Rhythms section), Mar. 5, 1999.

139. For example, the transcript of Mrs. Kao's interview is thirty-two pages long, much longer than the transcripts of the interviews of Officer Shields and Lynch combined. Even though they were supposed to be investigating the officers, the detectives asked Mrs. Kao many more questions than they asked the officers, including questions that seemed designed to use against her on cross-examination if later necessary. Moreover, two detectives were used to interview Mrs. Kao, while only one detective interviewed each of the officers. The investigation seemed more of an attempt to exonerate, rather than build a case against, the officers. *See* Transcript of Sonoma County Sheriff's Department's Interview with Ayling Wu Kao, conducted by Detectives Roy Gourley and Tom Dulaney on June 11, 1997 (CR 97- 0429-06).

140. *Id.; see also* J. K. Yamamoto, *Community Groups Hold Rally to Protest Kao Slaying*, HOKUBEI MAINICHI, Aug. 16, 1997, at 1 (noting that "[a] subsequent police search of Kao's home did not turn up any martial arts equipment"). In her interview with detectives from the Sheriff's Office, Mrs. Kao affirmed that her husband had no martial arts experience. *See* Transcript of Sonoma County Sheriff's Department's Interview with Ayling Wu Kao, conducted by Detectives Roy

Gourley and Tom Dulaney on June 11, 1997, at page 12 of thirty-two pages (CR 97-0429-06).

## NOTES TO CHAPTER 7

1. Les Payne, *Black Youths Have Good Reason to March*, NEWSDAY, Sept. 6, 1998, at B6.

2. Elizabeth Kolbert, *The Perils of Safety*, NEW YORKER, Mar. 22, 1999, at 50.

3. *Diallo Jurors Say Race Not an Issue*, THE AUSTRALIAN, Feb. 29, 2000, at 11.

4. James J. Fyfe, *Police Use of Deadly Force: Research and Reform*, 5 JUST. Q. 165, 189 (1988).

5. *Id. See also* CHARLES J. OGLETREE, JR., ET AL., CRIMINAL JUSTICE INSTITUTE AT HARVARD LAW SCHOOL FOR THE NATIONAL ASS'N FOR THE ADVANCEMENT OF COLORED PEOPLE, BEYOND THE RODNEY KING STORY: AN INVESTIGATION OF POLICE CONDUCT IN MINORITY COMMUNITIES 14 (1995) (hereinafter "NAACP Report"); James J. Fyfe, *Race and Extreme Police-Citizen Violence*, *in* READINGS ON POLICE USE OF DEADLY FORCE 176 (James J. Fyfe ed. 1982).

6. Fyfe, *Police Use of Deadly Force*, *supra* note 5, at 189–90, *citing* W. A. GELLER & K. J. KARALES, SPLIT-SECOND DECISIONS: SHOOTINGS OF AND BY CHICAGO POLICE (CHICAGO LAW ENFORCEMENT STUDY GROUP 1981).

7. SAMUEL WALKER ET AL., THE COLOR OF JUSTICE: RACE, ETHNICITY, AND CRIME IN AMERICA 85 (1996) (noting that minorities are "shot and killed three times as often as whites by police in the big cities"); *see also* Paul Takagi, *A Garrison State in a "Democratic" Society*, *in* READINGS ON POLICE USE OF DEADLY FORCE 201 (James J. Fyfe ed. 1982)("Black men have been killed by police at a rate some nine to ten times higher than white men").

8. WALKER, THE COLOR OF JUSTICE, *supra* note 7, at 92, *citing* GELLER & KARALES, SPLIT-SECOND DECISIONS 119 (studying Chicago police shootings during the late 1970s); WILLIAM A. GELLER & MICHAEL S. SCOTT, DEADLY FORCE: WHAT WE KNOW 149–50 (1992)(Police Executive Research Forum, Washington, D.C.)(studying police shootings in New York City and Los Angeles).

9. AMNESTY INTERNATIONAL, USA, RACE, RIGHTS AND POLICE BRUTALITY (September 21, 1999); HUMAN RIGHTS WATCH, SHIELDED FROM JUSTICE: POLICE BRUTALITY AND ACCOUNTABILITY IN THE UNITED STATES (1998) *available at* http://www.hrw.org/reports98/police/uspo40.htm].

10. John S. Goldkamp, *Minorities as Victims of Police Shootings: Interpretations of Racial Disproportionality and Police Use of Deadly Force*, 2 JUST. SYS. J. 169 (1976).

11. Takagi, *A Garrison State in a "Democratic" Society*, *supra* note 7, at 203.

12. Fyfe, *Race and Extreme Police-Citizen Violence*, *supra* note 5, at 190.

13. *See, e.g.,* R. James Holzworth & Catherine B. Pipping, *Drawing a Weapon: An Analysis of Police Judgments,* 13 J. POLICE SCI. & ADMIN. 185 (1985); Michael F. Brown, *Use of Deadly Force by Patrol Officers: Training Implications,* 12 J. POLICE SCI. & ADMIN. 133 (1984); George A. Hayden, *Police Discretion in the Use of Deadly Force: An Empirical Study of Information Usage in Deadly Force Decision Making,* 9 J. POLICE SCI. & ADMIN. 102 (1981); Fyfe, *Race and Extreme Police-Citizen Violence, supra* note 5, at 190 (finding that Blacks make up a disproportionate share of police shooting victims reportedly armed with guns or engaged in robberies); Mark Blumberg, *Race and Police Shootings: An Analysis in Two Cities, in* CONTEMPORARY ISSUES IN LAW ENFORCEMENT 152 (James J. Fyfe ed. 1981) (finding that similarly situated Blacks and Whites receive the same types and amount of force from police). Several of the studies that reach this conclusion, however, involve self- reporting by police officers about whether the race of the suspect would influence their own decision to use force.

14. Daniel Georges-Abeyie, *Foreword to* RACE AND CRIMINAL JUSTICE ix (Michael J. Lynch & E. Britt Patterson eds. 1991).

15. *See, e.g.,* Takagi, *A Garrison State in a "Democratic" Society, supra* note 7, at 203; James J. Fyfe, *Blind Justice: Police Shootings in Memphis,* 73 J. CRIM. L. & CRIMINOLOGY 707 (1982).

16. Federal News Service, *Attorney General Janet Reno Speech at Justice Department Police Integrity Conference,* Marriott Wardman Park, Washington, D.C. (June 9, 1999), *available at* http://www.usdoj.gov/ag/speeches/1999/agpoliceinteg.html.

17. Charles R. Lawrence, III, *The Id, the Ego, and Equal Protection: Reckoning with Unconscious Racism,* 39 STAN. L. REV. 317 (1987). *See also* Linda Hamilton Krieger, *The Content of Our Categories: A Cognitive Bias Approach to Discrimination and Equal Employment Opportunity,* 47 STAN. L. REV. 1161, 1187–90 (1995) (explaining the human tendency to categorize); Linda Hamilton Krieger, *Civil Rights Perestroika: Intergroup Relations after Affirmative Action,* 86 CAL. L. REV. 1251 (1998).

18. *See, e.g.,* Susan Bandes, *Patterns of Injustice: Police Brutality in the Courts,* 47 BUFF. L. REV. 1275 (1999).

19. Paul G. Chevigny, *Police Violence: Causes and Cures,* 7 J. L. & POL'Y 75, 86 (1998) (symposium).

20. *See supra* note 9.

21. Lawrence, *The Id, the Ego, and Equal Protection, supra* note 17, at 322.

22. *Id.* at 330 (defining racism as "a set of beliefs whereby we irrationally attach significance to something called race").

23. *Id.* at 331–36.

24. *Id.* at 323.

25. Anthony G. Greenwald, Mark A. Oates, & Hunter Hoffman, *Targets of*

*Discrimination: The Effect of Race on Detecting Presence of Weapons*, at 4–5 (unpublished manuscript on file with author), *available at* http://faculty.washington .edu/agg/unpublished.htm.

26. *Id.* at 11.

27. *Id.*

28. *Id.* at 12, *citing* J. Correll et al., *The Police Officer's Dilemma: Using Ethnicity to Disambiguate Potentially Threatening Individuals*, 83 J. PERS. & SOC. PSYCHOL. (2002); B. K. Payne, *Prejudice and Perception: The Role of Automatic and Controlled Processes in Misperceiving a Weapon*, 81 J. PERS. & SOC. PSYCHOL. 181 (2001) (finding that participants identified guns faster when primed with Black faces compared with White faces and misidentified tools as guns more often when primed with Black faces than with White faces); B. K. Payne et al., *Best Laid Plans: Effects of Goals on Accessibility Bias and Cognitive Control in Race-Based Perceptions of Weapons*, J. EXPERIMENTAL SOC. PSYCHOL. (forthcoming).

29. Cynthia Kwei Yung Lee, *Race and Self-Defense: Toward a Normative Conception of Reasonableness*, 81 MINN. L. REV. 367, 402–3, 441–43 (1996) (discussing stereotypes about African Americans and Latinos).

30. On any given day in 1994, one out of every three Black men in their twenties was in prison or jail, or on probation or parole. MARC MAUER & TRACY HULING, THE SENTENCING PROJECT, YOUNG BLACK AMERICANS AND THE CRIMINAL JUSTICE SYSTEM: FIVE YEARS LATER 3 (1995). Blacks are arrested for murder, robbery, and rape at a disproportionately high rate. In 1998, African Americans constituted 53.4 percent of those arrested for murder and non-negligent manslaughter, 55.3 percent of those arrested for robbery, and 37.5 percent of those arrested for forcible rape. FEDERAL BUREAU OF INVESTIGATION, CRIME IN THE UNITED STATES: 1998 UNIFORM CRIME REPORTS 228 (1998).

31. Lee, *Race and Self-Defense, supra* note 29, at 411–12.

32. MAUER & HULING, THE SENTENCING PROJECT, *supra* note 30, at 14.

33. Birt L. Duncan, *Differential Social Perception and Attribution of Intergroup Violence: Testing the Lower Limit of Stereotyping of Blacks*, 4 J. PERSONALITY & SOC. PSYCHOL. 590 (1976); H. Andrew Sagar & Janet Ward Schofield, *Racial and Behavioral Cues in Black and White Children's Perceptions of Ambiguously Aggressive Acts*, 39 J. PERSONALITY & SOC. PSYCHOL. 590 (1980); Charles F. Bond et al., *Responses to Violence in a Psychiatric Setting: The Role of Patient's Race*, 14 PERSONALITY & SOC. PSYCHOL. BULL. 448 (1988).

34. FEDERAL BUREAU OF INVESTIGATION, CRIME IN THE UNITED STATES: 1998, *supra* note 30, at 210 ("Race distribution figures for the total number of national arrests during 1998 showed 68 percent of the arrestees were white, 30 percent were black, and the remainder were of other races. (See Table 43.) Whites accounted for 63 percent of the Index crime arrestees, 65 percent of the property crime arrestees, and 58 percent of the violent crime arrestees").

35. Dennis Duggan, *Black, Unarmed, and Often a Target*, NEWSDAY, Feb. 9,

1999, at A6. There is some dispute as to the precise words that Deputy Marshal Cannon shouted before shooting Burgess. Cannon told prosecutors that he shouted, "U.S. Marshals. Drop the gun." Burgess, however, told police that Cannon yelled, "Hey you" or "Hold it." Burgess stated, "It was not 'Police' or 'Freeze.'" Selwyn Raab, *Marshal Who Shot Youth Faced '94 Beating Charge*, N.Y. TIMES, Nov. 11, 1997, at B3.

36. peter noel, *"I Thought He Had a Gun*," VILLAGE VOICE, Jan. 13, 1998, at 44.

37. Kit R. Roane, *Deputy Marshal Is Cleared in Shooting of Queens Teenager*, N.Y. TIMES, Mar. 5, 1998, at B5.

38. Raab, *Marshal Who Shot Youth Faced '94 Beating Charge, supra* note 35.

39. Bandes, *Patterns of Injustice, supra* note 18 (noting the judicial tendency to view instances of police misconduct as isolated incidents rather than a systemic problem); David Dante Troutt, *Screws, Koon, and Routine Aberrations: The Use of Fictional Narratives in Federal Police Brutality Prosecutions*, 74 N.Y.U. L. REV. 18 (1999)(arguing that authority narratives are used to justify acts of police brutality).

40. City of Los Angeles v. Lyons, 461 U.S. 95 (1983).

41. DAVID COLE, NO EQUAL JUSTICE: RACE AND CLASS IN THE AMERICAN CRIMINAL JUSTICE SYSTEM 162 (1999) ("By the time Lyons case reached the Supreme Court, sixteen persons had been killed by police use of the chokehold; twelve of the victims were black men"). According to Human Rights Watch, the Los Angeles police department still permits its officers to use the chokehold. HUMAN RIGHTS WATCH, SHIELDED FROM JUSTICE, *supra* note 9 (this cite comes from the online summary of SHIELDED FROM JUSTICE, the section on U.S. Law, Civil Remedies, endnote 11. "Of the fourteen city police departments examined by Human Rights Watch, only four (San Francisco, District of Columbia, Los Angeles, and Minneapolis) still allow chokeholds, according to [the] 1993 Law Enforcement Management and Administrative Statistics, 1993, Bureau of Justice Statistics, Washington, D.C. pp. 169–180").

42. Robert D. McFadden, *After Man Is Slain by Officer, Anger and Calls for Patience*, N.Y. TIMES, Dec. 27, 1997, at B1; Robert D. McFadden, *Panel Finds Officer Was Justified in Unarmed Man's Fatal Shooting*, N.Y. TIMES, Jan. 31, 1998, at A1; noel, "I Thought He Had a Gun," *supra* note 36.

43. McFadden, *After Man Is Slain by Officer, Anger and Calls for Patience, supra* note 42; AMNESTY INTERNATIONAL, RIGHTS FOR ALL: POLICE BRUTALITY AND EXCESSIVE FORCE IN THE NEW YORK CITY POLICE DEPARTMENT (1999) (online summary of United States of America: Police Brutality and Excessive Force in the New York City Police Department (1996)) *available at* http://www.amnestyusa.org/rightsforall/police/nypd/nypd- summary.html.

44. McFadden, *After Man Is Slain by Officer, Anger and Calls for Patience, supra* note 42.

45. *Id.*

46. *Id.*

47. Rodney Foo, *Disagreement over Necessity for Killing by Police*, S.J. Mer-cury News, Sept. 18, 1999, at 1A.

48. Bill Romano, Geoffrey Tomb, & Raoul V. Mowatt, *S.J. Police Reviewing Shootings, Sixth Fatality*, S.J. Mercury News, July 3, 1999, at 1A.

49. *Id.*

50. Todd Lighty, *Untold Story of Haggerty Shooting, Report Shows Witnesses Don't Back Cop's Account*, Chi. Trib., Sept. 12, 1999, at 1; Jennifer Vigil & James Janega, *2 Killed in Run-Ins with City Police; Victims' Families Demanding Answers*, Chi. Trib., June 6, 1999, at 1. In March 2000, Officer Daniels was fired by a civilian police board which found her guilty of shooting Haggerty without justification. The board concluded, "The use of deadly force here was not warranted because, in light of all the evidence, the Board does not find that Officer Daniels reasonably believed that deadly force was necessary." Gary Marx & Terry Wilson, *3 Fired in Haggerty Case* (Sept. 20, 2000), *available at* http://chicagotribune .com/news/metro/chicago/article/0,2669,ART- 43581,FF.html.

51. Lighty, *Untold Story of Haggerty Shooting*, *supra* note 50.

52. Todd Lighty & Steve Mills, *Witness Surfaces in Shooting by Cop*, Chi. Trib., June 12, 1999, at 1.

53. Hubert G. Locke, *The Color of Law and the Issue of Color: Race and the Abuse of Police Power*, *in* Police Violence: Understanding and Controlling Police Abuse of Force 129, 142 (William A. Geller & Hans Toch eds. 1996).

54. *Id.*

55. *District Attorney's Report on the Officer Involved Shooting of Tyisha Miller*, Press-Enterprise (Riverside, Calif.), May 7, 1999, at A19; The Report on the Tyisha Miller Shooting by the Riverside County District Attorney's Office (May 6, 1999), *available at* http://www.inlandempireonline.com/; Darryl Fears & Greg Krikorian, *Family Asks Why Police Shot Woman in Riverside*, L.A. Times, Dec. 31, 1998, at B1; Dara Akiko Williams, *Woman Killed by Police, Kin Want Answers, 27 Bullets Believed Fired at Woman*, Ariz. Republic, Dec. 30, 1998, at A4; Don Terry, *Officers' Killing of Woman in Car Leads to Dispute over Facts and Motives*, N.Y. Times, Dec. 30, 1998, at A1; Dara Akiko Williams, *Leaders Call for Patience after Riverside Shooting*, Orange County Reg., Dec. 30, 1998, at A1; Phil Pitchford & Sandra Stokley, *Police Defend Officers' Actions*, Press-Enterprise (Riverside, Calif.), Dec. 30, 1998, at A1; Ana A. Lima and Phil Pitchford, *Questions Over Police Slaying*, Press-Enterprise (Riverside, Calif.), Dec. 29, 1998, at A1.

56. The Report on the Tyisha Miller Shooting by the Riverside County District Attorney's Office (May 6, 1999), *available at* http://www.inlandempireon line.com/.

57. Jason W. Armstrong, *Riverside Police Shooting Results in No Charges*, L.A. Daily J., May 7, 1999, at 1.

58. *D.A. Clears Riverside Officers in Fatal Shooting of Black Woman*, S.F. CHRON., May 7, 1999, at A7. While no one accused the four officers directly involved in the shooting of making racial comments or jokes, another officer and a police supervisor reportedly made racially insensitive remarks after the shooting, including some at the scene. One officer referred to expressions of grief by family members at the scene as "the Watts wail" and the supervisor commented that the gathering was like being at a Kwanzaa celebration. Associated Press, *Riverside Cops Probe Racial Remarks, Jokes*, S.J. MERCURY NEWS, Apr. 20, 1999, at 3B.

59. Associated Press, *Sergeant at Fatal Shooting Is Informed He'll Be Fired*, S.D. UNION TRIB., July 28, 1999, at A4.

60. Jeff McDonald, *Standoff Snarls N. County*, S.D. UNION TRIB., July 2, 1999, at A1; Greg Moran, *Woman Pleads Not Guilty in Chase, Standoff*, S.D. UNION TRIB., July 8, 1999, at B1; Alex Roth, *Road Rage before 78 Standoff Described*, S.D. UNION TRIB., Aug. 27, 1999, at B2; Alex Roth, *Woman in Long Route 78 Standoff Is Ordered to Stand Trial*, S.D. UNION TRIB., Sept. 1, 1999, at B2; Alex Roth, *Tape-Recorded Message from Lucero's Father Ended 78 Standoff, Witness Says*, S.D. UNION TRIB., Mar. 15, 2000, at B2.

61. Greg Moran, *Woman Pleads Not Guilty in Case*, S.D. UNION TRIB., July 8, 1999, at B1.

62. Kim Peterson, *Woman in Route 78 Police Standoff Is Released from Jail*, S.D. UNION TRIB., March 28, 2000, at B1.

63. Onell R. Soto, *Woman in Standoff to Be Evaluated*, S.D. UNION TRIB., June 9, 2000, at B1.

64. Alex Roth, *Woman in '99 Standoff on Freeway Gets Prison*, S.D. UNION TRIB., Aug. 12, 2000, at B1.

65. Roth, *Woman in Long Route 78 Standoff Is Ordered to Stand Trial*, supra note 60, at B2.

66. Gregory Alan Gross, *Long Route 78 Standoff Still Rankles Some*, S.D. UNION TRIB., July 10, 1999, at B1.

67. noel, "*I Thought He Had a Gun*," supra note 36.

68. This account is largely drawn from Mark Singer, *A Year of Trouble: A City Subverts Itself*, NEW YORKER, May 20, 2002, at 42.

69. *Id.*

70. *Id.*

71. *Id.*

72. *Id.*

73. *Id.*

74. *Id.* Cincinnati police union spokesperson Keith Fangman defended the department, saying that most of the Blacks killed by Cincinnati police were armed. Fangman also stated that twelve of the last fourteen Cincinnati officers killed were shot by Black men. *Id.*

75. Francis X. Clines, *Officer Charged in Killing That Roiled Cincinnati*, N.Y. TIMES, May 8, 2001, at A16.

76. Robert E. Pierre, *Officer Is Acquitted in Killing That Led to Riots in Cincinnati*, WASH. POST, Sept. 27, 2001, at A2 (noting that Judge Winkler told a packed courtroom that Officer Roach made a split-second decision to shoot Timothy Thomas because the youth made a sudden movement that startled Roach during a chase through a dark alley in an "especially dangerous section of Cincinnati").

77. *Id.*

## NOTES TO CHAPTER 8

1. U.S.C. § 44935 (2002).

2. Sara Kehaulani Goo, *Federal Screeners Take Up Posts at BWI Checkpoints*, WASH. POST, May 1, 2002, at A10.

3. *Id.* A bill passed Senate Commerce, Science, and Transportation Committee on September 19, 2002, however, would "allow non–U.S. citizens to apply for federal airport-screening jobs, reversing a restriction imposed last fall." Sara Kehaulani Goo, *Senate Panel Votes to Exempt 40 Airports from Deadline*, WASH. POST, Sept. 20, 2002 at A6.

4. The jury's vision of the average person is likely to be a reflection of juror preferences and experiences. *See* Andrew E. Taslitz, *A Feminist Approach to Social Scientific Evidence: Foundations*, 5 MICH. J. GENDER & L. 1, 26 (1998) ("When jurors name a mental state as 'premeditation,' 'heat of passion,' or a 'belief in the imminent need to use deadly force in self-defense,' they are crafting an interpretation that partly embodies their own assumptions, attitudes, and beliefs").

5. Nancy S. Ehrenreich, *Pluralist Myths and Powerless Men: The Ideology of Reasonableness in Sexual Harassment Law*, 99 YALE L.J. 1177, 1210 (1990), *citing* GUIDO CALEBRESI, IDEALS, BELIEFS, ATTITUDES, AND THE LAW 23 n. 94 (1985), *citing* Hall v. Brooklands Auto Racing Club [1933] 1 K.B. 205, 224.

6. *Id.* at 1211.

7. *Id.*

8. *Id.* at 1212.

9. *Id.* at 1212–13.

10. Dolores A. Donovan & Stephanie M. Wildman, *Is the Reasonable Man Obsolete? A Critical Perspective on Self-Defense and Provocation*, 14 LOY. L. REV. 435 (1981) (arguing that the Reasonable Man standard is not an appropriate standard to apply to the defenses of provocation and self-defense).

11. *See, e.g.*, Anderson v. State, 43 S.E. 835 (Ga. 1903) (holding that the trial court's use of a Reasonable Man standard in its jury instruction on self-defense, even though the defendant was a woman, was proper).

12. Most courts seem to have embraced the view that the Reasonable Person is the ordinary or average person, a position which I critique later in this chapter.

13. *See* Kevin Jon Heller, *Beyond the Reasonable Man? A Sympathetic but Critical Assessment of the Use of Subjective Standards of Reasonableness in Self-Defense and Provocation Cases*, 26 Am. J. Crim. L. 1 (1998).

14. J. Contemp Legal Issues 1 (1994) (symposium entitled "Harm v. Culpability: Which Should Be the Organizing Principle of the Criminal Law?").

15. Cynthia K. Y. Lee, *The Act-Belief Distinction in Self-Defense Doctrine: A New Dual Requirement Theory of Justification*, 2 Buff. Crim. L. Rev. 192, 208–12 (1998).

16. *See* Richard Delgado, *Shadowboxing: An Essay on Power*, 77 Cornell L. Rev. 813 (1992) (arguing that objective standards reflect the values of powerful actors and their culture).

17. Irish courts have embraced a completely subjective test for provocation. As long as the defendant was actually provoked into a heat of passion, the appropriate verdict is manslaughter rather than murder. It is unnecessary for the jury to find that a "reasonable man" in the defendant's shoes would have been provoked. People v. MacEoin 1978 1 IR 27; People v. Davis 2001 1 IR.

18. Model Penal Code § 210.3(1)(b).

19. The drafters of the Code admit that the extreme mental or emotional disturbance defense is more subjective than the modern test for provocation, but insist that the test is still objective. They explain, "There is a larger element of subjectivity in the standard than there was under prevailing law, though it is only the actor's 'situation' and 'the circumstances as he believed them to be,' not his scheme of moral values, that are thus to be considered. The ultimate test, however, is objective; there must be a 'reasonable' explanation or excuse for the actor's disturbance." Model Penal Code § 210.3 cmt. 3.

20. State v. Simon, 646 P.2d 1119 (Kan. 1982).

21. *Id.*

22. People v. Goetz, 68 N.Y.2d 96, 111 (1986).

23. *Id.*

24. State v. Leidholm, 334 N.W.2d 811 (N.D. 1983). A number of states have adopted the Model Penal Code's test for self-defense which allows exculpation based on the defendant's subjective belief that it was immediately necessary to use force to protect against a threat of bodily harm. *See* Model Penal Code § 3.04(1). As long as the defendant honestly believed it was immediately necessary to use force in self-defense, the jury can find him not guilty of the charged offense. *Id.* The Model Penal Code approach to self-defense, however, does not use a subjective standard of reasonableness; it does not require reasonableness at all. *See, e.g.*, Moor v. Licciardello, 463 A.2d 268 (Del. 1982). Although the Code does not require a defendant claiming self-defense to show that his belief was

reasonable as well as honest, if the defendant was reckless or negligent in believing that the use of force was necessary, that defendant may be found guilty of an offense for which recklessness or negligence suffices to establish culpability. MODEL PENAL CODE § 3.09.

25. State v. Leidholm, 334 N.W.2d 811, 818 (N.D. 1983) (emphasis added).

26. Such a distinction was suggested in an earlier edition of JOSHUA DRESSLER, UNDERSTANDING CRIMINAL LAW 203 (1987).

27. *See, e.g.,* State v. Bourque, 636 So.2d 254, 268 (La. App. 1994) (excluding the "peculiar psychological characteristics of a particular defendant" from the Reasonable Person test); People v. Thomas C., 183 Cal. App. 3d 786, 798 (1986) (concluding that the defendant's "clinical depression is not the ordinary man's average disposition"); People v. Dooley, 944 P.2d 590, 595 (Colo. Ct. App. 1997) (holding that "the trial court properly concluded that the 'reasonable person' language in the heat of passion manslaughter statute refers to an objectively reasonable person, and not a person suffering from the defendant's chronic mild depression and polysubstance abuse").

28. State v. Wanrow, 559 P.2d 548 (Wash. 1977).

29. State v. Simon, 646 P.2d 1119 (Kan. 1982).

30. A growing number of academics think of race as a social construction, rather than a matter of biology. For an extensive discussion of the social construction of race, *see* MICHAEL OMI AND HOWARD WINANT, RACIAL FORMATION IN THE UNITED STATES: FROM THE 1960s TO THE 1990s (1994).

31. State v. Hundley, 693 P.2d 475 (Kan. 1985). While others have argued persuasively to the contrary, I feel such instructions are generally appropriate even though the physical-mental distinction would not necessarily lead to this result. *Compare* Joshua Dressler, *Battered Women Who Kill Their Tormentors: Reflections on Maintaining Respect for Human Life While Killing Moral Monsters, in* CRIMINAL LAW THEORY: DOCTRINES OF THE GENERAL PART 269 (2002) ("[I]t is a contradiction in terms to describe the 'reasonable person' as one who suffers from emotional paralysis or whose fear causes her to misperceive reality").

32. Camille A. Nelson, *(En)raged or (En)gaged: The Implications of Racial Context to the Canadian Provocation Defence,* 35 U. RICH. L. REV. 1007, 1025 (2002). Fifteen years earlier, M. Naeem Rauf made the same point, noting that a crucifix desecrated before an agnostic might be a matter of indifference to him, but the same act before a religious person might be extremely provocative. M. Naeem Rauf, *The Reasonable Man Test in the Defence of Provocation: What Are the Reasonable Man's Attributes and Should the Test Be Abolished?* 30 CRIM. L. Q. 73, 74 (1987).

33. R. v. Hill [1986] 1 S.C.R. 313 (Can.).

34. *Id.* at 331–32.

35. *Id.*

36. Dir. of Pub. Prosecutions v. Camplin [1978] 2 All E.R. 168, 175.

37. Katharine T. Bartlett, *Feminist Legal Methods*, 103 HARV. L. REV. 829, 837 (1990).

38. *Id.*

39. For an excellent discussion of the sameness and difference approaches, *see* MARTHA CHAMALLAS, INTRODUCTION TO FEMINIST LEGAL THEORY (1999); ROY L. BROOKS, CRITICAL PROCEDURE (1998). For a critique of the sameness/difference paradigm, *see* Joan C. Williams, *Dissolving the Sameness/Difference Debate: A Post-Modern Path Beyond Essentialism in Feminist and Critical Race Theory*, 1991 DUKE L.J. 296.

40. CAROL GILLIGAN, IN A DIFFERENT VOICE: PSYCHOLOGICAL THEORY AND WOMEN'S DEVELOPMENT (1982). Others have observed differences in communication styles between men and women. *See, e.g.,* DEBORAH TANNEN, YOU JUST DON'T UNDERSTAND: WOMEN AND MEN IN CONVERSATION (2001); *see also* JOHN GRAY, MEN ARE FROM MARS, WOMEN ARE FROM VENUS 16 (1992).

41. CHAMALLAS, INTRODUCTION TO FEMINIST LEGAL THEORY, *supra* note 39, at 49.

42. Ironically, the Reasonable Person is also constructed as the Ordinary Man with ordinary emotions, *not* the man who always exercises reason and cautious prudence.

43. In 1991, the Ninth Circuit Court of Appeals announced that in cases involving claims of hostile workplace environment sexual harassment, the severity and pervasiveness of sexual harassment should be determined from the viewpoint of a reasonable woman. Ellison v. Brady, 924 F.2d 872, 879 (9th Cir. 1991). Embracing the argument of difference feminists, the court explained that it had decided to adopt a Reasonable Woman standard "primarily because we believe that a sex-blind reasonable person standard tends to be male-biased and tends to systematically ignore the experiences of women." *Id.*

44. *See, e.g.,* State v. Wanrow, 559 P.2d 548 (Wash. 1977).

45. *Id.* at 558.

46. *Id.*

47. CAROLINE A. FORELL & DONNA M. MATTHEWS, A LAW OF HER OWN: THE REASONABLE WOMAN AS A MEASURE OF MAN xvii (2000).

48. *Id.* at xx.

49. *Id.*

50. CATHARINE A. MACKINNON, FEMINISM UNMODIFIED: DISCOURSES ON LIFE AND LAW 34 (1987).

51. *Id.* at 5.

52. For an excellent critique of essentialism in traditional feminist legal theory, *see* Angela Harris, *Race and Essentialism in Feminist Legal Theory*, 42 STAN. L. REV. 581 (1990).

53. *See, e.g.,* Kimberlé Crenshaw, *Demarginalizing the Intersection of Race and Sex: A Black Feminist Critique of Anti- Discrimination Doctrine*, 1989 U. CHI. LEGAL

F. 139 (using the concept of "intersectionality" to illustrate the various ways in which race and gender interact to shape Black women's employment experiences); Tam B. Tran, *Title VII Hostile Work Environment: A Different Perspective*, 9 J. CONTEMP. LEGAL ISSUES 357 (1998) (arguing that courts should apply a "reasonable minority woman" standard in sexual harassment cases).

54. *See, e.g.,* Stephanie M. Wildman, *Ending Male Privilege: Beyond the Reasonable Woman*, 98 MICH. L. REV. 1797 (2000) (reviewing Forell & Matthews, A LAW OF HER OWN, *supra* note 47); STEPHANIE M. WILDMAN, PRIVILEGE REVEALED: HOW INVISIBLE PREFERENCE UNDERMINES AMERICA (1996); Donovan & Wildman, *Is the Reasonable Man Obsolete, supra* note 10 (arguing that the Reasonable Man standard is not an appropriate standard to apply to the defenses of provocation and self-defense).

55. Wildman, *Ending Male Privilege, supra* note 54.

56. *Id.*

57. *See* text accompanying notes 36–38 in chapter 1.

58. *Id.*

59. Deborah W. Denno, *Gender, Crime, and the Criminal Law Defenses*, 85 J. CRIM. L. & CRIMINOLOGY 80, 154 (1994) (noting that sentencing severity studies "'repeatedly find' that females are less likely than males to receive prison sentences, and more likely to receive shorter terms when they are sentenced"); Wendy Keller, *Disparate Treatment of Spouse Murder Defendants*, 6 S. CAL. L. & WOMEN'S STUD. 255, 269 (1996) ("The chivalry and paternalism hypotheses assume that judges have a benevolent or condescending attitude towards women and believe women defendants are in need of guidance and protection from the harshness and stigma associated with prison sentences. The naiveté theory involves the belief that judges view women as 'less capable than men of committing criminal acts' and are somehow less responsible"); Jenny E. Carroll, *Images of Women and Capital Sentencing among Female Offenders: Exploring the Outer Limits of the Eighth Amendment and Articulated Theories of Justice*, 75 TEX. L. REV. 1413, 1418 (1997) (noting that one explanation for leniency in the sentencing of women in capital cases is "the gender stereotype of women as the weaker, more passive sex, both submissive to and dependent on men"); Fleischer Seldin, *A Strategy for Advocacy on Behalf of Women Offenders*, 5 COLUM. J. GENDER & L. 1, 25 (1995) (noting that "[b]ecause of cultural stereotypes, it is easier for the public to accept that women criminals deserve another chance"). *But compare* Myrna S. Raeder, *Gender and Sentencing: Single Moms, Battered Women, and Other Sex-Based Anomalies in the Gender-Free World of the Federal Sentencing Guidelines*, 20 PEPP. L. REV. 905, 923–24 (1993) (arguing that more women are being incarcerated under the Federal Sentencing Guidelines).

60. Letter dated May 2, 2002 from Alafair Burke to Cynthia Lee (on file with author); e-mail from Alafair Burke to Cynthia Lee dated June 21, 2002.

61. Angela Harris defines "essentialism" as "the notion that a unitary, 'es-

sential' women's experience can be isolated and described independently of race, class, sexual orientation, and other realities of experience." Harris, *Race and Essentialism in Feminist Legal Theory, supra* note 52, at 585. Harris argues that essentialism not only silences some voices in order to privilege others, but also silences the same voices which are silenced by the mainstream, namely "the voices of black women." *Id.*

62. Christina Pei-Lin Chen, *Provocation's Privileged Desire: The Provocation Doctrine, "Homosexual Panic," and the Non-Violent Unwanted Sexual Advance Defense,* 10 Cornell J. L. & Pub. Pol'y 95 (2000).

63. *Id.* at 231–32.

64. *Id.* at 232.

65. While Chen presumably would require judges to engage in role reversal or sexual orientation–switching pretrial to determine whether a defendant ought to be precluded at trial from arguing provocation, I would use gender-, race-, and sexual orientation–switching at the jury instruction stage.

66. *Bill to Address Prison Rape,* Wash. Post, June 13, 2002, at A4 (noting that "[u]nder the Prison Rape Reduction Act, proposed by Sen. Edward M. Kennedy (D-Mass.), Rep. Robert C. "Bobby" Scott (D-Va.), Rep. Frank R. Wolf (R-Va.) and Sen. Jeff Sessions (R-Ala.), national standards would be established for the first thorough study of the problem, and federal funding would be cut for states where prison wardens ignore the issue.").

67. *See* Robert B. Mison, *Homophobia in Manslaughter: The Homosexual Advance as Insufficient Provocation,* 80 Cal. L. Rev. 133 (1992).

68. *See* Neil Gotanda, *A Critique of "Our Constitution Is Color-Blind,"* 44 Stan. L. Rev. 1 (1991). In an insightful essay on color blindness, Victor Romero points out that in the affirmative action context, traditionalists (conservatives and liberals) tend to argue the law should be color-blind while race crits (Critical Race Theorists) argue the law should take race into consideration. The two camps switch positions when it comes to racial profiling, with conservatives arguing that police officers are right to take race into account when stopping suspects and race crits arguing that police officers should be color-blind when it comes to stopping suspects. Victor C. Romero, *Racial Profiling: "Driving While Mexican" and Affirmative Action,* 6 Mich. J. Race & Law 195 (2000).

69. *See* Randall Kennedy, *Racial Critiques of Legal Academia,* 102 Harv. L. Rev. 1745 (1989); *Colloquy: Responses to Randall Kennedy's* Racial Critiques of Legal Academia, 103 Harv. L. Rev. 1844 (1990); Richard Delgado, *When Is a Story Just a Story: Does Voice Really Matter?* 76 Va. L. Rev. 95 (1990).

70. Richard Delgado & Jean Stefancic, Critical Race Theory: The Cutting Edge (2000).

71. *See, e.g.,* Derrick Bell, *Xerces and the Affirmative Action Mystique,* 57 Geo. Wash. L. Rev. 1595 (1989) (defending affirmative action). *But compare* Richard Delgado, *Affirmative Action as a Majoritarian Device: Or, Do You Really Want to Be*

*a Role Model?* 89 MICH. L. REV. 1222 (1991) (criticizing the role model argument for affirmative action because it fosters assimilation); Richard Delgado, *Derrick Bell Lecture: Derrick Bell's Toolkit—Fit to Dismantle That Famous House?* 75 N.Y.U. L. REV. 283 (2000) (arguing that box-checking affirmative action programs misappropriate benefits to those who have not suffered from social stigma or exclusion).

72. Steve Geissinger, *Proposition 209 Passes, as Does Medical Marijuana Initiative,* ORANGE COUNTY REG., Nov. 6, 1996, at G4.

73. V. Dion Haynes, *Affirmative-Action Foe Is Targeting Racial Data; Plan Would Ban Classification by Race in California,* CHI. TRIB., Dec. 26, 2001, at A1 (noting that Proposition 209 inspired a similar initiative in the state of Washington); Kim Murphy, *Resignation over Admissions Policy Splits Seattle Education: The Principal Decried a Court's Order to Not Use Race as a Factor in Who Gets Into His School,* L.A. TIMES, May 13, 2002, at A1 (noting that "Washington in 1998 passed a voter initiative similar to California's Proposition 209").

74. *See, e.g.,* Trujillo-Garcia v. Rowland, No. 93-15096, 1993 WL 460961, at *1 (9th Cir. Oct. 10, 1993) (rejecting defendant's argument that he should be judged according to a reasonable Mexican male standard rather than a Reasonable Person standard); People v. Natale, 18 Cal. Rptr. 491, 494 (Cal. Ct. App. 1962) (rejecting defendant's argument that he should be compared to a reasonable Italian American).

75. Nelson, *(En)Raged or (En)gaged, supra* note 32, at 1038.

76. *Id.* at 1047.

## NOTES TO CHAPTER 9

1. Wolf v. Colorado, 338 U.S. 25, 27 (1949), *overruled by* Mapp v. Ohio, 367 U.S. 643 (1961).

2. *See* GEORGE FLETCHER, RETHINKING CRIMINAL LAW 759 (1978) ("A justification speaks to the rightness of an act"); Joshua Dressler, *New Thoughts about the Concept of Justification in the Criminal Law: A Critique of Fletcher's Thinking and Rethinking,* 32 UCLA L. REV. 61, 66, and 68 n. 37 (1984) (discussing the distinction between justification and excuses).

3. Joshua Dressler, *Rethinking Heat of Passion: A Defense in Search of a Rationale,* 73 J. CRIM. L. & CRIMINOLOGY 421 (1982); Joshua Dressler, *Provocation: Partial Justification or Partial Excuse?* 51 MOD. L. REV. 133 (1987).

4. Whether the defense of provocation ought to be characterized as a partial excuse or a partial justification is a matter of considerable debate. *See* Dressler, *Provocation: Partial Justification or Partial Excuse? supra* note 3 (arguing that the defense of provocation is correctly viewed as a partial excuse); Joshua Dressler, *Why Keep the Provocation Defense? Some Reflections on a Difficult Subject,* 86 MINN.

L. Rev. 959 (2002) (arguing that "provocation doctrine should not be (and, generally, is not today) understood in justificatory terms"); Finbarr McAuley, *Anticipating the Past: The Defence of Provocation in Irish Law*, 50 Mod. L. Rev. 133 (1987) (arguing that the defense of provocation ought to be viewed as a partial justification); A. J. Ashworth, *The Doctrine of Provocation*, 35 Cambridge L.J. 292 (1976) (arguing that provocation has elements of both justification and excuse).

5. Joshua Dressler, a critic of the view that the modern test for provocation ought to be viewed as a partial justification, acknowledges that the early common law categorical approach to provocation can be viewed in justificatory terms. He explains:

> [S]ome aspects of the [early] common law doctrine are best (or, perhaps, only) explained on justificatory grounds. For example, the old English rule that a husband's sight of his wife's adultery constitutes adequate provocation to kill the paramour, which mitigated the homicide to manslaughter, but a similar sighting of unfaithfulness by a fiancée did not result in mitigation. This contradiction is explainable on the antiquated patriarchal ground that, because adultery was considered "the highest invasion of [a husband's] property," the deceased paramour's actions constituted "a form of injustice perpetrated upon the killer . . ., whereas 'mere' sexual unfaithfulness out of wedlock [did] not." According to this approach, the husband was justified in protecting his property, but the excessiveness of his efforts reduced the justification to a partial defense only."

Dressler, *Why Keep the Provocation Defense? supra* note 4, at 967–68.

6. Rex v. Scriva [1951] V.L.R. 298.

7. In contrast to the modern test for provocation, the Model Penal Code's extreme emotional disturbance defense focuses on the defendant's emotional upset and is accurately characterized as an excuse.

8. Dressler, *Why Keep the Provocation Defense? supra* note 4, at 971.

9. *Id.* at 969.

10. George P. Fletcher, *Domination in the Theory of Justification and Excuse*, 57 U. Pitt. L. Rev. 553, 569 (1996) (arguing that actual necessity is or ought to be required); Paul H. Robinson, *Competing Theories of Justification: Deeds v. Reasons, in* Harm and Culpability 45, 46–47 (1996) (arguing that a person is justified in acting in self-defense only if he is actually right about the existence of the justifying circumstances); Heidi M. Hurd, *Justification and Excuse, Wrongdoing and Culpability*, 74 Notre Dame L. Rev. 1551, 1551 (1999) (arguing "that an action is justified if and only if it is permitted by our best moral theory, regardless of the beliefs of the actor").

11. I wish to thank Professor Alafair Burke at Hofstra University School of Law for suggesting this helpful distinction.

12. Laurie J. Taylor, Comment, *Provoked Reason in Men and Women: Heat-of-Passion Manslaughter and Imperfect Self-Defense*, 33 UCLA L. Rev. 1679 (1986); Deborah E. Milgate, Note, *The Flame Flickers, but Burns On: Modern Judicial Application of the Ancient Heat of Passion Defense*, 51 Rutgers L. Rev. 193, 193 (1998) ("The passion in the heat of passion defense refers to an induced uncontrollable rage that overcomes an ordinary man's reason momentarily and causes him to kill").

13. Dressler, *Provocation: Partial Justification or Partial Excuse? supra* note 3, at 472 n. 28 ("The act of self-preservation is nearly instinctual and therefore, is largely an unfree act").

14. Brown v. United States, 256 U.S. 335, 343 (1921).

15. Dan M. Kahan & Martha C. Nussbaum, *Two Conceptions of Emotion in Criminal Law*, 96 Colum. L. Rev. 269 (1996).

16. *Id.* at 279–80.

17. Michael S. Moore, *Causation and the Excuses*, 73 Cal. L. Rev. 1091, 1149 (1985).

18. *Id.*

19. Joshua Dressler, *When "Heterosexual" Men Kill "Homosexual" Men: Reflections on Provocation Law, Sexual Advances, and the "Reasonable Man" Standard*, 85 J. Crim. L. & Criminology 726, 748 (1995). Dressler still seems to view provocation largely in mechanistic terms, but also acknowledges an evaluative component to the provoked killer's anger. In his most recent work on the doctrine of provocation, Dressler compares provocation to the defense of duress and suggests that provocation involves a mechanistic loss of self-control while duress involves more of a rational choice.

> I believe that provocation is better understood in loss-of-self-control (more accurately, partial-loss-of-capacity-for-self-control) terms than in lack-of-fair-opportunity terms. In duress cases, we sense that the coerced party *chooses* to accede to the coercer's threat; it is in a real sense a *rational*, albeit perhaps socially unjustifiable, choice. We excuse the actor because her choices were unfairly hard. In contrast, with provocation, the killing is the result of an emotional explosion almost immediately following the provocation. The homicidal act here is the antithesis of rationality.

Dressler, *Why Keep the Provocation Defense? supra* note 4, at 974 n. 68. Dressler also recognizes the evaluative nature of the provoked killer's emotions. In another section of the article, he writes, "[i]n the provocation context, however, anger is preceded by some judgment by the provoked party, even if it occurs instantly, that he or another to whom he feels emotional attachment has been wronged in some manner by the provoker." *Id.* at 972.

20. Lynn v. Commonwealth, 499 S.E.2d 1 (Va. App. 1998).

21. *Id.* at 5 n. 1 (emphasis added).

22. Febre v. State, 30 So.2d 367 (Fla. 1947).

23. *Id.* at 369 (emphasis added).

24. Kahan & Nussbaum, *Two Conceptions of Emotion in Criminal Law, supra* note 15, at 328.

25. *Id., quoting* 3 WILLIAM BLACKSTONE, COMMENTARIES *3–4 (1966).

26. *Id.* at 285.

27. *Id.* at 308–18.

28. *Id.* at 329.

29. *Id.* at 330.

30. McAuley, *Anticipating the Past, supra* note 4, at 134.

31. Jody Armour calls the person who argues that his actions are reasonable because most people would act the same way he did a "Reasonable Racist." JODY DAVID ARMOUR, NEGROPHOBIA AND REASONABLE RACISM: THE HIDDEN COSTS OF BEING BLACK IN AMERICA (1997).

32. NORMAN J. FINKEL, COMMONSENSE JUSTICE: JURORS' NOTIONS OF THE LAW 8–9 (1995).

33. RONALD DWORKIN, LAW'S EMPIRE 177–78 (1986).

34. *Id.* at 177.

35. *See, e.g.,* DINESH D'SOUZA, THE END OF RACISM: PRINCIPLES FOR A MULTICULTURAL SOCIETY 67–114 (1995) (asserting that slavery in the United States was not racist). In response to the call for reparations for slavery, D'Souza writes, "It makes little sense to say that the United States has an obligation to place African Americans in the economic and social positions they would occupy 'but for' slavery, since 'but for' slavery they would probably be worse off in Africa." *Id.* at 113.

36. Popular opinion was reflected in the U.S. Supreme Court's *Korematsu* decision, upholding the constitutionality of the internment. *See* Korematsu v. United States, 323 U.S. 214 (1944); *see also* ERIC K. YAMAMOTO, MARGARET CHON, CAROL L. IZUMI, JERRY KANG, AND FRANK H. WU, RACE, RIGHTS AND REPARATION: LAW AND THE JAPANESE AMERICAN INTERNMENT (2001).

37. Walter Pincus, *Silence of 4 Terror Probe Suspects Poses Dilemma for FBI,* WASH. POST, Oct. 21, 2001, at A6 ("Among the alternative strategies under discussion are using drugs or pressure tactics, such as those employed occasionally by Isaeli interrogators, to extract information").

38. Camille A. Nelson, *(En)raged or (En)gaged: The Implications of Racial Context to the Canadian Provocation Defence,* 35 U. RICH. L. REV. 1007, 1023 (2002), *citing* Joanne St. Lewis & Sheila Galloway, *Reforming the Defence of Provocation, in* ONTARIO WOMEN'S DIRECTORATE 7 (1994), *citing* Rosemary Cairns Way, *The Criminalization of Stalking: An Exercise in Media Manipulation and Political Opportunism,* 39 McGILL L.J. 379 (1994).

39. People v. Logan, 164 P. 1121, 1122 (Cal. 1917) (emphasis added).

40. *See infra* chapter 10 (discussing the act-emotion distinction).

41. JOSHUA DRESSLER, UNDERSTANDING CRIMINAL PROCEDURE § 7.03, at 92 (2d ed. 1998) (noting that "the Court's approach to the issue is mixed").

42. Katz v. United States, 389 U.S. 347, 361 (1967) (Harlan, J., concurring) (emphasis added). The two-pronged test outlined in Justice Harlan's concurring opinion has been cited as *the test* for a search. *See, e.g.,* Minnesota v. Olson, 495 U.S. 91, 95 (1990) ("Since the decision in *Katz v. United States,* it has been the law that 'capacity to claim the protection of the Fourth Amendment depends . . . upon whether the person who claims the protection of the amendment has a legitimate expectation of privacy in the invaded place'").

43. *Katz,* 389 U.S. at 353.

44. State v. Campbell, 759 P.2d 1040, 1044 (Or. 1988).

45. JOSHUA DRESSLER, UNDERSTANDING CRIMINAL PROCEDURE § 30[D][3] at 61 (1991)(emphasis added).

46. California v. Greenwood, 486 U.S. 35 (1988).

47. My own intuitions about this might be off-base. In a survey seeking to measure expectations of privacy and attitudes about the intrusiveness of various types of government action, Christopher Slobogin and Joseph Schumacher found that most respondents felt that going through garbage was relatively unintrusive. Christopher Slobogin & Joseph E. Schumacher, *Reasonable Expectations of Privacy and Autonomy in Fourth Amendment Cases: An Empirical Look at "Understandings Recognized and Permitted by Society,"* 42 DUKE L.J. 727 (1993). In 1975, however, when "a reporter for a weekly tabloid seized five bags of garbage from the sidewalk outside the home of Secretary of State Henry Kissenger," JEROLD H. ISRAEL, YALE KAMISAR, & WAYNE R. LAFAVE, CRIMINAL PROCEDURE AND THE CONSTITUTION: LEADING SUPREME COURT CASES AND INTRODUCTORY TEXT 87, n. 4 (2001), *citing* WASH. POST, July 9, 1975, at A1, a number of individuals felt that Kissenger's expectation of privacy in his trash was eminently reasonable.

48. JEFFREY ROSEN, THE UNWANTED GAZE: THE DESTRUCTION OF PRIVACY IN AMERICA 61 (2000).

49. United States v. Miller, 425 U.S. 435 (1976).

50. Slobogin & Schumacher, *Reasonable Expectations of Privacy and Autonomy in Fourth Amendment Cases, supra* note 46.

51. Hoffa v. United States, 385 U.S. 293 (1966); United States v. White, 401 U.S. 745 (1971).

52. Mison further argues that the use of a provocation argument in this context of a nonviolent homosexual advance reinforces and institutionalizes homophobia. To counter such institutional endorsement of heterosexism, Mison argues that judges ought to rule as a matter of law that a nonviolent homosexual advance does not constitute legally adequate provocation. Under Mison's proposal, men who kill gay men in response to a nonviolent sexual ad-

vance would be precluded from arguing that they were provoked into a heat of passion. Robert B. Mison, *Homophobia in Manslaughter: The Homosexual Advance as Insufficient Provocation*, 80 CAL. L. REV. 133 (1992).

53. *Id.* at 160–61 (emphasis added).

54. Holmes v. Dir. of Pub. Prosecutions [1946] A.C. 588.

55. *Id.* at 601 (emphasis added).

56. *Id.* at 599 (emphasis added).

57. *Id.* at 600. Even the *Holmes* court, however, described the Reasonable Man as the ordinary reasonable man. *Id.* at 589.

58. R. v. S. (R.D.) [1997] 3 S.C.R. 484.

59. *Id.* at 509 (L'Heureux-Dube & McLachlin, Justices).

60. *Id.*

61. Dressler, *When "Heterosexual" Men Kill "Homosexual" Men, supra* note 19, at 753 (emphasis added).

62. *See infra* chapter 10 (discussing the focus on emotion reasonableness in provocation cases).

63. Dressler notes that "use of the word 'reasonable' reinforces the important point that the objective standard contains a normative component and is not merely descriptive." Dressler, *Why Keep the Provocation Defense? supra* note 4, at 973 n. 65.

64. Dressler, *When "Heterosexual" Men Kill "Homosexual" Men, supra* note 19, at 757 (emphasis added).

65. *See infra* chapter 10.

66. Andrew Taslitz argues that the jury is better than a single judge because twelve heads are more likely than one to recognize the fullness of the context. Andrew Taslitz, *A Feminist Approach to Social Scientific Evidence: Foundations,* 5 MICH. J. GENDER & L. 1, 47 (1998).

67. FLETCHER, RETHINKING CRIMINAL LAW, *supra* note 2, at 243 (emphasis added).

68. *See* discussion regarding act reasonableness in chapter 10.

69. *See* discussion regarding emotion reasonableness and act reasonableness in chapter 10.

70. *See* Cynthia K. Y. Lee, *The Act-Belief Distinction in Self-Defense Doctrine: A New Dual Requirement Theory of Justification,* 2 BUFF. CRIM. L. REV. 191, 235–44 (1998).

71. Alan C. Michaels, *"Rationales" of Criminal Law Then and Now: For a Judgmental Descriptivism,* 100 COLUM. L. REV. 54 (2000).

72. *Id.* at 47.

73. MD. ANN. CODE art. 27 § 387A (1997). In a similar attempt to carve out categories of things that do not constitute legally adequate provocation, the Minnesota legislature specifies that the crying of a child does not constitute legally adequate provocation. MINN. STAT. ANN. § 609.20(1) (1987).

74. Rather than legislative action, Robert Mison argues for judicial action. Under Mison's view, judges should rule as a matter of law that a nonviolent homosexual advance does not constitute legally adequate provocation. Mison, *Homophobia in Manslaughter, supra* note 52.

75. FINAL REPORT OF THE "HOMOSEXUAL ADVANCE DEFENCE" WORKING PARTY, NEW SOUTH WALES ATTORNEY GENERAL'S DEPARTMENT 31 (September 1998) (report on file with author; also available through the NSW Attorney General's Department, Criminal Law Division, or on the internet at http://www.lawlink.nsw.gov.au/clrd at "Papers and Reports"). The Working Party also recommended excluding "a homicidal response to *any* form of nonviolent sexual advance, not just a homosexual one," from the defense of provocation. *Id.*

76. NORMAN FINKEL, COMMONSENSE JUSTICE: JURORS' NOTIONS OF THE LAW (1995).

77. *See, e.g.,* JEFFREY ABRAMSON, WE THE JURY: THE JURY SYSTEM AND THE IDEAL OF DEMOCRACY (1994). Paul Butler has also written about the importance of jury nullification. Butler argues that Black jurors should exercise their power of nullification when sitting in judgment of a Black male defendant charged with a nonviolent crime. Paul Butler, *Racially Based Jury Nullification: Black Power in the Criminal Justice System,* 105 YALE L.J. 677 (1995).

78. *See, e.g.,* Apprendi v. New Jersey, 530 U.S. 466 (2000) (holding that the Constitution requires that any fact that increases the penalty for a crime beyond the prescribed statutory maximum, other than the fact of a prior conviction, must be submitted to a jury and proven beyond a reasonable doubt).

79. Taslitz, *A Feminist Approach to Social Scientific Evidence, supra* note 66.

80. *Id.* at 26.

81. *Id.* at 39.

82. *Id.* at 36–37, *quoting* ADAM SMITH, THE THEORY OF MORAL SENTIMENTS 22 (1774).

83. *Id.* at 40.

84. RICHARD A. POSNER, OVERCOMING LAW 381 (1995).

85. *Id.* Posner, however, never adequately explains why a jurisprudence of empathy lacks normative significance.

86. *See, e.g.,* Stephen J. Morse, *Undiminished Confusion in Diminished Capacity,* 75 J. CRIM. L. & CRIMINOLOGY 1, 7 (1984) ("In an adversary system of criminal justice, where liberty and stigma are at stake, it is a violation of the defendant's sixth and fourteenth amendment rights to prevent him from introducing competent and relevant evidence to defeat the state's case unless there are powerful justifications for their prohibition"); Montana v. Egelhoff, 518 U.S. 37 (1996) (affirming state statute that precluded defendants in criminal cases from presenting evidence of their voluntary intoxication to show that they lacked the mental state required for commission of the charged offense).

87. I wish to thank my friend and colleague Angela Harris for suggesting this valuable insight.

88. JEREMY HORDER, PROVOCATION AND RESPONSIBILITY 197 (1992) ("So the doctrine of provocation should be abolished, and the effect of provocation in murder cases left as a matter for mitigation in sentence").

89. Morse, *Undiminished Confusion in Diminished Capacity, supra* note 86, at 33 ("I would abolish this hoary distinction [between murder and voluntary manslaughter based on provocation/passion] and convict all intentional killers of murder").

90. *Id.* at 30.

91. *Id.* at 33.

92. *Id.* at 34.

93. *Id.* at 30–31.

94. *Id.* at 34.

95. Dressler, *Why Keep the Provocation Defense? supra* note 4.

96. Cynthia Kwei Yung Lee, *Race and Self-Defense: Toward a Normative Conception of Reasonableness*, 81 MINN. L. REV. 367 (1996).

97. JOHN GRISHAM, A TIME TO KILL 503–4 (1989).

98. *Id.* at 513.

99. Letter dated October 20, 1997, from attorney James H. McComas, Attorney at Law, to Professor Cynthia Lee (copy on file with author). *See also* James McComas & Cynthia Strout, *Combating the Effects of Racial Stereotyping in Criminal Cases,* CHAMPION 22 (1999).

100. McComas & Strout, *Combating the Effects of Racial Stereotyping in Criminal Cases, supra* note 99, at 23.

101. *Id.*

102. Lee, *Race and Self-Defense, supra* note 96, at 482.

103. Jury Instruction No. 36 in State of Alaska v. Denarius Lockhart, Case No. 3AN-S96-2362 Cr. (copy on file with author).

104. Letter dated October 20, 1997, from attorney James H. McComas, Attorney at Law, to Professor Cynthia Lee (copy on file with author).

105. Mari J. Matsuda, *Looking to the Bottom: Critical Legal Studies and Reparations*, 22 HARV. C.R.–C.L. L. REV. 323, 324 (1987).

106. *Id.* at 325.

107. Laurens Walker & John Monahan, *Social Frameworks: A New Use of Social Science in Law*, 73 VA. L. REV. 559 (1987).

108. Jody Armour, *Stereotypes and Prejudice: Helping Legal Decision-Makers Break the Prejudice Habit*, 83 CAL. L. REV. 733 (1995).

344 NOTES TO CHAPTER 10

## NOTES TO CHAPTER 10

1. This hypothetical comes from GAVIN DE BECKER, THE GIFT OF FEAR 1–7 (1997).

2. *Id.* at 288 ("[O]nce one has granted that a given emotional response is appropriate, one needs to ask many further questions before one can determine that a given related action is appropriate").

3. English courts, for example, require act reasonableness. Section 3 of the Homicide Act of 1957 instructs:

> Where on a charge of murder there is evidence on which the jury can find that the person charged was provoked (whether by things done or by things said or by both together) to lose his self-control, the question whether the provocation was enough to make a reasonable man *do as he did* shall be left to be determined by the jury; and in determining that question the jury shall take into account everything both done and said according to the effect which, in their opinion, it would have on a reasonable man.

Homicide Act, 1957, § 3 (emphasis added).

4. Maryland Criminal Pattern Jury Instructions § 4:17.4(C)(2) (1999) (emphasis added).

5. West Virginia Criminal Jury Instructions 557 (5th ed. 1997).

6. WAYNE R. LaFAVE & AUSTIN W. SCOTT, JR., CRIMINAL LAW § 7.10(b) at 654 (2d ed. 1986) (emphasis added).

7. *See* ALASKA STAT. § 11.41.115(f)(2) (Michie 1988) ("'serious provocation' means conduct which is sufficient to excite an intense *passion* in a reasonable person in the defendant's situation") (emphasis added); Colorado Jury Instructions (Criminal), No. 9:08 (1983) (provocation must affect the defendant "sufficiently to excite an irresistible *passion* in a reasonable person") (emphasis added); Lacy v. State, 387 So.2d 561, 562 (Fla. Dist. Ct. App. 1980) (defining legally adequate provocation as "something which would naturally and instantly produce in the mind of an ordinary person the highest degree of *anger, rage, resentment or exasperation*) (emphasis added); GA. CODE ANN. § 16-5-2(a) (1968) (defendant must act "solely as the result of a sudden, violent, and irresistible *passion* resulting from serious provocation sufficient to excite such passion in a reasonable person") (emphasis added); Illinois Pattern Jury Instructions (Criminal), No. 7.03 (4th ed. 2000) (defining "serious provocation" as "conduct sufficient to excite an intense *passion* in a reasonable person") (emphasis added); Iowa Criminal Jury Instructions, No. 700.16 (1996) ("a 'serious provocation' is conduct that would cause a reasonable person to have a sudden, violent and irresistible *passion*") (emphasis added); Commonwealth v. Whitman, 722 N.E.2d 1284, 1291 (Mass. 2000) (defining legally adequate provocation

as "provocation such as is likely to produce in an ordinary person that state of *passion, anger, fear, fright or excitement* as might lead to an intentional homicide") (emphasis added); ME. REV. STAT. ANN. tit. 17-A, § 201(1)(C)(3) (West 1983) (provocation is adequate when the defendant acts "under the influence of *extreme anger or extreme fear*") (emphasis added); Pattern Jury Instructions for Criminal Cases (North Carolina), No. 206.10 (1977) (defining adequate provocation as "anything which has a natural tendency to produce such *passion* in a person of average mind and disposition") (emphasis added); Oklahoma Uniform Jury Instructions (Criminal), No. 4-98 (2d ed. 1996) ("Adequate provocation" refers to any improper conduct of the deceased toward the defendant(s) which naturally or reasonably would have the effect of arousing a sudden heat of *passion* within a reasonable person in the position of the defendant(s)) (emphasis added).

8. Febre v. State, 30 So.2d 367, 369 (Fla. 1947).

9. Drye v. State, 184 S.W.2d 10, 13 (Tenn. 1944).

10. Illinois Pattern Jury Instructions (Criminal), No. 7.03 (4th ed. 2000) (emphasis added).

11. ALASKA STAT. § 11.41.115(f)(2) (1988)(emphasis added).

12. *See* Recommended Arizona Jury Instructions (Criminal), No. 11.032 (1989) (defining adequate provocation as "conduct or circumstances *sufficient to deprive a reasonable person of self-control*") (emphasis added); Criminal Jury Instructions for the District of Columbia, No. 4.18 (4th ed. 1993) (defining adequate provocation as "conduct that would cause an ordinary, reasonable person in the heat of the moment *to lose his/her self-control* and act on impulse and without reflection") (emphasis added); N.M. STAT. ANN. § 14-222 (Michie 2001) (defining sufficient provocation as that which "would affect the ability to reason and to cause a temporary *loss of self control* in an ordinary person of average disposition") (emphasis added); State v. Hatcher, 706 A.2d 429, 433 (Vt. 1997) (defining adequate provocation as circumstances "that would cause a reasonable person to *lose control*") (emphasis added); Instructions for Virginia and West Virginia, § 24-242 (4th ed. 1996) (defining adequate provocation as such as would "reasonably deprive [the defendant] of the power of *self-control*") (emphasis added); Wisconsin Jury Instructions (Criminal), No. 21 (2001) (defining adequate provocation as that which would "cause complete *loss of self-control* in an ordinary person") (emphasis added).

13. State v. McDermott, 449 P.2d 545, 548 (Kan. 1969).

14. *See* California Standard Jury Instructions (Criminal), CALJIC No. 8.42 (6th ed. 1996) (defining adequate provocation as that which would "cause the ordinarily reasonable person of average disposition *to act rashly* and without deliberation and reflection, *and from passion* rather than from judgment") (emphasis added); Michigan Criminal Jury Instructions, No. 16.9 (2d ed. 1989) ("a reasonable person might have *acted on impulse*, without thinking twice, *from passion*

instead of judgment") (emphasis added); State v. Hoyt, 1868 WL 1872, *3 (Minn. 1868) (defining legally adequate provocation as that passion which disturbs or obscures reason "to an extent which *might render* ordinary men, of fair average disposition, *liable to act rashly*, or without due deliberation or reflection, and from passion rather than judgment"); New Jersey Pleading and Practice Forms § 93:161 (1999) ("The provocation must be so gross as to cause the ordinary reasonable person to lose his or her self-control and *to use violence with fatal results*") (emphasis added); Ohio Jury Instructions (Criminal), No. 503.02(6)(E)&(F) (2001) (defining serious provocation as that which "is reasonably sufficient to incite a person into *using deadly force*" and "sufficient to arouse the *passion* of an ordinary person beyond the power of his/her control") (emphasis added).

15. New Jersey Pleading and Practice Forms § 93:161 (1999) (emphasis added).

16. *Id.*

17. Ohio Jury Instructions (Criminal), No. 503.02(6) (2001) (emphasis added).

18. *Id.*

19. Joshua Dressler, *Why Keep the Provocation Defense? Some Reflections on a Difficult Subject*, 86 MINN. L. REV. 959 (2002), *citing* People v. Casassa, 49 N.Y.S.2d 668, 679 n. 2 (1980).

20. JEREMY HORDER, PROVOCATION AND RESPONSIBILITY 44 (1992).

21. *Id.* at 45.

22. *Id.* at 51.

23. *Id.* at 49–50.

24. *Id.* at 50.

25. Richard Singer attributes the proportionality doctrine in provocation law to two writers, East and Russell. Richard Singer, *The Resurgence of Mens Rea: I—Provocation, Emotional Disturbance, and the Model Penal Code*, 27 B.C. L. REV. 243, 262–63 (1986).

26. A. J. Ashworth, *The Doctrine of Provocation*, 35 CAMBRIDGE L.J. 292, 297 (1976) (quoting the Criminal Law Commissioners of 1839).

27. Phillips v. The Queen [1968] 2 A.C. 130, 132.

28. Mancini v. Dir. of Pub. Prosecutions [1942] A.C. 1, 9.

29. *See* Phillips v. The Queen [1968] 2 A.C. 130 ("it may be prudent to avoid the use of the precise words of Viscount Simon in *Mancini v. Director of Public Prosecutions* 'the mode of resentment must bear a reasonable relationship to the provocation' unless they are used in a context which makes clear to the jury that this is not a rule of law which they are bound to follow, but merely a consideration which may or may not commend itself to them"); Regina v. Brown [1972] 2 Q.B. 229, 233 ("Plainly, one vital element for the jury's consideration in all these cases is the proportion between the provocation and the retaliation").

30. Regina v. Smith [2001] 1 A.C. 146.

31. *Id.* at 178.

32. Finbarr McAuley, *Anticipating the Past: The Defence of Provocation in Irish Law*, 50 MOD. L. REV. 133, 154–56 (1987). *See also* People v. Davis 2000 1 I.R. ("The accused must use no more force than is reasonable having regard to the effect the provocation had on him"); People v. MacEoin 1978 I.R. 27 ("When the defence of provocation is raised, we think that the trial judge at the close of the evidence should rule on . . . whether the provocation bears a reasonable relationship to the amount of force used by the accused").

33. People v. Matthews, 314 N.E.2d 15 (Ill. App. Ct. 1974).

34. *Id.* at 19 (emphasis added).

35. U.S. ex rel. Peery v. Sielaff, 615 F.2d 402 (7th Cir. 1979).

36. *Id.* at 405.

37. Phillips v. The Queen [1968] 2 A.C. 130, 137–38 (finding false the premise that loss of self-control is absolute and that there is no intermediate stage between icy detachment and going berserk). *See also* Regina v. Brown [1972] 2 Q.B. 229 (wherein the prosecutor argued, "[i]t must be wrong to state that there can be no limit to loss of self-control and that, once self-control within the meaning of section 3 of the Act of 1967 [*sic*] is lost, the acts following are beyond any control at all. . . . [The ordinary] man, even when provoked into acting as he would not have done had he not lost self-control, nevertheless retains some degree of control over his ensuing acts").

38. NORMAN J. FINKEL, COMMONSENSE JUSTICE: JURORS' NOTIONS OF THE LAW 305 (1995).

39. In using the term "normatively" to qualify reasonable, I invoke a normative conception of reasonableness, a concept discussed in chapter 9.

40. *See* Cynthia K. Y. Lee, *The Act-Belief Distinction in Self-Defense Doctrine: A New Dual Requirement Theory of Justification*, 2 BUFF. CRIM. L. REV. 191 (1998).

41. A survey of model jury instructions on self-defense in the fifty states indicates that most jurisdictions focus upon the reasonableness of the defendant's fear (or the reasonableness of his belief in the need to act in self-defense), rather than on the reasonableness of the defendant's acts. *See* Cynthia Kwei Yung Lee, *Race and Self-Defense: Toward a Normative Conception of Reasonableness*, 81 MINN. L. REV. 367, 470 n. 404 (1996) (listing the model jury instructions which focus on the reasonableness of the defendant's beliefs or fears).

42. Lee, *The Act-Belief Distinction in Self-Defense Doctrine*, *supra* note 40.

43. State v. Dill, 461 So. 2d 1130 (La. App. 1984).

44. *Id.* at 1133 (emphasis added).

45. *Id.* at 1137 (emphasis added).

46. *Id.* at 1138.

47. State v. Garrison, 525 A.2d 498 (Conn. 1987).

48. It is interesting that the trial court couched its decision in the language of beliefs, rejecting Garrison's self-defense claim because Garrison "knew" he

could retreat into an adjoining room and "knew" he could disarm Sharp. However, it is difficult to state with certainty what Garrison knew or didn't know. Most likely, the trial court simply thought Garrison's act of shooting Sharp a second time was not reasonably necessary. *See* Lee, *The Act-Belief Distinction in Self-Defense Doctrine, supra* note 40, at 228 n. 116.

49. Lee, *The Act-Belief Distinction in Self-Defense Doctrine, supra* note 40, at 236–37.

# Bibliography

Abramson, Jeffrey. *We the Jury: The Jury System and the Ideal of Democracy*. New York: Basic Books, 1994.

Abu-Odeh, Lamu. "Comparatively Speaking: The 'Honor' of the 'East' and the 'Passion' of the 'West.'" 2 *Utah Law Review* 287 (1997).

Adams, Henry E., et al. "Is Homophobia Associated with Homosexual Arousal?" 105 *Journal of Abnormal Psychology* 440 (1996).

Addis, Adeno. "'Hell Man, They Did Invent Us': The Mass Media, Law, and African Americans." 41 *Buffalo Law Review* 523 (1993).

Aguero, Joseph E., et al. "The Relationships among Sexual Beliefs, Attitudes, Experience, and Homophobia." 10 *Journal of Homosexuality* 95 (1984).

Alexander, Larry. "Self Defense, Justification, and Excuse." 22 *Philosophy & Public Affairs* 53 (1993).

Alfieri, Anthony V. "Defending Racial Violence." 95 *Columbia Law Review* 1301 (1995).

———. "Race Trials." 76 *Texas Law Review* 1293 (1998).

Alschuler, Albert W. "Racial Quotas and the Jury." 44 *Duke Law Journal* 704 (1995).

Amnesty International. *Rights for All: Police Brutality and Excessive Force in the New York City Police Department*, 1999.

———. *USA: Race, Rights and Police Brutality*, 1999.

Angel, Marina. "Abusive Boys Kill Girls Just Like Abusive Men Kill Women: Explaining the Obvious." 8 *Temple Political and Civil Rights Law Review* 283 (1999).

Armour, Jody David. *Negrophobia and Reasonable Racism: The Hidden Costs of Being Black in America*. New York: NYU Press, 1997.

———. "Stereotypes and Prejudice: Helping Legal Decision-Makers Break the Prejudice Habit." 83 *California Law Review* 733 (1995).

Ashworth, A. J. "The Doctrine of Provocation." 35 *Cambridge Law Journal* 292 (1976).

Bailey, Frankie Y. "Law, Justice, and 'Americans': An Historical Overview." In *Race and Criminal Justice*. New York: Harrow and Heston, 1991.

Baldus, David C., et al. *Equal Justice and the Death Penalty: A Legal and Empirical Analysis.* Boston: Northeastern University Press, 1990.

―――., et al. "Comparative Review of Death Sentences: An Empirical Study of the Georgia Experience." 74 *Journal of Criminal Law & Criminology* 661 (1983).

Bandes, Susan. "Patterns of Injustice: Police Brutality in the Courts." 47 *Buffalo Law Review* 1275 (1999).

Banks, Taunya Lovell. "Two Life Stories: Reflections of One Black Woman Law Professor." 6 *Berkeley Women's Law Journal* 46 (1990–91).

Bartlett, Katharine T. "Feminist Legal Methods." 103 *Harvard Law Review* 829 (1990).

―――, and Angela P. Harris. *Gender and Law: Theory, Doctrine, Commentary.* New York: Aspen Law and Business, 1998.

Baynes, Leonard M. "Paradoxes of Racial Stereotypes, Diversity and Past Discrimination in Establishing Affirmative Action in FCC Licensing." 52 *Administrative Law Review* 979 (2000).

Bell, Derrick A. "Brown v. Board of Education and the Interest Convergence Dilemma." 93 *Harvard Law Review* 518 (1980).

―――. "Xerces and the Affirmative Action Mystique." 57 *George Washington Law Review* 1595 (1989).

Berril, Kevin T., and Gregory M. Herek. "Primary and Secondary Victimization in Anti-Gay Hate Crimes: Official Response and Public Policy." In *Hate Crimes: Confronting Violence against Lesbians and Gay Men.* Newbury Park, Calif.: Sage, 1992.

Blumberg, Mark. "Race and Police Shootings: An Analysis in Two Cities." In *Contemporary Issues in Law Enforcement.* Beverly Hills: Sage, 1981.

Bond, Charles F., et al. "Responses to Violence in a Psychiatric Setting: The Role of Patient's Race." 14 *Personality & Social Psychology Bulletin* 448 (1988).

Brenner, Claudia. *Eight Bullets: One Woman's Story of Surviving Anti-Gay Violence.* Ithaca, N.Y.: Firebrand Books, 1995.

Brooks, Roy L. *Critical Procedure.* Durham, N.C.: Carolina Academic Press, 1998.

Brown, Michael F. "Use of Deadly Force by Patrol Officers: Training Implications." 12 *Journal of Police Science & Administration* 133 (1984).

Brown, Richard Maxwell. *No Duty to Retreat: Violence and Values in American History and Society.* New York: Oxford University Press, 1991.

Browne, Angela. *When Battered Women Kill.* New York: Free Press, 1987.

Burke, Alafair S. "Rational Actors, Self-Defense, and Duress: Making Sense, Not Syndromes, Out of the Battered Woman." 81 *North Carolina Law Review* 211 (2002).

Burr, Sherri L. "Scarlett's Code, Susan's Actions." In *Critical Race Feminism: A Reader.* New York: NYU Press, 1997.

Buss, David M., et al. "Sex Differences in Jealousy: Evolution, Physiology, and Psychology." 3 *Psychological Science* 251 (1992).

Butler, Paul. "Racially Based Jury Nullification: Black Power in the Criminal Justice System." 105 *Yale Law Journal* 677 (1995).

Buunk, Bram P., et al. "Sex Differences in Jealousy in Evolutionary and Cultural Perspective." 7 *Psychological Science* 359 (1996).

Carroll, Jenny E. "Images of Women and Capital Sentencing among Female Offenders: Exploring the Outer Limits of the Eighth Amendment and Articulated Theories of Justice." 75 *Texas Law Review* 1413 (1997).

Chamallas, Martha. *Introduction to Feminist Legal Theory*. Gaithersburg, Md.: Aspen Law & Business, 1999.

Chang, Robert S. *Disoriented: Asian Americans, Law, and the Nation-State*. New York: NYU Press, 1999.

———. "Toward an Asian American Legal Scholarship: Critical Race Theory, Post-Structuralism, and Narrative Space." 81 *California Law Review* 1243 (1993).

Chen, Christina Pei-Lin. "Provocation's Privileged Desire: The Provocation Doctrine, 'Homosexual Panic,' and the Non-Violent Unwanted Sexual Advance Defense." 10 *Cornell Journal of Law & Public Policy* 95 (2000).

Chevigny, Paul G. "Police Violence: Causes and Cures." 7 *Journal of Law & Policy* 75 (1998).

Chew, Pat K. "Asian Americans: The 'Reticent' Minority and Their Paradoxes." 36 *William & Mary Law Review* 1 (1994).

Chiu, Daina C. "The Cultural Defense: Beyond Exclusion, Assimilation, and Guilty Liberalism." 82 *California Law Review* 1053 (1994).

Cho, Sumi K. "Korean Americans vs. African Americans: Conflict and Construction." In *Reading Rodney King/Reading Urban Uprising*. New York: Routledge, 1993.

Coker, Donna K. "Heat of Passion and Wife Killing: Men Who Batter/Men Who Kill." 2 *Southern California Review of Law & Women's Studies* 71 (1992).

Cole, David. *No Equal Justice: Race and Class in the American Criminal Justice System*. New York: New Press, 1999.

Coleman, Doriane Lambelet. "Individualizing Justice through Multiculturalism: The Liberals' Dilemma." 96 *Columbia Law Review* 1093 (1996).

"Colloquy: Responses to Randall Kennedy's *Racial Critiques of Legal Academia*." 103 *Harvard Law Review* 1844 (1990).

Comstock, Gary David. "Dismantling the Homosexual Panic Defense." 2 *Law & Sexuality* 81 (1992).

———. *Violence against Lesbians and Gay Men*. New York: Columbia University Press, 1991.

Correll, J., et al. "The Police Officer's Dilemma: Using Ethnicity to Disambiguate Potentially Threatening Individuals." 83 *Journal of Personality and Social Psychology* (2002).

Cose, Ellis. *The Rage of a Privileged Class.* New York: HarperCollins, 1993.

Cotten-Huston, Annie L., and Bradley M. Waite. "Anti-Homosexual Attitudes in College Students: Predictors and Classroom Interventions." 38 *Journal of Homosexuality* 117 (2000).

Coughlin, Anne M. "Excusing Women." 82 *California Law Review* 1 (1994).

Crenshaw, Kimberlé. "Demarginalizing the Intersection of Race and Sex: A Black Feminist Critique of Anti-Discrimination Doctrine." 1989 *University of Chicago Legal Forum* 139 (1989).

Daniels, Roger. *Asian America: Chinese and Japanese in the U.S. since 1850.* Seattle: University of Washington Press, 1988.

David, Deborah S., and Robert Brannon. "The Male Sex Role: Our Culture's Blueprint of Manhood and What It's Done for Us Lately." In *The Forty-Nine Percent Majority: The Male Sex Role.* New York: Random House, 1976.

Davis, Angela J. "Benign Neglect of Racism in the Criminal Justice System." 94 *Michigan Law Review* 1660 (1996).

———. "Race, Cops and Traffic Stops." 51 *University of Miami Law Review* 425 (1997).

Davis, Peggy. "Law as Microaggression." 98 *Yale Law Journal* 1559 (1989).

De Becker, Gavin. *The Gift of Fear.* New York: Dell Publishing, 1997.

Delgado, Richard. "Affirmative Action as a Majoritarian Device: Or, Do You Really Want to Be a Role Model?" 89 *Michigan Law Review* 1222 (1991).

———. "Derrick Bell Lecture: Derrick Bell's Toolkit—Fit to Dismantle That Famous House?" 75 *New York University Law Review* 283 (2000).

———. "Making Pets: Social Workers, 'Problem Groups,' and the Role of the SPCA—Getting a Little More Precise about Racialized Narratives." 77 *Texas Law Review* 1571 (1999).

———. "Shadowboxing: An Essay on Power." 77 *Cornell Law Review* 813 (1992).

———. "When Is a Story Just a Story: Does Voice Really Matter?" 76 *Virginia Law Review* 95 (1990).

———. "Words That Wound: A Tort Action for Racial Insults, Epithets, and Name-Calling." 17 *Harvard Civil Rights–Civil Liberties Law Review* 133 (1982).

Delgado, Richard, and Jean Stefancic. *Critical Race Theory: The Cutting Edge.* Philadelphia: Temple University Press, 2000.

Delgado, Richard, and Jean Stefancic, eds. *Critical White Studies: Looking Behind the Mirror.* Philadelphia: Temple University Press, 1997.

———. "Images of the Outsider in American Law and Culture: Can Free Expression Remedy Systemic Social Ills?" 77 *Cornell Law Review* 1258 (1992).

Denno, Deborah W. "Gender, Crime, and the Criminal Law Defenses." 85 *Journal of Criminal Law & Criminology* 80 (1994).

"Developments in the Law—Sexual Orientation and the Law." 102 *Harvard Law Review* 1519 (1989).

Donovan, Dolores A., and Stephanie M. Wildman. "Is the Reasonable Man Obsolete? A Critical Perspective on Self-Defense and Provocation." 14 *Loyola Law Review* 435 (1981).

Dressler, Joshua. "Battered Women Who Kill Their Tormentors: Reflections on Maintaining Respect for Human Life While Killing Moral Monsters." In *Criminal Law Theory: Doctrines of the General Part*. Oxford: Oxford University Press, 2002.

———. "New Thoughts about the Concept of Justification in the Criminal Law: A Critique of Fletcher's Thinking and Rethinking." 32 *UCLA Law Review* 61 (1984).

———. "Provocation: Partial Justification or Partial Excuse?" 51 *Modern Law Review* 133 (1987).

———. "Rethinking Heat of Passion: A Defense in Search of a Rationale." 73 *Journal of Criminal Law and Criminology* 421 (1982).

———. *Understanding Criminal Law*. New York: Matthew Bender, 1987.

———. *Understanding Criminal Law*. New York: Matthew Bender, 1995.

———. *Understanding Criminal Law*. New York: Lexis Publishing, 2001.

———. *Understanding Criminal Procedure*. New York: Matthew Bender, 1991.

———. *Understanding Criminal Procedure*. New York: Matthew Bender, 1998.

———. "When 'Heterosexual' Men Kill 'Homosexual' Men: Reflections on Provocation Law, Sexual Advances, and the 'Reasonable Man' Standard." 85 *Journal of Criminal Law & Criminology* 726 (1995).

———. "Why Keep the Provocation Defense? Some Reflections on a Difficult Subject." 86 *Minnesota Law Review* 959 (2002).

D'Souza, Dinesh. *The End of Racism: Principles for a Multicultural Society*. New York: Free Press, 1995.

Duncan, Birt L. "Differential Social Perception and Attribution of Intergroup Violence: Testing the Lower Limit of Stereotyping of Blacks." 4 *Journal of Personality & Social Psychology* 590 (1976).

Dworkin, Ronald. *Law's Empire*. Cambridge: Belknap Press, 1986.

Dwyer, Jim, Peter Neufeld, and Barry Scheck. *Actual Innocence: Five Days to Execution and Other Dispatches from the Wrongly Convicted*. New York: Doubleday, 2000.

Edwards, Susan. "Battered Women Who Kill." 140 *New Law Journal* 1380 (1990).

Ehrenreich, Nancy S. "Pluralist Myths and Powerless Men: The Ideology of Reasonableness in Sexual Harassment Law." 99 *Yale Law Journal* 1177 (1990).

Epps, Garrett. "Any Which Way but Loose: Interpretive Strategies and Attitudes towards Violence in the Evolution of the Anglo-American 'Retreat Rule.'" 55 *Law & Contemporary Problems* 303 (1992).

Evans-Pritchard, Deirdre, and Alison Dundes Renteln. "The Interpretation and Distortion of Culture: A Hmong 'Marriage by Capture' Case in Fresno, California." 4 *Southern California Interdisciplinary Law Journal* 1 (1994).

Ewing, Charles P. *Battered Women Who Kill.* Lexington, Mass.: Lexington Books, 1987.

———. "Psychological Self-Defense: A Proposed Justification for Battered Women Who Kill." 14 *Law & Human Behavior* 579 (1990).

Faigman, David L. "The Battered Woman Syndrome and Self-Defense: A Legal and Empirical Dissent." 72 *Virginia Law Review* 619 (1986).

Falk, Patricia J. "Novel Theories of Criminal Defense based upon the Toxicity of the Social Environment: Urban Psychosis, Television Intoxication, and Black Rage." 74 *North Carolina Law Review* 731 (1996).

Faludi, Susan. *Stiffed: The Betrayal of the American Man.* New York: W. Morrow, 1999.

Feagin, Joe R., and Hernan Vera. *White Racism.* New York: Routledge, 1995.

Federal Bureau of Investigation. *Crime in the United States: Uniform Crime Reports.* 1998.

———. *Crime in the United States: Uniform Crime Reports.* 1999.

———. *Crime in the United States: Uniform Crime Reports.* 2000.

Ficarrotto, Thomas J. "Racism, Sexism, and Erotophobia: Attitudes of Heterosexuals towards Homosexuals." 19 *Journal of Homosexuality* 111 (1990).

Finkel, Norman J. *Commonsense Justice: Jurors' Notions of the Law.* Cambridge: Harvard University Press, 1995.

Fletcher, George P. *A Crime of Self-Defense: Bernhard Goetz and the Law on Trial.* New York: Free Press, 1988.

———. "Domination in the Theory of Justification and Excuse." 57 *University of Pittsburgh Law Review* 553 (1996).

———. "Proportionality and the Psychotic Aggressor: A Vignette in Comparative Criminal Theory." 8 *Israeli Law Review* 367 (1973).

———. *Rethinking Criminal Law.* Boston: Little, Brown, 1978.

———. "The Right to Life." 13 *Georgia Law Review* 1371 (1979).

Forell, Caroline A., and Donna M. Matthews. *A Law of Her Own: The Reasonable Woman as a Measure of Man.* New York: NYU Press, 2000.

Fyfe, James J. "Blind Justice: Police Shootings in Memphis." 73 *Journal of Criminal Law & Criminology* 707 (1982).

———. "Police Use of Deadly Force: Research and Reform." 5 *Justice Quarterly* 165 (1988).

———. "Race and Extreme Police-Citizen Violence." In *Readings on Police Use of Deadly Force.* Washington, D.C.: Police Foundation, 1982.

Geller, W. A., and K. J. Karales. *Split-Second Decisions: Shootings of and by Chicago Police.* Chicago, Ill.: Chicago Law Enforcement Study Group, 1981.

Geller, William A., and Michael S. Scott. *Deadly Force: What We Know.* Washington, D.C.: Police Executive Research Forum, 1992.

Georges-Abeyie, Daniel. "Foreword." In *Race and Criminal Justice.* Monroe, N.Y.: Library Research Associates, 1991.

Gilligan, Carol. *In a Different Voice: Psychological Theory and Women's Development.* Cambridge: Harvard University Press, 1982.

Goldberg, Stephen. *The Inevitability of Patriarchy.* New York: Morrow, 1973.

Goldkamp, John S. "Minorities as Victims of Police Shootings: Interpretations of Racial Disproportionality and Police Use of Deadly Force." 2 *Justice System Journal* 169 (1976).

Gotanda, Neil. "A Critique of "Our Constitution Is Color-Blind." 44 *Stanford Law Review* 1 (1991).

———. "Re-Producing the Model Minority Stereotype: Judge Joyce Karlin's Sentencing Colloquy in *People v. Soon Ja Du.*" In *Reviewing Asian America: Locating Diversity.* Pullman, Wash.: Washington State University Press, 1995.

Gray, John. *Men Are from Mars, Women Are from Venus.* New York: HarperCollins, 1992.

Greene, Dwight L. "Naughty by Nurture: Black Male Joyriding—Is Everything Gonna Be Alright?" 4 *Columbia Journal of Gender & Law* 73 (1994).

Greenfield, Lawrence A., et al. *U.S. Department of Justice, Office of Justice Programs Bureau of Justice Statistics, Violence by Intimates.* 1998.

Grisham, John. *A Time to Kill.* New York: Doubleday, 1989.

Harris, Angela. "Race and Essentialism in Feminist Legal Theory." 42 *Stanford Law Review* 581 (1990).

Harris, David A. "The Stories, the Statistics, and the Law: Why 'Driving While Black' Matters." 84 *Minnesota Law Review* 265 (1999).

———. "When Success Breeds Attack: The Coming Backlash against Racial Profiling Studies." 6 *Michigan Journal of Race & Law* 237 (2001).

Harris, Paul. *Black Rage Confronts the Law.* New York: NYU Press, 1997.

Harrison, James. "Roles, Identities, and Sexual Orientation: Homosexuality, Heterosexuality, and Bisexuality." In *A New Psychology of Men.* New York: J. Wiley, 1995.

Hayden, George A. "Police Discretion in the Use of Deadly Force: An Empirical Study of Information Usage in Deadly Force Decision Making." 9 *Journal of Police Science & Administration* 102 (1981).

Heller, Kevin Jon. "Beyond the Reasonable Man? A Sympathetic but Critical Assessment of the Use of Subjective Standards of Reasonableness in Self-Defense and Provocation Cases." 26 *American Journal of Criminal Law* 1 (1998).

Herek, Gregory M. "Beyond 'Homophobia': A Social Psychological Perspective on Attitudes toward Lesbians and Gay Men." 10 *Journal of Homosexuality* 1 (1984).

Hite, Shere. *The Hite Report on Male Sexuality.* New York: Knopf, 1981.

———. *The Hite Report: Women and Love: A Cultural Revolution in Progress.* New York: Knopf, 1987.

Holmes, Oliver Wendell. "The Path of the Law." 10 *Harvard Law Review* 457 (1897).

Holzworth, R. James, and Catherine B. Pipping. "Drawing a Weapon: An Analysis of Police Judgments." 13 *Journal of Police Science & Administration* 185 (1985).

Horder, Jeremy. *Provocation and Responsibility.* New York: Oxford University Press, 1992.

Howe, Adrian. "More Folk Provoke Their Own Demise (Homophobic Violence and Sexed Excuses—Rejoining the Provocation Law Debate, Courtesy of the Homosexual Advance Defense.)" 19 *Sydney Law Review* 336 (1997).

Human Rights Watch. *Shielded from Justice: Police Brutality and Accountability in the United States.* 1998.

Hurd, Heidi M. "Justification and Excuse, Wrongdoing and Culpability." 74 *Notre Dame Law Review* 1551 (1999).

Hutchinson, Darren Lenard. "Identity Crisis: 'Intersectionality,' 'Multidimensionality,' and the Development of an Adequate Theory of Subordination." 6 *Michigan Journal of Race & Law* 285 (2001).

———. "Ignoring the Sexualization of Race: Heteronormativity, Critical Race Theory and Anti-Racist Politics." 47 *Buffalo Law Review* 1 (1999).

Ikemoto, Lisa C. "Traces of the Master Narrative in the Story of African American/Korean American Conflict: How We Constructed 'Los Angeles.'" 66 *Southern California Law Review* 1581 (1993).

Johnson, Kevin R. "'Aliens' and the U.S. Immigration Laws: The Social and Legal Construction of Nonpersons." 28 *University of Miami Inter-American Law Review* 263 (1997).

———. "Public Benefits and Immigration: The Intersection of Immigration Status, Ethnicity, Gender, and Class." 42 *UCLA Law Review* 1509 (1995).

———. "Some Thoughts on the Future of Latino Legal Scholarship." 2 *Harvard Latino Law Review* 101 (1997).

Johnson, Paula C. "The Social Construction of Identity in Criminal Cases: Cinema Verite and the Pedagogy of Vincent Chin." 1 *Michigan Journal of Race & Law* 347 (1996).

Johnson, Peter. "'More Than Ordinary Men Gone Wrong': Can the Law Know the Gay Subject?" 20 *Melbourne University Law Review* 1152 (1996).

Johnson, Sheri Lynn. "Black Innocence and the White Jury." 83 *Michigan Law Review* 1611 (1985).

Joseph, Shelan Y. "Six Flags Magic Mountain: A Family Entertainment Park, but Only If You Wear the Right Clothes." 16 *Loyola of Los Angeles Entertainment Law Journal* 359 (1995).

Kahan, Dan M., and Martha C. Nussbaum. "Two Conceptions of Emotion in Criminal Law." 96 *Columbia Law Review* 269 (1996).

Kang, Jerry. "Racial Violence against Asian Americans." 106 *Harvard Law Review* 1926 (1993).

Keller, Wendy. "Disparate Treatment of Spouse Murder Defendants." 6 *Southern California Review of Law & Women's Studies* 255 (1996).

Kempf, Edward J. *Psychopathology.* St. Louis: C. V. Mosby, 1920.

Kennedy, Randall. *Nigger.* New York: Pantheon Books, 2002.

———. "Racial Critiques of Legal Academia." 102 *Harvard Law Review* 1745 (1989).

———. "The State, Criminal Law, and Racial Discrimination: A Comment." 107 *Harvard Law Review* 1255 (1994).

Kipnis, Aaron. "Men, Movies and Monsters: Heroic Masculinity as a Crucible of Male Violence." 29 *Psychological Perspective* 38 (1994).

Krieger, Linda Hamilton. "Civil Rights Perestroika: Intergroup Relations after Affirmative Action." 86 *California Law Review* 1251 (1998).

———. "The Content of Our Categories: A Cognitive Bias Approach to Discrimination and Equal Employment Opportunity." 47 *Stanford Law Review* 1161 (1995).

Kwan, Peter. "Complicity and Complexity: Cosynthesis and Praxis." 49 *DePaul Law Review* 673 (2000).

———. "Invention, Inversion and Intervention: The Oriental Woman in the World of Suzie Wong, M. Butterfly, and the Adventures of Priscilla, Queen of the Desert." 5 *Asian Law Journal* 99 (1998).

———. "Jeffrey Dahmer and the CoSynthesis of Categories." 48 *Hastings Law Journal* 1257 (1997).

LaFave, Wayne R., and Austin W. Scott, Jr. *Criminal Law.* St. Paul, Minn.: West Publishing, 1986.

Langan, Patrick A., and John M. Dawson. *Spouse Murder Defendants in Large Urban Counties.* U.S. Department of Justice, 1995.

Lawrence, Charles R. "The Id, the Ego, and Equal Protection: Reckoning with Unconscious Racism." 39 *Stanford Law Review* 317 (1987).

———. "The Word and the River: Pedagogy as Scholarship and Struggle." 65 *Southern California Law Review* 2231 (1992).

Lee, Cynthia Kwei Yung. "Beyond Black and White: Racializing Asian Americans in a Society Obsessed with O. J." 6 *Hastings Women's Law Journal* 165 (1995).

———. "Race and Self-Defense: Toward a Normative Conception of Reasonableness." 81 *Minnesota Law Review* 367 (1996).

Lee, Cynthia K. Y. "The Act-Belief Distinction in Self-Defense Doctrine: A New Dual Requirement Theory of Justification." 2 *Buffalo Criminal Law Review* 191 (1998).

———. "Race and the Victim: An Examination of Capital Sentencing and Guilt Attribution Studies." 73 *Chicago-Kent Law Review* 533 (1998).

Levant, Ronald F. "Toward the Reconstruction of Masculinity." In *A New Psychology of Men*. New York: Basic Books, 1995.

Levine, James P. *Juries and Politics*. Pacific Grove, Calif.: Brooks/Cole, 1992.

Locke, Hubert G. "The Color of Law and the Issue of Color: Race and the Abuse of Police Power." In *Police Violence: Understanding and Controlling Police Abuse of Force*. New Haven, Conn.: Yale University Press, 1996.

Loffreda, Beth. *Losing Matt Shepard: Life and Politics in the Aftermath of Anti-Gay Murder*. New York: Columbia University Press, 2000.

Logan, Colleen R. "Homophobia? No, Homoprejudice." 31 *Journal of Homosexuality* 31 (1996).

Maccoby, Eleanor Emmons, and Carol Nagy Jacklin. *The Psychology of Sex Differences*. Stanford: Stanford University Press, 1974.

MacKinnon, Catharine A. *Feminism Unmodified: Discourses on Life and Law*. Cambridge: Harvard University Press, 1987.

Maguigan, Holly. "Battered Women and Self-Defense: Myths and Misconceptions in Current Reform Proposals." 140 *University of Pennsylvania Law Review* 379 (1991).

———. "Cultural Evidence and Male Violence: Are Feminist and Multiculturalist Reformers on a Collision Course in Criminal Courts?" 70 *New York University Law Review* 36 (1995).

Mahoney, Martha R. "Legal Images of Battered Women: Redefining the Issue of Separation." 90 *Michigan Law Review* 1 (1991).

Mann, Coramae Richey. *Unequal Justice: A Question of Color*. Bloomington: Indiana University Press, 1993.

Margolis, Jeffrey R. "Closing the Doors to the Land of Opportunity: The Constitutional Controversy Surrounding Proposition 187." 26 *University of Miami Inter-American Law Review* 363 (1994–95).

Matsuda, Mari J. "Looking to the Bottom: Critical Legal Studies and Reparations." 22 *Harvard Civil Rights–Civil Liberties Law Review* 323 (1987).

———. "Public Response to Racist Speech: Considering the Victim's Story." 87 *Michigan Law Review* 2320 (1989).

Matsumoto, Alison. "A Place for Consideration of Culture in the American Criminal Justice System: Japanese Law and the Kimura Case." 4 *Journal of International Law & Practice* 507 (1995).

Mauer, Marc. *Young Black Men and the Criminal Justice System: A Growing National Problem*. Washington, D.C.: The Sentencing Project, 1990.

Mauer, Marc, and Tracy Huling. *Young Black Americans and the Criminal Justice System: Five Years Later.* Washington, D.C.: The Sentencing Project, 1995.

McAuley, Finbarr. "Anticipating the Past: The Defence of Provocation in Irish Law." 50 *Modern Law Review* 133 (1987).

McComas, James, and Cynthia Strout. "Combating the Effects of Racial Stereotyping in Criminal Cases." *Champion* 22 (August 1999).

Michaels, Alan C. "'Rationales' of Criminal Law Then and Now: For a Judgmental Descriptivism." 100 *Columbia Law Review* 54 (2000).

Milgate, Deborah E. "The Flame Flickers, but Burns On: Modern Judicial Application of the Ancient Heat of Passion Defense." 51 *Rutgers Law Review* 193 (1998).

Miller, Emily L. "(Wo)manslaughter: Voluntary Manslaughter, Gender, and the Model Penal Code." 50 *Emory Law Journal* 665 (2001).

Mison, Robert. "Homophobia in Manslaughter: The Homosexual Advance as Insufficient Provocation." 80 *California Law Review* 133 (1992).

Moore, Michael S. "Causation and the Excuses." 73 *California Law Review* 1091 (1985).

Morse, Stephen J. "Undiminished Confusion in Diminished Capacity." 75 *Journal of Criminal Law & Criminology* 1 (1984).

Mullen, Paul E. "Jealousy: The Pathology of Passion." 158 *British Journal of Psychiatry* 593 (1991).

Nelson, Camille A. "(En)raged or (En)gaged: The Implications of Racial Context to the Canadian Provocation Defence." 35 *University of Richmond Law Review* 1007 (2002).

Nilsen, Eva S. "The Criminal Defense Lawyer's Reliance on Bias and Prejudice." 8 *Georgetown Journal of Legal Ethics* 1 (1994).

Nisbett, Richard E., and Dov Cohen. *Culture of Honor: The Psychology of Violence in the South.* Boulder, Colo.: Westview Press, 1996.

Nourse, Victoria. "Passion's Progress: Modern Law Reform and the Provocation Defense." 106 *Yale Law Journal* 1331 (1997).

Nussbaum, Martha C. "'Secret Sewers of Vice': Disgust, Bodies, and the Law." In *The Passions of Law.* New York: NYU Press, 1999.

Ogletree, Charles J., et al. *Criminal Justice Institute at Harvard Law School for the National Ass'n for the Advancement of Colored People, Beyond the Rodney King Story: An Investigation of Police Conduct in Minority Communities.* Boston: Northeastern University Press, 1995.

Omi, Michael, and Howard Winant. *Racial Formation in the United States: From the 1960s to the 1990s.* New York: Routledge & Kegan Paul, 1994.

Payne, B. K., et al. "Best Laid Plans: Effects of Goals on Accessibility Bias and Cognitive Control in Race-Based Perceptions of Weapons." *Journal of Experimental Social Psychology* (forthcoming).

————. "Prejudice and Perception: The Role of Automatic and Controlled Processes in Misperceiving a Weapon." 81 *Journal of Personality & Social Psychology* 181 (2001).

Perkins, Rollin M. *Criminal Law.* Mineola, N.Y.: Foundation Press, 1969.

Posner, Richard A. *Overcoming Law.* Cambridge: Harvard University Press, 1995.

Raeder, Myrna S. *"Gender and Sentencing: Single Moms, Battered Women, and Other Sex-Based Anomalies in the Gender-Free World of the Federal Sentencing Guidelines."* 20 *Pepperdine Law Review* 905 (1993).

Ramsey, Carolyn. "The Discretionary Power of 'Public' Prosecutors in Historical Perspective." 39 *American Criminal Law Review* 1309 (2002).

Rapaport, Elizabeth. "Capital Murder and the Domestic Discount: A Study of Capital Domestic Murder in the Post-Furman Era." 49 *Southern Methodist University Law Review* 1507 (1996).

Rauf, M. Naeem. "The Reasonable Man Test in the Defence of Provocation: What Are the Reasonable Man's Attributes and Should the Test be Abolished?" 30 *Criminal Law Quarterly* 73 (1987).

Reinisch, June M. *The Kinsey Institute New Report on Sex: What You Must Know to Be Sexually Literate.* (1990).

Rennison, Callie Marie, and Sarah Welchans. *Intimate Partner Violence.* Washington, D.C.: U.S. Department of Justice, Bureau of Justice Statistics Special Report, 2000.

Renteln, Alison Dundes. "A Justification of the Cultural Defense as Partial Excuse." 2 *Southern California Review of Law & Women's Studies* 437 (1993).

Rivera, Jenny. "Domestic Violence against Latinas by Latino Males: An Analysis of Race, National Origin, and Gender Differentials." 14 *Boston College Third World Law Journal* 231 (1994).

Robinson, Paul H. "Competing Theories of Justification: Deeds v. Reasons." In *Harm and Culpability.* New York: Oxford University Press, 1996.

————. *Criminal Law Defenses.* St. Paul, Minn.: West Publishing, 1984.

Robinson, Paul H., and John M. Darley. *Justice, Liability, and Blame: Community Views and the Criminal Law.* Boulder, Colo.: Westview Press, 1995.

Robinson, Reginald Leamon. "'The Other against Itself': Deconstructing the Violent Discourse between Korean and African Americans." 67 *Southern California Law Review* 15 (1993).

Roman, Ediberto. "Who Exactly Is Living La Vida Loca? The Legal and Political Consequences of Latino-Latina Ethnic and Racial Stereotypes in Film and Other Media." 4 *Journal of Gender Race & Justice* 37 (2000).

Romer, Daniel, et al. "The Treatment of Persons of Color in Local Television News: Ethnic Blame Discourse or Realistic Group Conflict?" 25 *Communication Research* 286 (1998).

Romero, Victor C. "Racial Profiling: "Driving While Mexican" and Affirmative Action." 6 *Michigan Journal of Race & Law* 195 (2000).

Rosen, Cathryn J. "The Excuse of Self-Defense: Correcting a Historical Accident on Behalf of Battered Women Who Kill." 36 *American University Law Review* 11 (1986).

Rosen, Jeffrey. *The Unwanted Gaze: The Destruction of Privacy in America*. New York: Random House, 2000.

Rosen, Richard A. "On Self-Defense, Imminence, and Women Who Kill Their Batterers." 71 *North Carolina Law Review* 371 (1993).

Russell, Katheryn K. *The Color of Crime: Racial Hoaxes, White Fear, Black Protectionism, Police Harassment, and Other Macroaggressions*. New York: NYU Press, 1998.

———. "The Racial Hoax as Crime: The Law as Affirmation." 71 *Indiana Law Journal* 593 (1996).

Sagar, H. Andrew, and Janet Ward Schofield. "Racial and Behavioral Cues in Black and White Children's Perceptions of Ambiguously Aggressive Acts." 39 *Journal of Personality & Social Psychology* 590 (1980).

Schneider, Elizabeth. *Battered Women and Feminist Lawmaking*. New Haven: Yale University Press, 2000.

———. "Equal Rights to Trial for Women: Sex Bias in the Law of Self-Defense." 15 *Harvard Civil Rights–Civil Liberties Law Review* 623 (1980).

Schopp, Robert F. "Self-Defense." In *In Harm's Way*. New York: Cambridge University Press, 1994.

Schopp, Robert F., Barbara J. Sturgis, and Megan Sullivan. "Battered Woman's Syndrome, Expert Testimony, and the Distinction between Justification and Excuse." 1994 *University of Illinois Law Review* 45 (1994).

Schulhofer, Stephen J. *Unwanted Sex*. Cambridge: Harvard University Press, 1998.

Schwartz-Nobel, Loretta. *Forsaking All Others: The Real Betty Broderick Story*. New York: Villard Books, 1992.

Scrivner, Roy. "Gay Men and Nonrelational Sex." In *Men and Sex: New Psychological Perspectives*. New York: J. Wiley, 1997.

Seldin, Fleischer. "A Strategy for Advocacy on Behalf of Women Offenders." 5 *Columbia Journal of Gender & Law* 1 (1995).

Shields, Stephanie A., and Robert E. Harriman. "Fear of Male Homosexuality: Cardiac Responses of Low and High Homonegative Males." 10 *Journal of Homosexuality* 53 (1984).

Shipley, Patrick J. "Constitutionality of the Defense of Marriage Act." 11 *Journal of Contemporary Legal Issues* 117 (2000).

Siegel, Reva B. "The Rule of Love: Wife Beating as Prerogative and Privacy." 105 *Yale Law Journal* 2117 (1996).

Sing, James J. "Culture as Sameness: Toward a Synthetic View of Provocation and Culture in the Criminal Law." 108 *Yale Law Journal* 1845 (1999).

Singer, Richard. "The Resurgence of Mens Rea: I—Provocation, Emotional Disturbance, and the Model Penal Code." 27 *Boston College Law Review* 243 (1986).

———. "The Resurgence of Mens Rea: II—Honest but Unreasonable Mistake of Fact in Self Defense." 28 *Boston College Law Review* 459 (1987).

Sklansky, David A. "Traffic Stops, Minority Motorists, and the Future of the Fourth Amendment." 1997 *Supreme Court Review* 27 (1997).

Slobogin, Christopher, and Joseph E. Schumacher. "Reasonable Expectations of Privacy and Autonomy in Fourth Amendment Cases: An Empirical Look at 'Understandings Recognized and Permitted by Society.'" 42 *Duke Law Journal* 727 (1993).

Smith, Abbe. "Burdening the Least of Us: 'Race Conscious' Ethics in Criminal Defense." 77 *Texas Law Review* 1585 (1999).

———. "Criminal Responsibility, Social Irresponsibility, and Angry Young Men: Reflections of a Feminist Criminal Defense Lawyer." 21 *New York University Review of Law & Social Change* 433 (1995).

Smith, Adam. *The Theory of Moral Sentiments.* New York: Oxford University Press, 1774.

Smuts, Barbara. "Male Aggression against Women: An Evolutionary Perspective." In *Sex, Power, Conflict: Evolutionary and Feminist Perspectives.* New York: Oxford University Press, 1996.

Sneirson, Judd F. "Black Rage and the Criminal Law: A Principled Approach to a Polarized Debate." 143 *University of Pennsylvania Law Review* 2251 (1995).

Stearns, Peter N. *Jealousy: The Evolution of an Emotion in American History.* New York: NYU Press, 1989.

St. Lewis, Joanne, and Sheila Galloway. "Reforming the Defence of Provocation." In *Ontario Women's Directorate.* Ontario: N.p., 1994.

Stumbo, Bella. *Until The Twelfth of Never: The Deadly Divorce of Dan and Betty Broderick.* New York: Pocket Books, 1992.

Suffredini, Kara S. "Pride and Prejudice: The Homosexual Panic Defense." 21 *Boston College Third World Law Journal* 279 (2001).

Sunder, Madhavi. "Cultural Dissent." 54 *Stanford Law Review* 495 (2001).

Takagi, Paul. "A Garrison State in a 'Democratic' Society." In *Readings on Police Use of Deadly Force.* Washington, D.C.: Police Foundation, 1982.

Tannen, Deborah. *You Just Don't Understand: Women and Men in Conversation.* New York: Morrow, 2001.

Taslitz, Andrew E. "A Feminist Approach to Social Scientific Evidence: Foundations." 5 *Michigan Journal of Gender & Law* 1 (1998).

———. *Rape and the Culture of the Courtroom.* New York: NYU Press, 1999.

———. "What Feminism Has to Offer Evidence Law." 28 *Southwestern University Law Review* 171 (1999).

Taylor, Laurie J. "Provoked Reason in Men and Women: Heat of Passion Manslaughter and Imperfect Self-Defense." 33 *UCLA Law Review* 1679 (1986).

Thomas, Kendall. "Beyond the Privacy Principle." 92 *Columbia Law Review* 1431 (1992).

Tomsen, Steve. "Hatred, Murder and Male Honour: Gay Homicides and the 'Homosexual Panic Defense.'" 6 *Criminology Australia* 2 (1994).

Tonry, Michael. *Malign Neglect: Race, Crime, and Punishment in America.* New York and Oxford: Oxford University Press, 1995.

Tran, Tam B. "Title VII Hostile Work Environment: A Different Perspective." 9 *Journal of Contemporary Legal Issues* 357 (1998).

Troutt, David Dante. "Screws, Koon, and Routine Aberrations: The Use of Fictional Narratives in Federal Police Brutality Prosecutions." 74 *New York University Law Review* 18 (1999).

Tylor, Edward B. "Primitive Culture." In *High Points in Anthropology.* New York: Knopf, 1988.

Valdes, Francisco, "Afterword: Beyond Sexual Orientation in Queer Legal Theory: Majoritarianism, Multidimensionality, and Responsibility in Social Justice Scholarship or Legal Scholars as Cultural Warriors." 75 *Denver University Law Review* 1409 (1998).

———. "Queers, Sissies, Dykes, and Tomboys: Deconstructing the Conflation of 'Sex,' 'Gender,' and 'Sexual Orientation' in Euro-American Law and Society." 83 *California Law Review* 1 (1995).

Volpp, Leti. "Blaming Culture for Bad Behavior." 12 *Yale Journal of Law & Humanities* 89 (2000).

———. "Feminism and Multiculturalism." 101 *Columbia Law Review* 1181 (2001).

———. "(Mis)identifying Culture: Asian Women and the 'Cultural Defense.'" 17 *Harvard Women's Law Journal* 57 (1994).

———. "Talking 'Culture': Gender, Race, Nation, and the Politics of Multiculturalism." 90 *Columbia Law Review* 1573 (1996).

Walker, Laurens, and John Monahan. "Social Frameworks: A New Use of Social Science in Law." 73 *Virginia Law Review* 559 (1987).

Walker, Lenore. *The Battered Woman.* New York: Harper & Row, 1979.

Walker, Samuel, et al. *The Color of Justice: Race, Ethnicity, and Crime in America.* Belmont: Wadsworth Publishing, 1996.

Way, Rosemary Cairns. "The Criminalization of Stalking: An Exercise in Media Manipulation and Political Opportunism." 39 *McGill Law Journal* 379 (1994).

Wechsler, Herbert. "Toward Neutral Principles of Constitutional Law." 73 *Harvard Law Review* 1 (1959).

Welke, Barbara Y. "Unreasonable Women: Gender and the Law of Accidental Injury." 19 *Law & Social Inquiry* 369 (1994).

West, Cornel. *Race Matters.* New York: Vintage Books, 1993.

*Wharton's Criminal Law.* Rochester, N.Y.: Lawyers Co-Operative Publishing, 1979.

White, Gregory L., and Paul E. Mullen. *Jealousy: Theory, Research and Clinical Strategies.* New York: Guilford Press, 1989.

Wildman, Stephanie M. "Ending Male Privilege: Beyond the Reasonable Woman." 98 *Michigan Law Review* 1797 (2000).

———. *Privilege Revealed: How Invisible Preference Undermines America.* New York: NYU Press, 1996.

Williams, Joan C. "Dissolving the Sameness/Difference Debate: A Post-Modern Path beyond Essentialism in Feminist and Critical Race Theory." 1991 *Duke Law Journal* 296 (1991).

Williams, Patricia. *The Alchemy of Race and Rights* (1991).

———. "Spirit-Murdering the Messenger: The Discourse of Fingerpointing as the Law's Response to Racism." 42 *University of Miami Law Review* 127 (1987).

Wilson, Strong S., et al. *Human Sexuality: A Text with Readings* (1977).

Woo, Deborah. "The People v. Fumiko Kimura: But Which People?" 17 *International Journal of Sociological Law* 403 (1989).

Wu, Frank H. "Neither Black Nor White: Asian Americans and Affirmative Action." 15 *Boston College Third World Law Journal* 225 (1995).

Yamamoto, Eric K. "Korematsu Revisited—Correcting the Injustice of Extraordinary Government Excess and Lax Judicial Review: Time for a Better Accommodation of National Security Concerns and Civil Liberties." 26 *Santa Clara Law Review* 1 (1986).

Yamamoto, Eric K., et al. *Race, Rights and Reparation: Law and the Japanese American Internment* (2001).

Yen, Rhoda J. "Racial Stereotyping of Asians and Asian Americans and Its Effect on Criminal Justice: A Reflection on the Wayne Lo Case." 7 *Asian Law Journal* 1 (2000).

# Index

# About the Author

CYNTHIA LEE is Professor of Law at the George Washington University Law School in Washington, D.C. where she teaches Criminal Law, Criminal Procedure, and Professional Responsibility. Prior to moving to Washington, D.C., Professor Lee was Professor of Law at the University of San Diego School of Law. Professor Lee was born and raised in the San Francisco Bay Area. She graduated from Stanford University with a B.A. in political science and received her J.D. from the University of California at Berkeley, Boalt Hall School of Law.